THE LETTERS OF ST. ANTONY

STUDIES IN ANTIQUITY AND CHRISTIANITY

The Roots of Egyptian Christianity
Birger A. Pearson and James E. Goehring, editors

Gnosticism, Judaism, and Egyptian Christianity
Birger A. Pearson

Ascetic Behavior in Greco-Roman Antiquity
Vincent L. Wimbush, editor

Elijah in Upper Egypt
David Frankfurter

The Letters of St. Antony
Samuel Rubenson

THE INSTITUTE FOR ANTIQUITY AND CHRISTIANITY
Claremont Graduate School
Claremont, California

STUDIES IN ANTIQUITY & CHRISTIANITY

THE LETTERS OF ST. ANTONY

MONASTICISM AND THE MAKING OF A SAINT

Samuel Rubenson

MINNEAPOLIS FORTRESS PRESS

To Inga-Lill,
Mikael, Jonas, and Elisabet

THE LETTERS OF ST. ANTONY
Monasticism and the Making of a Saint

This Fortress Press edition, with the English translation of the letters of St. Antony, was first published in 1995. An earlier form of the book, without the translation of the letters, titled *The Letters of St. Antony: Origenist Theology, Monastic Tradition, and the Making of a Saint,* was published by Lund University Press, Sweden, in 1990.

Cover art: Icon of St. Antony, painted by the sisters of the monastery of St. Dimianah, Egypt, under the direction of Professor Issac Fanous, Higher Institute of Coptic Studies, Cairo.

Library of Congress Cataloging-in-Publication Data

Rubenson, Samuel.
The letters of St. Antony: monasticism and the making of a saint / Samuel Rubenson.
p. cm. — (Studies in antiquity and Christianity)
Includes bibliographical references and index.
ISBN 0-8006-2910-8 (alk. paper)
1. Anthony, of Egypt, Saint, ca. 250–355 or 6. Correspondence.
2. Anthony, of Egypt, Saint, ca. 250–355 or 6. 3. Monasticism and religious orders—Egypt—History. 4. Monasticism and religious orders—History—Early church, ca. 30–600. I. Anthony, of Egypt, Saint, ca. 250–355 or 6. Correspondence. English. II. Title.
III. Series.
BR65.A3573A4 1995
270.1'092—dc20 95-24837
CIP

The paper used in this publication meets the minimum requirements of American National Standard for Information Sciences—Permanence of Paper for Printed Library Materials, ANSI Z329.48-1984.

Manufactured in the U.S.A. AF 1-2910

99 98 97 96 95 1 2 3 4 5 6 7 8 9 10

CONTENTS

Foreword

As director of the Roots of Egyptian Christianity research project of the Institute for Antiquity and Christianity at the Claremont Graduate School I take great pleasure in welcoming the publication of this book by my Swedish colleague and friend in the Studies in Antiquity and Christianity series. An earlier version of this book, albeit without the translation of the letters, was published by Dr. Rubenson as a Lund University dissertation in 1990 and achieved international acclaim by reviewers as a work that revolutionizes our understanding of the life and thought of the great anchorite father of the Egyptian desert, Saint Antony. The republication of this book in a revised and enlarged version by Fortress Press will make Dr. Rubenson's work more accessible to readers in this country and abroad.

The Roots of Egyptian Christianity project is devoted to research in the history of Christian Egypt from the beginnings of Christianity in Egypt in the first century to the Arab conquest in the seventh. *The Letters of St. Antony* is the fifth volume to be published as a part of that project, and is a signal contribution to the expansion of our knowledge of Egyptian Christianity in the third and early fourth centuries.

Birger A. Pearson
Director, Roots of Egyptian Christianity Project
Professor of Religious Studies
University of California, Santa Barbara

καὶ γὰρ προσεῖχεν οὕτως τῇ ἀναγνώσει, ὡς μηδὲν τῶν γεγραμμένων ἀπ' αὐτοῦ πίπτειν χαμαί, πάντα δὲ κατέχειν, καὶ λοιπὸν αὐτῷ τὴν μνήμην ἀντὶ βιβλίων γίνεσθαι.

Vita Antonii 3

Therefore we ought to love one another warmly. For he who loves his neighbour loves God, and he who loves God loves his own soul.

Epistula Antonii VI:92

Introduction

In the late third century a young Egyptian sold his possessions and retreated into the desert. His name was Antony. He was not a distinguished theologian engaged in the formulation of Christian doctrine, nor a powerful politician concerned with the establishment of the Church. He wrote no theological treatises, nor did he participate in councils and controversies. He was a man of the desert, not of the city. In spite of this, the traces of his life and work are not covered by sand but manifest throughout the history of Christianity. His *Life,* written by the great Athanasius of Alexandria, has inspired Christians of all centuries in the West as well as in the East. Even in his lifetime his fame reached far outside Egypt, and within a century after his death he was known throughout the Christian empire as *the* father of monasticism, *the* ideal of *the* real Christian way of life. While his life story became an important model for Christian hagiography, the stories about his visions have never ceased to fascinate and inspire authors and painters, from St. Augustine and Matthias Grünewald to Gustave Flaubert and Max Ernst.[1]

It is, however, as an ideal, not as a historical figure that Antony has been handed down to posterity. At the turn of the century Henry Gwatkin, in a provocative note in his *Studies of Arianism,* even concluded from Weingarten's work on early monasticism, that Antony had never existed.[2] Although the historical existence of Antony has been universally accepted in later research, the traditional image of him, gained from Athanasius' *Vita Antonii,* has increasingly been questioned. The ideal of perfect life portrayed by the bishop, as well as Antony's long sermons and his concise discussions with the philosophers reported in the *Vita,* certainly reveal more about Athanasius' hagiographical and theological intent than about

1 See *i.a.* Reinhart Staats, 'Antonius', *Gestalten der Kirchengeschichte (hrsg. von M. Greschat),* I, Stuttgart 1984, pp. 236–249; Hermann Dörries, 'Die Vita Antonii als Geschichtsquelle', *NAWG,* Phil.-Hist. Klasse, Göttingen 1949, pp. 200–209 (quoted according to the revised edition in his *Wort und Stunde. Erster Band. Gesammelte Studien zur Kirchengeschichte des vierten Jahrhunderts,* Göttingen 1966, pp. 145–224); Jean Leclerq, 'Saint Antoine dans la monastique mediévale', *Antonius Magnus Eremita 356–1956* (*SA* 38), Rome 1958, pp. 229–247; and Marie Schütt, 'Vom heiligen Antonius zum heiligen Guthlac. Ein Beitrag zur Geschichte der Biographie', *Antike und Abendland* V, Hamburg 1956, pp. 75–91.

2 See Henry Gwatkin, *Studies of Arianism,* Cambridge [2]1900, pp. 102–107. The major refutation of Gwatkin's view came in Dom Cuthbert Butler, *The Lausiac History of Palladius,* I (*Texts and Studies* 6.1), pp. 215–228.

Antony himself. As a consequence Antony has disappeared into the obscure background of early monasticism, and of the *Vita* little more than a few uncertain dates and some uncontroversial statements on his background are left as reliable evidence of Antony's life and work.

With growing awareness of the limited value of the various *Lives* of saints as historical sources, scholars have tended to regard the different collections of the sayings of the desert fathers, the *Apophthegmata Patrum* as the best sources for early Egyptian monasticism. Generally viewed as recollections handed down in oral tradition, the *apophthegmata* are supposed to convey the very words of the first monks and to give an authentic image of their monastic tradition. The emphasis on reticence, humility and simplicity in the sayings and the fear they reveal of theological speculation, ecclesiastical dignitaries and city life, moreover, corresponds to the traditional emphasis on a contrast between Greek and Coptic, between cultured and illiterate, between philosophical and fanatical. But being a series of isolated aphorisms and anecdotes, the *apophthegmata* give no coherent view of the history or theology of the early monks. In them we find the portraits of rude and simple-minded peasants seeking forgiveness through harsh mortifications for their crude crimes, as well as the portraits of prudent masters of spiritual wisdom teaching their disciples through proverbs and parables. Although Antony was a prominent monk and accordingly well represented in the *Apophthegmata Patrum,* those sayings which are connected with his name do not differ from those of a great many other desert fathers. Like most of them he is depicted as a penitent, unlettered Egyptian peasant, who plagued by his conscience fled into the demon-haunted desert.[1]

Against the background of Antony's importance for early monasticism, and the conflict between the images of him presented in the *Vita* and in the *apophthegmata,* it seems strange, at first sight, that the *Letters of St. Antony* have hitherto received almost no attention in scholarly research. Although they have been printed in two Latin translations, one of them even reprinted now and again since the early 16th century, and in modern editions of the Coptic, Syriac, Georgian and Arabic versions, the seven

[1] Decisive for research on the monastic setting of Antony has been Karl Heussi, *Der Ursprung des Mönchtums,* Tübingen 1936. For Heussi the rise of monasticism has its roots in what he calls the radical determination of primitive and newly Christianized people—'unverbrauchte Bevölkerungsschichten'—to defeat the demons in their own land, the desert; see pp. 108-115. Based on Heussi's research and on Bousset's appreciation of the historical value and importance of the sayings: 'Man wird diese und jene nicht leicht zu hoch einschätzen können' (Wilhelm Bousset, *Apophthegmata. Studien zur Geschichte des ältesten Mönchtums,* Tübingen 1923, p. 91) Hermann Dörries in the hitherto most important study on Antony came to the conclusion that the *apophthegmata* in contrast to the *Vita* give a reliable image of Antony ('Die Vita Antonii als Geschichtsquelle', pp. 193–199).

letters have not previously been the subject of any major study.[1] The reasons for this are both their dubious authenticity and the poor transmission of the text. Of the Coptic version a fragment only is preserved, of the Greek translation nothing at all, and of the very early translation into Syriac only one letter. The text of the Latin version is, moreover, as obscure as the languages of the two other full versions, the Arabic and the Georgian, are unknown to most church historians and theologians.

The content of the letters is, moreover, hard to reconcile with the traditional image of Antony and the early monastic tradition gained from the *Vita*, the *Apophthegmata* and other sources. The obvious dependence on popular Platonic philosophy and Alexandrian theological tradition reveals that the author was no 'ignorant monk' who had simply exchanged the garb of the peasant for the monastic habit, but a teacher who wore a monk's garment as if it was the robe of a philosopher.[2] In his exhortations he urges his correspondents to 'know themselves' and meditate on their 'spiritual essence', and his allegorical exegesis shows him to be a disciple of the school of Origen. Given the image of Antony as a saintly, but simple-minded supporter of Athanasius, and of Egyptian monasticism as theologically naïve, scholars have either rejected the authenticity of the letters or tacitly avoided the problem they present for the established tradition. If the letters are genuine, they oblige us to redraw not only the image of Antony, but also much of the established picture of early Egyptian monasticism.

Against this background the present study is aimed at a thorough examination of the letters and a subsequent comparison of them with the other sources on Antony. The conflict between what the letters reveal and what the traditional sources tell—or are thought to tell—about Antony, and thus about early monastic tradition, has made it necessary to include an analysis of the historical setting of the first monks, an analysis based on contemporary evidence, not on the literature that grew out of the monastic tradition. As will be shown, the contrast between the letters on the one hand and the portraits and recollections of Antony on the other closely reflects the contrast between documentary evidence and historical retrospection. The letters cannot serve as a source for a new biography to replace the *Vita Antonii*. Their significance is that they document the

1 This in spite of the review by Jean Gribomont of Garitte's edition of the Georgian text, which emphasizes the importance of the text and anticipates many of my conclusions (*idem*, '*Lettres de S. Antoine. Version géorgienne et fragments coptes*, éd. et trad. par G. GARITTE. (*CSCO* 148–149) Louvain 1955', *RHE* 51 (1956), pp. 546–550 [comptes rendus]).

2 One of the canons of the council of Gangra in the mid-fourth century anathematizes him who: 'out of pretended ascesis wears the *peribolaion* and, as if he were righteous, despises those who in piety wear ordinary mantles and make use of normal clothing'. The background is probably the monastic tradition of Eustathius of Sebaste recorded in Socrates, *HE* II.43.

mental world of an Egyptian monk in the first decades of the fourth century and thereby support the new image of Egypt emerging from documentary papyri and the discovery of heterodox literature.[1] The fact, demonstrated below, that this monk is rightly identified with the father of monasticism, St. Antony, makes it possible to use his letters for a new interpretation of how his image was shaped by subsequent generations. A comparison of the letters with the *Vita,* the *apophthegmata,* and the other sources shows not only to what degree they preserved true reminiscences of the author of the letters, but above all it demonstrates the process by which his image was transformed, the forces behind 'the making of a saint'.

In accordance with the double aim of the study it is divided into two parts. Part One begins with the attempt to establish the history and reliability of the different versions of Antony's letters by a comparative analysis of the texts based on the manuscripts as well as on the editions. On the basis of linguistic and text-critical arguments it is suggested that the letters were originally composed in Coptic although the early date and speculative content of them would indicate a Greek original. In the second chapter the question of the authenticity of the letters is treated together with an analysis of the evidence for their date and of what they reveal about their recipients. Not only is there—as will be shown—strong support for an Antonian authorship, there are also good reasons to question the general opinion that he was illiterate and lacked knowledge of Greek. The evidence of the letters even suggests that he was himself aware of the issues of the Arian controversy, and expected his correspondents to be familiar with current theological and philosophical concepts.

In the third chapter the style and structure of the letters is discussed in an attempt to understand the purpose of the letters and the tradition in which they were written. The first part is then concluded by a chapter devoted to the teaching of the letters, with an emphasis on the philosophical and theological views that lie behind their exhortations to repentance, self-knowledge, and a proper understanding of the history of salvation. Although the letters are no theological treatises, and contain no systematic discussions on the major issues of contemporary theology, it can be shown that they represent a coherent view on man and salvation. The central ideas in the letters amply demonstrate that Antony shared a Platonic view of man, his origin, nature and destination, and that for his integration of Christian thinking into this framework he was dependent on

1 The major representatives of this reorientation are Philip Rousseau in his *Pachomius. The Making of a Community in Fourth Century Egypt,* Berkeley 1985, and James E. Goehring, whose articles are listed in the bibliography. See also C. Wilfred Griggs, *Early Egyptian Christianity. From its Origins to 451 C.E.* (*Coptic Studies* 2), Leiden 1990.

Clement of Alexandria and Origen. As a result he is brought closer to Athanasius and his theology.

In the second part the major section deals with Antony's historical background. On the basis of recent studies of the documentary evidence preserved in the papyri from late third and early fourth century Egypt, the attempt is made to understand the socio-economic and cultural situation in which Antony lived.[1] The aim is not to present a comprehensive view of Egyptian society at this time, but on the one hand to examine to what degree the letters, and the image of Antony gained from them, represent that society, and on the other to see whether the traditional image of the early monks is concordant with what the documents reveal. The emphasis in the chapter is thus on the level of literacy and cultural exchange, and on the question of social mobility. The main questions are 'What kind of monk is likely to have come out of Egypt on the threshold of the fourth century?' and 'What legacy was there at hand for someone who sought spiritual direction?' As will be demonstrated there is little evidence that the first monks were destitute and illiterate farmers who fled a degenerate society, or that, before Evagrius of Pontus settled in Egypt in the last decades of the century, Origenism was restricted to a few intellectuals of little importance.

In the subsequent chapters the traditional sources on Antony are discussed and compared with his letters. In Chapter Six the complex state of research on the *Vita Antonii* is discussed and the suggestion made that the letters constitute a significant contribution to the understanding of the *Vita.* The aim of the chapter, however, is not to solve the many open questions in regard to the text, authenticity, structure and purpose of the *Vita,* but to see to what degree the theology of the letters, and the Antony image gained from them, is preserved, and according to what rules it is transformed. The suggestion is here that the two major factors are the theological implications of the Arian controversy and the victory of Christianity over paganism. Chapter Seven deals with the *apophthegmata* and their reliability as historical sources. After a critical discussion on the methods of earlier research, the sayings on Antony in the collections are presented, analysed and compared to the letters. As a result the traditional view of the sayings as 'the authentic voices of the desert' is questioned, and the character of the collections as literary compilations representing later tradition is emphasized. The last chapter briefly discusses the references to Antony in other sources written within a hundred years of his death.

[1] For this part I rely on the papyrological studies by Arthur Boak, Jean van Haelst, Colin Roberts, Eric G. Turner, Ewa Wipszycka, and others. For a general survey I have used Alan K. Bowman, *Egypt after the Pharaohs,* London 1986, and Naphtali Lewis, *Life in Egypt under Roman Rule,* Oxford 1983.

While all of them demonstrate the importance attached to Antony, some of them also connect him with the later Origenist tradition of Nitria, a connection strongly supported by the letters.

The significance of the new image of Antony which emerges from the analysis of the letters and the criticism of previous views on the historical reliability of the other sources, poses a number of questions merely indicated in this study. The first question is to what degree the teaching of Antony in general, and the letters in particular, has been of importance to the development of monastic theology. In the conclusion the possibility of a dependence on Antony on the part of important monastic theologians such as Ammonas, Evagrius, Macarius, John Cassian and Dorotheus of Gaza is suggested on the basis of a few examples of similarities with the letters. The decision to exclude a study of the large Arabic corpus of texts attributed to Antony does not imply that they are of no importance for the legacy of the letters; it is based on the lack of editions and the difficulties inherent in the dating and the analysis of them.

Unless otherwise indicated, all quotations of the sources are according to the editions listed in the bibliography. All translations of the sources not explicitly quoted from others are my own.

PART ONE

THE LETTERS OF ST. ANTONY

I. THE VERSIONS

1. THE COPTIC VERSION

In Coptic, the seven letters written by Antony are preserved only in a fragment on two folios of a papyrus codex dating presumably from the seventh century.[1] The other parts of this codex are either lost or hidden in the piles of unidentified Coptic papyri kept in museums and libraries all over the world. The two folios contain the end of one letter, one complete letter, numbered Letter IV, and the beginning of a letter called Letter V. A comparison with the other versions of the letters shows that the fragments correspond to the end of Letter III, Letter IV, and the beginning of Letter V, according to how they are numbered in the Arabic version. It can thus be assumed that the letters were numbered identically in Coptic and Arabic and this Copto-Arabic sequence will be adhered to throughout the present study.[2] The numbering of the Coptic folios shows that the codex originally contained at least the first five letters, and most probably all seven letters. The folios are numbered on recto and verso 57-60, which makes the folios no. 29-30. This gives more than enough space for the

[1] See Georgio Zoega, *Catalogus codicum copticorum manu scriptorum qui in Museo Borgiano Velitris adservantur,* Rome 1810, no. 171, p. 363 (*Cod. Copt. Napol.* I.B. 1, 345). The date is the one given by Zoega, unchallenged by the subsequent editors of the text.

[2] The Copto-Arabic sequence of the letters corresponds to the other versions as follows:

Copto-Arabic	1	2	3	4	5	6	7
Georgian	1	2	6	7	3	4	5
Latin	1	4	6	7	5	2	3
Syriac	1	-	-	-	-	-	-

Within each letter the text is quoted according to the division in verses adapted by Garitte in his edition of the Coptic and Georgian texts (Gérard Garitte, *Lettres de Saint Antoine. Version géorgienne et fragments coptes* (*CSCO* 148), Louvain 1955). In the parts missing in the Georgian version of Letters I and VII, I have followed the division into verses in the Dutch translation by Christofoor Wagenaar (*Leven, getuignissen, brieven van de heilige Antonius abt* (*Monastieke cahiers* 17), Bonheiden 1981). The translation by Wagenaar as the English translation by Derwas Chitty preserve the Copto-Arabic sequence of the letters, while the French translation by André Louf and the Italian by Lisa Cremaschi (see bibliography) follow the different sequence of the Georgian version. The versions are in the notes given the sigla A=Arabic; C=Coptic; G=Georgian; L=Latin; S=Syriac; and Gr*=Greek.

preceding letters, if we take for granted that they had the same relation in length to the Georgian text as the preserved Coptic fragment has. The Coptic manuscript may have included also some of the Pseudo-Antonian material preserved with the Arabic translations of the letters.

The Coptic fragment was first published by Zoega, and subsequently by Winstedt and Garitte.[1] In addition to the fragment quotations from the Coptic version of the sixth letter are preserved in two letters from Besa, Shenoute's successor, one to Antinoë and one to Heraï.[2] The comparison of the quotations with the other versions of the letters shows that Besa quoted the original faithfully. A Coptic version of all seven letters is attested by Jerome, who writes about seven letters translated from Coptic into Greek.[3] That the Coptic corpus also included the thirteen letters which in Arabic are attributed to Antony, but in Greek and Syriac to Ammonas, his disciple, is evident from the notes in the Arabic manuscripts, as well as from a reference by the late medieval Coptic encyclopaedist Abū-l-Barakāt Ibn Kabar to a Coptic version of twenty letters by St. Antony still extant in his lifetime.[4] The Coptic text of one of these additional letters is, moreover, found in a quotation in the writings of Shenoute.[5]

2. The Syriac Version

In Syriac, only the first letter is preserved, and there is no trace of any translation of the other letters into Syriac. The letter is found in seven different manuscripts containing other early monastic texts:[6]

A = *British Library, add.* 12.175 (Wright, *Catalogue,* II, no. 727, p. 637.)
B = *Berlin syr.* 27 [Sachau 302] (Sachau, *Katalog,* p. 109)
L = *British Library, add.* 14.621 (Wright, *ibid.,* no. 779, p. 758)
M = *Ming. syr.* 605 (Mingana, *Catalogue,* I, p.1162)
P = *Par. syr.* 201 (Zotenberg, *Catalogues,* p. 150)
V = *Vat. syr.* 123 (Assemani, *Catalogus,* p. 142)
Z = *Vat. syr.* 126 (*ibid.,* p. 173)

1 Zoega, *op.cit.,* p. 363; E. O. Winstedt, 'The Original Text of One of St. Antony's Letters', *JTS* 7 (1906), pp. 541–545; Garitte, *Lettres de Saint Antoine,* pp. 41–46, and 11–12.

2 See K. H. Kuhn, *Letters and Sermons of Besa* (*CSCO* 158), Louvain 1956, pp. 97, 99–100, 100–101. For a discussion see, Gérard Garitte, 'A propos des lettres de S. Antoine l'ermite', *Le Muséon* 52 (1939), pp. 11–31.

3 Hieronymus, *De viris illustribus,* 88.

4 See below, p. 20f., for the Arabic texts, and Abū-l-Barakāt Ibn Kabar, *Miṣbāḥ al-ẓulmah fī īḍāḥ al-ḫidmah* VII (Riedel, p. 647, and Samir, p. 294).

5 See Garitte, 'A propos des lettres de S. Antoine l'ermite', pp. 20–22. In another passage Shenoute also refers to what Antony wrote, but no equivalent to his quotation can be found in the letters preserved. Nor does the quotation in the *florilegium* in *Cambridge, Univ. Lib. Add. 1876.2* come from the preserved letters. See Paulí Bellet, 'Nou Testimoni de les lletres de Sant Antoni', *Studia Monastica* 31 (1989), pp. 251–257.

6 It is worth noting that the letter in the oldest manuscript is transmitted together with writings by Evagrius, Macarius and Ammonas, as part of a very early collection of sayings.

The text was edited by Nau in 1909, but the edition is unsatisfactory.[1] Apparently, Nau did not have access to the oldest manuscript (A), dated 534, and made no attempt to work out the relations between the four manuscripts (B, L, P and V) he used. Moreover, he did not relate the Syriac letter to the other versions of the same text, merely suggesting that it was a translation from the Coptic original, and the basis of the Arabic version.[2] A new edition of the letter is thus sorely needed, but would go beyond the limits of this study. In order to evaluate the Syriac version and relate it to the others it has, however, proved necessary to make a collation of the oldest manuscript, Nau's apparatus, and the other versions.[3]

The manuscripts differ considerably from each other, and at least four of them contain serious *lacunae*.[4] The differences reveal that we are dealing with three families of manuscripts, A + V, B + P, and L. It is also clear that B is closer to A and V than are P and L, and that L is the least reliable manuscript. If we compare the Syriac texts with the other versions, it is further obvious that A, V, and to some extent B as well, have preserved the Syriac original better than the other manuscripts.[5] Nau, however, based his text primarily on L, checked against P, while B and V were made accessible to him shortly before publication, and A not at all. Until a new edition is made, we have to rely on A, checked against the readings of B and V in Nau's apparatus.

The dependence of the modern translations on the Syriac version of Letter I in the edition of Nau is thus without a firm basis. The early date of the oldest Syriac mss. is, moreover, no guarantee that the Syriac translation gives a reliable text of the letters.

1 F. Nau, 'La version syriaque de la première lettre de saint Antoine', *ROC* 14 (1909), pp. 282–297. The edition lacks a critical discussion on the mss., and is full of misprints. An examination of L also reveals that Nau sometimes neglected variant readings.

2 *Ibid.*, pp. 282–284. In both cases Nau was mistaken, see below, pp. 29–33

3 I have not been able to examine all the mss. myself, but have relied on an examination of A (dated 534) and L (dated 802) for comparisons with the text and apparatus of Nau and the other versions of the letter. Ms. B should, according to Sachau, be dated to the seventh or eighth century, P is by Zotenberg dated to the 13th century, while V is dated to the eighth century by the Assemani brothers . M is a copy of Z, which is a fairly late (13th century) ms. containing the large collection of monastic texts attributed to ᶜEnānīšōᶜ.

4 A, B, L and V. Larger *lacunae* are found in A, where the verses 54 and 55 as well as 57–71 are missing.

5 The most important examples are the verses where A and V agree with the Georgian and Latin versions against the other Syriac manuscripts. See *i.a.* v. 21 (Nau, p. 291, l. 5–6), 25 (p. 291, l. 12), 30 (p. 292, l. 3), 50 (p. 294, l. 5), 53 (p. 294, l. 16), 74 (p. 297, l. 1). In two other cases V agrees with the Georgian and Latin versions where A is missing: 57 (p. 295, l. 6) and 62 (p. 295, l. 16). Two other examples of the close affinity between A and V are verses 2 (p. 289, l. 6) and 6 (p. 289, l. 16). B agrees with A and V in two of the cases mentioned above (v. 53 and 57).

3. THE GEORGIAN VERSION

In Georgian, the letters are preserved in two manuscripts from the monastery of St. Catherine in the Sinai, both dated to the tenth century:[1]

A = *Sin.geo.* 35 + *Graz* (Garitte, *Catalogue*, pp. 97–122)
B = *Sin.geo.* 25 (*ibid.*, pp. 60–66)

A critical edition of the Georgian version, including the Coptic fragments and a Latin translation, was published by Garitte in 1955.[2] In this version the sequence of the letters is different from the Copto-Arabic tradition. Letters III and IV are placed at the end of the collection as nos. VI and VII, making letters V, VI and VII into III, IV and V. There is no information in the manuscripts on the source of the Georgian translation. However, in one of the manuscripts, *Sin. geo.* 35, by Garitte designated as A, some of the letters have titles written in Greek letters. This is an indication that the scribe was bilingual, and suggests, if the titles are original, a Greek source for the translation.[3] The fact that the Georgian version is known only from the library of the monastery of St. Catherine in the Sinai also makes it likely that the text was translated from Greek. Unfortunately none of the Georgian manuscripts has the complete text of all the seven letters. The best preserved manuscript, A, is mutilated at the beginning and at the end. The other manuscript, *Sin.geo.* 25, which Garitte called B, contains Letters IV and V only (in the Georgian version the seventh and the third). Together, the two manuscripts give us the complete text, except for the beginning of Letter I and a large part of Letter VII (the fifth in the Georgian version), which is missing, probably due to corruption in the text of the source for the Georgian translation. In the fourth letter there is also a sentence missing, obviously the result of haplography.[4]

In his edition Garitte made no attempt to establish the relation of the two manuscripts to each other. A collation of the parts common to both manuscripts clearly shows that they represent the same translation. However, the differences between them are such as to make it impossible to regard either of them as the direct source for the other. When the texts of

[1] A single folio, belonging to the first ms. is found among the Georgian manuscripts removed from the monastery of St. Catherine in the late 19th century and donated by Prof. Schuchardt to the university library of Graz in 1927. See Gérard Garitte, 'Les lettres de Saint Antoine en géorgien', *Le Muséon* 64 (1951), pp. 267–278, and Gregor Peradze, 'Über die georgischen Handschriften in Österreich', *Wiener Zeitschrift für die Kunde des Morgenlandes* 47 (1940), p. 219–232 with reference to the catalogue of A. Schanidze printed in Georgian in the *Bulletin de l'université de Tiflis* 9 (1929), pp. 310–353, and the article by Schuchardt in *ibid.* 8 (1928), pp. 347–376.

[2] Garitte, *Lettres de saint Antoine. Version géorgienne et fragments coptes, CSCO* 148–149, Louvain 1955. Cf. the important review by Jean Gribomont in *RHE* 51 (1956), pp. 546–550.

[3] For this usage see R. P. Blake, 'Greek Script and Georgian Scribes on Mt. Sinai', *HTR* 25 (1932), pp. 273–276.

[4] The passages missing are *Ep. Ant.* I.1–11, IV.11b, and VII.58b–58u.

the other versions are taken into account it becomes evident that neither of the manuscripts has preserved the original translation faithfully, since both deviate, but in different places, from what we find in the Coptic and Latin versions. In a number of cases, B (the readings of which Garitte gives in his footnotes) preserves the original rendering. In Letter V (the third in the Georgian version) there are two important cases in which B agrees with the Latin version against A, which Garitte used as his base.[1] In Letter IV (the seventh in the Georgian version) two words found in the other versions are missing in A but extant in B.[2] In two other cases B has kept a more difficult reading than A.[3] A preference for B is, moreover, supported by the curious fact, apparently not noticed by Garitte, that the two letters extant in B were copied according to the Copto–Arabic numbering of the letters (Letter IV and V), although their titles identify them as the seventh and the third letter.

4. THE LATIN VERSION

In 1516 Symphorianus Champerius published the Latin version of the letters. According to him they had been translated from Greek into Latin for the first time in 1475 by Valerio de Sarasio. Unfortunately neither de Sarasio's manuscript nor his source seems to be preserved.[4] The translation has been characterized as obscure and not easily understood. The large number of awkward grammatical constructions and strange words are probably due to misunderstandings of the Greek text, and/or to an unsuccessful attempt at too literal a translation of the source.[5] The letters are in this version numbered differently from both the Copto-Arabic tradition and the Georgian version. Letters III and IV are again placed at the end of

1 See V.5 (G: III.5) where A has omitted სეწევნაჲ 'helper', συνεργός (L: adjutorium), and V.32 (G: III.32), where it has added და ამას გიწამედ თქუენ 'and this I tell you', which is not found in the Latin version but strangely enough has a corresponding phrase in the Arabic version! This must be pure coincidence; the addition is rather natural in the context.

2 See IV.1 (G: VII.1) ყოველთა and IV.7 (G: VII.7) კრული.

3 See IV.8 (G: VII.8), B: მოჲღოთ for A: მოვიღოტ and IV.9 (G: VII.9), B: მათ for A: მას.

4 Symphorianus Champerius, *Epistolae Sanctissimorum,* Paris 1516 (the preface is dated April 1515, giving rise to a certain confusion in the references). In addition to the letters the book includes an introduction and commentaries. Champerius' text was reprinted several times (*i.a.* Köln 1536, Venice 1546, Basel 1550, 1555, 1569, Paris 1575, 1589 and 1610, London 1677; see *i.a.* M. Martini Lipenii *Bibliotheca Realis Theologica,* Frankfurt 1685) and finally by Migne in PG 40, 977–1000. A new edition was made by A. Erdinger, *Epistolae septem quae sub nomine Antonii abbatis circumferuntur,* Innsbruck 1881. The only Latin manuscript I have been able to find is a copy of Letter VII in a 16th century ms.: *Vat. Lat.* 3848, f. 40v–55r. In spite of its confused text, I have relied on the edition of 1516. The later reprints of the text show numerous alterations by the subsequent editors.

5 Otto Bardenhewer, *Geschichte der altchristlichen Literatur,* III, Freiburg 1923[2], p. 80, calls the translation 'barbarischen Latein', while Franz Klejna, 'Antonius und Ammonas. Eine Untersuchung über Herkunft und Eigenart der ältesten Mönchsbriefe', *ZKT* 62 (1938), p. 309, calls it 'mißglückt', and Johannes Quasten, *Patrology,* III, p. 150, 'very poor'.

the collection, as in the Georgian version, but the pairs made up by Letters II and V, and VI and VII, have been switched around, leaving only Letter I in the original position. Part of the second letter has also been interchanged with a related part of the third letter, probably due to dislocated folios in the Greek manuscript.[1] There are, furthermore, a great number of minor omissions in the text, as well as a case of obvious haplography.[2]

5. The Arabic Version

In Arabic, the seven letters are part of a large collection of texts attributed to Antony and preserved in a great number of manuscripts.[3]

Copt. Mus. Lit. 88 (Simaika, *Catalogue,* no. 193; Graf, *Katalog,* no. 93),
Copt. Patr. Theol. 221 (Simaika, *ibid.,* no. 385; missing in Graf),
Copt. Patr. Theol. 289 (Simaika, *ibid.,* no. 461; Graf, *ibid.,* no. 484),
Mingana syr. 177 (karšūnī)(Mingana, *Catalogue,* I, cols. 388–392),
Sbath 1015 (see Sbath, *Catalogue de manuscrits,* no. 1015),
St. Ant. Theol. 177 (according to the inventory by Yassā ᶜAbd al-Masīḥ)
St. Ant. Theol. 178 (*ibid.*), *St. Ant. Theol.* 179 (*ibid.*), *St. Ant. Theol.* 180 (*ibid.*),
St. Ant. Theol. 181 (*ibid.*), *St. Ant. Theol.* 182 (*ibid.*), *St. Ant. Theol.* 184 (*ibid.*),
St. Ant. Theol. 185 (*ibid.*), *St. Ant. Theol.* 186 (*ibid.*), *St. Ant. Theol.* 187 (*ibid.*),
St. Ant. Theol. 188 (*ibid.*), *St. Ant. Theol.* 191 (*ibid.*), *St. Ant. Theol.* 192 (*ibid.*),
St. Ant. Theol. 298 (*ibid.*),
St. Mac. Hom. 23 (Zanetti, *Les manuscrits de Dair Abû Maqâr,* no. 344),
Vat. ar. 398 (Mai, *Scriptorum veterum nova collectio,* IV.2, no. 398).

There is no critical edition of the Arabic version, but the Arabic text of one of the manuscripts from the Coptic Patriarchate was printed in Cairo in 1899, and the text of the manuscript of the monastery of St. Macarius was published by the monastery in 1979.[4] According to a colophon appearing in most of the manuscripts, the Arabic translation was done from two Sahidic manuscripts in the monastery of St. Antony and finished at the end of the year 986 A.M. (A.D. 1270/1271).[5] A comparison

[1] *Ep. Ant.* II.11b–27 has been interchanged with III.17–36. Klejna, who did not know of the Georgian version of the letters, used this passage as a decisive argument against the Arabic version by claiming that it was evident that the Latin version had preserved the original context. See his 'Antonius und Ammonas', p. 331f..

[2] See *i.a. Ep. Ant.* IV.18–20, V.9, 32, 33, VI.92, VII.22–23, 36, 50–51; haplography in VI.80–81.

[3] See *GCAL* I, 456 and Samuel Rubenson, 'The Arabic Version of the Letters of St. Antony', *Actes du deuxième congrès international d'études arabes chrétiennes, OCA* 226, Rom 1986, pp. 19–29. The mss. of the monastery of St. Antony are neither included in Graf nor in Rubenson. For the Arabic corpus, see *idem,* 'Arabic Sources for the Theology of the Early Monastic Movement in Egypt', *Actes du 3e congrès international d'études arabes chrétiennes. Ed. par S. Khalil Samir S.J.* (*Parole de l'Orient* XVI), Kaslik 1991, pp. 40–45.

[4] Anbā Murqus al-Anṭūnī, *Kitāb rauḍat al-nufūs fī rasā'il al-qiddīs Anṭūniyūs,* Cairo 1899, and *Rasā'il al-qiddīs Anṭūniyūs*, Dayr al-qiddīs Anbā Maqār, 1979.

[5] ونص الكاتب انه نقلها من اللسان الصعيدي القبطي الي اللسان العربي في آخر سنة ست وثمانين وتسعماية للشهدا الابرار بديره المعروف بالعربة. *St. Mac. Hom.* 23, f. 128v.. This note occurs in a large number of the manuscripts, see *i.a. St. Ant. Theol.* 177, f. 82rv., 178, f. 86v. In *Copt. Mus. Lit.* 88, f. 126v. and *Copt. Patr. Theol.* 289, f. 81r. the note continues with a reference to the

between the Arabic manuscripts reveals that they are all dependent on the same translation. The differences are almost negligible and do not go beyond variations in spelling and the exchange of single words for synonymous expressions.[1] The numbering of the letters is the same in the Arabic version as in the Coptic. A Latin translation of the Arabic text on the basis of *Vat. ar.* 398 was made by Abraham Ecchellensis (Ibrāhīm al-Ḥāqilānī). It was printed in Paris in 1641, and later reprinted by Migne.[2]

The Arabic version is much shorter than the Georgian and Latin versions, as observed already by Klejna.[3] This is due mainly to a tendency in the Arabic version to omit some of the numerous repetitions in the letters, and to condense others.[4] The Arabic text also avoids difficult expressions, and adds explanations.[5] For the passage missing in the Georgian it is, however, the only witness besides the Latin version.[6]

6. THE GREEK VERSION

The only part of the letters preserved in Greek is the one which was included as a saying in the alphabetical collection, *Apophthegmata Patrum*.[7] The existence of a complete Greek version is, however, attested by the Latin text, which refers to a Greek original in the Vatican library from which it was translated. Although there is no note in the Georgian

---

method of translation and the two mss. used as sources. The date 1070 given by Georg Graf (*Catalogue de manuscrits arabes chrétiens conservés au Caire* (*Studi e testi* 63), the Vatican 1934, p. 35, and in *GCAL* I, p. 456), and adopted by most scholars, is evidently a mistake. From where Abraham Ecchellensis had his information giving the date as *c.* 800, repeated in *PG* 40, 957, is uncertain; no date is given in the ms. he used (*Vat. ar.* 398). See *idem, Sanctissimi patris nostri Beati Antonii magni ... epistolae viginti. Nunc primum ex Arabico Latini juris factae,* Paris 1641, p. â iii j.

1 See Rubenson, 'The Arabic Version', p. 24f., and *idem,* 'Arabic Sources'.

2 Abraham Ecchellensis, *Sanctissimi patris nostri Beati Antonii magni ... epistolae viginti,* Paris 1641. Reprinted in *PG* 40,999–1066. His translation is fairly faithful, but occasionally he smoothes the text and inserts minor explanations.

3 Klejna, 'Antonius und Ammonas', p. 330.

4 See *i.a. Ep. Ant.* V.4, 16–28, VI.5, 6b, 7, 9–12, 15, 34–36, 42–43, 60, 78–81, 83, 87–91, 93–100, 103, VII.16, 26–31b, 40–42.

5 See *i.a.* I.34 (omitting a passage on sexual sin), II.25 ('come to know this in the truth' for 'know his own mind' in G); III.3 (adding: that you strive for that which is your duty towards the Lord), III:11 (omitting 'they have not been able to discover themselves as they were created'), III:39 ('understand what is written' for 'understand oneself' in G), III:45 (that 'satan rages' for 'the power of the devil lies in the matter of this world' in G; V.38 (adding 'we were all given the freedom to do the deeds of the saints'); VI.77 (adding 'a man bringing water from the divine spring'), VI:109 (adding 'for them there is no possibility except through humility'); VII.5 (omitting 'Israelite children according to your spiritual substance'), VII:38 (adding 'and it has been made perfect within us because of our ignorance, and has taken possession of us').

6 In this passage (*Ep. Ant.* VII.58*b*–58*u*) the Arabic, however, lacks the section summarizing the history of salvation, a recurrent passage lacking also in some of the other letters, obviously this is the result of an attempt to avoid repetitions.

7 *AP/G* Antonius 22.

version directly referring to a Greek source, the use of Greek letters in some of the titles, as well as the close affinities between the Latin and the Georgian version, suggest that they had a common Greek source. The relationships between the Syriac and the Georgian and Latin versions suggest a Greek source also in this case. Further evidence for a Greek version is the note by Jerome which has already been mentioned, and which refers to a Greek translation of seven letters by Antony. If, as we assume, he is referring to these particular letters, we are also able to date the Greek version to before 390.

From the context of the letters it is clear that the quotation transmitted as a saying is an original part of Letter I, which was extracted from there and transmitted independently in the *Apophthegmata Patrum.* That this saying is independent of the tradition of the *apophthegmata* is evident not only from the form and the content but also from the fact that the saying is missing both in the small independent Latin collections and in the Syriac collection.[1] A comparison of the Greek saying with the four extant versions of the parallel text of Letter I shows that the transmission of the saying is independent of the versions of the letter, and thus irrelevant for their textual criticism. The other versions of the saying, the Coptic as well as the Latin, confirm this conclusion.[2] Our only access to the Greek rendering of the letters is by reconstruction. In the parts where we have a Coptic text this is not too difficult, as long as the Georgian or the Latin agrees with it; elsewhere we have to confine ourselves to reconstructing some of the Greek terms that were used.

7. COMPARATIVE ANALYSIS

Of these different versions either the Coptic fragments or the Greek quotation represents the text of the letters in their original language. A Coptic original has been postulated by most scholars, usually on the basis of Jerome's testimony that Antony wrote seven letters in Coptic, and the statements on his lack of Greek that are found in the *Vita Antonii* and the *Historia Lausiaca.*[3] These arguments for a Coptic original rest, however, entirely on the assumption that the letters are authentic. Likewise, the arguments for a Greek original for the letters are usually combined with

1 See appendix on the Antonian *apophthegmata.* Cf. Hermann Dörries, 'Die Vita Antonii als Geschichtsquelle', pp. 156, 215–217, 219.

2 See *AP/Bo* 22 (Amélineau, p. 25f.) and *AP/PJ* V.1.

3 A Coptic original is proposed by Winstedt, 'The Original Text'; Nau, 'La version syriaque', p. 284; Garitte, 'A propos des lettres', p. 29; *idem., Lettres de S. Antoine,* p. IV; Derwas Chitty, *The Desert a City,* Oxford 1966, p. 27; and among the modern translators by Christofoor Wagenaar, *Leven, getuigenissen, brieven van de Heilige Antonius abt,* pp. 261ff., and Lisa Cremaschi, *Vita di Antonio, Apoftegmi, Lettere,* p. 79. For Antony's suggested lack of education and knowledge of Greek, see below, pp. 38–42.

doubts concerning their authenticity.[1] If it had not been for the attribution of the letters to Antony and the wide-spread opinion that he did not know Greek, suggestions about a Coptic original might have been dismissed out of hand on the basis of the strong Greek influence in the terminology and philosophical reasoning in the letters. No unlettered monk without knowledge of Greek could be expected to have been so familiar with Greek philosophical ideas. In the cultural situation of Egypt in the first half of the fourth century Greek would, moreover, have been the medium for texts such as these. On the other hand, the translations into Coptic of texts such as the Nag Hammadi corpus, as well as the fact that even Egyptians of some influence and education were unable to write Greek—this is attested for both village clerks and church readers—cautions against discarding the possibility of a Coptic original.[2]

Because of the strong influence Greek had on Coptic, and the bilingual situation prevalent in Egypt in antiquity, it is often impossible to ascertain whether a Coptic text is an original Coptic work or a translation of a Greek text.[3] Research in Coptic language and literature has shown that it is impossible to regard influence of Greek in a text as an indication of a Greek source. Without access to a Greek version of the text, scholars have to depend on external evidence—what is known of the linguistic proficiency of the author, the environment from which the text comes, or the recipients of the text—in order to decide whether it can be regarded as a Coptic original.[4] Although we do not possess a Greek version of Antony's letters, we can compare the Coptic text with the Georgian and Latin versions, regarding them as representatives of the lost Greek version. Since there is no Syriac version of Letter IV, the only letter preserved in Coptic, the position of the Syriac version in the transmission of the letters must be decided through a comparison with the Georgian, Latin, and Arabic versions in a subsequent step.

1 Dörries argued that a number of passages were so Greek that they could not have been possible 'im Munde eines Kopten' ('Die Vita Antonii', p. 219). André Louf, *Saint Antoine: Lettres*, p. 20, leaves the question of original language open, without, however, affecting the question of authenticity, and so does Tito Orlandi, 'Coptic Literature', *The Roots of Egyptian Christianity'*, Philadelphia 1986, p. 63f.

2 See below, chapter V for languages and literacy in Egypt in Antony's times.

3 See Martin Krause, 'Koptische Literatur', *LÄ* III, p. 694. An exception is the Sahidic version of the *Apophthegmata Patrum*, but here the Greek text is preserved together with a faithful Latin translation. See Maurice Chaine, 'Le texte original des Apophthegmes des Pères', *Mélanges de la faculté orientale (Université Saint-Joseph, Beyrouth)*, V,2, Beirut 1912, pp. 541–569.

4 See *i.a.* K. H. Kuhn, *A Panegyric on Apollo, Archimandrite of the Monastery of Isaac, by Stephen, Bishop of Heracleopolis Magna* (*CSCO* 394), Louvain 1978, pp. xi–xii, and D. W. Johnson, *A Panegyric on Macarius, Bishop of Tkow, attributed to Dioscorus of Alexandria* (*CSCO* 416), Louvain 1980, pp. 11*–13*.

The Coptic, Georgian and Latin Versions

Since the fourth letter is the only one fully preserved in Coptic, a comparison of the versions must start here. A detailed analysis of this letter has shown that the Coptic must be regarded as the original, and that the Georgian and Latin versions derive from the same Greek translation.[1] The arguments for the connection between the Georgian and the Latin versions are their adoption of identical insertions and a strikingly parallel word-order. It is even possible to reconstruct, albeit hypothetically, the lost Greek text with the help of its Coptic source and its two translations. That the Coptic text must be given priority over the lost Greek version can be proved by a number of instances in the source of the Georgian and Latin versions, in which words have been inserted. In some cases, moreover, the Coptic could not possibly be a translation from the Greek.[2] Some of the more obvious passages illustrate this. The first column gives the Coptic, the second the Georgian, and the third the Latin text.[3]

Letter IV,2-3:

Coptic	Georgian	Latin
ϯⲟⲩⲱϣ ⲉⲧⲣⲉⲧⲛⲉⲓⲙⲉ ⲉⲧ- ⲁⲅⲁⲡⲏ ⲉⲧⲟⲩⲧⲱⲓ ⲛⲙⲙⲏⲧⲛ ϫⲉⲛⲟⲩⲁⲅⲁⲡⲏ ⲁⲛ ⲧⲉ ⲛⲥⲱⲙⲁ- ⲧⲓⲕⲏ, ⲁⲗⲗⲁ ⲟⲩⲁⲅⲁⲡⲏ ⲧⲉ ⲙⲙⲛⲧⲣⲉϥϣⲙϣⲉⲛⲟⲩⲧⲉ. ⲧⲙⲛⲧϣⲃⲏⲣ ⲅⲁⲣ ⲛⲥⲱⲙⲁ ⲙⲙⲛⲧⲥⲧⲁϫⲣⲟ ⲟⲩⲇⲉ ⲛⲥ- ⲥⲙⲟⲛⲧ ⲁⲛ, ⲉⲥⲕⲓⲙ ⲉⲃⲟⲗ ϩⲓⲧⲏⲛϩⲉⲛⲧⲏⲩ ⲛϣⲙⲙⲟ.	და უწყებაჲ თქუენი მნებავს სიყუარულისაჲ რომელი მა- ქუს თქუენდა მიმართ რაჲმეთუ არა არს კორცი- ელი, არამედ სულიერი ღმრთისმსახურებისაჲ. რაჲ- მეთუ კორცთა ჩუენთა სი- ყუარული დაუმთკიცებელ არს და დაუდგომ და შერყე- ულ[4] უცხოთა გან ქართა.	Agnoscere autem vos volo dilectionem quam habeo in vobis quia non est corpo- rea, sed est dilectio spiritus culturae dei. Corporum quippe nostro- rum amicitia in substantia et in constantia saepe ab extraneis ventis.[5]
I want you to know the *love* I have for you, that it is not a bodily *love*, but that it is a *love* of divine service. For the friendship of the *body* has no firmness, nor is it stable, it is moved around by alien winds.	I want you to know the *love*, which I have for you, that it is not bodily, but *spiritual*, of divine service. For the friendship of *our bodies* is unsettled and unstable, and is moved by alien winds.	I want you to know the *love*, which I have for you, that it is not corporeal, but the *love* of the *spirit of* divine service. For the friendship of *our bodies* is unsubstantial and inconsistent, constantly (moved) by alien winds.

[1] See Samuel Rubenson, 'Der vierte Antoniusbrief und die Frage nach der Echtheit und Originalsprache der Antoniusbriefe', *OC* 73 (1989), pp 124–155. This is also suggested by Gribomont in his review of Garitte's edition (*RHE* 51, p. 547).

[2] In addition to the examples quoted below the following verses are discussed in the article cited above: IV.1, 7, 9, 11, 12, 13, 15, 17.

[3] The texts are from the editions of Champerius and Garitte, where I follow ms. B in Garitte's apparatus. The translations are mine. Differences between the versions are in italics.

[4] Ms B: შეურყეულ (unmoved).

[5] The edition in *Orthodoxia Theologiae,* Basel 1555 has 'in substantia et in constantia est, quae movetur saepe ab extraneis ventis', and *PG* 40, 999, has 'in insubstantia et inconstantia est, quae movetur saepe ab extraneis ventis'.

The accord between the Georgian and Latin versions in their use of the word 'spiritual/spirit' as a definition of 'divine service' and of the attribute 'our' for 'body' indicates a common source. Since the first is a natural addition made to correspond with 'bodily', and the second more likely to be an addition than a word suppressed, the differences suggest a Coptic original for the common Greek source of the two versions.[1] The second difference is that the Coptic text has 'love' three times, the Latin twice, and the Georgian once. This could be a natural reduction to smoothe the text; an expansion seems less likely. The position of the Latin between the Coptic and the Georgian indicates that the Latin version is translated from a manuscript of an earlier stage in the transmission than the one used for the Georgian translation, an inference which, as we will see, is supported by the comparison of the Georgian and the Latin with the Syriac version.

Letter IV,6:

Coptic	Georgian	Latin
ⲉⲧⲃⲉⲡⲁⲓ ⲛⲓⲕⲉⲡⲣⲟⲫⲏⲧⲏⲥ ⲙⲛⲛⲁⲡⲟⲥⲧⲟⲗⲟⲥ, ⲡⲉⲭⲟⲣⲟⲥ ⲉⲧⲟⲩⲁⲁⲃ, ⲛⲁⲓ ⲛⲧⲁⲡⲛⲟⲩⲧⲉ ⲥⲟⲧⲡⲟⲩ ⲉⲧⲁⲛϩⲟⲩⲧⲟⲩ ⲉⲩⲕⲏⲣⲩⲅⲙⲁ ⲛⲁⲡⲟⲥⲧⲟⲗⲓⲕⲏ, ϩⲛⲧⲙⲛⲧⲁⲅⲁⲑⲟⲥ ⲙⲡⲛⲟⲩⲧⲉ ⲡⲉⲓⲱⲧ ⲁⲩϣⲱⲡⲉ ⲉⲩⲙⲏⲣ ϩⲙⲡⲉⲭⲣⲓⲥⲧⲟⲥ ⲓⲏⲥⲟⲩⲥ.	ამის თჳსცა წინაწარმეტყუელნი და მოციქულნი და ყოველნი ქრებულნი წმიდათანი, რომელნი ღმრთისა მიერ გამორჩეულ იყვნეს და რწმონებულ იყო მათთა სამოციქულოჲ იგი ქადაგებაჲ, მამისა და ღმრთისა სახიერებითა კრულ იყვნეს იგინი ქრესტე იესუს თჳს.	Propter quod et prophetae et apostoli, omnisque sanctorum chorus deo suscepti, ut crederetur ei apostolica praedicatio per voluntatem Patris, vincti Christi effecti sunt.
For this reason the prophets too, and the apostles, the *holy choir*, these whom God chose in order to entrust to them the apostolic preaching, in the *goodness* of God the Father, became prisoners in Christ Jesus.	For this reason the apostles and prophets *and* all the *assemblies of the saints,* who were chosen by God and entrusted with this apostolic preaching, through the *grace* of the Father and God, were made prisoners for the sake of Christ Jesus.	For this reason the prophets too and the apostles, and all the *choir of the saints*, taken up by God, that the apostolic preaching might be entrusted to *it*, through the *will* of the Father, were made prisoners of Christ.

In the Georgian and Latin versions 'choir/assembly' is modified by 'all', and instead of the adjective 'holy' a noun is employed, 'the saints'. That this resulted in a change from the singular to the plural was not observed by the Latin translator, who kept the indirect object in the subsequent phrase in the singular, thus creating a lack of concord. In the Georgian version the change is, however, carried through and 'the saints' are made the subject of the next phrase. Again the Coptic text can hardly be a

1 The Greek text can thus have been something like: γνῶναι ὑμᾶς θέλω τὴν ἀγάπην ἣν ἔχω εἰς ὑμᾶς, ὅτι οὐκ ἐστὶν σωματική, ἀλλὰ ἀγάπη τῆς θεοσεβείας πνευματικῆς (or λογικῆς). τῶν γὰρ σωμάτων ἡμῶν φιλία οὐκ ἐστηρίχθη, οὐδὲ ἐστάθη, σαλευομένη ὑπὸ ξενῶν ἀνέμων.

translation of the common source of the two others, and again the Latin text seems closer to the Coptic than does the Georgian.[1]

Though it seems plausible that the Latin version derives from a Greek text antedating the source of the Georgian version, a closer analysis of the entire corpus shows clearly that the Latin text is far less reliable than the Georgian. It is often very obscure, and in a number of cases the translator seems to have misunderstood his text, or simply omitted phrases.[2] Occasionally there are, however, verses where the Latin version preserves the original, while the Georgian omits words or reinterprets the meaning of the text.[3] For the long passage at the end of Letter VII, which is missing in the Georgian, the Latin version is the only source besides the Arabic.

The precedence of the Coptic version over the Greek source behind the Georgian and Latin versions is illustrated by a furher example from the same letter.

Letter IV, 8:

ϩⲱⲥⲧⲉ ⲡⲉⲥϩⲁⲓ ⲛⲧⲉⲡⲛⲟⲙⲟⲥ ⲛϥⲉⲣϩⲱⲃ ⲛⲙⲙⲁⲛ ϩⲛⲟⲩⲙⲛⲧϩⲙϩⲁⲗ ⲉⲛⲁⲛⲟⲩⲥ, ϣⲁⲛⲧⲛϭⲙϭⲟⲙ ⲉⲣϫⲟⲉⲓⲥ ⲉϫⲛⲡⲁⲑⲟⲥ ⲛⲓⲙ ⲁⲩⲱ ⲛⲧⲛϫⲱⲕ ⲉⲃⲟⲗ ⲛⲟⲩϣⲙϣⲉ ⲉⲛⲁⲛⲟⲩϥ ⲛⲧⲉⲧⲁⲣⲉⲧⲏ ⲉⲃⲟⲗ ϩⲓⲧⲟⲟⲧϥ ⲙⲡⲉⲓⲁⲡⲟⲥⲧⲟⲗⲓⲕⲟⲛ.	რაჲთა დაწერილი იგი რჩუ-ლი შეეწე თქუენდა იყოს კეთილითა მით მონებითა, ვიდრემდის შეუძლოთ უფლებად ყოველთა ვნებათა ზედა კორცთასა, და სრულე-ბაჲ იგი მოვიღოთ კეთილითა მით მსახურებითა სათნოე-ბისაჲთა სამოციქულოჲთა მით ცხორებითა.[4]	Scripta itaque lex coopera-trix fiat vobis in hoc servi-tio, usquequo dominari possimus omni vitio, et perficiamur in optimo ministerio virtutis per apo-stolicum mandatum.
Thus the text of the law works *with us* in a good service, until we are able to control every passion and *fulfill* the good ministry of virtue through this *apostolikon.*	Thus the written law is an assistant *to you* in this good service until we are able to control all the passions *of the bodies* and *accept the fulfillment of* the good ministry of virtue through the *apostolic life.*	Thus the written law is an assistant *to you* in this service until we are able to control all passions and *become perfected* in the highest ministry of virtue through the apostolic *command.*

[1] In Greek: διὸ (or διὰ τοῦτο) καὶ οἱ προφῆται καὶ οἱ ἀπόστολοι καὶ πᾶς ὁ χορὸς τῶν ἁγίων, οἱ ὑπὸ θεοῦ ἐκλεκτοὶ καὶ πιστευθέντες τὸ ἀποστολικὸν κήρυγμα διὰ τὴν ἐπιείκειαν τοῦ θεοῦ τοῦ πατρός, ἐγένοντο δέσμιοι ἐν Χριστῷ Ἰησοῦ.

[2] Also in Letter IV some examples of the lack of reliability of the Latin version can be given. See IV.2: C and G both read θεός and L reads κύριος; IV.5: C and G have similar non-verbal constructions while L has a verbal sentence; IV.6: C and G read ἀγαθός while L reads βουλή; IV.6 and 7: L has dropped the names Jesus and Paul; IV.7: L lacks a word for καλός; IV.13: L has *mala vita* for C and G βίος σαρκικός/σωματικός; IV.17: L has totally misunderstood the text. For other examples see the discussion of the Syriac and Arabic texts.

[3] This can be shown by comparisons with the preserved Coptic fragments and with the Arabic version. See *i.a.* VI,99 where the Latin has 'laetificationem ac requiem', corresponding to Coptic ⲟⲩⲛⲟϥ ⲁⲩⲱ ⲙⲧⲟⲛ to be found in the quotation preserved by Besa. The Georgian has only სახარებაჲ ('joy').

[4] Ms B: მსახურებითა (ministry).

In the Georgian and Latin versions the lack of concord between the pronoun in the second person plural and the verb in the first person must be due to a confusion, intentional or not, of ὑμῖν and ἡμῖν in their Greek source. Another difference that might be regarded as significant is that the Coptic version uses the active voice of the verb 'to fulfill' (ϫωκ ⲉⲃⲟⲗ), while the other two have the passive (სრულებაჲ იგი მოვიღვთ and 'perficiamur). Since there is no passive voice in Coptic, Greek passive forms were regularly translated into the active; the distinction was observed by other means (usually the use of third person + object). It is, however, unlikely that a passive should have been turned into the active of the *same* person, as in this case. But the opposite is not at all improbable. In the last sentence the Georgian and Latin translators have found it necessary to provide 'apostolic' with a noun (*life* and *ministry* in the two Mss. of G and *command* in L), but their different solutions make it probable that the Greek source agreed with the Coptic. It is, however, easier to imagine the use of ἀποστολικόν as a noun in a Coptic original than in a Greek.[1]

In all comparisons of early Christian texts Biblical quotations constitute a special case. Though there are exceptions, it can generally be assumed that versions which conform to the established text of the Bible are secondary to versions which do not conform to the text. Authors usually quoted the Bible from memory, while copyists tended to revise the text they were copying according to what had become the standard rendering. Moreover, the early authors did not usually have the version of the Bible which later became the established. As for the text of the Coptic version or versions of the Bible which existed in the fourth century, very little is known.[2] In Antony's letters there is no marked difference between quotations and allusions to Biblical texts, and throughout the letters the Biblical language is strongly present.[3] A good example of how Biblical texts are treated in the different versions is given by the quotation from Sap. 1:4-5 in the fourth letter. To facilitate the comparison, the text of the Septuagint is given underneath in each of the versions, as well as in the text of the Septuagint.

1 A Greek reconstruction might give the following: ὥστε τὰ γράμματα τοῦ νόμου (ὁ γεγραμμένος νόμος) συνεργὰ ἐγένετο ὑμῖν ἐν τῇ δουλείᾳ τῇ καλῇ ἕως ἂν δυνώμεθα κυριεύειν παντὸς πάθους καὶ τελειώμεθα ἐν τῇ ἀγαθῇ διακονίᾳ τῆς ἀρετῆς διὰ τὸ ἀποστολικόν.

2 See Bruce M. Metzger, *The early Versions of the New Testament. Their Origin, Transmission, and Limitations,* Oxford 1977, pp. 99–152. His use of the story about how Antony became an ascetic as told in *VA* 1 is, however, based on Antony's proposed lack of Greek. As will be shown below, this view must be questioned on the basis of the letters.

3 I have been able to detect almost one hundred different Biblical passages quoted or alluded to in the letters. The fact that many of them repeatedly occur and the way they are used suggest that Antony is not directly dependent on his own reading of the Bible, but on exegetical and homiletical tradition. See below, chapter IV for examples.

Letter IV, 14

ⲙⲉⲣⲉⲡⲉⲡⲛⲉⲩⲙⲁ ⲅⲁⲣ ϩⲱⲛ ⲉϩⲟⲩⲛ ⲉⲟⲩⲯⲩⲭⲏ ⲉⲣⲉⲡⲉⲥϩⲏⲧ ϫⲁϩⲙ ⲟⲩⲇⲉ ⲟⲩⲥⲱⲙⲁ ⲛⲣⲉϥ- ⲣⲛⲟⲃⲉ, ⲟⲩⲁⲅⲓⲟⲛ ⲛⲇⲩⲛⲁⲙⲓⲥ- ⲡⲉ ⲉϥⲥⲁϩⲏⲩ ⲉⲃⲟⲗ ⲛⲕⲣⲟϥ ⲛⲓⲙ.	ხოლო ბოროტისა მოქმედსა სულსა არა შევიდის სული ღმრთისაჲ არცა დაიმკვდრეს კორცთა შინა ცოდვითა განკაფულთა,რაჲმეთუ წმი- დაჲ ძალი არს და ევლტის ყოვლისა გან ზაკვისა.	*In malam enim animam non* *intrabit spiritus Dei, nec* *habitabit in corpore sub-* *dito peccatis, sancta quippe* *est virtus, fugiens ab omni* *dolo.*
For the spirit does not enter *a soul whose heart is de-* *filed, nor a body which sins.* *It is a holy power, which* *removes itself from all guile.*	*For into an evil-doing soul* *does not the spirit of God* *enter, nor does it live in a* *body affected by sin, since it* *is a holy power and flees* *from all guile.*	*For into an evil soul does* *not the spirit of God enter,* *nor does it live in a body* *subjected to sin, indeed it is* *a holy power, fleeing from* *all guile.*

Sapientia 1:4-5:[1]

ϫⲉ ⲙⲉⲣⲉⲧⲥⲟⲫⲓⲁ ⲃⲱⲕ ⲉϩⲟⲩⲛ ⲉⲩⲯⲩⲭⲏ ⲉⲥϩⲟⲟⲩ ⲟⲩⲇⲉ ⲙⲉⲥⲟⲩⲱϩ ϩⲛⲥⲱⲙⲁ ⲛⲣⲉϥⲣ- ⲛⲟⲃⲉ. ⲡⲉⲡⲛ̅ⲁ̅ ⲉⲧⲟⲩⲁⲁⲃ ⲛⲧⲥⲟⲫⲓⲁ ϣⲁϥⲡⲱⲧ ⲉⲃⲟⲗ ⲛⲕⲣⲟϥ...	რაჲმეთუ ბოროტისმოქმედსა სულსა არა შევიდეს სიბრძნე, არცა დაიმკვდრონ კორცთა შინა განკაფულთა ცოდვათა. რამეთუ წმიდა სული სწავლისა ევლტინ ზავუასა...	Quoniam in malivolam ani- mam non intrabit sapientia nec habitabit in corpore subdito peccatis. Sanctus enim spiritus disciplinae effugiet fictum...

ὅτι εἰς κακότεχνον ψυχὴν οὐκ εἰσελεύσεται σοφία οὐδὲ κατοικήσει ἐν σώματι καταχρέῳ ἁμαρτίας. ἅγιον γὰρ πνεῦμα παιδείας φεύξεται δόλον...

Here all three versions have changed σοφία (ⲥⲟⲫⲓⲁ, სიბრძნჱ, sapientia) to πνεῦμα (ⲡⲛⲉⲩⲙⲁ, სული, spiritus), and πνεῦμα (ⲡⲛⲉⲩⲙⲁ, სული, spiritus) to δύναμις (ⲇⲩⲛⲁⲙⲓⲥ, ძალი, virtus). In the Georgian and the Latin versions 'of God' is added to 'the spirit', a change probably influenced by 1.Cor. 1:24. Like the Biblical original, but unlike C, both G and L have the passive voice in the following line, and the verb 'to flee' in the last line. For κακότεχνον the Coptic text, moreover, has a genuinely Coptic construction, ⲉⲣⲉⲡⲉⲥϩⲏⲧ ϫⲁϩⲙ, which is not found in the Coptic Bible and unlikely to be attributed to a Greek source. Here, too, a Coptic original for the letters seems more likely than a Greek. A last verse which can hardly be explained by proposing priority for the Greek version behind the Latin and the Georgian text is verse 17, to which we will return later in connection with the dating of the letters.[2]

This comparison of the versions thus supports the evidence for a Coptic original, which is usually associated with the attribution of the letters to

[1] The Coptic text is taken from *The Coptic (Sahidic) Version of Certain Books of the Old Testament from a papyrus in the British Museum* (ed. by Sir Heribert Thompson), Oxford 1908. The Georgian text comes from the edition by E. Dočanašvili Tiflis 1985. The Latin text is from the Vetus Latina edition, Freiburg 1980. The Greek text comes from the Septuagint edition by A. Rahlfs, Göttingen 1935.

[2] See below, p. 44.

Antony.[1] Moreover, there is nothing in the vocabulary or syntax which can't be found in other Coptic originals. The arguments for a Greek original, *i.e.* the Greek flavour and Greek ideas found in the letters, can easily be explained by supposing that the author's background was heavily influenced by Greek thought. In the early fourth century this would not have been uncommon among the Coptic-speaking population of Egypt. It is even possible that the author, while fully capable of writing his letters in Greek, wrote them in Coptic for the benefit of his audience. Unfortunately the lack of a Coptic text for the other letters, as well as the greater differences between the Latin and the Georgian in most of the letters, reduce further reconstructions of the lost Greek version to mere guesswork.

The Syriac and Arabic versions

The first translation that was made, besides the lost Greek one, was no doubt the Syriac, which on the basis of the oldest and fortunately dated manuscript goes back at least to the beginning of the sixth century. The editor of the Syriac text suggested that it might have been translated directly from the Coptic.[2] Since there is no part of the letters preserved in both Coptic and Syriac, it is difficult to prove or disprove this suggestion. Through the publication of the Georgian version it has become evident that the differences between the Syriac and the Latin pointed to by Nau as an argument for a Coptic source are not conclusive. But although the Syriac can be shown to be close to the common source of the Georgian and Latin, it can still go back to a more primitive form. For historical reasons it is, however, rather unlikely that the translation was made from anything but the Greek text. Actually, no convincing examples are known of Syriac translations made directly from the Coptic.[3] The few Greek words which occur also suggest a Greek source for the translation, though they can be found in Coptic texts as well.[4]

In his edition Nau also suggested that the Arabic text was a translation of the Syriac text. This opinion is disproved not only by a comparative

1 Even though the Coptic text could hypothetically be regarded as a translation of a lost Greek original, and the Greek source of the Georgian and Latin versions as a retranslation of the Coptic translation, this seems a bit farfetched.

2 Nau, 'La version syriaque', p. 284. His suggestion was based on the differences between the Syriac and the Latin versions, the Georgian being unknown to him.

3 The suggestion that the *Vita Antonii* was translated directly from Coptic into Syriac is dealt with in chapter VI. The theories put forward by René Draguet on traces of Coptic language in Greek and Syriac translations of monastic texts has not found much approval. See his 'Le chapitre de l'*Histoire Lausiaque* sur les Tabennésiotes dérive-t-il d'une source copte?', *Le Muséon* 57 (1944), pp. 53–145, and 58 (1945), pp. 15–95; *idem, Les cinq recensions de l'ascéticon syriaque d'abba Isaïe* (*CSCO* 122), pp. 44*–73* and *idem, La vie primitive de saint Antoine conservée en syriaque* (*CSCO* 418), Louvain 1980, pp. 25*–98*.

4 The two Greek words which occur are πολιτεία (I,9) and χωρίς (I,74).

analysis of the texts,[1] but also by the fact that the Arabic manuscripts state that the translation was made from Coptic. Furthermore, there is no evidence whatsoever for any translation of more than the first letter into Syriac, while the larger Arabic corpus is attested in Coptic as well. The accord of the Arabic numbering of the letters with the Coptic, in contrast to the two versions derived from the lost Greek translation, also implies a Coptic source for the Arabic version. Thus it is clear that the Arabic version is the only one deriving directly from the Coptic; all the others are dependent on the lost Greek translation. Unfortunately, it does not present a reliable text. As noted above, its omissions and its tendency to summarize make it shorter than the other versions. Also, a close comparison of the Arabic text of Letter IV with the Coptic original shows that the Arabic translator was not very accurate or faithful, but tried to make the text easy to understand.[2] This tendency is even more pronounced in some of the other letters.[3] This does not, however, mean that—as has often been said—the Arabic version is without value. In a large number of cases it is the only version which can be used to decide if it is the Georgian or the Latin version which best preserves the original text. In the cases where they differ from each other, and one of them agrees with the Arabic, we can be sure that this is the original text, since the Arabic was transmitted quite independently of the Greek tradition.[4]

Once it has been established that the Arabic translation was made directly from the Coptic original, it can be used to determine the position of the Syriac text. As will be shown by the following examples, when the Latin and the Georgian disagree, the Syriac text usually agrees with the Georgian. In a number of these cases the Arabic tends to agree with the Latin, which suggests that the Georgian and the Syriac have common de-

1 The Arabic text preserves the portions which are missing in the Syriac version. These amount to the verses 39–40, 60 and 63–65. In I,12–13, the Syriac has another combination of quotations from the Psalter than the Georgian and Latin versions, a combination not reflected in the Arabic. In I,16, the Arabic has preserved the longer text, also known from the Georgian, but summarized (differently) in the Latin and the Syriac versions. There is also a large number of agreements between the Latin and Georgian on one hand and the Arabic on the other against the Syriac, see *i.a.* the verses 2, 9, 10, 26, 37, 42, 53, 59, 62, 72.

2 It is even possible to distinguish between the different ways in which the translator has interfered with the text:

a) Omission of words: IV.2, 6, 9, 12, 17;

b) Additional comments: IV.9, 18, 19;

c) Reinterpretation: IV.5, 13.

3 In addition to the examples given above, p. 21, n. 5, typical examples are:

a) Om.: I.34, III.45, VII.11;

b) Expl.: III.9, 28, V.9, 12, 40, VI.71, VII.8, 44;

c) Interpr.: II.23, 25. III.9, 20, 28, 45, V.7, 17, VI.16, 21, 62, 70, VII.4, 53.

4 Examples where the Arabic supports L against G are found in II.3, III.6, III.14, V.30, VII.34, and examples where A supports G against L are found in V.9, V.33, V.35, VI.36, VII.22–23, VII.57. In the last case we have an allusion to Biblical texts (Luk 21:19; Hebr. 10:36) and thus L could be correct even though A and G agree.

viations from the original. Moreover, there are no examples of an agreement of the Syriac and the Latin against the Arabic and the Georgian. It can further be observed that, though the Syriac text is the oldest preserved version, it is less reliable than has usually been taken for granted.[1]

In the following examples the first column gives the Latin text, the second the Georgian, the third the Syriac, and the fourth the Arabic text.[2]

Letter I,26-27:

Tum vero ille de- ductor spiritus in- cipit adaperire ani- mae oculos ad poenitentiam exhibendam, et ut sanctificetur etiam sensus, discretionem intermediam praebet, incipiens doceri a spiritu sanctificare corporis et animae poenitentiam	მაშინ წინამძღუარ- მან სულთამან იწყის ახილვად თუალთა სულისა მათისათა, რაჲთა მოსცეს მათ თჳსი სინანული რაჲთა წმიდა იყოს; და გონებამან განწვალებაჲ შორის მათსა მოსცის, და იწყის სწავლად სულითა მით განწმედად კორცთა და სულისა სინან- ულითა;	ܗܝܕܝܢ ܪܘܚܐ ܡܕܒܪܢܐ ܡܫܪܐ ܦܬܚ ܥܝ̈ܢܐ ܕܢܦܫܐ ܡܛܠ ܕܢܬܠ ܐܦ ܠܗ̇ ܬܝܒܘܬܐ ܕܬܬܕܟܐ. ܐܦ ܗܘܢܐ ܕܠܒܐ ܡܫܪܐ ܦܪܫ ܒܝܬ ܬܪܝܗܘܢ ܒܗ̇ ܐܦ ܠܒܐ ܡܫܪܐ ܕܢܐܠܦ ܡܢ ܪܘܚܐ ܡܛܠ ܕܢܕܟܐ ܬܪܝܗܘܢ ܒܬܝܒܘܬܐ ܠܦܓܪܐ ܘܠܢܦܫܐ	وتفتح عيني النفس ايضاً للتوبة الحقيقة لكي تُطهّر مع الجسد ويكونا كلاهما في الطهر واحداً لان هذا هو تعليم روح القدس
Then truly the guid- ing spirit begins to open the eyes of the soul to show it repentance. And, that it may be purified, even the mind effects a distinction between them by beginning to learn from the spirit to sanctify the repentance of the body and soul.	Then the guide *of* *the souls* begins to open the eyes of their soul(s) in order to grant them its repentance so that it becomes pure. And the mind grants a separation between them and begins to learn from the spirit to purify the body and the soul through repentance.	Then the guiding spirit begins to open the eyes of the soul to give also to it repentance so that it may be purified. Also the mind of the heart begins to sepa- rate the two. Through it also the heart begins to learn from the spirit to pu- rify them both through repentance, body and soul.	It (the spirit) also opens the eyes of the soul to the *true* repentance, so that it becomes purified *with the body.* And they *both be-* *come one* in purity since this is the teaching of the *Holy* Spirit.

[1] The Syriac text is usually the basis of the modern translations, see Chitty, Louf, and Wagenaar. Besides the texts quoted and the omissions mentioned above the following examples of unreliability can be mentioned: I.2: S lacks the passage about 'the calling of the Word of God' found in L as well as in A; I.9: S has introduced a reference to the ascetic life, not found in the other versions; I.28–30: the Syriac has reinterpreted the text; and I.62: S drops the reference to the Spirit speaking through the mouth of David.

[2] The Latin text is given according to Champerius, the Georgian according to Garitte (for the first letter ms. B is missing), the Syriac according to ms. A, and the Arabic according to the edition in *Kitāb rauḍat al-nufūs.* The translations are my own. Different readings are in the translations marked by italics.

The close relations between the Georgian, Latin and Syriac versions are obvious. They all refer to the Spirit as a 'guide', and they all make the mind the subject of the separation. The independence of the Arabic version, and its tendency to simplify the text, are also borne out clearly. The recurrent use in the Syriac of 'heart' or 'the mind of the heart' (ܠܒܐ and ܠܒܐ, ܗܘܢܗ), which is exemplified here, is not reflected in the other versions, except in the Biblical quotations and the expression 'of all his heart'. The Georgian version consistently uses გონებაჲ (the mind, νοῦς), the Latin 'sensus', and the Arabic العقل , or in this case, ارادة العقل (the mind, or the will of the mind).[1] Since in Coptic the same word, ϩΗΤ, means both heart and mind, the Syriac use could be taken as an argument for a direct translation from Coptic into Syriac. However, Syriac ܠܒܐ is possible as a translation of both νοῦς and καρδία.[2] In addition, there are signs of a close relationship between the Georgian and the Syriac versions. In this case they both use the verb 'give' in verse 26, as well as the expression 'to purify body and soul through repentance'. This relationship between the Georgian and the Syriac is more evident in a number of other verses.[3]

Letter I,43:

Sin vero dimiserit semetipsum sensus a testimoniis quibus spiritus testificatur ei; tunc maligni spiritus super-sederunt (?) con-gregationi corporis, et oppugnant illo motu	უკუეთუ დააცადოს თავით თჳსით გონე-ბამან წამებათა მათ შინა რომელთა სუ-ლი იგი უწამებს მას, მაშინ უკეთურთა მათ სულთა შეუთესიან შესვარ-ულებასა მას კორც-თასა და ჰბრძვანედ მით აღძრვითა	ܐܢ ܕܝܢ ܒܣܐ ܠܒܐ ܒܗܠܝܢ ܬܠܬܐ ܙܘܥܝ̈ܢ ܒܡܐ ܕܪܘܚܐ ܡܣܗܕܐ ܠܗ ܡܫܬܠܛܝܢ ܒܗ ܪܘܚܐ ܕܒܝܫܬܐ ܘܙܪܥܝܢ ܒܡܫܠܡܘܬܗ ܕܦܓܪܐ ܟܠ ܚܫܐ ܘܡܥܝܪܝܢ ܘܡܚܝܝܢ ܒܗ ܩܪܒܐ ܥܙܝܙܐ	فان غفل الانسان عن الشهادات والتعليم التي قد سمعها هذه فحينئذٍ تقوى عليه الارواحُ الردية وتنجس جسده
If the mind turns itself from the testimonies which the spirit testifies to it, then the evil spirits *override the constitution* of the body and attack through this motion.	If, however, the mind keeps away from itself regarding the testimonies which the spirit testifies to it, then the evil spirits *sow in the constitution* of the body and attack through this motion.	But if the heart spurns by*these three motions,* what the spirit testifies to it, the evil spirits *take dominion over it and sow in the constitution* of the body all passions. They stir up and bring to life intense warfare against it.	But if man ignores these testimonies and *instructions* which *he has heard,* then the evil spirits *prevail over him and defile his body.*

1 See *Ep. Ant.* I.26, 32, 42, 43, 47, 48, 56, and 66.

2 See R. Payne Smith, *Thesaurus Syriacus* II, Oxford 1901, p. 1877.

3 See *Ep. Ant.* I.15, 37, 43, 51, 53, 59, and 74.

The close relationship between the Latin, Georgian and Syriac is obvious, as well as the attempt by the Arabic translator to make the text easier to understand. The important passage common to the Georgian and the Syriac texts is the use of the expression 'to sow into the mass of the body'. Either this expression is something original, which in the Arabic and Latin has been simplified into 'override/prevail', or it is an expression peculiar to the source of the Syriac and the Georgian versions. The fact that the Syriac has added the expression 'take dominion over' as a gloss, as well as the possibility that the Latin *congregatio* reflects the same expression as 'mass' in Georgian and Syriac, makes the first alternative the most likely.

Other passages, however, make it unlikely that the agreements of the Latin and Arabic against the Georgian and Syriac are the result of unrelated revisions of the original. In verse 53 the Latin and the Arabic, in contrast to the other two, both have the word 'always', albeit in a somewhat different context, since the Arabic has interfered heavily with the passage. In verse 59 the Latin says: 'in orationibus et misericordiis moveantur' (moved in prayers and mercy), and the Arabic has ورفعها للصلاة وفعل الرحمة (and their raising for prayer and acts of mercy). Neither the Georgian nor the Syriac has any equivalent of 'moving/raising'. If the Syriac version had been a translation independent of the source of the Georgian, we would also have expected instances of agreement of the Syriac with the other versions against the Georgian.

Conclusions

In the attempt to establish a stemma of the different versions of Antony's letters, Letter IV has been used as a point of departure since it is the only letter preserved in Coptic. The analysis of this letter shows that the Georgian and Latin versions of the letters derive from a common Greek source, now lost. It also shows that the Coptic version must be accepted as having priority over the lost Greek text. The Syriac and Arabic versions have been located in the stemma by means of Letter I. A comparison of the versions of this letter shows that the Syriac version is fairly close to the Georgian and Latin versions, particularly to the former. It is further evident that the Arabic version is completely independent of the Syriac, and has to be regarded as a free and abridged translation of the original Coptic version.

As for the relations between the Syriac and Greek textual traditions, it can be noted that there are some instances of agreement between the Latin version and the Arabic against the Syriac and the Georgian, making it likely that the Syriac is based on a text closer to the Georgian version than to the Latin. There are, moreover, no instances of agreement between the Syriac and the Latin version against the Georgian. It can thus be assumed that the Latin translation derives from a Greek text of an earlier stage in the transmission than the one used by the Syriac and Georgian translators. But even if the Arabic and the Latin versions are translations of texts closer to the original than the Georgian and the Syriac versions, this does not make them more reliable. The Arabic version is a very free translation and the Latin is often confused, probably due to a poor source. Although the Syriac version of Letter I is not only the one preserved in the oldest extant manuscripts, but, no doubt, the oldest preserved translation, it does not present the most reliable text. In a number of passages and in important expressions the accord between the three other versions shows that the Syriac translator was less accurate than has been supposed. Except for the parts preserved in Coptic, the best witness to the original text is no doubt the Georgian version. Only when at least two of the other versions agree against the Georgian should we be obliged to reject its readings.

The result of the comparative analysis gives the following stemma:

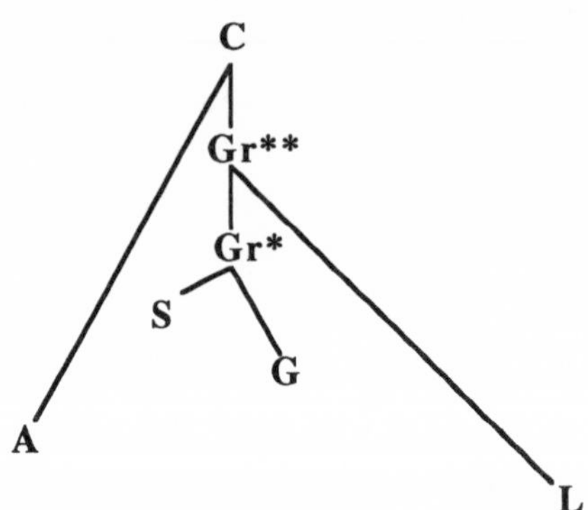

C	= the Coptic version, *c.* 340.
Gr**	= the Greek translation, *c.* 360.
Gr *	= the Greek source for S and G, early fifth century.
S	= the Syriac translation, late fifth century.
G	= the Georgian translation, sixth–eighth century.
A	= the Arabic translation, 1271.
L	= the Latin translation, 1475.

II. The Historical Setting

The Author of the Letters

The authenticity of the letters attributed to Antony, like that of so many other early Christian writings, was questioned by the patrologists of the turn of the last century. To Otto Bardenhewer they were too long, too theoretical, and too moderate to have been written by a vigorous monk such as Antony.[1] Although Ludwig von Hertling and Franz Klejna regarded them as authentic and von Hertling even used them as sources for the life and work of Antony, they have since been neglected.[2] The lack of a more extensive text in the original language—whether Greek or Coptic—the need for more exhaustive philological investigations, and the fact that the letters are inconsistent both with the description of Antony in the *Vita Antonii* and, more decisively, with the concept of the early monks in the *Apophthegmata Patrum*, caused scholars such as Karl Heussi and Hermann Dörries to remain cautious about their authenticity.[3] Gérard Garitte, however, apart from publishing the complete Georgian version, was able to show, from external evidence—especially the quotations of the letters in the writings of Besa and Shenoute—that the letters ought to be considered genuine, and that the statements in the *Vita Antonii* that Antony had no education and thus was to be regarded as illiterate (ὅτι μὴ μεμάθηκε γράμματα and ἰδιώτης) were not to be taken at face value.[4]

1 'Diese Briefe, welche mit wenig Variationen immer wieder denselben, ziemlich eng umschriebenen Gedankenkreis durchlaufen, sind fast zu lang, zu theoretisch, zu saft- und kraftlos, als daß man sie einem Manne wie Antonius zueignen könnte.' Bardenhewer, *Geschichte der altchristlichen Literatur,* p. 81. This is echoed in Gustave Bardy, 'Antoine', *DSp* I,705: 'Il semble bien que toutes ces lettres, trop longues, trop lénifiantes, n'aient rien à voir avec saint Antoine et ne soient que des compilations assez tardives'.

2 See von Hertling, *Antonius der Einsiedler,* pp. 56–60, and Klejna, 'Antonius und Ammonas', p. 326–341. In addition to the text-critical works quoted already quoted, the only studies of the letters are J. Kraus, *Der heilige Geist in den Briefen des heiligen Antonius des Einsiedlers* (*Festschrift zum 50-jährigen Bestandsjubiläum des Missionshauses St. Gabriel*), Kaldenkirchen 1939; Fabio Giardini, *La dottrina spirituale di S. Antonio Abate e di Ammonas nelle loro lettere. Contributi allo studio della Spiritualità dei Padri del Deserto,* Florence 1957; and Guerric Couilleau, 'La liberté d'Antoine', *Commandements du Seigneur et libération évangélique* (*SA* 70), Rome 1977, pp. 13–46.

3 See Karl Heussi, *Der Ursprung des Mönchtums,* Tübingen 1936, p. 78, and Dörries, 'Die Vita Antonii', p. 218f.

4 Garitte, 'A propos des lettres de Saint Antoine', pp. 11–31.

Although the far-reaching implications of Garitte's research have not been given due consideration, most scholars today accept the letters as genuine.[1]

The arguments for the authenticity of the letters can be summarized as follows:

1. The manuscript tradition in all the languages attributes the letters to Antony. The oldest evidence is the Syriac manuscript, dated 534.[2] The fact that the Copto-Arabic as well as the Greek tradition attributes the letter to Antony proves that this attribution must date back before the Greek translation, which was known to Jerome already in the early 390's.

2. In his *De viris illustribus,* written in 392, Jerome mentions seven letters by Antony, written in Coptic and translated into Greek. Since he is the only writer explicitly mentioning the letters, it is likely that he had his information directly from the monks in Egypt, with whom he is known to have had close contacts.[3]

3. Passages from the letters are quoted with an attribution to Antony by Shenoute, and by Besa, his successor. In quoting the letters Shenoute, who became a monk in 370 and superior of the large monastery in 388, explicitly refers to 'what Antony wrote'. The quotations are, moreover, astonishingly literal, and thus the letters must have been present in the library of the White Monastery in *c.* 400.[4]

4. Passages from the letters are found in some of the sayings attributed to Antony in the great collections of the fifth century. The most obvious case is the saying mentioned above as representing the lost Greek text of the letters. Here the literal agreement rules out the possibility of an oral tradition as a common source for both, and there is nothing in the letter to suggest that a saying has been incorporated into an existing text. The

1 *CPG* 2330; J. Quasten, *Patrology* III, pp. 148–152; Theofried Baumeister, 'Die Mentalität des frühen ägyptischen Mönchtums. Zur Frage des Ursprungs des christlichen Mönchtums', *ZKG* 88 (1977), p. 149; Tito Orlandi, 'Coptic Literature', *The Roots of Egyptian Christianity,* Philadelphia 1986, pp. 63–64. A summary of my own arguments are found in S. Rubenson, 'Der vierte Antoniusbrief', p. 125–130.

2 W. Wright, *Catalogue of the Syriac Manuscripts in the British Library,* II, London 1871, p. 637, No. 727 (British Library, Add. 12175).

3 'Antonius monachus, cuius vitam Athanasius Alexandriae episcopus insigni volumine prosecutus est, misit Aegyptiacas ad diversa monasteria apostolici sensus sermonisque epistulas septem, quae in Graecam linguam translatae sunt, quarum praecipua est ad Arsenoitas. Floruit Constantino et filiis eius regnantibus'. Hieronymus, *De viris illustribus* 88 (Richardson, *TU* 14:1, p. 45). On Jerome and his contacts with the monks, see chapter VIII.

4 See Garitte, 'A propos des lettres de S. Antoine l'ermite', pp. 11–31. Shenoute explicitly says: ⲁⲗⲗⲁ ⲛ̄ⲧⲁϥⲥϩⲁⲓ ⲛ̄ⲧⲉⲓϩⲉ 'but this is what he wrote'. The letters of Besa have since been edited by K. H. Kuhn, *Letters and Sermons of Besa* (*CSCO* 158), Louvain 1956, and the quotations from the letters are found on p. 97 and 99–100. The quotation in Shenoute is from the additional thirteen letters attributed to Antony in the Arabic corpus of Antonian writings. But there seems to be no reason to question the existence, already in his lifetime, of the complete Coptic version of the twenty letters attributed to Antony known to have existed in the eleventh century as shown by the marginal notes in the Arabic mss. and in the thirteenth and fourteenth century as evidenced by Abū-l-Barakāt (see above, p 16, note 5).

structure and style of the letters, moreover, make it clear that they are genuine letters and cannot be regarded as collections of sayings by Antony, edited as letters by someone else.[1]

5. A comparison of the letters and the *Vita Antonii* also reveals a number of affinities.[2] These are found mainly in the long sermon attributed to the saint by his biographer. Since they do not belong to the parts of the *Life* often used as arguments for an Athanasian authorship, there seems to be little reason to deny their authenticity. The idea that the letters might be dependent on the *Life* can easily be dismissed. There is no reference in the letters to the principal theological ideas of the *Life*; on the contrary, we find a number of conflicting ideas. Moreover, the main arguments of the letters are missing in the *Life*.

6. An analysis of the content of the letters shows that their theological outlook and their emphasis on repentance, self-knowledge, and endurance in the struggle against the demons have close parallels in the early monastic tradition known to us from the *Apophthegmata*. The more speculative parts of the letters, and their obvious Origenist flavour, have their closest parallels in Evagrius of Pontus. It is thus likely that their author was a forerunner of the Origenist tradition in Nitria, in which Evagrius was later to develop his teaching. The rather confused and somewhat heterodox teaching of the letters also makes it difficult to see why, if unauthentic, they should have been preserved and attributed to Antony. Their author must, in any case, have been a monastic father of importance, and if the title of one of the letters, mentioned already by Jerome, is to be trusted, he can even be identified as a monastic father related to the monks of Arsinoë, *i.e.* of the area close to where Antony had his 'outer' monastery.

7. Evidence that Antony wrote letters is found in several early sources. Firstly, a short letter by Antony is preserved in Greek translation in the *Letter of Ammon* dated to the end of the fourth century.[3] Secondly, two letters by Antony are mentioned in the *Vita Pachomii*, one to Athanasius and another to Theodore. The last-mentioned even seems to presuppose the seven letters.[4] Thirdly, a Coptic letter from Antony is quoted in a *florilegium* variously attributed to Shenoute or his successor Besa.[5] Furthermore there are in the *Vita Antonii*, in the *Apophthegmata Patrum*, in the *Vita Pachomii*, as well as in the *Historia Ecclesiastica* by Sozomenus, references

1 See below, chapter VII for a detailed discussion.

2 See below, chapter VI for a detailed discussion.

3 For a discussion on the *Epistula Ammonis* see below, chapter VIII.

4 See *Ep. Amm.* 29 and *VP/G* 120, *VP/SBo* 133 (S^5 17, Lefort, *S. Pachomii vitae sahidice scriptae*, p. 183f.). These passages will be discussed below in connection with the references to Antony in Pachomian literature.

5 *Cambr. Univ. Lib. Add. 1876.2*; see Bellet, 'Nou testimoni de les lletres de Sant Antoni'.

to an exchange of letters between Antony and the imperial court.[1] Several letters from Antony to Gregory, the Arian bishop of Alexandria from 339 to 345, are mentioned in Athanasius' *Historia Arianorum;* how one of them was received is recalled in the *Vita Antonii.*[2] A correspondence between Antony and Hilarion is mentioned by Jerome, and, although fictitious, the report makes it clear that a monk like Antony was expected to have corresponded with monks abroad.[3] Finally, there are in the *Vita Antonii,* as well as in the *Vita Pachomii,* references to Antony intervening through letters on behalf of people in need of help.[4]

Turning to the arguments against the authenticity of the letters we have to deal with the character of early monasticism and the image of Antony in other sources. Firstly, there is little evidence for literary activity of this kind in Coptic as early as the first half of the fourth century. Greek was still the only language of education and literary culture, and Coptic only beginning to be used, primarily for translations of religious texts. The only other original Coptic texts that can be dated earlier than the mid-fourth century are a few short letters by or to monks, among them the letters of Pachomius.[5] In content, however, none of these are similar to Antony's letters. The fact that a great number of Biblical texts, as well as texts such as the Nag Hammadi codices, were translated into and copied in Coptic in this period nevertheless proves that there was a Coptic literary culture in the making, and that there was a demand for religious and philosophical texts in Coptic. Thus there is, on the one hand, no need to presuppose that the letters have been written in Greek; on the other, it seems rather unlikely that the writer can have been ignorant of Greek.

But even if it is admitted that the letters could have been composed in Coptic, it has been generally felt that they do not fit the traditional concept of the Egyptian monks as illiterate and uneducated.[6] Although this concept has been challenged by research on the Pachomian material, the *Apophthegmata,* generally relied upon as the best sources for the earliest monastic tradition, produce a different image of the first monks. There is, how-

1 See *VA* 81, *AP/G Antony* 31, *VP/G 120* and Sozomenus, *HE* I.13. This correspondence is discussed below, pp. 154 and 183.

2 See Athanasius, *Historia Arianorum* 14. The same story is told differently in *VA* 86. Since *VA* is the later text, and the fact that Antony wrote several letters to Gregory could have been regarded as less coherent with the *VA,* I would regard the version of the *Historia Arianorum* as more trustworthy.

3 See Hieronymus, *Vita Hilarionis* 24.

4 See *VA* 84–86, *VP/ SBo* 127 (S^5 16, Lefort, *S. Pachomii vitae sahidice scriptae,* p. 178).

5 Edited by H. Quecke, *Die Briefe Pachoms* (*Textus Patristici et Liturgici* 11), Regensburg 1975.

6 Especially in earlier literature the monks are dismissed as illiterate, and with them Antony. In addition to Bardy and Bardenhewer quoted above (p. 35) we find the same opinion in Bousset, *Apophthegmata,* p. 76f. and Hugh G. Evelyn White, *The Monasteries of the Wâdi Natrûn,* II, New York 1932, p. 13.

ever, reason to question the reliability of the *Apophthegmata* far more than has hitherto been done.[1] The collection and recording of the sayings took place as late as in the second half of the fifth century, and the complicated manuscript tradition, with variants in different languages, cautions against regarding them as literal and authentic reminiscences of the mid-fourth century. Though there is little doubt that a number of the sayings can date back to this period, there is every reason to suspect theological and ecclesiastical tendencies at work in the sifting and transmission of the material over more than a hundred years. Thus the overall picture given in the sayings, even if only the earliest stratum is used, reflects the way the leading monastic circles wanted their forerunners to be remembered and used as models rather than the actual conditions of the early period. In addition there is the fact that the collections were made after the devastating Origenist controversy, which involved a great number of the leading monks, whose sayings form the base of the *Apophthegmata.*[2]

As for the Pachomian material, primarily the *Vita Pachomii,* it must be emphasized that Antony did not belong to the same tradition. There is even in the *Vita Pachomii* a cautious criticism of the monastic tradition represented by Antony. [3] The suspicions of heresy that the Pachomians had towards Antonian monks are particularly striking. Still, there is sufficient evidence in the letters of Pachomius, as well as in the *Vita Pachomii,* for the existence of numerous educated monks and for theological discussions and reading among monks in their vicinity.[4] In view of this and our knowledge of contemporary ascetic groups, such as the followers of Hieracas, the Manichaeans, the Gnostics, the Meletians and the Arians, there is no reason to deny that the letters of Antony could have been composed in the early monastic setting. On the contrary, the fact that Origenism had a firm hold on the leading monks of Nitria long before Evagrius settled there in 383 makes it likely that the letters came from this environment.[5]

But even if the concept of the early monks as uneducated peasants, with an unsophisticated faith based on a literal interpretation of the Bible and a great fear of all kinds of theological speculation and wisdom, can be dis-

1 Modern research on the *Apophthegmata* started with Bousset, as part of the program of the *religionsgeschichtliche Schule* to emphasize the priority of popular oral tradition over the theological literary activity in the shaping of the New Testament. Bousset's appreciation of the sayings was taken over by Heussi in his work on the origins of monasticism, and is now generally accepted. For a more cautious stand see Philip Rousseau, *Ascetics, Authority and the Church in the Age of Jerome and Cassian,* Oxford 1978, pp. 12–14, 68–76.

2 See below, chapter VII for a discussion on the reliability of the sayings.

3 See *VP/G* 120 and more explicitly in the Sahidic version, *VP/SBo* 126 (S^5 16, Lefort, *S. Pachomii vitae sahidicae scriptae,* p. 177f.).

4 See Clemens Scholten, 'Die Nag-Hammadi-Texte als Buchbesitz der Pachomianer', *JAC* 31 (1988), pp. 144–172.

5 See below, chapter V for a discussion of literacy and literature among the monks.

missed as one-sided, based on uncritical reading of the sources and prejudice, the description of Antony in the *Vita Antonii* has been regarded as a valid argument against his authorship. Though there is no lack of studies questioning the value of the *Life* as a historical source, the statements about Antony's lack of education and his rejection of wisdom and reasoning (σοφία and συλλογισμός) in favour of faith, as well as the lack of any reference to the seven letters in the *Life*, are still regarded as decisive.[1]

The statements on Antony's lack of education, however, fit rather too well into the general tendency of the *Life*—to enhance the concept of Antony as taught exclusively by God—to have any value of their own. The absence of any reference to the letters only shows that the biographer either did not know about them—which is not unlikely, since they were sent to monastic communities still quite independent of the official Church—or that they did not fit his design.[2] On the other hand, the reference in the *Life* to discussions with philosophers is an argument for the authenticity of the letters, and the image of Antony as a teacher is quite consistent with the long sermon the *Life* reports him to have preached to his disciples.[3] Parts of this sermon, often considered the least authentic part of the *Life*, are remarkably close to the letters, not only in style but also in content.[4] Antony's visitations of the monastic communities in the area, reported both in his own *Life* and in the *Vita Pachomii*, and the emphasis at the end of the *Life* on Antony's responsibility for them, also give us a plausible setting for the letters.[5]

It is, however, more difficult to reconcile the eager and speculative teacher of the letters with the sayings and their emphasis on silence and self-denial, or their warnings against theological speculation and teaching; these are the very traits in the sayings which are regarded as the most authentic, and used to reject the image of the Antony gained from the sermons and controversies in the *Vita Antonii*.[6] On the other hand, one finds in the *apophthegmata* a constant flow of visitors to Antony seeking his

1 VA 1 and 72–73. Of special importance is the expression that he had not 'learned letters', γράμματα μαθῶν. This can, however, not be understood literally, since Antony is characterized as capable of reading and writing in a number of other passages in the *Vita*. He writes and receives letters and even exhorts his disciples to write down their thoughts! See *VA* 81, 86, and 55. The statement rather refers back to the Gospel of John 7:15, where it is said about Jesus that he had not studied: μὴ μεμαθηκώς. See also below pp. 141–144.

2 For a full discussion on the relation between the *Vita* and the letters see below, chapter VI.

3 *VA* 16–43, 55. Even a pagan philosopher like Synesius writing in about 400 looked back on Antony as a man who like Hermes and Zoroaster was renowned for his wisdom, his source most probably being no other than the *VA*. See Synesius, *Dion* 10.

4 For the critical view on the sermons see Heussi, *Der Ursprung des Mönchtums*, p. 87, and Dörries, 'Die Vita Antonii', *passim*.

5 *VA* 14–15, 44, 54, 63 and 89; *VP/G* 120, *VP/SBo* 127 (S[5] 16, Lefort, *S. Pachomii vitae sahidice scriptae*, p. 178)

6 See *AP/G Antony* 2, 6, 17, 18 and 30, discussed by Dörries, *op.cit.*, pp. 149–157.

spiritual advice and his answers to their questions on the interpretation of the Scriptures and the salvation of the soul.[1] Even if some monks might later untruthfully have styled themselves disciples or friends of Antony, the large number of monks who, in the *apophthegmata* as well as in the *Historia Monachorum,* the *Historia Lausiaca* and the writings of Jerome, Rufinus and others, are said to have been his disciples is proof of an intense contact between Antony and his environment.[2] According to the Pachomian documents, Antony kept in touch with members of their *koinonia,* and did not hesitate to write to them about what God had revealed to him. The designation 'a true Israelite' which Antony, according to the *Vita Pachomii,* used for Horsiesius, and the subsequent interpretation as 'a mind that sees God', also recalls the way he designates his correspondents in the letters.[3]

The strongest argument used against an attribution of the letters to Antony is no doubt the statements that he did not know Greek, a statement that can hardly be true about the author of the letters. The sources are, however, not as unequivocal as earlier research implies.[4] The only source which explicitly states that Antony did not know Greek is the *Historia Lausiaca,* where Kronios presents himself as his interpreter.[5] Since also the *Vita Antonii* and Jerome speak about interpreters working for Antony, it seems evident that he spoke Coptic and was translated for the benefit of non-Coptic speaking visitors.[6] On the other hand, according to the same source, he communicated with leading theologians and secular authorities, discussed with philosophers and heretics, and emphasized the need for studies. Thus it seems unlikely that he had no background in Greek, even if he is likely to have preferred to speak in his own mother tongue, and

1 See *AP* 12, 17, 19, 26, 27.

2 These references to Antony are discussed in chapter VIII.

3 See *Ep. Amm.* 29 and *VP/G* 120, *VP/SBo* 133 (S^5 17, Lefort, *S. Pachomii vitae sahidice scriptae,* p. 183f.). See below, chapter VIII for a full discussion of the Pachomian material and p. 69 for the background of this interpretation.

4 The literature is unanimous in its verdict that Antony did not know Greek. Besides Bardenhewer, Bardy, Bousset and Evelyn White, quoted above (p. 35, 38), see von Hertling, *Antonius der Einsiedler,* p. 13, Heussi, *Der Ursprung des Mönchtums,* p. 101, Gustave Bardy, *La question des langues dans l'Église ancienne,* I, Paris 1948, pp. 45–46, and Dörries, 'Die Vita Antonii', p. 219.

5 ἔμαθεν οὖν ὁ Κρόνιος καὶ ἐξέστη· καὶ λαβὼν εὐαγγέλιον καὶ θεὶς ἐν μέσῳ τῆς ἀδελφότητος διωμόσατο ἀφηγούμενος τὸ συμβὰν ὅτι *τῶν λόγων τούτων ὅλων ἑρμηνεὺς γέγονα τοῦ μακαρίου Ἀντωνίου, ἑλληνιστὶ μὴ εἰδότος· ἐγὼ γὰρ ἠπιστάμην ἀμφοτέρας τὰς γλώσσας, καὶ ἡρμήνευσα αὐτοῖς, τοῖς μὲν ἑλληνιστί, ἐκείνῳ δὲ αἰγυπτιστί* (*HL* 21). But this was written in the 420's by someone who had read the *Vita Antonii.*

6 See Hieronymus, *Vita Hilarionis* 30 and *VA* 74. This is the only instance in the *Vita Antonii* where an interpreter is mentioned, and the purpose is clearly to defend the reliability of the author of the *Vita* in reproducing the words of Antony. It is never said that he did not receive the letters of the emperors because he did not know Greek, as Garitte implies ('A propos des lettres de S. Antoine', p. 15, n. 13), only that he did not know how to reply.

that of his disciples. In the bilingual situation of the Egypt of the third and fourth centuries insufficient knowledge of Greek was undoubtedly more common among Copts than no knowledge at all.[1]

If we summarize the arguments on the authenticity it is evident that at the end of the fourth century the letters were attributed to Antony both in their Coptic original and in their Greek translation. The letters can also be located to the early Coptic-speaking monastic circles, to a tradition close to the leading fathers in the *Apophthegmata,* but also related to material found in the *Vita Antonii.* It is also clear that the letters must be attributed to an educated monastic leader of importance, acquainted with the philosophical ideas of his time, as well as with the Arian heresy. Furthermore there is no source on Antony with sufficient credibility to dismiss the authenticity of the letters.[2]

2. The Date

In order to date the letters we must examine what is known about the chronology of Antony's life. Since the *Vita Antonii* is virtually the only source, scholars have generally relied on whatever evidence it provides. The chronology of the *Life* is, however, only relative, as it gives Antony's age at various stages of his career. The only episode that can be dated from other sources is his visit to Alexandria. According to the account given in the index to Athanasius' *Festal Letters,* it took place in 337 or 338. His age at that time is, however, not given in the *Life.* All other dates rest on the combination of the date of his death and the relative chronology of the *Life.* According to Jerome's chronicle, Antony died in 356.[3] This date is corroborated by a letter from Serapion of Thmuis to Antony's disciples prompted by Antony's death.[4] Since the *Life* says that he died at the age of 105, he would have been born in 251. From the other information in the *Life* we can gather that in *c.* 271 he sold his possessions to live as an ascetic near the village and that around 285 he entered the deserted fortress, which he left in *c.* 305.[5] After this he is reported to have gone down to Alexandria at the time of the persecutions (311–313) and then to

1 See below, chapter V for a discussion.

2 It is worth noting that the archives of monastic correspondence published by Bell and by Kramer & Shelton give examples of letters written *to* a monastic leader, letters that could have prompted replies similar to Antony's. See Harold I. Bell, *Jews and Christians in Egypt. The Jewish Troubles in Alexandria and the Athanasian Controversy,* London 1924; and Bärbel Kramer & John C. Shelton, *Das Archiv des Nepheros und verwandte Texte* (*Aegyptiaca Treverensia* 4), Mainz 1987.

3 Hieronymus, *Chronicon* ad annum 356.

4 The letter is edited by René Draguet, 'Une lettre de Sérapion de Thmuis aux disciples d'Antoine (A.D. 356) en versions syriaque et arménienne, *Le Muséon* 64 (1951), pp. 1–25.

5 *VA* 2 gives his age as between 18 and 20, *VA* 10 gives the age as 35 and *VA* 14 says that he stayed nearly twenty years in the fortress.

have retreated into the interior desert. It is, however, very unlikely that Athanasius could have had exact information about Antony's age; most probably even Antony himself did not know when he was born.[1]

In addition to the above-mentioned visit to Alexandria, the only reliable information about a date in Antony's life is what we know about a visit a group of Pachomian monks paid him. In the *Vita Pachomii* this visit is said to have taken place shortly after Pachomius' death in May 346, at about the time Athanasius returned from his second exile in October 346.[2] To this might be added a letter to Theodore (*c.* 354), if it is authentic and the story told by Ammon reliable, but the letter gives no clue to his age.[3] Even if the statement in the *Life of Antony* that he died at the age of 105, and thus was born in 251, is open to doubt, it is clear from the account in the *Vita Pachomii* that he was an old man in 346.[4] The way his name is mentioned in the *apophthegmata,* as well as in the *Historia Monachorum* and the *Historia Lausiaca*, as the ultimate authority and the father of the monks shows that he must have belonged to an earlier generation than Macarius the Egyptian and his contemporaries. As early as the 320's he must have been a monastic master, an *abba.*[5]

The letters themselves give no hint as to when they were written. They are exhortations to monastic disciples, modelled on the Pauline epistles, and except for a reference to Arius, which will be discussed below, they contain no historical information. The structure and content common to Letters II to VII suggest, however, that these letters were written at roughly the same time but sent to different monasteries. From the way the writer addressed his correspondents, as well as from the general tone and content of the letters, it is obvious that he had already been acknowledged as a master, and was widely known and respected. From what we know about the emergence of monasticism this can hardly have been the case before the 330's. Moreover, since many disciples of his, known from other sources, lived on until the end of the century, they can hardly have stayed

[1] That even fairly well-off landowners serving in official duties did not know their own age is evidenced by the documents from the archive of Aurelius Isidorus of Karanis, who gave his age as thirty-five in 297, thirty-seven in 308, forty in 308, forty-five in 309 and forty again in 309. The tendency to round off to fives or tens is manifest. See Alan K. Bowman, *Egypt after the Pharaohs*, London 1986, p. 138 with reference to the sources (*P. Cair. Isid.* 81, 97, 125, 91 and 8).

[2] *VP/G* 120 and *VP/SBo* 123–134 (S[5] 16–17, Lefort, *S. Pachomii vitae sahidice scriptae,* p. 174–185). See below, pp. 167–169, for a full discussion

[3] *Ep. Amm.* 29. See below, pp. 169–172, for a full discussion.

[4] See *VP/G* 120. Even if *VA* 93 states that his health was unbroken when he died at the age of 105, the same text actually admits his advanced age and need for special food long before, see *VA* 51.

[5] See chapter VIII for the information about Antony in *HM, HL,* and other sources.

with him before then.[1] Thus the letters were probably not written before the end of the 330's. Perhaps a passage at the end of the sixth letter, where the author seems to have accepted the fact that he would not see his friends again before dying, indicates an advanced age:

> 'I had hoped to see you face to face in the body, but I look forward to the time, which is near, when we shall be able to see one another in that vision, when pain and sorrow and sighing shall flee away, and joy shall be upon the heads of all.[2]

The only historical reference in the letters is the important passage in Letter IV where Antony reports about Arius' preaching in Alexandria and denounces him as someone who 'does not know himself'.

Letter IV.17

Coptic	Georgian	Latin
ⲉⲧⲃⲉⲁⲣⲓⲟⲥ ⲅⲁⲣ ⲛⲧⲁϥⲧⲱⲟⲩⲛ ϩⲛⲣⲁⲕⲟⲧⲉ ⲁϥϫⲱ ⲛϩⲉⲛϣⲁϫⲉ ⲛϣⲙⲙⲟ ⲉⲧⲃⲉ ⲡⲙⲟⲛⲟⲅⲉⲛⲏⲥ ϫⲉⲡⲉⲧⲉⲙⲙⲛⲧϥⲁⲣⲭⲏ ⲁϥϯⲁⲣⲭⲏ ⲛⲁϥ ⲡⲁⲧϣⲁϫⲉ ⲙⲙⲟϥ ϩⲛⲛⲣⲱⲙⲉ ⲁϥϯⲧⲉⲗⲟⲥ ⲛⲁϥ ⲡⲓⲁⲧⲕⲓⲙ ⲁϥϯⲕⲓⲙ ⲛⲁϥ.	ხოლო არიოზის თჳს რომელი ალდგა ალექსანდრიას და ითყოდა სითყუათა უცხოთა მხოლოდშობილისა თჳს; რაჲმეთუ რომელსა ჟამ არა აქუნდა სცა მას ჟამი, და დაუსრულებელსა მას დაბადებულთა თანა მოსცა ალსასრული, და ურყეველი იგი თქუა შერყეულად.	De Arrio vero, qui in Alexandria surrexit et loquitur aliena verba de unigenito, cui qui est et qui sine tempore est, tempus non adscivit, et ineffabilis finem inter creaturas non dedit, immobilis, immobilitatem non affixit.
But as for Arius, who stood up in Alexandria, he spoke strange words about the Only-begotten: to him who is without beginning he gave a beginning (ἀρχή), to him who is ineffable among men he gave an end (τέλος), to him who is immovable he gave movement.	But as for Arius who stood up in Alexandria and spoke strange words about the Only-begotten: to him to whom time did not exist he gave *time*, and the *infinite* among creatures he gave an end and the immovable he told to move.	But as for Arius who has stood up in Alexandria and speaks alien words about the Only-begotten: to him who is and who exists without time, he *did not ascribe* time (?) and the ineffable he *did not give an* end (?) among the creatures, to the immovable he *did not attach* motion (?).[3]

Since this letter, even before the passage on Arius, deals with the question of self-knowledge, which is the essence of the quotation, there is no reason to regard the passage as an interpolation.[4] The account of Arius' main

[1] As his earliest disciples are mentioned Kronides, who was still living in 394 and Macarius, who died in *c.* 390. See *HM* 20.13 and 21.

[2] *Ep. Ant.* VI.115.

[3] The Latin text is evidently corrupt, and ends, moreover, in the middle of the sentence. The Coptic text with its use of ἀρχή comes closer to the expressions used by Arius as we know them from Alexander and Athanasius. The priority of ἄρρητος 'ineffable' is shown by its common use in the Coptic and the Latin version, whereas the Georgian 'eternal' must be seen as an accommodation to τέλος in the next line. The Greek text might have been something like: περὶ Ἀρείου γάρ, ὃς ἀνέστη ἐν Ἀλεξανδρείᾳ καὶ ἔλεγεν λόγους ἀλλοτρίους περὶ τοῦ μονογενοῦς· τῷ ἀνάρχῳ ἔδωκεν ἀρχήν· τῷ ἀρρήτῳ ἐν ταῖς κτίσεσι ἔδωκεν τέλος· ὃς ἀκίνητός ἐστιν ἔδωκεν αὐτῷ κίνησιν.

[4] Moreover, the strange combination of ἄρρητος and τέλος can hardly be the work of a redactor. Probably it is meant to say that according to Arius, Christ could be reduced to the

propositions is very close to what we find in Athanasius' reports on what Arius taught. In these the terms ἄρρητος, ἄναρχος and τρεπτός usually appear, terms which could well have been the sources for the Coptic expressions in Antony's letters, although atkim was then probably translated ἀκίνητος or ἀσάλευτος, which are the usual Greek equivalents. It is also worth noting that, according to Athanasius, one of Arius' principal tenets was that the Son did not know his own οὐσία.[1] There is, however, no trace of a direct literary influence from Athanasius on the letter, and most of the Arian ideas reproduced here were mentioned already by Alexander of Alexandria in his encyclica. There is a notable difference between the language of Antony's letter and the words his biographer puts in his mouth in the *Vita Antonii*, arguments closely related to the later stages of the polemic.[2] The letter thus seems to belong to the earlier part of the Arian conflict. There is nothing in it of the crude and bitter abuse and condemnation typical of the later stages. Moreover, it is evident from the text that the recipients were not supposed to be acquainted with Arius, and the passing reference to him—as an example of deficient self-knowledge—makes it unlikely that the Arian conflict had already permeated the Egyptian scene.

Unfortunately we do not know when the monks were first involved in the Arian controversy, only that in 337 Antony acted in defence of Athanasius, and that, during his third exile in 356, the bishop was hidden by the monks.[3] If, however, the letters had been of a later date, they would have shown a greater influence from the controversy and from Athanasian theology in general. It is thus unlikely that this letter was written much later than at the end of the 330's.[4] Although no precise dating is possible, we can thus conclude that the letters were written in the fourth or at the latest the fifth decade of the the fourth century, which makes them one of

---

role of a Redeemer. As will be demonstrated in Chapter IV, Antony's theology *was* anti-Arian, even though it did not exactly match Athanasius'.

1 See *i.a.* Athanasius, *De Synodis* 15.3 (ed. H.-G. Opitz, *Athanasius Werke*, II, 1, Berlin 1935–1941, p. 242). A useful table on Arius' teaching as given by Athanasius and Alexander is found in Rudolf Lorenz, *Arius judaizans. Untersuchungen zur dogmengeschichtlichen Einordnung des Arius*, Göttingen 1980, pp. 38–47.

2 *VA* 69. See Dörries, *Die Vita Antonii*, pp. 178–179.

3 The evidence for Arian inroads among the monasteries of Upper Egypt is very slight, and later than Antony's death. It is not before the late 350's that Athanasius writes to the monks against the Arians, and relates their heresy and history. The attempt in Robert C. Gregg & Dennis E. Groh, *Early Arianism—A View of Salvation*, Philadelphia 1981, p. 133ff., to see the *Vita Antonii* as an anti-Arian tractate motivated by a strong Arian bid for monastic support is unconvincing. At the time when the *Vita* was written the presence of attacks on the Arians in an Athanasian writing cannot prove anything about the monks. Antony's anti-Arian position as related in the *Vita* is corroborated by the evidence of the letters.

4 Klejna's attempt to date the letters more precisely to shortly after the sudden death of Arius in 336 on account of the urgency of the tone, as well as the stress on the decisiveness of the present time, is not convincing. See his 'Antonius und Ammonas', pp. 335–339.

the earliest known Coptic literary texts, and Antony probably 'the first real Coptic author'.[1]

3. THE CORRESPONDENTS

According to Jerome, Antony sent his letters to different monasteries, the most important to the monks in the region of Arsinoë.[2] The sixth letter, which is by far the longest, actually begins, in all the versions: 'Antony greets all his beloved who are in Arsinoë and its neighbourhood, and those who are with them'.[3] That Antony was regarded as the spiritual father of a number of monastic communities, especially in the region of Arsinoë, is well attested in the *Vita Antonii*, and in the traditions of the monasteries of the Fayyūm.[4] Antony's rule, preserved in the Arabic corpus of Antonian writings, was, moreover, addressed to the monks of the monastery of Naqlūn, the most important early monastic sites in the Arsinoë/Fayyūm area.[5] Unfortunately, very little is known about the monastic communities in this region in the first half of the fourth century, but it is clear from the *Historia Monachorum* that long before the 390's a monastic tradition had been established. Jerome's evidence and the parallel structure of the letters show, moreover, that they were sent to different monasteries. The reputation which Antony had reportedly acquired makes it likely that he could have sent letters to monasteries situated anywhere between the Delta and Upper Egypt. His contacts with the Pachomians as well as the Nitriotes are known from the sources, and he might very well have sent letters to monastic communities such as the ones mentioned in the archives of Paphnutius, Paieous and Nepheros.[6]

In the letters Antony generally refers to the addressees either as 'beloved sons in the Lord', or as 'beloved brothers'. This is a practice adhered to also in the letters to Theodore in the *Epistula Ammonis* and to the Pachomians in the *Vita Pachomii.* Since this is a common tradition in monastic letters, with roots in wisdom literature, it cannot be drawn on to prove that the recipients were all literally disciples of Antony's. What is

1 The quotation is from Tito Orlandi, 'Coptic Literature', p. 64. For a discussion of it see Samuel Rubenson, 'St. Antony, "The First Real Coptic Author"?' (*Actes du IVᵉ congrès copte, Louvain-la-Neuve, 5-10 septembre 1988. Ed. par M. Rassart–Debergh et J. Ries, Vol II De la linguistique au gnosticisme*), Louvain-la-Neuve 1992, pp. 16–27.

2 '...misit Aegyptiacas ad diversa monasteria..., quarum praecipua est ad Arsenoitas.' Hieronymus, *De viris illustribus,* c. 88.

3 *Ep. Ant.* VI.1.

4 *VA* 15. Cf. Nabia Abbott, *The Monasteries of the Fayyum* (*SAOC* 16), Chicago 1937, p. 27f., based on the evidence of the Egyptian and of the Ethiopic Synaxarium.

5 For the monastery of Naqlūn, see Abbott, *op. cit.*, pp 28–35, and Stefan Timm, *Das christlich-koptische Ägypten in arabischer Zeit,* II Wiesbaden 1984, pp. 762–767.

6 For these see Bell, *Jews and Christians in Egypt,* pp. 38–99, and Kramer & Shelton, *Das Archiv des Nepheros und verwandte Texte,* pp. 11–20.

evident is that they were monks, but the lack of references to a communal life, to superiors, or to monastic rules makes it impossible to tell whether or not they belonged to organized monasteries. The recipients are, however, expected to regard the writer as an authoritative teacher in much the same way as they are in the letter to Theodore. Repeatedly he exhorts them to understand his words and not neglect his teaching.[1]

In order to know more about the recipients and the context of the letters we have to turn to an interpretation of their contents. While Letter I is an introduction to monastic life, it is evident that the readers of Letters II to VII are supposed to be mature monks and experienced ascetics, who have to be warned against relying exclusively on ascetical practices. What Antony emphasizes is the need for insight and discernment; seemingly, he finds it necessary to impart to his correspondents a more profound theological understanding. The expressions used in these letters also presuppose that the readers are acquainted with the philosophical and theological language of the Platonic and, in particular, the Origenist tradition. This is confirmed by the passage in which Antony praises his correspondents for their inquiry into the spiritual essence (οὐσία νοερά).[2] Thus not only the author, but also the recipients of the letters must have been part of an intellectual tradition and well acquainted with contemporary theological language.[3]

[1] A favourite expression for this is ცხად იყავნ თქუენდა (let it be manifest to you), see *i.a.* *Ep. Ant.* II.20, 31; III.4, 14, 41; V.8, 32; VI.82, 93; VII.35, 63.

[2] *Ep. Ant.* VI.5: დიდ არს ესე თქუენდა კითხვად გულისხმისყოფისა თჳს გონიერისა მის თჳს არსებისა (it is great for you to attempt the self-understanding of the spiritual essence). The Latin version has *'cognitione sensualis exstantiae'*, while the Arabic has omitted the passage.

[3] Some of the important Greek terms appear in Coptic form in the Coptic fragments. These include οὐσία (ⲟⲩⲥⲓⲁ), νοῦς (ⲛⲟⲩⲥ), νοερός (ⲛⲟⲉⲣⲟⲥ), and λογικός (ⲗⲟⲅⲓⲕⲟⲥ). A large number of Greek terms of theological significance can be reconstructed, with a high degree of probability, with the help of the Coptic, Georgian and Latin expressions and comparisons with their Greek equivalents in other texts, especially in the Bible. Examples of these are ἀνάπαυσις, ἄναρχος, ἀόρατος, ἀρχή, ἀποκαλύπτω, ἀσάλευτος, γνῶσις, εἰκών, καιρός, καταβολή, κίνησις, μορφή, νόμος ἔμφυτος, παρουσία, σοφία, υἱοθεσία, φύσις. Evidently it was taken for granted that these terms would be correctly interpreted by the recipients. See below, chapter IV for a discussion on their content in the letters.

III. The Text

1. The Style

In contrast to many other ancient texts written in the guise of letters, but aimed at a wider readership, like *i.a.* the *Vita Antonii,* the letters of St. Antony are, no doubt, genuine letters. They are filled with direct exhortations to their readers, and marked by an urgency and an concern on the part of the author that his correspondents follow his advice and understand his teaching. Repeatedly he implores them to seek knowledge, and to act accordingly, sometimes threatening condemnation, sometimes extending promises. He is also anxious to make it clear to them that he really loves them and cares for them, with a love which is not 'bodily' but 'spiritual'. In one passage one of the letters is said to have been written in reply to a request for teaching,[1] and twice the author mentions writing his letters as a means of recreation and consolation for his disciples.[2] Both the uniform structure of the letters and the many repetitions, even in the same letter, of the author's favourite themes and expressions, make it unlikely that they were intended to be anything more than casual letters to genuine correspondents. This is particularly the case with the letters II to VII, which are so close to each other in structure and expressions that they must have been written within a short span of time.

A remarkable feature of the letters is that they give the impression of having been modelled on the epistles of St. Paul. Not only are these quoted abundantly—the quotations being sometimes almost indiscernible from the author's own use of Pauline expressions—but there is also, throughout the letters, a manifest imitation of the structure and style of the epistles.[3] In particular the phrases he uses at the beginning and at the end of several of the letters are very similar to those used by Paul. The author certainly feels that he is in the same position towards his communities as Paul to his congregations, and occasionally he even puts the quotations from Paul in

[1] *Ep. Ant.* VI.5.

[2] *Ep. Ant.* VI.84 'rest' (G: განსუენებაჲ; L: requiem; Gr*: ἀνάπαυσις); VII.58b 'consolation' (G missing; L: consolatio).

[3] Almost half of the Biblical quotations and allusions in the letters—they number about one hundred—are from the epistles of St. Paul. The Pauline model is obvious in the beginning and at the end of each letter, as well as in the style. As in Paul's epistles passages on Christ, on the Holy Spirit and on salvation are interwoven with personal exhortations. See *i.a.* *Ep.Ant.* III.17–20, IV.1–3, V.1–2, VI.1–3, 45–48, VII.1–2, 18–22, 37–38.

the first person, appropriating them as his own.[1] It is to what he himself thinks, knows and has experienced that he constantly refers, and his readers are supposed to regard this as authoritative.[2] Nowhere does he quote an author outside the Bible, and nowhere does he refer to tradition, or to the Church, to support his own teaching.

Of the writings more or less contemporary with the letters of Antony it is the *Teachings of Silvanus* that has the greatest stylistic similarities with the letters. Although Antony's letters are real letters and Silvanus' text a theological treatise we find the same rhetorical style linking passages with one another by using the expression 'my son', followed by an exhortation to know and to understand. Like the *Teachings* the letters are obviously intended as a wise man's instructions to his disciples, his spiritual children. Both texts are part of the wisdom literature of Hellenized Egypt which includes texts of Jewish wisdom like *Proverbs, Ecclesiastes,* the *Wisdom of Salomo* and *Jesus Sirach,* as well as the Egyptian wisdom literature of texts such as the *Instructions of Ankhsheshonqy* and *P. Insinger*, and Greek apophthegmatic collections of wisdom such as the *Sententiae Menandri* and the *Sentences of Sextus.*[3] In the *Teachings of Silvanus,* as in Antony's letters, this kind of collections of aphorisms are recast into a piece of unsystematic theological teaching.

That this legacy was important to the making of monastic tradition is obvious. Silvanus and Sextus are found among the ascetic texts of Nag Hammadi and the wisdom texts of the Septuagint are repeatedly encountered in early monastic literature.[4] It has also been argued that the *Apophthegmata Patrum* have a background in Egyptian wisdom literature.[5] A close connection between Silvanus and the monastic tradition is,

1 *Ep. Ant.* III.17, VI.47,

2 See *i.a. Ep. Ant.* I.2, 18, 35, 71, VI.81, 107, and VII.52, where he even refers to what he himself has seen.

3 For this background see Robert L. Wilken 'Wisdom and Philosophy in Early Christianity', *Aspects of Wisdom in Judaism and Early Christianity (ed. by R. L. Wilken),* Notre Dame/London 1975, pp. 143–167 and William R. Schoedel, 'Jewish Wisdom and the Formation of the Christian Ascetic', *ibid.,* pp. 169–199. The late Egyptian texts are discussed by Miriam Lichtheim, *Late Egyptian Wisdom in the International Context* (*Orbis Biblicus et Orientalis* 52), Fribourg 1983. See especially pp. 184–196 where she argues for a Demotic background for at least parts of Silvanus. For Silvanus see also Jan Zandee, 'Die Lehren des Silvanus. Stoischer Rationalismus und Christentum im Zeitalter der frühkatholischen Kirche', *Essays on the Nag Hammadi Texts in Honour of Alexander Böhlig* (*NHS* 3), Leiden 1972, pp. 145.

4 Of the Old Testament quotations in Antony's letters, three are from the historical books, thirteen are from the Psalms, sixteen from the prophets, and eleven from Proverbs, Wisdom and Ecclesiastes. The same tendency is also to be found in the Pachomian writings, see Rousseau, *Pachomius,* pp. 87–104.

5 See Theofried Baumeister, 'Die Mentalität des frühen ägyptischen Mönchtums, pp. 145–160. See also the examples quoted in Helmut Brunner, 'Ptahhotep bei den koptischen Mönchen' *ZÄS* 86 (1961), p. 146ff.; M. Kaiser, 'Agathon und Amenemope', *ZÄS* 92

moreover, evidenced by the inclusion of an identic wisdom passage in the *Teachings of Silvanus* and in a text known as the *Teachings of Antony*, only preserved in Arabic, but no doubt originally composed in Coptic.[1]

The frequent use of repetitions and stereotype expressions, the large amount of Biblical quotations, as well as the lack of systematic treatment of the themes discussed, have led scholars to dismiss the letters as long-winded, narrow-minded, and feeble.[2] There is, however, every reason to question this opinion. The use of stereotypes and repetitions should not be dismissed as a sign of narrow-mindedness or senility; rather, it is a typical feature in the tradition of wisdom, of which the early monastic fathers were certainly a part. Many of the phrases also have manifest rhetorical functions, signalling important passages or constituting smooth transitions to new themes. The most obvious example of this rhetorical style is the use of the exhortation to understand. Especially in Letters II to VII new passages are usually introduced and often also concluded with a reference to knowledge and understanding:

II, 20-23	Let this word be manifest to you...
	— ...teaching us that we are members of one another.
24-30	I beseech you in the name of our Lord, understand this great...
	— Now, therefore, O God, we know what Thou hast given us: ...
31-36	Let this word be manifest to you:...
	— *Give occasion to a wise man and he will be yet wiser.*
III, 7-14	I believe that you are not unaware that...
	— Let this word be manifest to you, my beloved...
26-38	I beseech, my beloved in the Lord, to understand this writing, since...
	— But you, my beloved in the Lord, know yourselves so that...
39-48	Truly, my beloved in the Lord, I write to you as to wise men, who...
	— Therefore, know the time in which we are.
IV, 15-20	Truly, my beloved, *I write to you as to wise men,* who are able to know...
	— It is, however, manifest that he did not know himself.
V, 15	That you may know that...
32	Truly, my children, *I talk to you as to wise men,* so that you understand...
40	Now, therefore, understand that...
VI, 5	It is great for you to attempt to understand the spiritual essence...
17	I want you to know, my children,...
21-26	*As to wise men I talk to you,* that you may know...
	— They know the indulgence of our Creator,...
27-44	I want you to know, my children, that...
	— so that you may teach yourselves to know what is truly right.

(1966); and *idem*, 'Ein altägyptisches Idealbild in christlicher Gewand', *ZÄS* 99 (1973), pp. 88–94.

1 See Wolf-Peter Funk, 'Ein doppelt überliefertes Stück spätägyptischer Weisheit', *ZÄS* 103 (1976), pp. 20–21; Yvonne Janssens, 'Les leçons de Silvanos et le monachisme', *Colloque international sur les textes de Nag Hammadi* (*BCNH*, Études 1), Quebec 1979, pp. 352–353; and Armand Veilleux, 'Monasticism and Gnosis in Egypt', *The Roots of Egyptian Christianity*, Philadelphia 1986, p. 294.

2 See *e.g.* the quotation from Bardenhewer above, p. 35, n. 1, and Klejna, 'Antonius und Ammonas', p. 339.

82-84	Let this word be manifest to you, that
	— thus, they who know themselves know that...
85	I want you to know that Jesus Christ is the true mind of the Father.
93	Let this word be manifest to you, my dear children in the Lord,...
102	Now, my children, I want you to know that...
106	Truly, my children, I also want you to know that...
111-116	...to open for you the eyes of your hearts that you may know...
	— *If one gives occasion to a wise man he will be yet wiser.*
VII, 1	Know, my children, the grace of our Lord Jesus Christ.
16	I pray you all in the Lord, my beloved, that you understand what...
31	Therefore, we all, who approach our Creator, have to strain our minds and faculties in order to know :::
58	*Give occasion to a wise man and he will be yet wiser.*

Of these recurring expressions the most significant are the quotations from Prov. 9:9 and 1 Cor. 10:15.[1] While this use of the latter is an original contribution by Antony to Christian rhetoric, the former is repeatedly used by Origen in a similar way, *i.e.* as a remark on the brevity and incompleteness of the exposition, combined with a reference to the writer's confidence in the ability of his readers to bring his teaching to completion.[2]

Another rhetorical feature in the letters is the use of a tripartite division, encountered in Antony's description of how man is summoned by God, in his teaching on the three motions in the body, and on the three stages of the history of salvation. The clear and well realized structure of the first letter, as well as the evident common plan behind the other six letters, also reveal a careful and logical mind behind the letters. The choice of Biblical texts, their use and often unusual combination, moreover, show the author to have been well acquainted, not only with the Bible, but also with allegorical exegesis.[3]

2. The Structure and Contents

Letter I

Within the group of seven letters the first letter stands distinctly apart from the others. It contains few references to the readers, and no direct exhortations. Instead of being a typical letter, it is written as an introduction on monastic life. In it the author stresses the need for wholeheartedness and the purification of mind, soul and body. The main themes of Letters II to VII—man's need for salvation, God's dispensations, and the dangers of the age—are completely absent. On the other hand the detailed instructions on ascesis and purity of this first letter are missing in

1 See *Ep. Ant.* II.36, III.49–50, VI.116, VII.58 and 62.

2 See Origenes, *Commentarii in Ioannem* 32.181; *Homiliae in Leviticum* 1.1; and *Homiliae in Numeros* 14.1, 27.13 and 28.1.

3 See the examples cited below, pp. 72–81.

the other six letters. In comparison with them the greeting of Letter I is very brief, and there is no formal conclusion. Of the Biblical quotations, hardly any are common to the first letter and the other six. It is also worth noting that the first letter is the only letter transmitted separately, albeit only in the Syriac version.

However, these differences can be explained by different purposes and addressees; there is no need to look for a different author. While in the other letters Antony speaks in general terms about the history of salvation and the need for knowledge, he here sets out to give precise instructions, apparently to monastic novices. In spite of this, many of the traits typical of the other letters appear here as well. Thus we find the same references to the author's own ideas, the same emphasis on the need for the readers to understand, and the same method of quoting the Bible. An analysis of the instructions of the letters also shows that there is a clear agreement between the teaching on repentance in this letter and the more general theological views put forward in the Letters II–VII. The loss of the original version, and of the Greek translation, precludes a detailed linguistic comparison between the letters. There is, however, no evidence in the Georgian and Latin versions of the entire collection for any significant differences in expressions between this first letter and the other six. On the contrary, the strange expression 'the law of promise' (or 'the law of the covenant') (აღთქუმისა რჩული, *testamenti lex*)—or in the Syriac and Arabic 'the law of nature' (ܢܡܘܣܐ ܕܟܝܢܐ. ناموس الطبيعة) or the 'spiritual law' (الناموس العقلي)—which in all the versions appears in the first as well as in the other letters, strongly supports the unity of the collection.

What we have in the first letter is actually a carefully planned treatise on repentance and purification. After a description of how men are called to repentance, Antony describes how the 'Spirit of repentance' acts in man, and how this affects mind, soul and body. The teaching is strictly limited to the practice of repentance, which is described for each member of the body, and there are no references to the history of salvation, to Christ or to eschatology. Antony first describes the three ways in which men come close to grace through the calling of God.[1] There is no reason to interpret this as a reference to monastic life, even if it was later understood and used as such.[2]

The first calling is by the natural and original law, or as it is called the 'law of love' or the 'law of promise', implanted in man at his creation (νόμος ἔμφυτος). The second calling is by the written law and its threats

[1] *Ep.Ant.* I.1. In L we have the expression 'apprehenderit gratia Dei', which in S is given as ܕܢܩܪܒ ܠܚܢܢܗ ܕܐܠܗܐ ('come close to the mercy of God'). G is missing and A has greatly simplified the entire passage.

[2] See the discussion in Guerric Couilleau, 'La liberté d'Antoine', *Commandements du Seigneur et libération Évangélique* (*SA* 70), Rome 1977, pp. 22–24 and p. 41f.

and promises, and the third calling is by the afflictions laid upon man because of his sin. With regard to the first it is explicitly said that it exists for all men 'until now', making it clear that the Fall has not obliterated the original law in man.[1] But even if these three vocations are different, the way to repent, and to purify body and soul in ascesis, is the same.

Antony then presents the 'Spirit of repentance' as a teacher and guide, and gives a brief summary of the work of the Spirit, in which he introduces his teaching on the relation between mind, soul and body. It is the Spirit that calls man and begins the work of repentance, by showing him how to be purified. This purification is achieved with the help of the mind as soon as it accepts the teaching of the Spirit and becomes its instrument. It thus becomes the task of the mind to discriminate between soul and body and bring them back to their original constitution by cleansing them and by purifying each part of the body. Before the analysis of the purification of the single members of the body, which constitutes the main part of the letter, Antony presents his view on the motions of the body; this passage is also incorporated into the *Apophthegmata Patrum*. Man is subject to three kinds of motions, the natural, which are controlled by the soul and not harmful in themselves, the motions which are generated by greed and gluttony, and the motions roused by the temptations of the evil spirits. Through the mixing of these in his body and his soul man has been wounded; he is in need of healing, which can be achieved only through careful purification of soul and body under the guidance of the Spirit.

In the remaining part of the letter Antony teaches how man can purify the different parts of his body. Starting with the eyes, he then proceeds to write about the ears, the tongue, the hands, the belly, the genitals—referred to in the Latin version as 'what is below the belly'[2]—and finally the feet. In each passage Antony first refers to the passions of the member and then gives one or two Biblical references regarding its purification. The description of the purification of the body concludes with the statement that a body which has received the fullness of the Spirit and is fully purified takes on something of the spiritual body which it is to assume at the resurrection. In a last short paragraph Antony enumerates other passions which are not mingled into the body but peculiar to the soul. He then concludes the letter with an emphasis on God's mercy on all who strive in repentance, promising the help of the 'Spirit of repentance'. Man's toil, endurance and obedience to the Spirit are necessary, but he is still dependent upon God's mercy and deliverance.

1 *Ep. Ant.* I.6 according to L and A. S has dropped this reference to the continuous existence of the calling by the natural law, and G is missing for the entire passage.

2 *Ep. Ant.* I.66. Of the other versions S and A avoid any reference, while G speaks about the belly მუცელი. Behind *sub alvo* in L stands the Greek term ὑπογαστρίδιος.

The structure of Letter I can be summarized as follows:

The three modes of God's calling	1-17
The natural law	*2- 8*
The written law	*9-14*
The afflictions	*15-16*
The way the Spirit guides a man to repent	18-34
The ascetic practise	*18-25*
The restoration of man's original constitution	*26-34*
The three motions in the body	35-45
The first belongs to the original nature and is good	*35-36*
The second comes from greed and gluttony	*37-40*
The third comes from the devil	*41*
The need to control the motions in obedience to the Spirit	*42-45*
The way the mind purifies the members of the body	46-71
The partnership of Spirit and mind	*46-49*
The purification of the eyes	*50*
The purification of the ears	*51-52*
The purification of the tongue	*53-58*
The purification of the hands	*59-60*
The purification of the belly	*61-65*
The purification of the genitals	*66-68*
The purification of the feet	*69-71*
The purification of the soul	72-78
The passions of the soul apart from the body	*72-74*
The compassion of the Creator for him who repents	*75-78*

Letters II to VII

The structures of Letters II to VII are virtually the same, and a number of passages are almost identical. The only convincing explanation for this fact is that they were written by the same writer, most probably at the same time, for the same purpose, and to similar audiences. As can be seen from the following table Letters VI and VII actually seem to consist of two letters each. Particularly in the case of letter VII this at first sight seems obvious since the quotation from Prov. 9:9, usually marking the end of a letter, occurs twice.[1] But if the part that comes after the first quotation was originally a separate letter, it must have been incorporated into Letter VII already in the first decades of the transmission, since Jerome gives the number of the letters as seven and all versions include it as part of that letter. This seems unlikely. The fact that most of the text after the first quotation from Proverbs is missing in the Georgian version does not support the view that it was originally a separate letter, since it is only the passage 58*a*–58*u* that is omitted, while the passage designated as a separate

[1] See *Ep. Ant.* VII.58 and 62. In his French edition Louf regards the second part of the Letter VII (the fifth letter in his edition) as a separate letter.

letter, VIIb, also includes the verses 59–62. Since this part of the letter contains a unique passage on baptism, the omission cannot be due to an attempt by the Georgian translator to summarize the letter. Either he must have suppressed this passage, or a folio or two must have been missing in his source. The fact that most of the verses 58*b*–58*i* are missing also in the Arabic version is, however, undoubtedly due to the general tendency of the Arabic text to summarize the letters. A closer examination of the Letters VI and VII shows that both are less carefully structured than the other four, and especially in the case of Letter VII the second part gives the impression of being a short repetition of what the letter was intended to teach, to which the short passage on baptism is added. Instead of being separate letters, the closing sections of these two letters are most likely original parts of them. They will here be called VIb and VIIb.

All the the Letters II–VII are divided into two distinct sections, preceded by an introduction intended to create a close relationship between the author and the readers, and concluded with a passage which stresses the paucity of what he has been able to say and his conviction that the readers will make up for what is lacking. The first section consists of a summary of the history of salvation, and the second of a series of exhortations.[1] In his greetings Antony refers to the spiritual insight of his readers, to their spiritual names, and to his own spiritual love towards them. The theme of the letters is thus introduced as the shared spiritual knowledge and the spiritual relationship between the author and his readers. On what is bodily there is no need to write at all. After the greetings Antony describes the history of salvation as the history of God's repeated attempts to care for man. In the beginning the natural law or, as it is usually called, 'the law of promise' was implanted in man. This law, however, 'froze' or 'whithered'. God then sent Moses with the written law and through him founded the 'house of truth', the Church. But neither Moses, nor the prophets after him, could accomplish salvation; like John the Baptist, they were only the forerunners of God's only-begotten Son. The sending of the Son is by Antony referred to as the result of the inability of all others to heal the wound of mankind and of the prayers of 'the holy' (presumably the angels) for the coming of the Son. Christ's mission is then described with the help of Is. 53:5, Rom. 8:32, Phil. 2:6-11, and Heb. 4:15. Here the emphasis is on Christ's humility and his becoming like us. The result is the remission of sin, the resurrection of the mind, the reconstitution of unity and liberty, and the granting of the 'Spirit of adoption'.

[1] In this respect Antony's letters are similar to some of the epistles of the New Testament, especially the epistles to the Romans, the Ephesians and the Hebrews.

In this first part on the history of salvation, the text of several letters is almost identical. Letter II and III in particular agree almost *verbatim* as is shown by the following example:

Letter II. 2-8	Letter III.8-12
Truly, my beloved in the Lord, God did not visit his creatures only once, but since the beginning of the world, as soon as anyone has turned through the law of promise to the Creator of all, God embraces him in his benevolence, grace and Spirit. As for those rational beings in whom the law of promise grew cold and whose faculties of the mind thus died, so that they can no longer know themselves after their first formation, they have all become irrational and serve the creatures instead of the Creator. But in his great benevolence the Creator of all visited us through the law of promise, for our essence is immortal. Those who have become worthy of grace and have been fortified with the law of promise and taught by the Holy Spirit and accepted the Spirit of adoption, they have become able to worship the Creator as is proper.	Therefore God has not visited his creatures only once, but from the creation of the world some have prepared themselves to come to the Creator through covenant of his promise, learning from that how to worship their Creator as is proper. But through much weakness, the heaviness of the body and the concern for evil the law of promise has grown cold and the faculties of the mind have been worned out. [1]Thus they have not been able to discover themselves as they were created, namely as an eternal substance, which is not dissolved with the body but still cannot be freed through its own righteousness. Therefore God in his benevolence turned to it with the law of Scripture to teach them to worship the Father as is proper.

In shorter, for the letters typical, passages all letters use precisely the same phrases, as is demonstrated by the following example:

Letter II. 22-23	Letter III.24-25	Letter V.27-28	Letter VI.91	Letter VII.30
and by the word of his power he gathered us from all lands, from one end of the earth to the other, resurrecting our minds, giving us remission of our sins, and teaching us that we are members of one another.	Through the word of his power he gathered us from all lands, from one end of the earth to the other, resurrecting our hearts from the earth and teaching us that we are members of one another.	and he gathered us from all lands, from one end of the earth to the other, resurrecting our minds from the earth and teaching us that we are members of one another.	And he gathered us from all lands, until he resurrected our hearts from the earth, and taught us that we are of one essence and members of one another.	and by the power of his word he gathered us from all lands, until he resurrected our minds from the earth and taught us that we are members of one another.

After relating the history of salvation, Antony interprets its meaning and exhorts his readers to understand and to act accordingly. His emphasis is here on the decisive character of the 'coming of Jesus' and on liberation or judgement as its result. Antony also mentions the great risk of false religion and of 'wearing the habit in vain'. Every man must know himself and his time; he must prepare himself in perfect purity as a spiritual sacrifice. In this connection he also writes about the intercessions of the saints (the angels) and the activities of the demons. The letters then conclude with the above-mentioned reference to the paucity of the author's words and his trust in the wisdom of his readers, for which he quotes Prov. 9:9.

But even if the general outline is common for these six letters, some of them contain major divergences from the design. As mentioned above, Letters VI and VII repeat most of the common contents in summaries at the end. Letter VI, moreover, contains a long section on the demons without parallels in the other letters. The passage on the concern of the author which usually introduces the exhortations is here developed into a detailed discussion on the art of the activities of the demons, the reasons for their onslaught on man, their dependence on the bodies of men, and finally their spiritual origin. Some of this is also found at the end of Letter V.[1] A passage which lacks parallels is also found in the latter part of Letter VII, where Antony speaks about baptism in connection with God's care for his creatures. Here the common themes of purification, sacrifice and the wearing of the habit of religion are interpreted as referring to baptism. This leads the author to emphasize the distinction between the baptism of John for the remission of sins and the baptism of Jesus granting the Spirit.[2]

Besides these two letters, it is Letter IV that differs most from the others. In this letter there is no description of the history of salvation, and the eager exhortations to the correspondents characteristic of the letters are also missing. Instead the letter has a short exposition on the difference between servitude and sonhood. The emphasis on self-knowledge, on the spiritual essence and the knowledge of the time is, however, the same as in all the letters. Several of the expressions repeatedly used in the other letters, as well as the same Biblical quotations, are also found in it. The most striking and unique passage in the letter—the one in which Arius is mentioned—has been discussed above.

1 *Ep. Ant.* VI. 27–43, and 49–62. A short summary of some of this teaching is also found in V.40. The passage on the origin of the demons is the probably most charactreristically Origenist in the letters. See below, pp. 64–68.

2 *Ep. Ant.* VII.58m–q. This passage is discussed in connection with Antony's teaching on the Spirit, see below, pp. 79–81.

The common outline of Letters II–VII is illustrated by the following table:

Theme	II	III	IV	V	VI	VIb	VII	VIIb
I. Greeting	1	1-6	1-2	1-3	1-4	78-87	1-5	58*b-d*
The spiritual knowledge		1-3		1	2	80,84		
'Holy Israelites'		6	(1)	1	2	78	5	58*b*
'My love towards you'		4	2	2		79		
II. History of salvation	2-30	7-31	(3-14)	4-28	5-16	88-92	6-45	58*e-k*
God's visits	2-8	8-16		4-16	5-7		6-21	58*f*
Moses and the prophets	9-12	17-19		17	8-9		(22-24)	
The prayer for the Son	13-17	20-21		20-24	10-11		(26-27)	
The kenosis *of Christ*	18-21	22-23		25-26	12-14	89-90	28-44	58*f*
The aims of his mission	22-24	24-26		27-28		91	30,44	58*g*
Liberation by His advent	25	27			(16)		32-34,45	58*h*
Servitude and sonhood	26-30	29-31	4-12				45	
III. Exhortations	31-35	32-48	15-20	29-42	17-77	93-110	46-57	58*l*–61
His advent a judgement	31-33	32-37					(35)	
Wearing the habit in vain	34	33		29		106	46-47	
'Know this time'	35	38,47f.	16	37				
'Prepare yourselves'		38		(33f.)	73-77	93	52	58*n*
Intercessors		41-44		(36)		98-101		
The demons		45f.		(40f.)	17-72	102-105		
IV. End	36-37	49-51				111-117	58	62-66
I have more to write	36	49				116	58	62

The close relationship between the six letters is also illustrated by their use of Biblical quotations and their allusions to Biblical texts. Most of the quotations common to more than one letter are even found in the same order in the letters.

Biblical ref.	II	III	IV	V	VI	VIb	VII	VIIb
Ps. 132:4				7	15	95		
Hebr. 11:39	8			9				
Jer. 8:22	16			21				
Jer. 51:9	17			22				
Ez. 12:3	18			24				
Phil. 2:6-8	19				12	89	39,43	58*k*
Rom. 8:32/Gal 1:4	20	22		25	13	90	28	58*f*
Is. 53:5	21	23		26	13	90	29	58*f*
2 Tim. 3:5		33		29			47	
Ps. 116:12				30			18	58*j*
Hebr. 4:15	24	26					32	
2 Cor. 8:9		28			14		1,41	
Hebr. 2:14		28					44	
John 15:15	27	30	9					
Rom. 8:15	29		11					
Rom. 8:17	30		12					
1 Cor. 10:15		39	15	32	21	114		
Prov. 9:9	36	50				116	58	62

IV. The *Gnosis*

1. Man and Cosmos

The Concept of Knowledge

Probably the most striking feature of the letters of Antony is their emphasis on knowledge, *gnosis.* The exhortations to know and to understand, which appear throughout the letters, and the recurring use of Prov. 9:9, 'Give occasion to the wise man, and he will be yet wiser', and 1 Cor. 10:15, 'As to wise men I speak to you', are not empty rhetoric or an intellectual façade, but rooted in a theology for which true knowledge is at the centre. Without knowledge of himself, or as Antony says, of his own *spiritual essence,* a man cannot know God, he cannot understand God's acts of salvation, but by fully understanding himself a man knows his time and ultimately learns to worship God as is proper. It is not *credo quia absurdum* that is Antony's device and defence for Christianity, but γνῶθι σεαυτόν 'know thyself'.[1]

Our analysis of the contents of the letters must therefore proceed from three questions about knowledge: what it is, why it is essential, and how it is gained. The answers to these questions are closely linked with Antony's views on man and cosmos. It is here that we must look for the philosophical presuppositions for his views on God's acts of salvation and man's response to these. The letters are, however, unsystematic, and contain no definitions of the crucial concepts used, such as γνῶσις, νοῦς, νοερός, λογικός, οὐσία and φύσις. The way Biblical expressions are mixed with philosophical concepts often makes it extremely difficult to understand Antony's thinking. Thus it is necessary to draw upon the philosophical and theological background that is discernible behind the letters. While there is no evidence in them for a use of earlier philosophical or theological texts, the letters show Antony to have been acquainted with current ideas. As might be expected, his background must be sought in a popularized form of the Middle and Neo Platonic tradition.

[1] For the history of the maxim see L. de Bazelain, 'Connaissance de soi', *DSp* II, p. 1511–1543; and P. Courcelle, *Connais-toi toi-même de Socrate à Saint Bernard,* 1, Paris 1974; for a background, see also the passages on the Stoic and on the Gnostic use, pp. 51–57 and pp. 69–79. In his emphasis on self-knowledge and proper worship Antony is very much the heir of Clement of Alexandria. For parallels to the letters, see especially *Stromata* VII.1–12.

The links between the letters and Origen' theology were noted and commented upon by Symphorianus Champerius as early as 1516, but have since received little attention. With the traditional image of Antony and the early monks as illiterate and unaware of Greek theological tradition the Origenism of the letters has been seen as 'unexpected' and apparently of little consequence for the interpretation of early monasticism.[1] In addition to Origen, and to some extent Clement of Alexandria, it is in the theology of late third and early fourth century Alexandria that we find parallels to Antony's letters. In two important texts from this theological setting, the *Teachings of Silvanus* and Athanasius' *Contra Gentes*, we find the closest parallels to the theology of the letters. The opening lines of *Contra Gentes:* Ἡ μὲν περὶ τῆς θεοσεβείας καὶ ὅλων ἀληθείας γνῶσις ('knowledge about the worship of God and the true nature of the universe'), is a good definition of what the letters want to emphasize.[2]

According to Plato, for man to gain true knowledge is not to attain something new and previously unknown, but to wake up and realize what he originally beheld. Ignorance is to forget one's origin, knowledge is to remember what the soul once knew. The aim of man's quest for knowledge is thus the return to his original nature; philosophy is the transcendence of earthly life, the preparation for dying.[3] This emphasis on the return to what is original is fundamental to the theology of Origen, recurs in Silvanus and permeates Antony's letters. It is to his original nature, his 'first beginning', that man must be brought back, he must know himself according to his 'first creation'.[4] His ignominy and susceptibility to evil is the result of negligence and ignorance.[5] Behind this Platonic view lies the

1 See Chitty, *The Desert a City,* London 1966, p. 20. But see Gribomont's review of Garitte's edition for an accurate evaluation of what the letters imply.

2 A summary of the philosophical and theological tradition behind the letters is Andrew Louth, *The Origins of the Christian Mystical Tradition. From Plato to Denys,* Oxford 1981, pp. 1–74. The general background and most themes are covered in Jean Daniélou, *Message évangelique et culture hellénistique (idem, Histoire des doctrines chrétiennes avant Nicée* II), Paris 1961. For a study of Silvanus, convincingly dating the *Teachings* to the early fourth century, see Roelof van den Broek, 'The Theology of the Teachings of Silvanus', *VC* 40 (1986), pp. 1–23. A comparison of the letters with themes in the Nag-Hammadi codices is Wincenty Myszor, 'Antonius-Briefe und Nag-Hammadi-Texte', *JAC* 33 (1990), p. 74–88.

3 On Plato as a background, see Louth, *op.cit.,* pp. 1–1,7 and Daniélou, *Message évangelique,* pp. 103–122.

4 See *Ep. Ant.* I.30, II.4, 10, III.9, V.18 and VII.58*p*. The Arabic version also refers to the 'original creation' in I.36, III.12 and VII.50–51. Cf. *Teachings of Silvanus* 90–92.

5 *Ep. Ant.* VI.87: 'But if a member is estranged from the body, having no contact with the head, but delighting in the passions of the flesh, it has contracted an incurable wound and has forgotten its beginning and its end'; VI,106 'Truly, my children, I also want you to know that there are many who have endured great struggle in this way of life, but have been killed by lack of discernment' (უმეცრებაჲ; L: indiscretio; Gr*: ἄγνοια); VI,107 'I consider it not strange at all that, if you neglect yourselves (უდებ ვყვნეთ, the 1 pl. form is evidently a mistake; L: negligatis) and do not discern (განკითხვაჲ; L: discernere; Gr*: ἀνακρινεῖν) your works, you fall into the hands of the devil'. *Cf.* VI.22, 26.

conviction that true knowledge is only possible about what is truly real, *i.e.* what is above change and corruption, what is spiritual and not material. In Antony's letters this fundamental distinction in Platonic thought between the spiritual and the corporeal is echoed in his preference for the spiritual names of his correspondents over their names in the body, and his insistence on the spiritual nature of his love for them.[1] In the letters, as in the Platonic tradition, mutability, lack of firmness, and change are signs of an earthly nature; varying opinions or new doctrines are signs of falsehood.[2] Thus the true nature of things is not what we apprehend with our senses, and our own true nature lies not in our individual corporeal existence, but in what is immortal and unchangeable, the higher part of the soul, the *nous.* It is in Antony's words to his 'own spiritual essence', to what has an origin but no end, that man has to return.[3]

In Platonic thought knowledge presupposes participation in what is known. Only by being rational (λογικός) and possessing the capacity for spiritual knowledge (νοερός) can man know what is essentially spiritual, (νοητός).[4] To contemplate the true realities is to become like God.[5] This Platonic concept of an assimilation (ὁμοίωσις) to God was later linked to the Biblical phraseology of man created 'in the image of God'. Thus the essence of man's likeness to God was seen as consisting in his being rational, *i.e.* in his capacity for true knowledge.[6] For Antony it is by being rational, *logikos,* that man can know himself, *i.e.* know his 'spiritual essence' (οὐσία νοερά), while becoming irrational is the same as being condemned to death.[7] By knowing himself according to the 'spiritual

1 See *Ep. Ant.* III.4–5, 41, IV.2–3, V.1–2, VII.16. The distinction between spiritual and bodily love is akin to Plato's distinction between ἔρος πάνδημος and ἔρος οὐράνιος and is paralleled by Plotinus, *Enneades* VI.9.9, and Origenes, *Commentarii in Canticum canticorum,* Prologus. See Louth, *The Origins,* p. 66f.

2 See *i.a.* IV.2–3: bodily love has no firmness or stability, or IV.16: he who knows himself is able to stand firm and is not moved by 'shifty tongues', in contrast to Arius who spoke alien words about the Son of God.

3 *Ep. Ant.* III.11–12.

4 The distinction between νοερός ('intellectual') and νοητός ('mental') was emphasized by Jamblichus, who was a contemporary of Antony, and upheld by philosophers and theologians, but in general usage the two terms were often used synonymously to mean spiritual, *i.e.* what belongs to the mind, the *nous.* See Lampe, *Patristic Lexicon,* p. 917.

5 Plato, *Theaetetus* 176A–B.

6 Again we can turn to *Contra Gentes* to find a passage which summarizes what lies behind Antony's teaching: 'And through the likeness to Him He made man in such a way that he could behold and know that which is really, giving him also an idea and knowledge of his own eternity, that, preserving his identity, he may never abandon the contemplation of God and never turn away from life with the saints' (*Contra Gentes* 2, tr. by E. P. Meijering, *Athanasius: Contra Gentes,* Leiden 1984, p. 16f.).

7 That the letters used the expression οὐσία νοερά is evident from the Coptic version of *Ep. Ant.* IV.10: ⲛⲉⲛⲧⲁⲩϩⲱⲛ ⲉϩⲟⲩⲛ ⲅⲁⲣ ⲉⲁⲩⲇⲓⲇⲁⲥⲕⲉ ⲙⲙⲟⲩ ⲉⲃⲟⲗ ϩⲓⲧⲛⲡⲉⲡⲛⲉⲩⲙⲁ ⲉⲧⲟⲩⲁⲁⲃ ⲁⲩⲥⲟⲩⲱⲛⲟⲩ ⲕⲁⲧⲁⲧⲉⲩⲟⲩⲥⲓⲁ ⲛⲛⲟⲉⲣⲁ (Those who had come close, by being taught by the Holy Spirit, came to know themselves in their spiritual essence). The equivalent in the Georgian version is არსება გონიერი. არსება is the natural translation of οὐσία and გონიერი is related

essence' man is able to attain true knowledge, he is able to know God, to know all.[1]

In Platonic terms real knowledge thus implies an orientation of the whole person towards the spiritual world. Philosophy is not a theoretical exercise but a way of living, a participation in what is known. Virtue is not only necessary for knowledge, it *is* knowledge, and the pursuit of knowledge is as much a moral and spiritual as an intellectual exercise. In order to see true reality man must be set free, he must be detached from this world, he must purify himself. This purification has two aspects, a moral and an intellectual. Moral purification is the purification of the soul from undue bodily influence, the detachment of the soul from the body. To achieve this it is necessary to season the body by virtue and ascesis. Intellectual purification is the search for the essence of things, for what lies behind the forms apprehended by the senses; it is the quest for principles, ultimately for the highest principle. This is done through dialectics (abstraction) and contemplation. In both cases purification as the remedy for man consists in 'a movement from the material to the spiritual, from the external to the interior, from the transient to the eternal'.[2] In Antony's letters these basic concepts lie behind his teaching on repentance as a matter of purification. As in the philosophical tradition purification is the detachment of soul and body, the separation of what has become mingled, and the subjection of body and soul to the mind.[3]

In the development of the Platonic tradition self-knowledge emerged as the most important road to true knowledge, and thus to salvation. The spiritual is close at hand, it dwells in man as his essential nature, his real self, and only needs to be recognized and liberated.[4] The emphasis on self-knowledge in the letters has already been noted. In two passages in Athanasius, one of which has even been attributed to Antony, these Platonic foundations are manifest. In *Contra Gentes* Athanasius speaks about 'knowledge of the way of truth' as something within us, 'in no need of anything other than ourselves', in the *Vita Antonii* he reports that

to the word used in the Georgian version where the Greek must have had νοῦς (see *i.a.* III.6, where 'Israel' is interpreted as 'mens videns Deum' in L and as გონებაჲ მხედველი ღმრთისაჲ in G). The Latin text varies between 'sensualis essentia', 'sensualis substantia' and 'sensualis exstantia'.

1 Apparently Antony did not regard God as unknowable in principle, as did *i.a.* Origen or Silvanus, but remained in the tradition based on Plato, *Timaeus* 28c, according to which it is a difficult, but not impossible, exercise to find God. On the question of God as unknowable, see Daniélou, *Message évangelique,* pp. 297–316

2 Louth, *The Origins,* p. 26.

3 *Ep. Ant.* I.26–34.

4 The difference between Plato and Plotinus in this respect is described by Louth and shows that Antony had much of the same concern as Plotinus. See Louth, *The Origins,* pp. 36–51.

Antony taught about 'virtue' as being within us and arising from us.[1] The self is not only the most common object of knowledge mentioned in the letters, but self-knowledge is also repeatedly said to be a condition for, or closely connected with knowledge of other things. He who knows himself knows that he is of one immortal essence, he knows this time, the dispensations of the Creator for his creation, the gift of adoption, the truth about Christ; he is even said to know God himself, to know all.[2] Without discernment (διάκρισις) of his own acts, and the exertion of his heart and senses, man cannot attain purity, cannot 'discriminate between good and evil, right and left, the eternal and the passing', but is liable to fall into the hands of the devil.[3]

These basic concepts of knowledge explain the lack of any reference to authoritative teaching in the letters. Only once does Antony support his exhortation by calling it the commandment of God.[4] Instead, he invites and implores the reader to discover and understand himself. The chief criterion is experience, and Antony alluding to 1 John 1:1, refers to his own experience as the basis for his teaching.[5] At the same time the abundance of Biblical quotations, as well as the content of his teaching, clearly shows that Antony regarded the testimony of the Bible as a true revelation of this existential knowledge.[6] The Law is a witness to judgement and a guide to divine sonhood, and the history of revelation a witness to God's care for man. But what the Bible reveals is not something new and foreign to man's own perception of reality. The Bible elucidates what is difficult for man to grasp; it helps man to understand himself and God; it teaches him how to turn back to the original nature. In Antony's use of the Bible it is his teaching that is elucidated by the quotations, not the other way round, and very often it is extremely difficult to tell whether we have a quotation, an

1 *Contra Gentes* 30 and *VA* 20.

2 *Ep. Ant.* II.28, III.2, 38–40, IV.11, 15–16, 20, VI.69, 84, 20. For the same emphasis in Silvanus, see *Teachings of Silvanus* 92.

3 See *Ep. Ant.* III.43–44. The last antithesis constitutes a textual problem. G has სიმტკიცჱ და უძლურებაჲ ('firmness and infirmity'), while L has *substantia et insubstantia*, and A has الثبتين من غير الثبتين ('the stable from the unstable'). While სიმტკიცჱ is not used elsewhere in the Georgian text, *substantia* is used synonymously with *essentia*, and occasionally *exstantia* in Latin for Georgian არსებაჲ (οὐσία). Georgian უძლურებაჲ is common in the letters for 'weakness' as is the equivalent Latin word *infirmitas*. But *insubstantia* does not occur elsewhere in the letters. Could it be that the Greek text originally used ὑπόστασις where the Latin has *substantia*—in this verse together with ἀνυπόστασις—but that these terms were avoided in the subsequent transmission of the text and dropped before the Georgian translation was made?

4 *Ep. Ant.* VII.63.

5 *Ep. Ant.* VII.52.

6 As will be shown below, Antony is dependent upon Origen's exegetical theories and methods. The emphasis on revelation at the expense of tradition is characteristic of Origen. See Daniélou, *Message évangelique*, pp. 249–264, and, more extensively, Marguerite Harl, *Origène et la fonction révélatrice du verbe incarné*, Paris 1957, pp. 333–376.

allusion, or simply a reflection of Biblical language.[1] True understanding of revelation ultimately rests on self-knowledge.

This emphasis on knowledge is corroborated by the complete absence in the letters of the concept of 'faith'.[2] But it would be wrong to regard knowledge in the letters as *a priori* opposed to faith, as *i.a.* in the debate with the philosophers in the *Vita Antonii.*[3] The *gnosis* of the letters is not the kind of knowledge studied in the academies, it is not primarily knowledge about a theological system, certain doctrines or secret teachings, but knowledge about oneself and about one's own salvation. What counts is not the intellectual capacity but the state of mind, a state characterized by insight and true perception.

Unity and Diversity

The Platonic background of Antony's concept of knowledge and its affinities with the later developments of Platonism, culminating in the teachings of Plotinus, are also evident in what the letters reveal about Antony's views on unity and diversity. Unity is in this tradition the original, the highest level of being, while diversity is the result of movement, a sign of instability and disintegration. Everything is linked together: it emanates from the highest principle and strives to return to it. Unity is the beginning and the end. In Antony's words: 'God is one and the spiritual essence also exists through oneness.'[4] This Platonic concept of God as one and the cause of all is combined with the Biblical teaching of a *creatio ex nihilo.*[5] Antony explicitly confesses that he 'called everything into being

1 The most frequent phrase introducing a Biblical quotation is 'this is why it is said'. Quite often verses from different parts of the Bible are interwoven into one quotation, and there is no attempt to interpret the text itself. The fact that a small number of verses make up half of the quotations also shows that Antony uses the Bible primarily to confirm his favourite ideas.

2 In the three passages in the letters, where the verbs რწამს (to be persuaded, to be entrusted with, believe) and *credere* are found, it is clear that the meaning is 'to be entrusted' and 'to be persuaded'. See I.45 (G) 'then it is persuaded that this is its rest' (L 'dat', S and A a different reading); I.75 (L) 'if it entrusts itself to God' (G, S and A all have the simple word 'gives'); IV.6 (C, G, L, A) 'entrusted with the apostolic preaching' (C: ⲧⲁⲛϩⲟⲩⲧ).

3 *VA* 72–80. But here knowledge stands for pagan philosophical studies and reasoning, not for the spiritual self-knowledge emphasized in the letters. See below, chapter VI, for a discussion on the difference between the *VA* and the letters.

4 *Ep. Ant.* III.13. G: რამეთუ ღმერთი ერთ არს, და გონიერი იგი არსებაჲ არს ერთობითა; L: 'Sed quoniam Deus unus existit et secundum sensualem essentiam in id ipsum est unitas'; A: لان الله واحد هو والجوهر العقلي ايضاً كائن في الوحدانية . My translation is based on the accord between the Georgian and the Arabic, while Chitty has relied on the Latin text and translated as follows: 'God is One, that is to say, Unity of intellectual substance'. For a similar passage in Origen, see *De Principiis* I.1.6.

5 For the use of Platonic texts on creation by the Christian Middle Platonists, see Daniélou, *Message évangélique,* pp. 104–106. Louth argues that there is, in spite of earlier references, no articulate and unambigious doctrine of a *creatio ex nihilo* before Arius and Athanasius, since this doctrine demands a notion of a complete contrast between God and created order (Louth, *The Origins,* p. 77f.). The ambiguity of the pre-Arian period suggested by Louth is corroborated by Antony's view on the relationship between the mind and God, for which

out of nothingness.'[1] The sun, the moon and the stars, the holy heavens, angels and archangels, thrones and dominions, the devil and the evil spirits, men and women, from the beginning of their formation they all derive from one and the same.[2] Like Plotinus and Origen, Antony is sharply opposed to any dualist view on the origin and nature of creation. Not even for the evil beings can there be any other source than the original unity in God. With men and angels, the demons 'are all from one source in their spiritual essence'.[3]

The importance of the concept of unity is manifest throughout the letters. The original unity in essence of all that is spiritual is based on the fact that all rational nature (λογικὴ φύσις) was originally made in the image of God's mind (νοῦς), which is Christ.[4] Christ, the head of creation, is also the source of unity. The essence of Christ's mission in his descent to the world is to gather all men back to unity, a unity manifest in the metaphor of the Church as a body. This unity with one's fellow men, and with God in Christ, is repeatedly drawn upon in the letters to stress the need for love. As members one of another we must love one another; if we love our neighbour we love God and if we love God we love ourselves.[5]

Against the background of this Platonic view of unity as the original and ultimate reality, it becomes necessary to explain the plurality manifest

---

parallels are found in Origen, and more radically Silvanus. See Origenes, *De Principiis* I.1.7 'quod propinquitas quaedem sit menti ad deum', and the *Teachings of Silvanus* 93.25–27: ⲉⲓ̈ϣⲁϫⲉ ⲇⲉ ϫⲉ ⲡⲛⲟⲩⲧⲉ ⲡⲉ ⲡⲉⲡⲛⲁⲧⲓⲕⲟⲥ ⲡⲣⲱⲙⲉ ⲛ̄ⲧⲁϥϫⲓ ⲙⲟⲣⲫⲏ ⲉⲃⲟⲗ ϩⲛ̄ ⲧⲟⲩⲥⲓⲁ ⲙ̄ⲡⲛⲟⲩⲧⲉ ⲧⲯⲩⲭⲏ ⲛ̄ⲑⲉⲓⲟⲛ ⲥⲣ̄ⲕⲟⲓⲛⲱⲛⲓ ⲉⲡⲁⲓ̈ ϩⲛ̄ ⲟⲩⲙⲉⲣⲟⲥ ('Since, as I have said, 'God is spiritual, man has taken form from the essence of God; the divine soul participates partially in Him'). This relationship does not, however, mean that the mind is eternal; like everything else it is created, it has a beginning. See VI.5, 84. Origen's discussion on the need to postulate an eternal creation, since God is both eternal and Creator (*De Principiis* I.4.4–5), finds no echo in Antony's letters.

1 *Ep. Ant.* VI.69. He introduces this as a Scriptural quotation, probably referring to Sap. 1:14: ἔκτισεν γὰρ εἰς τὸ εἶναι τὰ πάντα, or 2 Makk. 7:28: οὐκ ἐξ ὄντων ἐποίσεν αὐτὰ ὁ θεός.

2 *Ep. Ant.* V.40.

3 *Ep. Ant.* VI.56.

4 *Ep. Ant.* VI.85. რაჲმეთუ იესუ ქრისტე უფალი ჩუენი იგი თავადი არს ჭეშმარიტი გონებაჲ მამისაჲ, რომლისა გან ყოველი სავსებაჲ ყოვლისა მეტყოელისა მის ბუნებისაჲ იქმნა ხატად თჳსისა მის ხატისა, რაჲმეთუ იგი თავადი არს თავ ყოვლისა დაბადებულისა (that Jesus Christ, our Lord, is himself the true mind (νοῦς) of the Father, by whom all the fullness (πλήρωμα) of the entire rational (λογική) nature (φύσις) is made to an image of his image, for he himself is the head of all creation). L: 'quod Jesus Christus dominus noster ipse patris verus est sensus in quo omnis plenitudo totius naturae rationabilis effecta est: eorum maxime qui sunt imaginis eius conformes effecti: caput totius creature'. See also II.14 and VII.10. The translation 'mind' is based on the use of the words (G. გონებაჲ, L: 'sensus' and A: عقل) throughout the letters. Christ as the νοῦς of the Father is an unusual expression. In Alexandrian theology God is usually called *Nous* and Christ *Logos*. It is, however, encountered in Theognostus, a late third century Alexandrian Origenist and in Arius. See Alois Grillmeier, *Jesus der Christus im Glauben der Kirche* I, Freiburg 1979, pp. 291–294, 412.

5 *Ep. Ant.* VI.86–92 *et. al.*

in creation as secondary. Clement regarded the spiritual, which he equated with Plato's world of ideas, as the creation of the first day, followed by increasing differentiation during the remaining five days.[1] The view that plurality and material nature are less real and subsistent than unity and spiritual nature led Origen to conclude that the cause for this differentiation and corporality must have been an original fall. The plurality of being was not intended from the beginning, it is a result of a departure from the original unity, a deviation from God.[2] In this Antony follows Origen closely, suggesting a direct contact with Origenist teaching. According to Origen all souls and spiritual beings were originally, before the material creation, pure minds, all equal and all contemplating God. Bored by this eternal bliss, they fell and became souls (ψυχή), allegedly so called since they were cooled (ψύχομαι). To halt their fall God gave men bodies, which enabled them to ascend once more to their contemplation. In his attempts to stress the unity of spiritual being and the fact that the demons have no origin of their own, and thus no source of power, Antony twice recalls this Origenist view. In origin all are the same, it is only because of the differences in their acts of 'flight' from God that there is a difference in names between them.[3]

In accordance with Platonic thought Antony in his letters regards unity as the equivalent of stability and peace. In contrast to Christ, who is 'the unaltered image of the Father', man is 'of changeable substance', he is 'easily moved', εὐκίνητος.[4] Arius' mistake, according to Antony, was precisely his suggestion that even in Christ, who is immovable (ⲁⲧⲕⲓⲙ), there was motion. Immovability is for man an ideal hard to attain; it is only possible for him who truly knows himself.[5] The fall is thus a sign of the soul's susceptibility to evil, evil being alien to the nature of the spiritual

1 See Daniélou, *Message évangelique,* p. 113, for Clement's use of Plato in his interpretation of Genesis.

2 For the background of Origen's views, see Daniélou, *op.cit.,* pp. 381–390.

3 *Ep. Ant.* V.40–42 and VI.56–62. The affinities with Origenes, *De Principiis* I.5.1–2 and I.8.2–4 are here obvious. Antony does not use ψύχομαι in this context, but to indicate that the natural law, 'the law of promise' had become ineffective in man. See below, pp. 74.

4 Antony does not use the expression εὐκίνητος, but the similarities between his thought and what we find in *Contra Gentes* 3–4, where the expression is used, suggest the same concept. For the Platonic background, see the comments by Meijering, *Athanasius: Contra Gentes,* p. 24, and Daniélou, *Message évangelique,* p. 382ff..

5 See *Ep. Ant.* IV.16–17 for Antony's accusations against Arius, and an emphasis on self-knowledge as the prerequisite for stability. Coptic atkim is the equivalent for ἀκίνητος or ἀσάλευτος. Although the former is the traditional term in philosophical language for things not subject to motion or change the latter is suggested by the preceding verse. Both terms are used about Antony's mind in the *Vita Antonii* (chs. 39 and 51). For a background and the use of the expression 'the immovable race' (ⲧⲅⲉⲛⲉⲁ ⲛ̄ⲁⲧⲕⲓⲙ, or ἡ ἀσάλευτος γενεά) as a designation of certain Gnostics in some of the Nag Hammadi texts, see Michael A. Williams, *The Immovable Race. A Gnostic Designation and the Theme of Stability in Late Antiquity* (*NHS* 29), Leiden 1985, especially pp. 14–25, where the Platonic background is treated with references to Philo, Plotinus and Plutarch. A Biblical parallel is found in Hebr. 12:25–28.

essence.[1] The motions (κινήσεις) are not originally evil, they are natural, it is only when they are wrongly directed and uncontrolled that they become passions (πάθη). The beginning of the evil motions is arrogance, the first motion away from God and the cause of the fall.[2] To Antony, the origin of evil is thus the free will which God gave to all spiritual beings. It is only because they were endowed with free will that they could move in the wrong direction.[3]

Although Antony gives no systematic explanation of his views on the results of the original fall and the creation of the material world, the close affinities with Origen already noted suggest that Origen's teaching can be regarded as the background of his thought. According to Origen, God created the world to correspond to the diversity among the spiritual beings, now no longer equal and united. In this order or hierarchy 'matter' is, in the Platonic manner, regarded as the lowest level of being.[4] But the material world is not evil. It is the result of God's providence, it is the attempt to establish an order in the diversity caused by the fall of the 'minds'. In Antony's letters matter is at one and the same time the source of 'the power of the devil', and the precondition for progress in virtue. To Antony the chief result of the fall is this ambivalence and insecurity. Man has not lost his likeness to God, his 'spiritual essence' or his 'mind', but the body 'weighs it down' from the spiritual to the material, and the motions of the soul and the body defy its control.

In Antony's letters this predominantly Platonic and Origenist concept of creation and fall is combined with a different and more Biblical view. While there is in the first concept no reference to sin against God, to punishment, or to any need for redemption, the second sees man as suffering from an incurable wound. His spiritual nature has died, he is condemned by his sin to perdition, and thus in need of resurrection and the remission of his sins through the coming of Christ. This tension between what could be called a mythical and a historical explanation is also encountered in Origen, and possibly in Athanasius as well.[5] Origen's solution is to regard Gen. 1:26–27 as referring to the original creation of man as purely mind, while the creation of the body is implied by the coverings of skin given by God to Adam and Eve and by their subsequent expulsion from Paradise in Gen. 3:21–24. While the original fall resulted in the material creation and the expulsion from Paradise, the fall into sin and

1 *Ep. Ant.* VII.11.

2 *Ep. Ant.* VI.109.

3 See *Ep. Ant.* V.39, VII.38 and 58*e*. Antony in this agrees completely with Origen, who states that nothing was created as fixed to good or evil. See *De Principiis* I.5.3, and for a similar view Athanasius, *Contra Gentes* 4.

4 Origenes, *De Principiis* II.9.2–6.

5 See *Contra Gentes* 2–4; Meijering, *Athanasius,* p. 19 and Louth, *The Origins,* p. 77–80.

condemnation came with Cain's murder of Abel in Gen. 4.[1] In the letters there is no attempt to explain how these two concepts are related to each other. The first is important only to stress man's spiritual essence and origin, and the unity of creation, while the second is the foundation of Antony's teaching on God's dispensations. Man's incurable wound and his need for redemption are attributed to the long history of his disobedience to the natural law implanted in him at his creation (the νόμος ἔμφυτος), rather than to a cosmic fall. It was since this law had 'withered away', and the written law was ineffective, that Christ had to come.

Man as mind, soul and body

The basis for Antony's anthropology is the Platonic dualism between the spiritual and the corporeal. As we have seen, man's real self, his nature, is his 'spiritual essence'. Though created, it is immortal: 'we are all created from one invisible essence, having a beginning but no end'.[2] This essence is now hidden in the body, but it does not belong to it, and will not be dissolved with it. Since it is purely spiritual, it has in itself no differentiation; it is 'a unity of spiritual essence'. Thus there is no distinction in it between male and female.[3] Apparently Antony regards individuality as a result of the fall and of diversity, and something that belongs to corporeal and transient existence; it is no part of the essence of man. Individuality is manifest in body and soul, while the 'spiritual essence' is manifest in the mind, which is created in the image of God's mind, Christ, and thus equal for all. Although Antony maintains that the mind is 'of changeable substance', he seems to imply that differentiation is only possible through the incarnation of the mind in a soul and a body.

This basic dualism is, however, in Platonic anthropology combined with a tripartite division of man. Plato propounded a divison of the soul into *nous, thymos,* and *epithymos.* The latter two were subsequently merged and out of the division *of the soul* into three parts emerged a division *of man* into three parts, the body, the (lower parts of the) soul, and the mind, a division found also in Antony's letters. While later Origenist theology fused this division with the Biblical concept of man as spirit, soul and body, the letters do not equate the mind with the spirit, but with a few exceptions reserve the term 'spirit' (πνεῦμα) for the gift given to man by

1 The reconstruction and interpretation of Origen's views remain hypothetical and a matter of dispute. See Henri Crouzel, *Origène,* Paris 1985, pp. 123–137, 216–236 and 267–284. A possible echo of Origen's teaching is the expression 'the skin of the corruptible flesh' (G: ტყავი ჴორცთაჲ განხრწნადი, L: 'pellicula carnis corruptibilis'), in *Ep. Ant.* V.37. It recalls Origen's views according to Epiphanius (see Origenes, *De Principiis* in the edition by Görgemanns and Karpp, p. 279) and Methodius, *De Resurrectione* I.29. For a cautious view see Tim Vivian, *St. Peter of Alexandria. Bishop and Martyr,* Philadelphia 1988, pp. 119–126.

2 *Ep. Ant.* VI.84.

3 *Ep. Ant.* V,15; VI,5–6, 70.

God. Therefore, the spirit (πνεῦμα) is according to Antony not a part of man, but a gift of God. When he turns to Biblical language, he uses the concept of 'the heart', which for him is synonymous with the Platonic *nous* and the Stoic concept for the authoritative part of the soul, τὸ ἡγεμονικόν or 'spiritus principatus', which also occurs in the letters. However, the lack of most of the Coptic, and all of the Greek text of the letters, prevent an exact definition of Antony's terminology.[1]

In Platonic tradition the mind is part of the soul, not a separate faculty outside the soul—to Origen it is even the origin of the soul itself—and it seems as though Antony, albeit not consistently, adhered to this tradition.[2] As we have seen, the mind is the centre of man, the manifestation of his spiritual essence. It is because man has a mind that he is rational, capable of knowledge, since true knowledge presupposes participation in what is known. Through his mind man is thus open to the divine, is capable of contemplating God. Antony combines this Platonic concept of contemplation with the Biblical expression 'to see God' by calling his correspondents 'Israelites', or 'holy Israelites in their spiritual essence', which he, like Origen, interprets as 'a mind that sees God'.[3]

But even if man's mind remains the image of God's mind, and preserves the capacity for knowledge of man's spiritual essence, it has been weakened, it has become spiritually dead when the natural law grew ineffective.[4] For man to regain knowledge about his origin and essence and achieve control of himself, his mind must be called back to life; it must learn how to purify soul and body. Consequently, the resurrection

1 In Coptic ϩⲏⲧ is used for both mind (νοῦς) and heart (καρδία). As is evident from *Ep. Ant.* VI.32, for which we have a Coptic text in Besa, it can also equate 'soul' ψυχή. Except for the cases where a Biblical text is the background, G has გული 'heart' 16 times (*Ep. Ant.* I.56, II.4, III.25, 35, 43, 44, V.38, VI.29 (twice), 31, 36, 41, 46 (twice), 91 and 105). In five cases L does not have *cor,* but 'anima' (thrice), 'sensus' and 'habitudo' (once). In the only three of these preserved in A, the Arabic supports L against G (I.56, III.44, V.38). In S ܠܒܐ 'heart' is used both for καρδία and νοῦς, as noted above, p. 32. The most common term in G is გონებაჲ 'mind' which can be used for διάνοια, φρόνησις, or νοῦς in Greek (see Joseph Molitor, *Glossarium Ibericum* (*CSCO* 228), p. 74). L in most of these cases has 'sensus'; 'mens' is used only four times, and in the passage missing in G another three times. In A the corresponding term is العقل (mind, intellect). The terminological difficulty is increased by the lack of any distinction between 'spirit' and 'soul' in Georgian, both rendered as სული.

2 The use of the expression 'the senses of the soul' (G: საცნობელნი იგი სულისა, L: 'sensus animae', A: حواس النفس) in *Ep. Ant.* III.10 suggests what is usually called 'the mind', and thus implies that the mind is regarded as a part of the soul. Also *Contra Gentes* 30 calls the mind 'part of the soul'. For Evagrius it has, however, become a completely separate part of man, equated with his πνεῦμα, his spirit.

3 This interpretation of the name Israel as 'a man who sees God' is encountered first in Philo (*De ebrietate* XX.82) and subsequently in Origen. (See *Commentarii in Ioannem* II,31; *Commentarii in Canticum canticorum,* Prologus; and extensively in *Homiliiae in Genesim* XV.3). It is also found in an anonymous untitled Alexandrian Gnostic text contemporary with Antony, the so-called *On the Origins of the World* (*NHC* II, 5, p. 105, l. 24).

4 *Ep. Ant.* III.10, V.16, VII.27. See below, p. 74 for Antony's metaphor.

that Christ brought is to Antony a resurrection of the mind,[1] and the task of the Spirit is to teach the mind and guide it in the acts of repentance. Through his mind man can have a partnership with the Spirit, and take himself back to his original nature.[2]

In a metaphor, first used by Plato, and often adduced by later writers, the mind is a charioteer who drives two horses, the two lower parts of the soul.[3] When Athanasius alludes to this metaphor in *Contra Gentes,* he sees the soul and the bodily members as a carriage that bolts if the charioteer neglects his goal.[4] Although Antony does not use the metaphor, his understanding of the relationship of body, soul and mind is close to the metaphor as used by Athanasius. Through neglect of the mind, soul and body are handed over to confusion.

In line with Platonic tradition, Antony sees the passions not as results of wrong judgement, but as irrational; they are the effects of confusion and lack of reason.[5] The terminology Antony uses for this confusion and its remedy is 'mixing' and 'separation'.[6] The passions originate in a soul no longer guided by reason, and affect man by being mingled with the members of the body, or with the will. Thus the first task of the mind, when it is led by the Spirit to purify soul and body, is to discriminate between the two and bring back the members of the body under its own authority.[7] For Antony it is this reconstitution of man that is the essence of repentance and Christian life.

The passions are thus not natural to man, not a necessary result of his corporeality. It is only when greed and temptation interfere with the natural and passionless motions of the body that the body becomes subject to evil. In a passage regarded as sufficiently decisive to be transmitted as a

1 *Ep. Ant.* II.23, III.25, V.28, VI.91, VII, 30. In two passages (III.25 and VI.91) we find in both G and L 'the resurrection of our hearts', while the other passages have 'the resurrection of our minds', a clear indication of the synonymous use of the terms; probably C had ϩⲏⲧ in all five. In the only passage that A has preserved (III.25), we have 'hearts' and not 'minds'.

2 *Ep. Ant.* I, 47–48. See also I.27–29, 32, 42–43, 56, 59, and 69. Close parallels to this teaching are found in the *Teachings of Silvanus* 85–87.

3 Plato, *Phaedros* 246–247. For the use of this metaphor in Clement see Lilla, *Clement of Alexandria. A Study in Christian Platonism and Gnosticism,* Oxford 1971, p. 97f., and for the more general use see Daniélou, *Message évangelique,* p. 117f.. None of them, however, mentions the use of it in the *Teachings of Silvanus* 90.

4 Athanasius, *Contra Gentes* 5.

5 For the philosophical background, see the treatment of the ethics of Clement of Alexandria in Salvatore R. C. Lilla, *Clement of Alexandria*, especially pp. 84–92.

6 Also Athanasius sees 'disorder' and 'mixing' as the results of man's turning away from God: ταῖς μὲν τοῦ σώματος ἡδοναῖς συνέκλεισαν ἑαυτῶν τὴν ψυχήν, τεταραγμένην καὶ πεφυρμένην πάσαις ἐπιθυμίαις (*Contra Gentes* 3). In Silvanus a man who falls from virtue 'mixes himself', see *The Teachings of Silvanus* 92f..

7 *Ep. Ant.* I.27–32. The Georgian version seems to make no distinction between 'body' and 'flesh' (σάρξ and σῶμα), but in the Latin text 'caro' is used when the derogatory sense is implied, which is usually only when there is an allusion to Biblical language (See I.29, III.35 and V.37).

saying in the *Apophthegmata Patrum*, Antony teaches that there are three sets of urges (movements, κινήσεις) in the body. The first are the natural urges, controlled by the soul; the second are the urges which are the result of excess and greed; and the third are those which the demons produce by their temptations and attempts to defile those who walk on the road of purity.[1] The passions are thus something foreign to the body, something that must be expelled.

Antony shared the basic Platonic view on corporeality, and thus often refers to the body as something 'heavy' which ties man down, something corruptible to be freed from.[2] At the same time it is clear that he did not share the contempt for the body manifest both in Plotinus and in Gnosticism. The body is to him not an irrelevant piece of matter, nor a prison of the soul, but a home to be cleansed, a sacrifice to be purified.[3] His contempt is not for the body, but for what has usurped it and made it into 'the house of the robber within us', 'a home of death', 'a house of darkness', 'a house of war', 'a store of evil'.[4]

The body is to Antony not evil *per se,* nor is it responsible for its misuse; it is created for a good purpose, and only needs to be brought back to its original nature. The body is not simply to be discarded; it can be transformed. In his letter on repentence (Letter I) he describes how each member of the body can be purified, how by ousting the evil it can be made a seat of virtue. The eyes, the ears, the tongue, the hands, the belly, the sexual organs and the feet, all can become pure through the work of the mind guided by the Spirit.[5] Like Origen he thought of ascesis as a matter of refining and transforming the body, ultimately making it less material and more spiritual.

1 *Ep. Ant.* I, 35–41. Cf. *AP/G* Antony 22. A close parallel to this teaching is found in *De Principiis* III.2.2–3, where Origen stresses that the demons are not responsible for all passions, but that some are the result excessive attendance to natural motions.

2 *Ep. Ant.* VI.42, 54, 61, 66. The 'heaviness' of the body is encountered also in Origen and in Pachomius. See Brown, *The Body and Society,* pp. 168 and 222, for references. A passage of striking similarity to Antony is found in the Pachomian *Paralipomena* 20 (Halkin, *Sancti Pachomii Vitae Graecae,* pp. 145–147).

3 For an excellent interpretation of the Christian ascetic view of the body and the difference between it and pagan, especially Platonic, thought, see Peter Brown, *The Body and Society,* New York 1988, especially pp. 30–32, 168–177, and 222–240. The body is to be freed, not simply controlled (p. 31); it is a temple, not a grain of mud (p. 176f.); it is to become transparent (p. 224).

4 *Ep. Ant.* V.5, 9, VI.37, 46, 48, 83, 97.

5 *Ep. Ant.* I.50–70.

2. God and His dispensations

In all his letters Antony, after greeting his correspondents, sets out to tell the story of 'God's visits to man', which is his way of referring to the history of salvation. Besides knowledge of the self, the 'spiritual essence', it is the acts of God for the salvation of man that are the most frequent objects of knowledge, of *gnosis,* in the letters.[1] Although Antony, as we have seen, was deeply influenced by his Platonic background, it is the Biblical message that is his message. But it is not a literal interpretation of the Scriptures that governs his thought. Not only what is 'manifest' but also what is 'hidden' in the preaching (κήρυγμα) must be understood as a revelation of God's acts of love to man.[2] Only through self-knowledge and a knowledge of the 'spiritual essence' can man attain true knowledge of God and his acts.

To Antony, as well as to Origen, it is the spiritual meaning, allegorized in the text, that is of importance.[3] The Bible is the story about how God as Creator cares for man and acts to restore him to his original constitution, how he seeks to resurrect man's spiritual essence, *i.e.* to restore order and knowledge. What God gives man through the natural law, through the written law, through Jesus Christ, and through the Spirit, is all the same; it is his summons to repentance (μετάνοια), purification (κάθαρσις), and knowledge (γνῶσις).[4] The description of God's acts as a history of salvation does not imply that Antony regarded them as acts which simply succeed and replace each other; on the contrary, like Athanasius he maintained that they all remain valid ways to knowledge about God.[5]

1 *Ep. Ant.* III.1, 40, IV.15, VI.21.

2 *Ep. Ant.* VI.21. Antony here alludes to Sap. 7:21 (ὅσα τέ ἐστιν κρυπτὰ καὶ ἐμφανῆ ἔγνων· ἡ γὰρ πάντων τεχνῖτις ἐδίδαξέν με σοφία), a verse also quoted by Origen. See his *Commentarii in Canticum canticorum* 3.12.

3 Behind the exegetical practice of Antony lies the cosmological and what Daniélou calls the *gnostic* tradition of Clement and above all Origen's allegorical method of interpretation. See Daniélou, *Message évangelique,* pp. 217–233 and 256–264. Although Antony nowhere discusses the methods of interpretation, the letters show that he was close to the program developed by Didymus on the basis of Origen. See Wolfgang A. Bienert, *«Allegoria» und «Anagoge» bei Didymos dem blinden von Alexandria* (*PTS* 13), Berlin 1972, pp. 154–164.

4 This view of the same principle behind all God's acts and its background in an understanding of all evil as deviation from the universal rule of reason is summarized by Lilla, *Clement of Alexandria,* p. 96: 'The different ways in which He (God) manifests Himself—the law of nature, the ten commandments, the κυριακαὶ ἐντολαί of the Old Testament and the teaching of Christ during His stay on earth—have one and the same aim: the healing of the πάθη, and consequently also the restoration of the harmony of the soul'.

5 Meijering's conclusion about Athanasius' view is valid for Antony too:'There is a history of God's adaptation to human weakness and in this sense the stages follow each other, but in consequence of human weakness, even after the incarnation of the Word the other ways of receiving knowledge of God should still be gone by man' (E.P. Meijering, *Athanasius: Contra Gentes,* p. 115).

The Natural Law

According to Antony, the care the Creator shows towards his creatures is manifest already in the law laid down in creation.[1] Everything has an original nature of its own, to which it should adhere. The background of this notion of a 'law of nature' is the Stoic concept of the *Logos* as a universal principle for physics and morals. Through Middle Platonism this concept had been integrated into the Platonic tradition. To the Jewish and Christian philosophers the *Logos* was, however, no longer an immanent principle, but God's link to the world and to man, the principle of creation and providence. It is not difficult to recognize Antony's dependence on this tradition, and especially the close affinities to the teachings of Clement of Alexandria. Like Clement Antony sees the virtues as natural to man; they are laid down by the law of nature; a virtuous life is a life according to nature.[2] Clement identified this law, the λόγος ὀρθός, with the highest part of the soul according to Platonic anthropology (the λογιστικόν or the νοῦς). To live according to nature is to be governed by the mind.

A similar connection between the natural law and the spiritual nature of man is made by Antony in his letters. The 'natural law' 'the discernment of the good inherent in them from their first formation' (νόμος ἔμφυτος ?) belongs to man from his creation by virtue of his spiritual essence;[3] it is since man has a spiritual and immortal essence that God can 'visit' him.[4] By virtue of this law man has spiritual insight, he knows himself according to his original nature, and he knows how to worship properly. It is thus a sign of unity between God and man, a sign

1 *Ep. Ant.* I.2, II.3, III.8f. The expression 'law of nature' occurs only in the Syriac and Arabic version of *Ep. Ant.* I.2 and I.3. The Georgian text is, unfortunately, missing, and the Latin has the usual expression 'testamentaria lex', but I.2 is here barely intelligible: 'Quidam enim per testamentariam legem et iuditium in eis semel bonum, a prima sui conditione pertingere verbo Dei ad eos morati non sunt, sed perrexerunt parati cum eo.'

2 *Ep. Ant.* IV.13; VII.11, 49–51. This is also in an important idea in the *Vita Antonii.* See *VA* 20, and the analysis in Johannes Roldanus, *Le Christ et l'homme dans la théologie d'Athanase d'Alexandrie,* Leiden 1968, pp. 300–303. As Roldanus points out there is a difference between how κατὰ φύσιν is used in *VA* 14 and 20 and how it is used in *De Incarnatione Verbi* 5. In the former, as in the letters, it is equivalent with the origin and goal of human life, in the latter it is man's corruptible nature unaffected by the grace given through Christ (*ibid.*, p. 344). This difference is related to the change in perspective between *Contra Gentes* and *De Incarnatione Verbi.* See *ibid.*, pp. 22–24, Louth, *The Origins,* pp. 77–79 and *idem,* 'The Concept of the Soul in Athanasius' *Contra Gentes — De Incarnatione'*, *Studia Patristica* XIII.2, Berlin 1975, pp. 227–231. The latter article is briefly and unconvincingly criticized by Meijering, *Athanasius,* p. 19.

3 *Ep. Ant.* II.4, III.10, V.16 and VII.7. Although different terms are used (საცნობელნი სულისა—'officia sensus (animae) and გონიერი ბუნებაჲ—'sensualis natura') what is meant must be the mind.

4 *Ep. Ant.* II.6. The last phrase in the verse has caused the translators problems. From the context, as well as from the parallels in III.12, V.15, VI.5–6 it is, however, clear that the phrase რამეთუ არსებაჲ არს უკუდავი or in L 'quoniam substantia immortalis exsistit' must refer to our 'spiritual essence', as it is otherwise called (so Wagenaar and Cremaschi against Chitty and Louf).

manifest in the expression constantly encountered in the letters: 'the law of promise' or 'the law of the covenant'.[1] Through the law God calls man back to his origin; to obey and return to God is simply to do to what is natural.[2] That, despite this law, man does not return, is explained by Antony as the result of the death of the 'law of promise. To use his expression, it has 'withered away' or 'frozen'.[3]

Since the law is an integral part of man, not a command he is ordered to obey, Antony views man's deviation from the law not as an offence but as a deterioration of his own mind, a loss of spiritual perception and true knowledge. Antony generally seems to imply that this has happened once and for all, but at the same time he states that some have abided by the law. Again we have a tension between an mythological (collective) and a historical (individual) point of view. The deterioration of the law is both something that belongs to the first stage of the common history of man, and a continuing process in anyone who does not follow his mind. Nowhere does Antony explicitly refer to a fall as the reason for this deterioration, or to a common guilt; he simply states that as a result of his infirmity and the 'heaviness of his body' man has succumbed to passions and evil cares.[4]

1 The term law occurs 22 times in the letters. In G the term used is რჩული, which is not the usual translation of νόμος in the NT, but of διαθήκη. However, the use of *lex* in L, ܢܡܘܣܐ in S and الناموس in A,.as well as nomos in the single occurance in the Coptic fragments supports the rendering *law*. It is more difficult to find a precise rendering of the recurrent expression generally translated by *the law of the covenant* (Louf: *loi d'alliance;* Wagenaar: *wet van het Verbond,* Cremaschi: *legge dell'alleanza*). This corresponds to L: *testamentaria lex,* and *testamentum,* while the expression in G: აღთქმისა რჩული could as well be translated *law of promise.* In the only two instances preserved in S we have ܢܡܘܣܐ ܕܟܝܢܐ (the law of nature) and ܢܡܘܣܐ ܕܚܘܒܐ (the law of love) and in A we have a variety of expressions: I.2, 3 *nāmūs al-ṭabīʿah.* (the law of nature); II.3 *taʿālīmuhu* (his instructions); II.6 *nawāmīs al-ḥayyah* (the living laws); III.9 *nāmūs qulūbihim* (the law of their hearts); III.10 *ḥawās al-jasad al-ẓāhirah* (the pure senses of the body); *al-nāmūs al-ʿaqlī* (the spiritual law). The most likely explanation for this confusion is that behind all these variants there is a Greek expression (ὁ νόμος τῆς ἐπαγγελίας ?), which Antony used as a loanword, but which apparently the Arabic and Syriac translators found impossible to translate.

2 *Ep. Ant.* I.3–9, II.7–8, III.9, VII.49–51.

3 *Ep. Ant.* II.4, III.10, V.16, VII.7. Except for the first instance G has განცვმობაჲ, which can go back either to ξηραίνομαι or ψύχομαι. Since L has 'refriguit' in all four instances, the latter alternative seems plausible. A has نشف 'dried up' in the single instance where the text is strictly parallel. The Coptic original probably had ϩⲱϭⲃ, which means 'whither, fade, expire' (Crum p. 744b). It is the term used in the Sahidic version of Matt. 24:12 for ψύχομαι, while the Vulgata has 'refrigere' and the Georgian New Testament განცვმობაჲ. Origen used the verb to denote what happened with the 'minds' when they fell and became souls, ψυχή. Either Antony was unaware of this Origenist etymology, or he did not clearly distinguish between the cosmic fall and the 'growing wound' in man.

4 The lack of any systematic treatment in the letters makes it impossible to know more precisely how Antony interpreted the Biblical message. In contrast to Moses, the prophets, Jesus and the apostles, the letters nowhere refer to Adam, Eve, Cain or Abel. Probably Antony regarded them as mythological figures only. Even in Athanasius, *Contra Gentes* 2, it is unclear if Adam is more than a symbol for man.

The Written Law

To Antony the written law is above all a sign of God's compassion for man. It is the response to the failure of the natural law. As we have seen, the result of this failure is generally described by Antony as 'an incurable wound' or 'a disease'. The background is, once more, Clement of Alexandria and Philo, who both used the Stoic notion of the passions as a disease of the soul.[1] Like Clement, Antony sees the written law as part of God's acts to heal man's disease. It is an integral part of what Antony refers to as God's visits to man. Like Athanasius, he regards the written law as a law not for the Jews only, but for all mankind. Probably in opposition either to Jews or to Gnostics, Antony emphasizes that there is a unity between the law and the prophets of the Old Testament on the one hand, and Christ on the other: 'Jesus sent forerunners before himself. I do not hesitate to say that Moses, who gave us the law, is one of them and that the same Spirit which was in Moses acted in the assembly of the saints when they all prayed for the Only-begotten Son of God'.[2] As in his view of man and cosmos, it is unity and knowledge that are at the centre of Antony's teaching. Through the written law Moses 'founded for us the house of truth, the spiritrual Church, which creates unity, since it is God's will that we turn back to the first formation'.[3] Except for the greeting in Letter IV and a reference to the Church as the body of Christ in Letter VI, this is the only reference to the Church in the letters.[4]

But to Antony the written law is, like the natural law, a failure. Moses could only lay a foundation, then he passed away. Although many built on this foundation, none was able to complete the house, to heal the wound. Thus the written law is above all a preparation for the coming of the Son. It shows the inability of any creature to heal the wound. This does not mean that Antony regards the law as of historical interest only. The tension, noted above, in Antony's view of man and salvation is here manifest in a tension between the historical and moral roles of the written law.

1 See Lilla, *Clement of Alexandria*, p. 98 with references.

2 *Ep. Ant.* III.17 (the verse belongs to the passage misplaced in the Latin version, where it follows upon II.19a, *i.e.* in the fourth letter according to the Latin numbering). G has წინაისწარმეტყუელი 'prophet', L 'praecursor' and A منذر 'warner'. As in Athanasius' *Contra Gentes* the saints are the angels (see Meijering, *Athanasius*, p. 15).

3 *Ep. Ant.* II.10. G: და გუიფუძნა ჩუენ სახლი ჭეშმარიტებისაჲ, რომელ იგი არს კათოლიკეჱ ეკლესსიაჲ, რომელმან იგი დაჰბადა ერთობაჲ, რამეთუ უნდა ღმერთსა მოქცევაჲ ჩუენი პირველსავე მას დასაბამსა; L: 'Et fundavit nobis veritatis domum quae est ecclesia catholica, quam creavit volens convertere Deus ad primum initium'; A: ووضع اساس البيت الحقيقي الذي هو الكنيسة الناطقة الواحدة وبمشيئته أن يرد الخليقة الى خلقة الاولى (Arabic text according to *Vat. ar.* 398 and *St. Ant. Theol.* 178). My translation above is as far as possible based on what is common to most of the versions. Only for 'the spiritual Church' instead of 'the catholic Church', have I preferred the reading solely attested in A. A similar passage, albeit without a reference to the Church, is found in Letter VI.9. See also below for Antony's concept of the Church.

4 *Ep. Ant.* IV.1, VI.85.

Through the written as well as through the natural law, man is still summoned by God. The threats and promises of the law are not abolished. But adherence to the law can only make man a servant of God, they cannot grant him perfection. There is no righteousness by the law alone, but it is a guide on the road to perfection, and cooperates with man in the good service of virtue.[1] To Antony there is thus a clear distinction between service under the law and perfect righteousness. From being servants of God men are called to be brothers and friends of Jesus, that is adopted sons of God. With a strange use of a quotation from St. Paul, Antony even refers to the service as an imprisonment, implying that man needs to be liberated from it.[2]

The Son

For Antony the history of God's visits, the history of salvation, has its climax in the coming of the Son. Vividly he describes how all other attempts to restore man had been failures. The natural law had 'frozen', the written law was an unfinished edifice, and man's wound had become incurable. Like Origen, Antony sees the Babylonian captivity of the Jews in the Old Testament as an allegory for man's captivity in sin.[3] The cry in Jer. 28:8–9 (LXX) for a physician and a remedy in captivity is the prayer of the prophets and the angels for the sending of the Son to heal man from his disease. In his love for man God listens to the prayer and, as he has made everything to minister to man, does not even spare his own Son.[4] As the prophet is sent into exile, so the Son is sent into the world: 'And you, son of man, make yourself a dress of captivity' (καὶ σύ, υἱὲ ἀνθρώπου, ποίησον σεαυτῷ σκεύη αἰχμαλωσίας, Ezek. 12:3; LXX).[5] Jesus is to Antony, as to Origen, the Son who has came down from heaven, humbled himself and assumed a human form. Like Origen, Antony has a predilection for the words of Phil 2:6–11.[6]

It is the coming of Christ, his presence (παρουσία), that is the focus of Antony's letters. Our access to his views on the Trinity and the preexistence of Christ is thus severely limited. That Antony believed in the doctrine of the Trinity is, however, evident not only from the single

1 *Ep. Ant.* IV.5. Cf. II.26.

2 *Ep. Ant.* IV, 4–12.

3 *Ep. Ant.* II.16–18, V.21–24.

4 Rom 8:32 quoted in *Ep. Ant.* II.20, III.22, V.25 and VII.28.

5 While Antony's use of Jer. 28:8–9 (LXX; probably also Jer. 26:11 lies behind) has parallels in Origen's exegesis of Jeremiah (see *i.a. Homiliae in Ieremiam* A.2), the quotation from Ezek. 12:3 does not appear in the preserved works of Origen, nor does it appear in any other early Christian writer according to *Biblia Patristica* I–IV. Most probably Antony had it from a lost text by Origen or one of his disciples (Pierius, Stephen or Hieracas ?).

6 See *Ep. Ant.* II.19, III.23, VI.12, 89, VII.39, 43. The copious use of this text in Origen is shown by the references in *Biblia Patristica* III.

reference in the letters, but also from his views on the Son and the Spirit.[1] For Antony's Christology, the perhaps most important passage is his attack, in Letter IV.17, on the teaching of Arius. Not only the fact that the passage belongs to the context of that letter, but also the accord between this passage and Antony's general theological outlook makes it unlikely that it is a later anti-Arian interpolation.[2] Antony's emphasis on the Son as ἄναρχος, ἀσάλευτος (or ἀκίνητος) and ἄρρητος is close to the criticism of Arius put forward by Athanasius as well as by Alexander of Alexandria, and is probably based on Origen.[3] It is also to Origen that we must turn to see the reasons behind Antony's anti-Arian position.

Like Origen, Antony saw 'the free will' not as a divine attribute but as a gift to the soul making it liable to fall, and both of them were eager to stress a permanent and ontological relation between God and creation. Thus Antony could not share Arius' concern for the concept of a free will in God, nor for God's detachment from creation.[4] To Antony it is the identity and unity between the Father and the Son, and between Jesus and man, that makes salvation real.

The crucial point in Christ's mission is his identification with man in his fallen state. To understand salvation is for Antony to understand the form Jesus took for the sake of man, to understand that he became like man in everything except sin.[5] Repeatedly Antony stresses that Christ assumed the weakness, foolishness and poverty of man to make man, once more, strong, wise and rich. His favourite quotation is from Isaiah: 'by his wounds we were healed' (Is. 53:5); in essence it contains Antony's emphasis on man as wounded and Christ as the physician. But to Antony these words do not refer only to the crucifixion; the identification with man in the incarnation is in itself a suffering. Already by assuming a human form, Christ assumed death. The vicarious suffering of Jesus is not confined to his death on the cross, it includes his life as well. Jesus, to Antony, is not a man who by virtue of his perfect life can serve as an expiatory offering for the sins of others; he is the divine physician who

1 *Ep. Ant.* V.40.

2 See above, p. 45, where the lack of evidence for Arianism in the earliest monastic tradition is also discussed.

3 See *i.a.* Origenes, *De Principiis* I.2.2–3 (ἄναρχος) and *Contra Celsum* VI.5 (ἄρρητος). For ἀσάλευτος, we can note that a central notion in Origen's Christology was that the soul of Christ did not take part in the original movement, but remained in fixed contemplation of God.

4 The completely different perspective in Arius and Antony is clearly borne out by a comparison of the letters with the analysis of Arius' motives in Rowan Williams, *Arius. Heresy and Tradition,* London 1987, especially pp. 95–116 and 181–232. In contrast to Arius, who in his philosophical presumptions was rather radical, Antony relied on older tradition and did not share Arius' notion of absolute unknowability and freedom in God.

5 Hebr. 4:15 quoted in *Ep. Ant.* II.24 and III.26.

heals their wounds.[1] It is probably only the Biblical language that causes Antony to speak about 'the remission of sins'.[2] The healing he sees in Jesus is not an act of reconciliation with a God demanding a sacrifice, but a way to reconciliate man with his origin, with his 'spiritual essence'.

To Antony, as to Origen, it is the spiritual meaning of the Biblical message, not the historical facts, that are important.[3] Through his life and death Jesus reveals God's continued compassion and his identification with man. By 'the Word of His power' he raises the minds of men from earth and restores the original unity.[4] Although Antony never mentions the Resurrection, his theological views plainly make it impossible that he denied it. But what is important to him is not what once happened—the simple facts that Jesus was born, that he died and was raised from death—nor any turn of history brought about through these events, but how in his own life man is able to experience God's regenerative work. The resurrection is not primarily the final resurrection at the end of time, but the raising of the mind and the subsequent restoration of man's original nature.[5] Through the purification of body and soul achieved by repentance, and through the reception of the Spirit, even the body takes part in this resurrection of man; it is assimilated to the spiritual body which it is to assume in the ultimate resurrection of the just.[6]

As noted above, the idea of unity is central to Antony's thought. With an allusion to Is. 49:6 the mission of Christ is seen as the 'gathering of men from the earth's farthest bounds'. Through Christ's teaching the original unity is restored and men realize that they 'are members of each other'. For this unity Antony adduces the Pauline use of the body as an image of the Church. But to Antony it is an image of the entire creation. As a member of the body dies when it is severed from the body and separated from the head, man dies as a result of his sin against his neighbour and of his neglect of the Creator. The Church is the restoration of this

1 The attempt by Robert Gregg and Dennis Groh to enlist the monastic theology in support of their notion of the Arian view on salvation (*Early Arianism*, pp. 142–153) is contradicted by the letters. Antony fully shared the theology of 'adoptive sonship' and imitation of 'unchangeable nature' of the anti-Arian position, and not the Arian insistence on the progress of Christ. The features of the *Vita* which they adduce as indicative of an Arian position are not coherent with the letters; they are not due to original monastic theology, but probably to a hagiographical bias contradicting Athanasius' emphasis. See below, chapter VI.

2 Besides the quotation of Rom. 8:32 occurring in most of the letters, II.23 is the only passage of all those dealing with the coming of Christ that mentions the remission of sins.

3 See below, p. 81–85, for Antony's understanding of the relation between history and 'the time in which we are' and its Origenist background.

4 *Ep. Ant.* II.20–23, III.22–25, V.24–28, VI.89–91, VII.28–30 and 58*f–g*. Except for III.25 G always has აღდგომაჲ გონებათა ჩუენთაჲ 'the resurrection of our *minds*'. L has *sensus nostri/ sensuum nostrorum,* except in III.25 and VI.91.

5 *Ep. Ant.* II.23, III.25, V.28, VI.91 and VII.30.

6 *Ep. Ant.* I.71.

bodily unity. As Christ is the head of creation, he is also the head of the Church.[1]

The restoration brought by Christ is thus in the letters seen as the result of revelation. Through Christ's teaching man learns to examine himself, to know his origin and 'spiritual essence'. The fire Christ came to send (Luke 12:49) is the Spirit which makes man able to discern good from evil, reality from unreality.[2] But Antony does not regard the essence of the revelation through Christ as restricted to the restoration of the original unity and knowledge; it is rather a communion, the communion with Christ by adoption as sons of God.[3] This communion is not possible, however, as long as man is far away. First he must be brought near through virtue and knowledge, so that he controls his passions and knows 'his spiritual essence'. When he receives the 'Spirit of adoption', he no longer fears God but understands the fullness of what Jesus received from his Father and reveals to man; he knows Christ no longer after the flesh, but after the Spirit.[4]

The Spirit

A characteristic of all three stages of the history of salvation—the granting of 'the law of promise, of the written law, and of the Son,—as well as of Antony's teaching about man's response through repentance is the activity of the Spirit. It is through the Spirit that God, from the foundation of the world, is present in those who come to their Creator.[5] The Spirit was in Moses and the prophets, and in the Spirit they prayed for the sending of the Son.[6] It is the Spirit that teaches man how to return to God, and it is in the fullness of the Spirit that man is able to worship God as is proper.[7] As noted above, Antony does not speak about the 'spirit' as a part of man.[8] Except for the expression 'evil spirits', he restricts the use of the term 'spirit' to the Spirit of God or the Holy Spirit.[9] Although the letters

1 Probably Antony is here also influenced by John 11:52. In the few passages (II.10, IV.1, VI.85) where Antony mentions the Church, there is no evidence that he regarded it as anything but this cosmic and spiritual unity. See also above, p. 75, n.3 and below, p. 81, n. 3

2 *Ep. Ant.* III.43–44.

3 Antony here combines Rom. 8:14–17 and John. 15:15 with 2. Cor. 5:16.

4 See *Ep. Ant.* II.25–30, III.27–31, IV.4–12, VII.45. The contrast between a serevant of God and a friend of God is made also by Clement in his *Stromata* VII.19.

5 *Ep. Ant.* II.3.

6 *Ep. Ant.* II.12–13, III.18–20

7 *Ep. Ant.* II.7, V.35

8 See above, p. 68f.

9 The fact that in Georgian the same word, სული, is used for both ψυχή and πνεῦμα makes it impossible to rely on G for Antony's use of the term. Besides 'spiritus maligni' and 'spiritus erroris', and the expression 'paupertate spiritus' in I.78 and 'et in toto spiritu tuo', an allusion to Deutr. 6:5 in VI.110, there are only two instances in L where 'spiritus' does not refer to the Holy Spirit: V.10: 'sed et mihi deterrimo, habitante in hac luteo domo, eam-

contain no explicit teaching on the divinity of the Spirit or the doctrine of the Trinity, there is no reason to believe that in these respects Antony differed from a contemporary Origenist theologian such as Didymus.[1]

Though he usually speaks simply about 'the Spirit' and occasionally about 'the Holy Spirit', Antony also makes use of a variety of other expressions such as 'the Spirit of repentance', 'the Spirit of wisdom', 'the Spirit of consolation', 'the Spirit of bondage' and 'the Spirit of adoption'. This variety in expression is the result of a view according to which the activity of the Spirit in man is a process of growing participation, consummated in the granting of 'the fullness of the Spirit'. It is through the Spirit that God from the beginning calls man to return to his origin. The 'Spirit of repentance' teaches man how to purify body and soul and assists him in all his warfare against evil. It has a loving partnership with the mind, and opens the eyes of the soul.[2] In order to discern his acts and come to know himself truly, man also needs the 'Spirit of wisdom', and Antony prays that it might be given to his disciples.[3] In all of this man has 'the Spirit of bondage', since he strives for righteousness through obedience. But this is only the road to communion signified by 'the Spirit of adoption'.[4]

Thus the Spirit is seen on the one hand as the initiator and guide to a life of virtue, and on the other as the gift granted to him who lives such a life. The Spirit summons man to repentance, but as 'a holy power' it cannot enter a man unless he prepares himself.[5] This tension raises the question of Antony's views on baptism. As we have noted, the Church of the letters is a spiritual communion of all who return to their spiritual origin. In a single passage (Letter VII.58*l-u*), unfortunately missing in the Georgian version, Antony sets baptism by John for the remission of sins in contrast to baptism by Jesus, which sanctifies man through the Spirit. The Arabic version, being more extensive than the Latin, makes it clear that to

---

dem laetitiam in spiritu meo' and V.38: 'Vere, filioli, quia anima mea phantasma patitur, et spiritus meus in pavore consistit'. Both are most likely the result of Biblical language.

1 There is an affinity between the letters and Didymus, *De Spiritu Sancto,* which undoubtedly has a background in Origen. But it is on the basis of the letters not possible to know Antony's position in regard to the subtle differences between Origen and Didymus in respect to the subordination of the Spirit. See Alisdair Heron, 'The Holy Spirit in Origen and Didymus: A Shift in Perspective From the Third to the Fourth Century', *Kerygma und Logos,* Göttingen 1979, pp. 298–310.

2 *Ep. Ant.* I.19, 25–28, 32, 42–48, 56–59, 66–70, 77.

3 *Ep. Ant.* III.3, VI.29, VII.63. The emphasis on the Spirit as a dispenser of knowledge is also prominent in Didymus and Origen, see Heron, *op.cit.,* p. 304–307 and Origenes, *De Principiis* I.1.9 and II.7.4.

4 *Ep. Ant.* II.7, 27–29, III.31, IV.11.

5 *Ep. Ant.* IV.14, quoting Sapientia 1:4–5. The text is discussed above, p. 28. This emphasis on purity and worthiness as a condition for the Spirit are also met with in Didymus. See Heron, *op.cit.,* p. 304. The same is found in Origenes, *De Principiis* I.3.7.

Antony baptism by Jesus is the granting of the Spirit, here called 'the Paraclete' (paracletus spiritus) and 'the Spirit of consolation' (spiritus consolantis). These expressions occur also in Letter VI, where Antony interprets the history of Elijah and the prophets of Baal (1 Kings 18:36–44) as an allegory for the sending of the Spirit, and probably also for baptism, since he explicitly refers to the 'spiritual' rain that came after the offering.[1] The image of the Spirit as a purifying fire is encountered in two other places; baptism is probably implied here as well. In Letter III Antony alludes to Luke 12:49 and the fire Jesus came to kindle, and in Letter V he writes about the invisible fire which consumes all impurity and makes man fit to be a dwelling for the Holy Spirit.[2] The collective evidence of these three passages indicates that Antony saw baptism as a spiritual experience of the ascetic, much the same as the granting of the 'Spirit of adoption', which is for him the fulfillment of communion.[3] Thus, while the Spirit acts on man from the beginning, the gift of the Spirit, and thus baptism, presupposes repentance.

3. THE TIME IN WHICH WE ARE

The history of salvation, *i.e.* the Biblical message, is to Antony, as to Origen, not primarily a history but a message about something spiritual and eternal. The true understanding of the Scriptures and of history is the spiritual understanding, since what is really true is spiritual and what is spiritual is eternal.[4] This principle of interpretation is evident not only in the use of allegorical exegesis of the Old Testament in Antony's letters but, as we have seen, also in how the coming of Christ, the παρουσία, is understood. The story told is a story about man, about ourselves. The history of God's acts has to be understood since it also speaks about the 'time in which we are'.[5] Antony repeatedly implores his readers to recognize their own situation, to became aware of their time. to 'know how it is'. He vividly paints the image of the hour of decision, the καιρός,

[1] *Ep. Ant.* VI.72–77. Antony here implores his correspondents to make themselves into altars and to pray to God to send 'his great invisible fire that it may descend from heaven and consume the altar and all that is on it'.

[2] *Ep. Ant.* III.43 where the fire makes man able to discern good and evil; V.34–35 where the Arabic version explicitly states that the fire is the Spirit.

[3] The text of the letters does not allow any further conclusions on how this view was related to the baptism administered in the Church. The emphasis on fire as a symbol and on the gift of the Spirit as the essence of baptism is close to Origen. See *i.a.* his *Commentarii in Ioannem* VI.43–44, and Crouzel, *Origène,* pp. 290–294. The distinction made by Origen between the crossing of the Red Sea and of Jordan as images of baptism, and the implication that the latter signifies the end of the wandering and the entrance to Paradise, fits the view of the letters.

[4] For this concept in Origen and its background in the Platonic tradition represented by Philo and Clement, see Daniélou, *Message évangelique,* pp. 256–264.

[5] See *Ep. Ant.* III.38, 48, and IV.16.

with its tension between despair and agony in the face of impending judgement, and its joy and peace through liberation and restoration. He teaches them to repent and to strain their hearts and minds, to distinguish between soul and body, to discern between good and evil. In order to outdo the enemies of his beloved brothers, he reveals the methods and plots of the demons, contrasting them with the bond of love and unity that belongs to man's true self, to his origin and future perfection.

In all this it is knowledge, *gnosis*, that is necessary. If a man does not know his time, if he does not realize the conditions in which he is, he cannot attain true self-knowledge and knowledge of God. Nothing is gained by ascesis without prudence, or by demon-hunting without insight. On the contrary, lack of discernment leads many astray. A man who knows his time is able to stand firm, but he who does not is easily moved by the changing ideas of men. Referring to the Arian heresy spread in his days, Antony implores his readers :

> My beloved in the Lord, know yourselves! Those who know themselves know their time, and those who know their time are able to stand upright without being moved by shifty tongues.[1]

In order to emphasize the dangers inherent in the present age and the need for knowledge Antony adduces a Platonic metaphor, similar to that of the charioteer. The mind is here likened to a helmsman κυβερνήτης, guiding his ship in the right direction (Plato, *Phaedrus* 247C). In the *Teachings of Silvanus* the two metaphors are combined in a similar emphasis on the difference between someone who knows himself and a fool:[2]

> Truly, my beloved, when it is calm all captains boast, but in high winds the true skill of the captain becomes manifest. Therefore, know the time in which we are.[3]

The Parousia of Jesus

Antony, in his interpretation of the New Testament message about Jesus, regularly refers to it as the 'coming (G: მოსლვაჲ, L: 'adventus', Gr* παρουσία) of Jesus'.[4] Throughout, the letters preserve the tension between

1 *Ep. Ant.* IV,16. C: ⲛⲁⲙⲉⲣⲁⲧⲉ ϩⲙ̄ⲡϫⲟⲉⲓⲥ, ⲥⲟⲩⲛⲧⲏⲩⲧⲛ̄. ⲛⲉⲛⲧⲁⲩⲥⲟⲩⲱⲛⲟⲩ ⲅⲁⲣ ⲁⲩⲥⲟⲩⲛ ⲡⲉⲩⲟⲩⲟⲉⲓϣ. ⲛⲉⲛⲧⲁⲩⲥⲟⲩⲛ ⲡⲉⲩⲟⲩⲟⲉⲓϣ ⲇⲉ ⲁⲩϭⲙ̄ϭⲟⲙ ⲛ̄ⲧⲁϩⲟⲟⲩ ⲉⲣⲁⲧⲟⲩ ⲛ̄ⲥⲉⲕⲓⲙ ⲁⲛ ⲉⲃⲟⲗ ϩⲓⲧⲛ̄ϩⲉⲛⲁⲥⲡⲉ ⲉⲩϣⲟⲃⲉ.

2 *Teachings of Silvanus* 90.

3 *Ep. Ant.* III, 47–48. G: ჭეშმარიტად, საყუარელნო, ჟამსა მას ქარისა დაყუდებისასა ნავისმხერველი იქადინ, ხოლო ქარისა ძლიერისა და წინააღმდგომისა ჟამსა ყოველივე მეცნიერი ნავისმხერვალი გამოჩნდის. აწ გულისხმაყავთ ჟამი ესე რომელსა მოვიწიენით რაჲ ესე არს. L: 'Vere, fratres, scitis quod tempore ventorum prosperitas, omnis gubernator plaudit sibi, in contraria vero quaeque ventorum, omnis gubernator manifestatur. Intelligite ergo tempus in quod advenimus, quale sit.'

4 *Ep. Ant.* III.1, 27, 29, 34, 37, V.9 (L), VI.16, VII.32, 34, 35, 45, 58*h* (L), 58*u* (L). In two other places we have the *parousia* of the Saviour: II.25, 31. I have preferred to translate მოსლვაჲ and 'adventus' as παρουσία and not as ἐπιδημία, which is the word Origen used to indicate that the 'coming of Jesus' revealed what was hidden in the words of the Old Testament (*De Principiis* IV.1.6).

a past and a future *parousia,* between 'already' and 'not yet', and Antony makes no distinction between the first and the second 'coming of Jesus'. The significance of the *parousia* is not a matter of history and eschatology but of the decisive moment; it is not the coming, but the presence of Jesus that is essential. The *parousia* is the hour of decision: 'to some it is foolishness, to others a stumblingblock, and to others gain and wisdom and power, and to some resurrection and life'.[1] It is an imperative, not an event.[2] In all the letters the *parousia* is connected with the notions of impending judgement and the promise of freedom. But there is no clear distinction between the judgement *brought* by his *parousia,* and the judgement *to be brought* by it, between the freedom *gained* by it and the freedom *expected.*[3] This does not imply that Antony denied a future coming, only that the content of the *parousia* is already anticipated. It is not as a historical but as a spiritual event that the *parousia* of Jesus has its deepest significance.

Antony's emphasis on a spiritual interpretation of the *parousia* is manifest in the marked difference between his views and those of other early monastic teachers. In contrast to the *Vita Pachomii* and the *Apophthegmata Patrum* there are in the letters no exhortations to the reader to fear the torments of everlasting punishment, not even an exhortation to fear God. It is not the fear of God but the knowledge of him that Antony impresses upon his correspondents. Through the *parousia* of Jesus man is made free to leave the fear of the 'Spirit of bondage' for the joy of the 'Spirit of adoption', the earlier knowledge 'according to the flesh' (κατὰ σάρκα) for a more profound and intimate knowledge according to the

1 *Ep. Ant.* VII, 34. Cf. 1. Cor 1:23–24. Antony has, however, added *gain* and *resurrection and life.* the last probably influenced by Luke 2:34, and 2 Cor. 2:16, quoted in another letter (II.31–33).

2 In connection with the noun *parousia* we find verbal tenses ranging from perfect and aorist to future with a preponderance for imperative and conjunctive forms. In III.37, VII.25, 32, and 34 the *parousia* is something that has happened; in III.29 and VII.58*u* it is something now present; in VI.83 it is future, and in II.25, 31, III.1, 27, 34, V.9, VI.16, VII.35, 58 *h,* it is an imperative. The background for Antony's views must be sought in the development from primitive Christian eschatology to what we find in the writings Clement and Origen. For a summary and references see Jaroslav Pelikan, *The Emergence of the Catholic Tradition* (*The Christian Tradition. A History of the Development of Dogma* 1), Chicago 1971, pp. 123–132 with references to R. P. C. Hanson, *Allegory and Event: A Study of the Sources and Significance of Origen's Interpretation of Scripture,* London 1959.

3 References to freedom by his *parousia* are found in *Ep. Ant.* II.25, III.1, 27, 34, VII.45, 58*h,* and references to judgement in *Ep. Ant.* II.31, III.35–37, VII.35, 58*t–u*. The identity between the present and the future is manifest in *Ep. Ant.* VII, 58*t–u*. G is missing; L: 'Manifestus siquidem sit vobis sermo iste, nec exspectare velitis judicium futurum in illa praesentia Jesu; jam etenim adventus illius omnibus nobis judicium exsistit'. A has changed the sentence to its opposite: 'Therefore, let no one of you say, o my children, that there is no judgement for us in the last advent of our Lord, rather you shall know that the first advent of Christ, our master, has concluded that there will be a judgement for us on that day, if we do not fulfill his precepts'. The secondary nature of A is here obvious. The background is probably John 3:18–19.

Spirit.[1] But in order to be set free by the *parousia* man must prepare himself; he must 'come near' through repentance and righteousness by obedience of the law; he must walk the road to adoption.[2] The decisiveness of the *parousia* is that it reveals if a man has prepared himself for freedom or for judgement. This revelation, however, presupposes spiritual insight. It is the man who has prepared himself and knows himself who understands the *parousia*.[3] It is to him that the true meaning of the past and the future is revealed; it is to him that Jesus has truly come.[4] Thus, if the essence of freedom is to have knowledge, the essence of judgement is to be ignorant. He who does not care for his spiritual life and neglects his own identity remains in darkness; he becomes a beast without reason.[5]

The interpretation in the letters of the *parousia,* with its emphasis on the present, does not imply that they lack an eschatological vision. The notion of the present time as the decisive time has its background in the fact that the end is near. This consummation of time is primarily connected with the two concepts: 'proper worship' and 'final rest'. The essence of all knowledge is 'to know how to worship the Father as is proper'.[6] Although Antony does not seem to have used the expression *theoria,* the teaching of Evagrius on the highest state of knowledge and worship can be seen as a development of what is implied in the letters. Although man can transform his body through purification, and while still in the body attain true knowledge through the 'Spirit of adoption', the consummation of vision and worship is purely spiritual and only possible when man is liberated from the restraint of corporeal life. For this final state Antony uses the expression 'rest', ἀνάπαυσις (G. განსჳენებაჲ, L: requiem). On the basis of the use of the term in the New Testament *anapausis* had become an important concept in Christian Gnosis. It is used by Clement to denote what true *gnosis* leads to and is a prominent term in Gnostic texts, almost exclusively with an eschatological connotation.[7] In

1 *Ep. Ant.* II.28–29 with an allusion to 2 Cor. 5:16. This contrast is prominent in Origen.

2 *Ep. Ant.* II.27, III.31, IV.9–10. The expression 'to come near' is characteristic. The final step is not anything man can do by his own righteousness; it is the act of God (cf. I.77–78).

3 *Ep. Ant.* II.24–25, III.1–2, 26–28, VII.31–32.

4 Cf. John 15:15 quoted in *Ep. Ant.* II.27, III.30, and IV.9.

5 *Ep. Ant.* II.31, III.35–37. Also Origen (*De Principiis* 1.8.4) uses the metaphor of animals for the souls which have become irrational, an imagery that has wrongly been interpreted as a doctrine of reincarnation (μετενσωμάτωσις). See Carl-Martin Edsman, 'Origenes och själavandringen', *Meddelanden från Collegium Patristicum Lundense* 4 (1989), pp 9–17.

6 See *Ep. Ant.* II.8, III.9, 12, 31, IV.15, V.34.

7 The term ἀνάπαυσις (Coptic mton) is closely linked to the concept of stability as the opposite of disorder and motion. For its use in Philo, Clement, the *Apocryphon of John,* the *Gospel of the Egyptians,* and the *Sophia of Jesus Christ,* see Williams, *The Immovable Race,* pp. 76f., 127–129, 138–140, 142f., 157, 171. For the Gnostic use and its background see also Heldermann, *Die Anapausis im Evangelium Veritatis* (*NHS* 18), Leiden 1984, pp. 51–65, 337–344.

the letters it is linked to the *parousia* and denotes what it brings for him who has prepared himself. The 'rest' is not only a rest for man, but also a rest for all the holy, *i.e.* the saints, who on account of our distress have not yet been able to find rest.[1]

The Time to Repent

In contrast to Letters II to VII, which emphasize the history of salvation, the coming of Jesus and the subsequent spiritual interpretation of his *parousia*, the first letter deals exclusively with repentance. Not once does Antony mention Jesus, nor does he refer to the concepts of freedom and judgement. Though at first sight this omission might be regarded as insignificant—it might be explained by the difference in scope and addressees—there are good reasons to see it as an expression of Antony's theology. As shown above, he shares not only the Platonic view on the necessity of a gradual seasoning and adaptation to true knowledge, but also the exegetical methods of Origen implied by it. Like Origen, he distinguishes between on the one hand the manifest and literal, on the other the hidden and spiritual meaning of the Scriptures; like Origen, he sees in Christ the focus of the spiritual meaning.[2] To understand the *parousia* is to Antony not the foundation but the consummation of spiritual growth.[3] Although there is no evidence that Antony shared the Gnostic emphasis on a secret revelation, it is significant that he avoids mentioning Christ in a letter addressed to novices.

That the teaching on repentance in Letter I is seen as a preparation for accepting Christ is confirmed by a comparison of what this letter says about the three 'gates' to repentance and what the other letters teach about the history of salvation.[4] According to this letter God calls on man to repent and return to his original nature by three different means. The first is the law of nature implanted in man from creation, the second the threats and promises of the written law, the third the afflictions which make man weary and ready to turn back. The correspondence between the first two of these and the first two stages of the history of salvation is obvious. Significantly, the third is not equated with Christ's call to repentance; it refers vaguely to those who return to God despite having discarded the natural and the written law.[5] The reason is, no doubt, that all three of

1 *Ep. Ant.* V.9. The background is probably Hebr. 11:40. The saints can not enjoy a real rest until all are assembled and unity restored. See also VI.16 and 83–84.

2 In *De Principiis* I.3.8 Origen also states that sanctification through the Spirit is necessary for participation in Christ.

3 See above, p. 84. The contrast with the *Vita Antonii* is striking.

4 See *Ep. Ant.* I.1–16.

5 Although John Cassian refers to Abba Paphnutius as his source he probably depends on this passage, or a later development of it, in his teaching about the three ways in which God summons man. But to Cassian the first summons, for which he adduces not only Abraham, as

them are introductions to what Antony viewed as a necessary preparation for his teaching on the *parousia* of Jesus.[1]

The protagonist of the first letter is thus not Jesus but the Spirit. While the laws and the afflictions are the instruments of God's call to repentance, it is the Spirit that from the beginning acts on man, guiding him and teaching him. Instead of a moral teaching based on the commandments we find an emphasis on the reconstitution of the inner man. It is the law that shows man the necessity of repentance and conversion, it is the Spirit that shows him how to turn back to his original nature. Behind this emphasis on the spiritual and the experienced, at the expense of the moral and normative, lies Antony's Platonic concept of knowledge and of the soul. Accordingly, repentance is the attainment of purity and knowledge, the control of soul and body, and the contemplation of the spiritual. This understanding of repentance as a process of spiritual growth is evident in the way in which Antony, at the end of the letter, concludes his description. When the whole body is purified, it receives the fullness of the Spirit and 'receives partially the spiritual body of the final resurrection'. If the soul endures and obeys the Spirit, the Creator has mercy upon it and delivers it.[2]

Angels and Demons

In Antony's view of cosmos man is not alone with God, he is surrounded by angels and demons. Although the subject of demons is not as prominent in the letters as for instance in the *Vita Antonii*, the long section on their nature and activities in Letter VI shows that Antony shared the emphasis on demonic activity known from other early monastic sources and systematically described by Evagrius.[3] The background of this tradition is

---

does Antony, but also Antony himself as example, is the direct summons from God. The second is the summons through the hands of man and the third is out of necessity (Cassian, *Conlationes* III.3–4). *Cf.* the discussion in Couilleau, 'La liberté d'Antoine', pp. 22–24.

[1] The correspondence between the three introductions and Antony's description of the history of salvation also confirms that he did not regard that history as successive stages of a historical development, but as an allegory for God's acts of salvation. The emphasis of Letter I that the introduction through the natural law persists until now is corroborated by the statement in II.2–3 that some have abided by the natural law. The corresponding passage in III.9 implies that this was only originally so. In I.16 and I.19 we even find parallels to the expression 'to draw near' encountered in the other letters as an expression of being prepared to receive the 'Spirit of adoption' and to know Jesus no longer in a bodily way.

[2] *Ep. Ant.* I.70–71, 77–78.

[3] *Ep. Ant.* VI.27–43. The prominence of demons in early Christian literature must be understood against the background of contemporary pagan religion. To the Christians it was the fear of the demons and the dependence on them that was the most obvious idolatry. The Judeo-Christian and Origenist roots of the monastic literature makes it unlikely that its demonology has a specific Egyptian foundation. Antony's letters, the *apophthegmata* and Evagrius show that the roots are to be looked for in a profound interest in psychology based on a Platonic concept of man. For this background see Daniélou, *Message évangelique,* pp. 391–403.

primarily the demonology of Origen with its roots in Judeo–Christian tradition.[1] As noted above, Origen and Antony regard the demons as spiritual beings who, like all rational nature, are created by God and share the same spiritual essence. In the original fall into diversity the 'minds' (νόες) that stayed closer to God became angels and those who moved furthest away became demons.[2] But while Origen thought that the demons could make progress and become angels, and that ultimately all would return to God, Antony seems to think that the demons are destined to perdition.[3] Man thus lives under the influence of two spiritual powers, the angels who help him and pray for him, and the demons who oppose the ministry of the angels and man's struggle for a return to God.

In a way similar to the *Vita* and to the writings of Evagrius, the emphasis in the letters is on the great variety among the demons, and on their manifold and artful cunningness. Knowledge of the demons is an essential part of spiritual knowledge and necessary for a life of virtue.[4] In contrast to the imagery of the *Vita,* where the demons are visible and audible, the letters present them as completely internalized.[5] They make themselves known through the thoughts (λογισμοί) and become part of man in as far as he consents to their influence.[6] Thus demonology is to Antony, as to Origen and Evagrius, closely linked to psychology. To know the demons is to discern between the natural and unnatural motions of body and soul. The demons are more or less equated with passions; they make themself known by disturbing thoughts and have their seat in the soul of man.[7] It is in the tensions of the soul and the diversity of ideas and thoughts that the

1 For the demonology of Origen and his dependance on Judeo-Christian tradition represented by texts such as the *Testament of the Twelve Patriarchs,* the *Shepherd of Hermas* and the *Epistle of Barnabas,* see Daniélou, *Message évangelique,* pp. 397–403.

2 *Ep. Ant.* V, 40–42, VI, 56–62. Cf. Origenes, *De Principiis* I.8.1 and I.6.2 and Daniélou, *op. cit.,* p.398. Antony explicitly links the various names ('archangels, thrones, dominions, principalities, powers and cherubim', or 'devil, satan, demons, evil spirits and princes of this world') to the fall; they are the result of different ways to respond to God.

3 See *Ep. Ant.* VI, 19–20. Antony here implies that the reason for demonic assault is precisely that man can make progress and return, while the demons cannot, and thus envy him. Origen's concept of a final return of everything, the ἀποκατάστασις τῶν πάντων, is also missing in the letters.

4 See *Ep. Ant.* VI.28f.

5 Although Antony does not explicitly say so, it is most likely that he followed Origen in regarding the angels and demons as having bodies, albeit of a thinner and invisible substance. In contrast to Athanasius he explicitly denies that they can be seen and he implies that they need men as bodily instruments for activity. See VI.49–51.

6 *Ep. Ant.* VI.46–48. Cf. the *Teachings of Silvanus* 85.

7 This does not mean that Antony regarded all passions as the result of demonic activity. In accordance with Platonic and Stoic tradition, as encountered for example in Clement, he saw passions primarily as the result of undue attendance to natural motions of the body. Of the three motions in the body he enlists, the demons are only responsible for the third. See *Ep. Ant.* I.35–41 and, for the same teaching in Origenes, *De Principiis* III.2.2–3. Cf. Lilla, *Clement of Alexandria,* pp. 84–92.

demons are palpable. In the description of the acts of the demons Antony does not emphasize the sensual temptations by which the demons create disorder in man. The greater danger lies in their attempts to antagonize men against each other, to create division instead of unity. Although not explicitly stated, Antony obviously links unity within man with unity between men. Ascesis and ethics are two sides of the same coin.[1]

It is against this background of a spiritual warfare fought in the souls and bodies of men that Antony's views on ascesis and virtue must be understood. Only in man is the spiritual and the material linked; only here can what is spiritual make itself manifest and what is corporeal be transformed and assimilated to what is spiritual. In man's life it becomes evident what kind of spirit dominates him. As the demons depend on the assent of the soul for their evil business of corruption, the soul depends on the body for its purification and return. For as long as man lives his corporeal life, the body and the soul are intimately linked to each other. What a man does to his body he does to his soul; what he does to his neighbour he does to himself and to God.[2]

[1] In the long passage on the demons and their cunningness all the examples given are temptations to act to the detriment of fellow men. Behind this emphasis lies, no doubt, Antony's view of unity as the original and ultimate state of men, and of Christ as the head of the creation and thus the head of the Church.

[2] *Ep. Ant.* VI.53, 63–71, *AP/G* Antony 9.

PART TWO

THE IMAGE OF ST. ANTONY

V. THE HISTORICAL BACKGROUND

In the late third and early fourth centuries Egypt was a society in transition and crisis. The sharp distinctions of the Ptolemaic and early Roman period between the Greek πόλις of Alexandria on the one hand and the 'despised and uncivilized countryside', Coptic Egypt, the χώρα, on the other, had gradually disappeared.[1] During the third century a series of reforms accelerated the integration of Egypt into Graeco–Roman economy and cultural life. The position of the Egyptian towns, the *metropoleis,* was strengthened by the introduction of local self-rule, Roman citizenship was conferred on virtually the entire population, a new system of taxation was introduced and the non-convertible Egyptian currency was abolished.[2] The immigration, growing bureaucracy and improved communications which accompanied Roman rule had also paved the way for the social mobility, cultural exchange and religious reorientation which characterized the period.[3] Rapidly, Egypt was emerging from being a colonial backwater of Rome into becoming a central part of the Byzantine state.

1 On Egypt in the third and fourth century the literature is abundant. For a general view, I have used Alan K. Bowman, *Egypt after the Pharaohs,* London 1986, and Naphtali Lewis, *Life in Egypt under Roman rule,* Oxford 1983, and for the administrative reaction to the crisis, Jacqueline Lallemand, *L'administration civile de l'Égypte de l'avènement de Dioclétien à la création du diocèse (284–382),* Brussels 1964. A more recent study covering much of the same ground is Roger S. Bagnall, *Egypt in Late Antiquity,* Princeton 1993. The importance of the period as a time of integration is emphasized by Colin Roberts, *Manuscript, Society and Belief in Early Christian Egypt,* London 1979, pp. 49–73, and Rousseau, *Pachomius,* pp. 1–36. The gloomy picture drawn by Harold Idris Bell and Edward Hardy must consequently be thoroughly revised. For details I have relied upon the work of the papyrologists quoted in the notes.

2 For the reform of Septimius Severus in 200, see Lallemand, *op.cit.,* pp. 23–25, for Caracalla's extension of Roman citizenship in 212, see pp. 25–27, and for the reforms of Diocletian including taxation, currency and administrative divisions, see pp. 34–40 and *passim.*

3 For the later Empire as a period of 'unprecedented flux' see Ramsay MacMullen, 'Social Mobility and the Theodosian Code', *JRS* 54 (1964), pp. 49–53.

At the same time the second half of the third century witnessed a growing economic and social crisis in Egypt, not to end until the late fourth century. The Roman exploitation of Egypt through heavy taxation and the direction of the economy towards export, coupled with military requisitions and the oppressive system of collective obligations, the liturgies (λειτουργίαι), were the reasons behind the desertion of many villages and the widespread escape from land and civic obligations, the *anachoresis* (ἀναχώρησις). Rapid inflation, corruption, neglect of irrigation, and indifference on the part of those responsible were obvious consequences, as well as a movement towards urbanization and the subsequent demotion of the traditional local aristocracy. The period was also plagued by repeated nomad incursions, and by domestic turmoil caused by Alexandrian usurpers. The integration of Egypt into the empire and the crisis shook the entire society and prepared the way for new structures and ideals.[1]

As a result of the crisis and the accelerated integration, the religious map of Egypt was completely redrawn. The diverse Egyptian, Greek and Roman cults (often merged with each other) which constituted the official religion increasingly gave way to new and vigorous religious movements which attracted growing numbers of people. From small sects defying the established tradition, these new philosophies grew into important religious movements, to face bitter external and internal conflicts. Famous temples and their sacred cults were scorned, celebrated philosophers and religious thinkers were denounced as heresiarchs, and previously persecuted Christians were rapidly taking over social obligations, education and trade. This transformation had been prepared by a long tradition of religious pluralism in which different social and philosophical traditions had met and merged. Through Alexandria, Egypt was not only in close contact with all parts of the Roman empire, with soldiers from Egypt serving on the border north of the Alps and Alexandrian merchants travelling on the British isles, but also a primary target for missionaries and philosophers from the East preaching new roads to salvation. In the politically strengthened and culturally flourishing Egyptian towns, in Arsinoë, Oxyrhynchus, Lycopolis and Panopolis, the mobility and crisis paved the way for the new religious movements which could draw upon the same sections of society. With their common social background and common

[1] The crisis is summarized in Lallemand, *op.cit.*, pp. 27–33 and amply illustrated in the papyri, *i.a.* in the archive of Aurelius Isidorus of Karanis. See Arthur E. R. Boak & Herbert Chaim Youtie, *The Archive of Aurelius Isidorus in the Egyptian Museum, Cairo, and the University of Michigan,* Ann Arbor 1960, and *idem*, 'Flight and Oppression in Fourth-Century Egypt', *Studi in onore di Aristide Calderini e Roberto Paribeni* (ed. Edoardo Arslan), II, Milano 1957, pp. 325–337. An example from a village, probably similar to that from which Antony came, is given in Peter van Minnen, 'Pelousion , an Arsinoite Village in Distress', *ZPE* 77 (1989), pp. 199–200.

religious language these new movements were not always easy to distinguish from each other.[1]

It is within this Egyptian society of the late third and early fourth centuries that we have to look for the socio–economic and cultural background of Antony and his followers. Though he was in many ways an outsider, nowhere mentioned in the contemporary documents, allegedly indifferent to society and taught by God alone, he had been formed by certain traditions and he related himself to the people of his environment, dukes as well as peasants, philosophers as well as fools.[2] The early monks, and with them Antony, are usually thought of as poor, uneducated peasants who, inspired by an unsophisticated fundamentalist theology, fled a degenerate society and a Church in disrepute. This view, based as much on prejudice about Coptic Egypt as on early monastic literature, has little room for the letters of Antony or any form of Origenist tradition among the monks. Can it be upheld, once the evidence from the papyri is taken into consideration? If not, the combined evidence of Antony's letters and the economic and cultural situation prevailing in Egypt in the late third and early fourth century prompts us to have a new look at the traditional sources for early monasticism, none of which is earlier than the second half of the century.

1. Crisis and Changes

Town and countryside

Of the reforms introduced by the Roman rulers the gradual augmentation of the power of the towns, and the decision to put the surrounding countryside under their administration, were probably the most important. Earlier, the entire province had been directly governed for the emperor by the prefect and his officers, and with the exception of the two Greek cities Antinoopolis and Ptolemais, none of the cities, not even Alexandria,

1 On this the lectures by Bell in his *Cults and Creeds in Graeco–Roman Egypt,* Liverpool 1953, are still unsurpassed. Rousseau, *Pachomius,* pp. 28–36, gives a cautious view on the new movements. In the early Christian papyri Oxyrhynchus and Arsinoë are most prominent, Lycopolis is known as the hometown of Plotinus and as the Manichaean centre in Upper Egypt, and Panopolis was the centre of the dialect of most Gnostic texts. See Roberts, *Manuscript, Society and Belief,* pp. 62–65, 70f., and J. Vergote, 'L'expansion du manichéisme en Égypte', *After Chalcedon. Studies in Theology and Church History Offered to Professsor Alois van Roey* (*OLA* 18), Louvain 1985, pp. 471–478.

2 These aspects are usually overlooked in most studies on the early monastic fathers. The most prominent exceptions are Rousseau, *Pachomius,* and the articles by Peter Brown. See especially his 'The Rise and Function of the Holy Man in Late Antiquity', *JRS* 61 (1971), pp. 80–101. My debt to both of them is readily admitted.

had been entitled to have a city council.[1] This was changed by Septimius Severus in 200, when Alexandria and each of the thirty-odd *metropoleis* were allowed to have a council, a βουλή of their own. The economic crisis and the subsequent inability of the central authority to rule the countryside forced Diocletian, almost a century later, to give the cities responsibility for the entire districts. This introduction of municipal and later provincial rule was followed by a recurring division of Egypt into smaller provinces weakening the central authority. The effect was further strengthened by the division of power within the provinces between a civil administrator and a military commander.[2] The towns were no longer privileged isles in a backward sea, but the centres of the districts on which their prosperity depended. Local rule was no longer kept in the hands of a few foreigners, but distributed among the leading persons in the new society that was emerging. The foundations were laid for a national renewal and a sense of shared community.[3]

The growing power and wealth of the *metropoleis*, as well as the agricultural crisis, led to increasing migration into the towns and cities. The recurring efforts by the rulers to dispatch all non-citizens does not seem to have helped much, and especially Alexandria and the towns in the Fayyūm grew rapidly. There is no evidence that the migration consisted only of destitute peasants and vagabonds. On the contrary, with growing unity of town and countryside through the reforms of Diocletian, mobility between towns and villages increased. Numerous wealthy countrymen were enrolled as *metropolitai* in a far-reaching movement upwards on the social ladder, and intermarriages between Greek citizens and Egyptians were frequent, often in conflict with rigid class regulations. Village land was frequently owned by 'townspeople' (πολίται), who served as officials at the local level and even settled in the villages.[4] An important result was the demotion of the traditional aristocracy and the rise of new classes without the same background. At the same time Greek culture and

[1] Possibly Naukratis, too, had been allowed to keep its council after the introduction of Roman rule. See Lewis, *Life in Egypt*, p. 27.

[2] See Lallemand, *L'administration civile de l'Égypte*, pp. 41–77, 96–138; Bowman, *Egypt after the Pharaohs*, pp. 68–84; and Lewis, *op.cit.*, pp. 45–51.

[3] See Rousseau, *Pachomius*, pp. 3–6. The diffusion of the so–called *Acts of the Pagan Martyrs*, in which Graeco-Egyptians defy the governors even indicates a national opposition. See Roberts, *Manuscript, Society and Belief*, p. 3f.. Another 'nationalistic' text circulating in places like Oxyrhynchus in the third century is *The Prophecy of the Potter* (*P.Oxy.* 2332), see Lewis, *Life in Egypt*, p. 206 f.. The latter is according to J. W. B. Barns, 'Egypt and the Greek Romance', *Akten des VIII. internationalen Kongresses für Papyrologie* (*MPER* New Series 5), Wien 1956, p. 35, echoed in the early Coptic apocryphon *The Apocalypse of Elijah*.

[4] As is shown by Arthur E. R. Boak, '*Politai* as landholders at Karanis in the Time of Diocletian and Constantine', *JEA* 40 (1954), pp. 11–14, there is no major difference in wealth between villagers and town people.

communications with Alexandria and other cities were opened to new groups. Through a distinction between so called 'gymnasiasts' and 'non-gymnasiasts' the illusion of a distinction between Greeks and Egyptians was still upheld, but cultural refinement, literacy, or even fluency in Greek was no longer a necessary condition for wealth and power.[1]

The migration and the social mobility were further enhanced by the most striking features of Later Roman Egypt, the oppressive system of liturgies and the 'flight' from obligations and land. *Anachoresis,* usually rendered 'flight', was the term in official language for illegal absence and thus for tax evasion, but there is no evidence that the absentees actually fled, still less that they went into hiding in the deserts. The liturgies were originally the honorary duties of the Greek city elite for the upkeeping of their city, but often they became costly obligations forced upon people who could hardly afford them. Largely as a result of the introduction of local rule and responsibility, the liturgies were extended even to the small towns and villages and reached a level unmatched elsewhere. The official duties were numerous and severe, and unfortunate individuals often had to serve several terms. Since the official serving was privately responsible for the fulfillment of his obligations, these appointments were—with the growing of the crisis and heavier duties—something most people tried to avoid. The more fortunate could have the privilege of an exemption; others tried to transfer these obligations to less fortunate villagers who, without any recourse, were often almost ruined by a term as an official. In the end an appointment, or even the mere rumor of an appointment, would cause a person to join the absentees, even if he was by no means a destitute peasant at the lowest level of the society.[2]

Anachoresis had long been a solution open to an Egyptian farmer who could not fulfill his obligations. As early as in the first century A.D. this was a problem as is shown by the violent reactions against the tax evaders reported by Philo. In the crisis of the third and early fourth century the instances of *anachoresis* and of attempts to find and resettle the 'fugitives' are numerous. Although it is impossible to estimate the scale of the *anachoresis*—the desertion of numerous villages, especially in the Fayyūm, probably had other reasons than tax evasion—the papyri show an administration seriously worried by the exodus of the farmers. The havens

1 See Rousseau, *Pachomius,* pp. 8–9. For the degradation of the local aristocracy, see Ewa Wipzycka, 'Le degré d'alphabétisation en Égypte byzantine', *REAug* 30 (1984), p. 284.

2 See Lallemand, *L'administration,* pp. 27–29. Through the archive of Isidorus of Karanis we have a good picture of the system of liturgies in the Arsinoë area in Antony's lifetime. See the analysis in Arthur E. R. Boak, 'Village liturgies in Fourth Century Karanis', *Akten des VIII. internationalen Kongresses für Papyrologie* (*MPER,* New. Ser. V), Wien 1956, pp. 37–40. The complaint of Isidorus against his being exploited for all kinds of liturgies is instructive, as is the gradual reduction of his obligation.

for these runaways were most often neighbouring villages or towns, or Alexandria; but some even took up the life as an outlaw on the fringes of the desert. Though it is clear that some of the 'fugitives' became bandits, and that others were prepared to reject traditional social life, it is evident that the intention of most of them was not at all to abandon their community. What they were looking for was a refuge from tax-collectors and a new way to earn a living, a new start without too heavy debts. For many this would mean to associate with persons or with a community able to take part of the responsibility.[1]

For the authorities *anachoresis* was a serious problem. Not only did the tax evasion disturb them, but also the presence of 'fugitives' as a potential mob in Alexandria, or as bandits along the roads and in the country. In order to resettle fugitives they used both threats and amnesties, and a number of papyri speak about farmers who cannot be found, or who have returned because of the promises. Officials at the local level were even paid a reward for each 'fugitive' restored to his proper jurisdiction.[2] Efforts were made not only to recover the fugitives, but also to prevent further abandonment of farming land. Thus the farmers were by law tied to their land, a system known as the *colonate,* introduced in the fourth century and further strengthened by the Byzantine emperors. Another remedy was found in the corporate responsibility of the village for the taxes, making fugitives a burden also for their fellow men. The flight of some thus led to added taxes for others and compulsory exploitation of abandoned land. This, however, tended to create an evil circle of pauperization, and to increase the numbers of fugitives.[3]

In the long run the inability of the small farmers to meet their obligations, and their difficulties in finding refuge and new possibilities after leaving their villages, led to the system of patronage. In exchange for their land and allegiances wealthy and influential land owners assumed responsibility for the oppressed and indebted farmers. But the transfer of

1 Cf. Lallemand, *op. cit.*, pp. 18–20, 227–228, Lewis, *Life in Egypt,* pp. 163–165, 202–204 and Boak–Youtie, 'Flight and Oppression', *passim.* In a number of papyri preserving repertories of questions to be put to the oracles, a recurring question is 'Shall I become a fugitive?' Rousseau, *Pachomius,* pp. 9–10, rejects the idea of widespread readiness to abandon village life and stresses the opposite development of cooperative ventures.

2 See the interesting letter of a *praepositus pagi* in the Arsinoite nome, who reminds his colleague of an imperial edict prescribing the repatriation of all strangers to the fiscus with a reward of five folles for each, and who states that his villagers have complained that some of their men are staying in the district of his addressee (Boak–Youtie, *op.cit.*, pp. 325–332)

3 In 215 Caracalla issued an edict to expel all 'countryfolk who have fled to Alexandria from other parts'; in 207 a committee of farmers from the village Soknopaiou Nesos in the Arsinoite nome refer to another imperial edict calling bandits back to farming work; and in 308/309 a *praepositus pagi* refers to a contemporary edict prescribing local commissions authorized to recover fugitives. See Lewis, *Life in Egypt,* pp. 202–204, and Boak–Youtie, *op. cit., p.* 328f. referring to *Cod. Theod.* XI.24.1. For the *colonate* see Lallemand, *L'administration,* pp. 231–232 referring to *Cod. Theod.* V.17 and *Cod. Just.* XI.51.

crown land to private and public land, introduced by Diocletian, did not at once create the great *latifundia* of absentee land owners, the patrons of Byzantine Egypt. Even if this was to become the ultimate result of the crisis, the first effect of the strengthening of local government and the transfer of land to private hands was an increased interaction between the towns and the villages, and the search for new ways to make a living among the farmers themselves. It is in this context that we must seek the roots for the establishment, in the mid-fourth century, of the chain of monasteries in the Nile valley and the cells of the desert fathers.[1]

Education and Literacy

For far too long the traditional disdain for Egypt and the Egyptians has hidden the fact that, in this period of transition and crisis, life in the Egyptian countryside was strongly affected by the world outside Egypt. In the *metropoleis* gymnasia and other Greek institutions were founded and cared for by a mixed population and prosperous Egyptians learned Greek and participated in its cultural manifestations.[2] Greek immigrants and military personnel recruited from abroad were gradually absorbed into the heterogeneous population of the towns and villages of Upper Egypt; Greek traditions and cults merged with Egyptian so that Greek poets and philosophers of the tradition of the *Stoa* even officiated in the cult of the Egyptian temples.

In the letters and literary texts preserved in the papyri, there is strong evidence for a much more extensive contact between Alexandria and the towns of Upper Egypt than hitherto supposed, a contact, moreover, not restricted to the wealthy, travelled or learned. Townspeople from Upper Egypt were resident in Alexandria, and a number of Alexandrians owned estates in Upper Egypt. Especially among minority groups, such as the Jews, the contacts were intensive. The rapid spread of ideas from abroad, such as Christianity, Gnosticism, and Manichaeism in the third and fourth century, also proves that an informed contact with the Greek world had prepared the way.[3]

There was also a movement in the other direction, Egyptians becoming known abroad and even playing important roles on the international stage.

1 For the system of patronage, and the monasteries as places of refuge, see Lallemand, *op.cit.*, pp. 228–235.

2 See Bowman, *Egypt*, pp. 125–128, and Lewis, *op.cit.*, p. 39f. The Oxyrhynchus papyri give us ample evidence for this mixed population, so deeply rooted in Greek culture. See *i.a.* Eric G. Turner, 'Scribes and Scholars of Oxyrhynchus', *Akten des VIII. internationalen Kongresses für Papyrologie* (*MPER*, New Ser. V), Wien 1956, pp. 141–146.

3 See Rousseau, *Pachomius*, pp. 6–8, and Roberts, *Manuscript, Society and Belief*, p: 3f. Examples of correspondence are found *i.a.* in the archive of Theophanes published by A. Moscadi, 'La lettere dell'archivio di Teofane', *Aegyptus* 50 (1970), pp. 88–154, and in the archive of Nepheros published by Kramer & Shelton, *Das Archiv des Nepheros.*

The first to be mentioned in our context is Valentinus in the early second century, who like so many young ambitious Egyptians was drawn to Alexandria, where he began a teaching career which was to take him to Rome and subsequent fame as the probably greatest thinker among the Gnostics.[1] Another distinguished teacher, Hieracas, who apparently shared some of the views of Valentinus, taught in Leontopolis in the Delta a century later. He is said to have been well versed in Greek and Egyptian philosophy, astronomy and magic, to have read Origen, and to have had a large following throughout Egypt.[2] A younger contemporary of his was Plotinus, the famous founder of Neo–Platonism. A native of Lycopolis he had studied in Alexandria with Ammonius Sakkas, the teacher of Origen, and after serving the emperor on an expedition to Persia he set up a school in Rome.

Some fifty years later, in *c.* 300, another philosopher, Alexander of Lycopolis, who had stayed in his hometown, wrote the first refutation of Manichaeism, comparing it to Christianity, which he thought a better philosophy.[3] It was at about the same time, half-way between Lycopolis and Alexandria, that an Origenist monk with the name of Antony retreated to the desert, but nonetheless kept in touch with bishops, philosophers and emperors and reached international fame before he died in 356. In addition to these famous individuals, a large number of other Egyptians were in close contact with the outer world: groups such as the literary school of Panopolis, the Christian community in Arsinoë, and the first monks of Nitria and Scetis, who were receiving visitors and disciples from abroad already a few decades after their first withdrawal into the desert. This evidence of close contacts between Alexandria, and even the world beyond, and the Egyptian countryside cautions us against repeating the traditional view of an opposition between Alexandria: urban, Greek, philosophical and international; and Egypt: rural, Coptic, illiterate and nationalistic.[4]

The towns of third century Egypt were no 'cultural wastelands'.[5] On the contrary, papyri and literature give ample evidence for the presence of a variety of scholars, philosophers, poets and bibliophiles. We meet with

1 According to Epiphanius, *Panarion* 31.2, Valentinus was born at Pharbaithus in the Delta and educated in Alexandria. In the Muratorian fragment he is connected with Arsinoë. See Griggs, *Early Egyptian Christianity from its Origins to 451 C. E.* (*Coptic Studies* 2), Leiden 1990, p. 82f.

2 Epiphanius, *Panarion* 67.

3 Lewis, *Life in Egypt,* p. 61, concludes that the towns in Upper Egypt 'can hardly have been cultural wastelands'. See also Roberts, *Manuscript, Society and Belief,* pp. 6–12, for numerous examples of scholarly papyri, and Turner, 'Scribes and Scholars of Oxyrhynchus', *passim.*

4 See Rousseau, *Pachomius,* p. 18, and his criticisms of Bell and Hardy.

5 Lewis, *Life in Egypt,* p. 61

professors and honorary members of the Museum of Alexandria: one a specialist on Attic orators, another an author of a famous lexicon; some studied medicine, others astronomy. In numerous papyri and ostraca the schools of elementary education, and occasionally of rhetoric, appear. Classical Greek, as well as Latin, texts were procured from Alexandria to build up libraries, but also to be used for the performance of the plays of Euripides and others, and in poetry contests the younger citizens were encouraged to become authors—several actually made it to international fame. In addition to these, there were the copyists, the bookdealers and the numerous scribes necessary in a highly bureaucratic society, scribes ranging from skilled calligraphers to almost illiterate clerks.[1]

Though classical education was initially limited to the elite of the towns, the Greek 'gymnasial' class, it certainly spread to the mixed population of the growing middle class, the members of which could be rather wealthy and influential, so that ultimately there was no strict correlation between social class and literacy. Even the rural areas were not cut off from literary activity. In addition to the constant need for official correspondence and documentary works, we also find examples of book trade, calligraphers and Greek literature in the villages.[2]

Although it is impossible to reach a firm conclusion about the degree of literacy in Egypt at this time, it is clear that Egypt was not less literate than other parts of the Graeco-Roman world. As we have seen, Greek influence was well established and strong everywhere, and the development of the bureaucratic system inherited from the Ptolemies, coupled with the augmented responsibilities of the local authorities, required a certain degree of knowledge of Greek and literacy even in the smaller towns and villages.[3] Even if the actual writing was generally done by scribes, and most people would have had great difficulties in writing Greek, it is evident that there were many who were semi-literate, or slow writers (βραδέως γράφων), as they were called, and others who did read,

1 For a survey, see Eric G. Turner, *Greek Papyri. An Introduction,* Princeton 1968, pp. 74–96; Lewis, *op.cit.,* pp. 59–64; and Wipszycka, 'Le degré d'alphabétisation, p. 279ff. For the important group of poets from Upper Egypt, see Alan Cameron, 'Wandering Poets: a Literary Movement in Byzantine Egypt', *Historia* 14 (1965), pp. 470–509, and for the 'impressive testimony to the level of teaching and literary appreciation at the end of the third century' in Oxyrhynchus, Turner, 'Scribes and Scholars', p. 142. It is worth noting that Oxyrhynchus was not only a centre of Greek culture, but also of emergent Christianity in Egypt.

2 Bowman, *Egypt after the Pharaohs,* p. 161f., Lewis, *Life in Egypt,* pp. 81–83.

3 Literacy in Egypt is dealt with by Wipzycka, 'Le degré d'alphabétisation', *passim.* To her, Egypt is best described as midway between a society of scribes and of literate people (*ibid.*, p. 280). For more negative views see H. C. Youtie, 'ΥΠΟΓΡΑΦΕΥΣ: The Social Impact of Illiteracy in Graeco-Roman Egypt', *ZPE* 17 (1975), pp. 201–221, and the general survey by William V. Harris, *Ancient Literacy,* Cambridge & London 1989, pp. 289–318. The latter tends to see Christianization as decline in literacy, confusing literacy with esteem for classical pagan literature. But evidence from Egypt before the fourth century is scarce.

but did not write. In most cases the knowledge of Greek would have been a passive one, that is an ability to understand, and probably also to make oneself understood in Greek, without being really a part of the literate community. Persons only able to read and write Egyptian or Coptic were regarded as illiterate (ἀγράμματος).

On the other hand, literacy was apparently not required even for membership in a town council.[1] Illiteracy was no social stigma, and literacy no evidence for high social status. There is, moreover, little evidence that literacy was decreasing in Egypt after the crisis of the third century. The spread of Christian, Gnostic and Manichaean ideas, the conflicts arising from their encounter and the later struggle between Christian groups, such as the Meletians and Arians, on the contrary contributed to a growing interest in books, especially after the introduction of Coptic literature. In the rapidly growing Church and in the monasteries people who were able to read and write were no doubt in high demand.[2]

In the towns of Upper Egypt, as in Alexandria, knowledge of more than one language can hardly have been something extraordinary. For a long time Egypt had been a bilingual society. With Roman rule Latin was added to Greek and Egyptian, not only as the result of attempts to enforce it as the official language, but also as the language of many immigrants and sections of the cultural elite.[3] Since Greek had been the official language for a long time, and the only language used for written communication, most people would have had some Greek. A person who was 'unlettered' or even 'illiterate' was therefore not necessarily ignorant of Greek language and literature. The very strong influence of Greek on Coptic, visible in the earliest texts, also suggests that not only the writers, but also the intended readers, were familiar with Greek. Even if the spoken language consisted of different Coptic dialects, Coptic was only slowly and with the spread of Christianity, emerging as a written

1 It is worth noting that illiteracy was perfectly acceptable also in families of high standing. There does not seem to have been any social obligation even among the wealthy to send their children to school (Bowman, *Egypt after*, p. 159, and Wipzycka, *Le degré d'alphabétisation*, p. 280ff.). Examples of village officials, among them Isidorus himself, and others who did not sign their documents themselves, since they were *agrammatos*, are found in Boak & Youtie, *The Archive of Aurelius Isidorus*, index on ἀγράμματος. But does ἀγράμματος always mean 'illiterate'? A possible translation in some cases could be 'unlettered', *i.e.* not having the education necessary for a proficiency in *writing* Greek.

2 Wipzycka, 'Le degré d'alphabétisation', pp. 285, 289–290, 295, with evidence for literacy as a prerequisite to ecclesiastical office. In a papyrus (*P. Lips.* 43), albeit from the mid-fourth century, we even have the curious case of a nun, an ἀειπάρθενος, from Hermopolis accused of having appropriated Christian books. See E. A. Judge, 'Fourth-Century Monasticism in the Papyri', *Proceedings of the Sixteenth International Congress of Papyrology*, Chico (California), 1981, p. 613.

3 For the use of Latin as an administrative language, see Lallemand, *L'administration*, p. 40, and for examples of Latin outside administration Lewis, *Life in Egypt*, p. 61; Rousseau, *Pachomius*, p. 8, n. 19, and below, p. 110.

language. Between the earliest translations into Coptic in the mid-third century, and the emergence with Shenoute of original Coptic literature, there is a period of some 150 years. Greek also remained the language of official documents even into Arabic times. The use of Coptic was largely restricted to the new religious movements and to private matters. But even for these and for the administration of the Church and the growing monastic communities knowledge of Greek was necessary.[1]

2. GODS AND GNOSIS

The Traditional Cult

The pagan cult in Later Roman Egypt is probably best described as a subtle interlock of a wide range of cults and practices accommodated to each other without losing their characteristic features.[2] The dominant tendency was inclusiveness: new Greek, Roman and Oriental gods were accepted, often identified with older ones and, if there was a lack of resources, worshipped in multiservice temples. Even if the cults were sometimes blurred, the difference in offices was strictly upheld. An Egyptian priest was ordained for a full-time profession and distinctly set apart from the population in general. Once an influential group, the priests saw their privileges and powers curtailed by the rulers, who restricted their activities to the duties connected with the cult in the temples and demanded compensation for appointments. The Graeco–Roman priests were, on the contrary, lay officials serving for a short period as part of their political duties.

The importance of the cult as a political instrument was acknowledged by the Ptolemies, who introduced the cult of Sarapis as a sign of unity between Greeks and Egyptians, and was later emphasized by the Romans, who included their emperors into the pantheon and upheld the cult as an expression of political submission. To an ordinary Egyptian in the third century, the Roman emperor was still the deified Pharaoh, who had his throne-room in the temple with his name in hieroglyphs in a cartouche, and as late as 373 a priest of Isis is reported to have covered with gold a

[1] Even if there certainly were Egyptians who never learned Greek, the evidence indicates that most did. See Bowman, *Egypt after the Pharaohs,* p. 126. The forces behind the emergence of Coptic literature are still obscure. See Roberts, *Manuscript, Society and Belief,* pp. 64–67. The strong Greek influence, the diversity in dialects, and even idiolects, and the slow emergence of original Coptic literature suggest that it is most likely to have started with local transcriptions (in Greek letters) of *ad hoc* translations into the vernacular, possibly as parts of teaching in church schools.

[2] Bowman, *Egypt after the Pharaohs,* p. 166.

statue of Cleopatra as the new Hatshepsut. But alongside these political Graeco–Roman features which by now probably dominated in the towns, the old Egyptian cults of the gods and their animal representations continued without interruption. Topography and daily life were still dominated by the numerous temples, of which even a small village with only 1,500 inhabitants could have more than ten covering an area of some 60,000 sq. meters. As late as the third century a number of temples were renovated and decorated; the last inscription in an Egyptian temple is found on an altar in the Luxor temple dated in the reign of Constantine.[1]

At the same time there was a clear move away from public worship towards more individual concern for personal security and salvation. The temples and priests lost much of their importance. Asceticism and the state of purity which, as a prerequisite for an intermediary between men and gods, had been a sign of priesthood, became something practised by others. Through oracles, dreams, horoscopes and amulets people found direct access to the divine. A number of lists of questions to oracles have been preserved as evidence of the high degree of formalization of the institution. There are also examples of private religious foundations of ascetics dedicated to the worship of a certain deity or providing opportunities for a philosophical life in a community.[2] The strongholds of pagan resistance to Christianity were mainly groups of conservative philosophers preserving and nurturing traditional culture. The temples and the cult had to be defended for what they represented, the national Hellenistic culture of the cities.[3]

Although traditional cult was losing ground, except as a political institution, and, moreover, tended to become very formalized and impersonal, it was still omnipresent and deeply rooted in the ideas and rituals of ordinary people. For the making of the new movements and their heroes, it was the inescapable background. The revelations of *gnosis* were first seen as gifts of the old gods, primarily Thoth–Hermes, and the

1 See Bowman, *op.cit.*, pp. 167–183; Lewis, *Life in Egypt*, pp. 84–95.

2 See Lewis, *op.cit.*, pp. 95–99. Bell, in particular, stresses this development as a 'preparation for Christianity' (see his *Cults and Creeds*, pp. 64–77). For an interesting case of a religious foundation in which a small group lived in seclusion outside Panopolis, followed an ascetic practice and devoted itself to serving their God, see C. B. Welles, 'The Garden of Ptolemagrius', *Transactions of the American Philological Association* 77 (1946), pp. 192–206. For another example, see E. Lüddeckens, 'Gottesdienstliche Gemeinschaft in Pharaonischen, Hellenistischen und Christlichen Ägypten', *ZRG* 20 (1968), pp. 198ff.

3 See Roger Rémondon, 'L'Égypte et la suprême résistance au christianisme', *BIFAO* 51 (1952), pp. 63–78, and Ewa Wipszycka, 'La christianisation de l'Égypte aux IVe–VIe siècles. Aspects sociaux et ethniques', *Aegyptus* 68 (1988), pp. 142–158. Wipszycka argues convincingly for a strong presence of paganism far into the fifth century against the general view of an almost complete Christianization in the fourth century. As she rightly points out all main sources about attacks on pagan cult by Christians belong to the late fourth and the fifth century. See also Trombley, *Hellenic Religion and Christianization*, I, pp. 108–147.

new movements all had to find ways to transform the old wisdom into the new knowledge. In the most successful of the new faiths, Christianity, and in the emerging monastic tradition, traces of old beliefs can hardly have been missing.

The probably most central notion in Egyptian religion, the importance of the preservation of the body for the life after death, certainly affected the religious debates on the resurrection in the fourth century, and mumification is reported to have been practised by Christians at least into the sixth century.[1] Some of the apocryphal texts circulating in Egypt at the turn of the fourth century, *i.a.* the *History of Joseph the Carpenter,* the *Ascension of Isaiah,* and the *Apocalypse of Elijah,* as well as the growing Coptic literature on martyrdom, are clear indications of this interest in the fate of the body after death. The death and burial of Joseph is actually carried out according to the ritual of the Osiris cult and the preservation of the different parts of the body are heavily emphasized.[2] In Egyptian hagiographical literature the preservation of the body of the holy man is an essential element; an echo of this is possibly found even in the *Vita Antonii.*[3]

The New Gnosis

The three religious systems which challenged and defeated the traditional cults of Egypt—Gnosticism, Christianity and Manichaeism—were not only related to each other, but in some respects almost indistinguishable. They all preached individual salvation with an emphasis on *gnosis* and *askesis;* they all stressed a spiritual and heavenly rather than a corporeal and earthly citizenship, and they all combined the language of contemporary religious philosophy and its Platonic concepts with older traditions based on the Jewish Scriptures. Gnostics and Manichaeans regarded themselves

1 See Lüddeckens, 'Gottesdienstliche Gemeinschaft', p. 297ff. with references, and Theofried Baumeister, *Martyr Invinctus. Der Märtyrer als Sinnbild der Erlösung in der Legende und im Kult der frühen koptischen Kirche. Zur Kontinuität des ägyptischen Denkens,* Münster 1972, p. 78f., who quotes Augustin, *De resurrectione mortuorum* 12 (Sermo 361, *PL* 39, 1599–1611) as evidence.

2 For the *History of Joseph the Carpenter*, see Siegfried Morenz, *Die Geschichte von Joseph dem Zimmermann* (*TU* 56), Berlin 1951. The Egyptian background of this apocryphal writing is stressed by Morenz, *op.cit.* as well as by Hennecke–Schneemelcher, *Neutestamentliche Apokryphen,* I, Tübingen 1968, p. 320; Baumeister, *op.cit.*, p. 79f., and C. J. Bleeker, 'The Egyptian Background of Gnosticism', *Le Origini dello Gnosticismo,* Leiden 1967, p. 243f.. A more cautious view is given in G. Giamberardini, 'San Giuseppe nella tradizione copta', *Studia Orientalia Christiana Aegyptiaca,* Cairo 1966, p. 21f., and Jan Zandee, *Death as an Enemy, Studies in the History of Religion. Supplement to Numen,* Leiden 1960, pp. 301–342.

3 For the martyr literature see Baumeister, *Martyr invictus*. In *VA* 93 (in connection with criticism of burial practise) it is said that Antony's body was unaffected by age, preserved in every member.

as Christians and later they had to disguise as such. It has, moreover, been suggested that the Manichaeans to a large degree 'took over' after the Gnostics when Gnosticism receeded. It is obvious that the limits of what was Christian were very obscure until the end of the persecutions: It was only with the subsequent rise of ecclesiastical power that the distinctions between orthodoxy and heresy, canonical and uncanonical, sharpened. In the case of Gnosticism the term is actually more of a label put on heterodox groups by ecclesiatical opponents than a religious movement of its own.[1]

In the second century Gnostic ideas were propagated in Alexandria and the papyri indicate that they were known in Upper Egypt as early as the beginning of the third century. The Coptic Gnostic codices show that the tradition was still of importance as late as the middle of the fourth century. The often repeated suggestions that Gnosticism was *the* form of Christianity existing in Egypt before the third century, and that the established Church only gradually managed to stamp out what it considered heretical, do not, however, have much support in the sources. There is furthermore no evidence that the Gnostics were the first to use Coptic in writing. Most likely the spread of pronounced Gnostic ideas in Egypt was far less dramatical than can be deduced from Epiphanius's writings.[2]

The first Manichaean missionaries are reported to have come to Egypt in 270 and to have established 'houses' or 'monasteries' (*mānistān*) there.[3] Within a few decades their presence provoked a number of anti-

[1] Even if the roots of Gnosticism are less Christian than earlier research has proposed, Gnosticism soon became predominantly a Christian 'heresy'. See Kurt Rudolf, *Die Gnosis. Wesen und Geschichte einer spätantiken Religion,* Leipzig 1980², pp. 295–296. It can also be said that the entire religious sentiment in the first and second century was Gnostic, and that the parting of the ways between Gnostic and non–Gnostic Christianity came only gradually (Rousseau, *Pachomius,* p. 20f.). For Manichaeans as Christians and their disguised persistences, see Gedaliahu Stroumsa, 'Monachisme et Marranisme chez les Manichéens d'Égypte', *Numen* 29 (1982), pp. 184–201, and *idem,* 'The Manichaean Challenge to Egyptian Christianity', *The Roots of Egyptian Christianity,* Philadelphia 1986, pp. 308–314.

[2] The literature on Gnosticism is abundant, but its history still obscure; Gnostic texts being void of historical information. The Gnostic character of early Egyptian Christianity was maintained by Walter Bauer, *Rechtgläubigkeit und Ketzerei im frühesten Christentum,* Tübingen 1934, whose opinion was accepted doctrine until the well documented criticism of Roberts, *Manuscript, Society and Belief in Early Christian Egypt,* esp. pp. 49–73. See below, p. 111f.. Epiphanius gives ample evidence for Gnostic traditions in the fourth century, suggesting that 'For a while it must have teemed with Gnostics in Egypt.' (Bleeker, 'The Egyptian Background of Gnosticism', p. 229). His credibility is, however, questionable. Gnosticism actually seems to have receded by the mid-fourth century (David W. Johnson, 'Coptic Reactions to Gnosticism and Manichaeism', *Le Muséon* 100 (1987), pp. 199–209).

[3] For Egyptian Manichaeism, see in addition to the two articles by Stroumsa, William Seston, 'L'Égypte manichéenne', *Chronique d'Égypte* 14 (1939), pp. 362–372; Ludwig Koenen, 'Manichäischer Mission und Klöster in Ägypten', *Das römisch–byzantinische Ägypten* (*Aegyptiaca Treverensia* II), Mainz 1983, pp. 93–108; and J. Vergote, 'L'expansion du manichéisme en Égypte', pp. 471–478, with references. The suggestion that the *mānistān* were the models for the Egyptian monasteries has proven false (see below, p. 122).

Manichaean writings such as the anonymous *Epistle against the Manichees*, assigned to the rule of Diocletian, and probably from the chancery of Theonas of Alexandria (bishop 282–300), and the two refutations of Manichaeism by the Greek philosopher Alexander of Lycopolis and bishop Serapion of Thmuis. The writings of Didymus and the later monastic sources give ample evidence for continued Manichaean presence.[1] The lack of documentary or archaeological evidence can easily be attributed to the continued severe persecution of everything Manichaean.[2]

Since a number of the most prominent Gnostic leaders are known to have been active in Egypt and almost all the Gnostic texts are preserved in Coptic only, a specific Egyptian background and colouring has been proposed for Gnosticism. Even if the original settings of many of the Nag Hammadi texts are still disputed, they were definitely not written in Coptic, and with some exceptions not even in Egypt. The proposed affinities, a strong emphasis on knowledge and insight—rather than belief—as a prerequisite for salvation, and a preoccupation with the journey of the soul to heaven and the obstacles to be overcome, are also too general to be regarded as decisive.[3] Nor does the fact that our major Manichaean sources were found in Egypt and largely preserved in Coptic, prove an Egyptian background. On the other hand, it can hardly be a coincidence that many of the leading Gnostics came from Egypt or that the major refutations of Manichaeism were written in Egypt. Egypt in the fourth century probably deserved to be regarded as the land of 'heresies' *par préférence.*

In the *Corpus Hermeticum* there is, moreover, an important link between older Egyptian religion and these new movements. Here Egyptian and Greek philosophical ideas are combined in a series of revelations by Thoth–Hermes which have close affinities with some of the Gnostic

1 See *P. Ryl.* 469; Alexander of Lycopolis, *Contra Manichaei opiniones disputatio;* Serapion, *Contra Manichaeos;* Didymus, *Contra Manichaeos; AP/G* Theodora 4; *AP/PJ* XIII.12; and *HM* X.30–32. For Shenoute, see J. Leipoldt, *Shenute von Atripe und die Enstehung des national-ägyptischen Christentums* (*TU* 25), Leipzig 1903, p. 87, and Stroumsa, 'Monachisme et Marranisme', p. 201. A subversive Manichaean activity in connection with the revolt of Domitianus in 296/297 is suggested by Seston, 'L'Égypte manichéenne', p. 368.

2 As early as 297 Diocletain directed a *rescriptum* against Manichaeans to his African proconsul, and later Theodosius took strong measures against them. For texts, literature and an analysis stressing their affinities with ascetic groups in general, see Per Beskow, 'The Theodosian Laws against Manichaeism', *Manichaean Studies. Proceedings of the First International Conference on Manichaeism (ed. P. Bryder)* (*Lund Studies in African and Asian Religion* 1), Lund 1988, pp. 3–11.

3 The Egyptian background is favoured by Bleeker, 'The Egyptian Background of Gnosticism', pp. 229–237, and L. Kakosy, 'Gnosis und ägyptische Religion', *Le Origini dello Gnosticismo,* Leiden 1967, pp. 238–247. Incidentally, both these aspects can be found in Antony, the first in his letters, the second in the *VA.*

writings.[1] That Hermetic treatises were read by the same groups as Gnostic is evident from their presence in the Nag Hammadi codices.[2] More decisive than this philosophical and religious affinity is, however, the evidence they give for the syncretistic setting in philosophy and religion that prevailed in Egypt in the third and fourth centuries.[3] The combination in the Nag Hammadi library of texts gathered from Plato, the Hermetic corpus, Syrian encratism, Gnostic sects, and the Alexandrian theological school in the early fourth century, is impressive.

The rapid spread of Gnosticism and Manichaeism also calls for an analysis relating the message to the social setting of late third century Egypt. Gnosticism is generally thought to have attracted the newly hellenized and literate middle class of the smaller towns. The critical attitude to cult and the egalitarian message with its 'Brüderethik' and mythological denouncement of powers and rulers is supposed to have fitted people who had lost their traditions and become uprooted by growing mobility, individualism, privatization and cultural confusion under Roman rule.[4]

Arising on the border between Hellenic and Oriental cultures in a time of vigorous exchange, Gnosticism can be seen as a natural reaction to the confusion of the old cults, Platonic ideology, and Jewish traditions. That there was much in Christianity that could be used as a vehicle for this reaction cannot be denied.[5] The towns of Upper Egypt with their philosophical and cultural life thus constitute a plausible setting for these new currents. This is corroborated by the fact that the Coptic Gnostic material is written in the dialect of Panopolis, and that the Coptic

1 For a profound analysis of Egyptian Hermetism see Garth Fowden, *The Egyptian Hermes. A Histotical Approach to the Late Pagan Mind,* Cambridge 1986, revised reprint Princeton 1993. For the relations to Gnosticism see especially pp. 104–115.

2 See J.-P. Mahé, *Hermès en Haute-Égypte,* I–II (*BCNH* 3 & 7), Quebec 1978 and 1982. *Cf.* Fowden, *The Egyptian Hermes,* pp. 193–195, and Bleeker, *op. cit.*, pp. 234–235.

3 Fowden warns against attempts to interpret Hermetica through Gnostic writings or vice versa: 'It would be a mistake, then, to imagine that Christian Gnosticism either substantially influenced Hermetism, or can be used to illuminate it, except by way of general analogy' (*idem, The Egyptian Hermes,* p. 114).

4 See the analysis by Kurt Rudolph, 'Zur Soziologie, sozialen Verortung und Rolle der Gnosis in der Spätantike', *Studie zum Menschenbild im Gnosis und Manichäismus (hrsg. von P. Nagel) (Wissenschaftliche Beiträge der Martin-Luther-Universität Halle-Wittenberg* 1979/39), Halle 1979, pp. 19–29. Rudolph's results are strikingly similar to those of Henry A. Green, 'The Socio-Economic Background of Christianity in Egypt', *The Roots of Egyptian Christianity,* pp. 100–113. See also *idem, The Economic and Social Origins of Gnosticism* (Society of Biblical Literature, Dissertation Series 77) 1985.

5 'In short, if you are a second century person anxious to fit all the diverse local cults of the empire into a single religious view, to set it in a framework of Platonic metaphysics, and also to allow for an interest in that most intractable, unassimilable of ancient religions, Judaism, whose god was nevertheless so potent, then you could be very likely to end up as some sort of Gnostic' (Henry Chadwick, 'The Domestication of Gnosis', *The Rediscovery of Gnosticism,* p. 13f.). Chadwick is, however, sceptical about the conclusions drawn on the basis of sociological interpretation since the evidence is scarce an not unambiguous.

Manichaean material shows Lycopolis to have been a strong centre of theirs.[1] With their general indifference towards cult, and their tolerant view about other religious ideas, the Gnostics were not easily distinguishable, and most followers, whether Christian or not, would have been interested in their *gnosis* without being professing Gnostics.[2]

3. Bishops and Believers

Wealth and Power

Though all the evidence has been carefully sifted, the early history of the Church in Egypt still remains obscure. Evidently even Eusebius knew nothing about the time before Pantaenus became head of the catechetical school (*c.* 180) and Demetrius bishop in Alexandria (189–231). On Egypt outside Alexandria he has no material before the second half of the third century, except a vague reference to martyrs during the persecution of Septimius Severus, and a quotation from a letter by Alexander of Jerusalem to the Christian community in Antinoopolis from *c.* 200.[3] It is only through the letters of Dionysius of Alexandria (247–264) that Eusebius is able to tell anything more substantial about the Church in Egypt.

In a long letter Dionysius tells about how a bishop by name of Nepos, 'bishop of the Egyptians', caused a schism by his millenarian teaching, and how he himself went to Arsinoë after Nepos' death, probably as a martyr in the persecution of 251, to heal the schism. From what he writes it is obvious that there must have been a Christian centre there with a bishop and probably a kind of Christian school as early as the 240's, and that there were presbyters and teachers serving the 'brothers' in the surrounding villages.[4] Dionysius also refers to bishops in Nilopolis, Hermopolis and the Pentapolis, as well as to a bishop Hierax, styled as 'bishop of the Egyptians'.[5] The first official document mentioning Christians is an order by the President of the Council of Oxyrhynchus dated 28 February 256, to arrest a Christian (χριστιανός).[6] The Christian community in Arsinoë is also known through a letter (dated *c.* 265) from Rome linking it with bishop Maximus, Dionysius' successor.[7] With the turn of the century the

1 Panopolis was the town of Zosimos, the most important representative of the Hermetic tradition in early fourth century Egypt in. See Fowden, *The Egyptian Hermes* pp. 120–126.

2 See Rudolph, 'Zur Soziologie', pp. 21–23.

3 Eusebius, *HE* VI.1 and VI.11.3.

4 *Ibid.*, VII.24 *passim*. Nepos is honoured by Dionysius as a man of Scripture and a famous hymn writer, and probably also as a victim of the persecution.

5 *Ibid.*, VI.42.3, 46.2, VII. 21.2 and 26.1–3.

6 *P. Oxy.* 48.3035. See Roberts, *Manuscript, Society and Belief*, p. 3.

7 *P. Amh.* 3a. See van Joseph van Haelst, 'Les sources papyrologiques concernant l'Église en Égypte à l'époque de Constantine', *Proceedings of the Twelfth International Congress of Papyrology*, Toronto 1970, p. 497.

documentary material on the Church grows rapidly, reveals two churches in Oxyrhynchus in *c.* 295, Christian communities in Panopolis and the Kharga oasis, and a village church in Khysis in the Oxyrhynchite nome. The story of the persecutions under Diocletian shows a massive Christian presence all over Egypt, and at the time of the synod of Nicaea there were no less than 72 bishoprics in Egypt.[1]

But even if the sources for Egyptian Christianity before the end of the third century are meagre, it is unlikely, considering the close relations between Alexandria and the country, that Christianity was not heard of in the towns of Upper Egypt before the end of the second century. Even in their lifetime teachers such as Valentinus, Clement of Alexandria, Basilides and Origen can hardly have been unknown there. The early spread of Christianity in Egypt is also attested by the Christian literary papyri.[2] These show that even before the third century Biblical and other Christian texts, including texts such as Irenaeus' *Adversus haeresis,* were copied in the towns of Upper Egypt, and with the third century there is an abundance of Christian texts, primarily Biblical, from places like Arsinoë, Oxhyrynchus, Antinoopolis and Hermopolis. The lack of documents referring to Christians is probably best explained by the fact that the Christians did not constitute a defined judicial or ethnic group and thus had little reason to pose as Christians in official correspondence.[3] With the beginning of the fourth century the documentary evidence for Christian communities grows steadily and even before the end of the persecutions and the edict of tolerance Christians are officially referred to with designations according to their various positions in the Church.[4]

The literary papyri not only show the existence of Christians in Upper Egypt in the third century, but also tell something about the people who wrote them. The papyri are with some exceptions based on the ordinary documentary style, not on the classical Greek or the Graeco–Jewish manuscript traditions, and must have originated with the middle classes of the towns. Evidently the Church did not have access to professional scribes but relied on its own literate members, who developed a scribal tradition of their own. Behind this development one can see the people of the documentary papyri trying to write literary texts intended for public reading, without being able to attain the level of the literary hands of the intellec-

1 See Annick Martin, 'Aux origines de l'église copte: L'implantation et le developpement du christianisme en Égypte (I[e] – IVe siècles)', *REAnc* 83 (1981), pp. 37f. and 43.

2 See Roberts, *Manuscript, Society and Belief,* pp. 1–25.

3 Roberts, *op.cit.,* p. 2f., and Wipszycka, 'La christianisation', pp. 117–120.

4 The papyri from the first decades of the century contain titles such as ἀναγνώστης, διάκων, ἐκλεκτός, ὁμολογητής and μοναχός. See van Haelst, 'Les sources papyrologiques', p. 498, and Judge, 'Fourth-century Monasticism', p. 614.

tual Greek elite.[1] The large proportion of private manuscripts indicates that the Scriptures were not copied exclusively, perhaps not even predominantly, for public use in the churches.[2] The urban middle class setting is also evident in the few documents showing the involvement of the Church in trade, social activity and education. But there is, in the literary papyri, also evidence for Christians from the highest classes: private parchment *de luxe* codices with edifying romances from the apocrypha.[3] The documentary material, moreover, shows that the Church, through donations of money, grain, valuable articles, animals, slaves, and above all of land, rapidly accumulated considerable wealth. As early as the turn of the century it is said to have been 'an ancient custom' to bequeath land to the Church.[4]

With the end of the persecutions the documents increasingly testify to the growing wealth and power of the Church. The administration of the revenue and the social, political and economic duties that came with it fell on the bishops, who in Egypt were appointed by the patriarch acting as a sort of governor of the only centralized and nation-wide body, the Church, after the divisions of Egypt and the political and economic decentralization of the third century.[5] The position of the bishops was further enhanced when Constantine introduced state contributions to church funds (designated for the poor) and the bishops were exempted from taxation. Apparently the office of the bishop was soon regarded as so attractive that people tried to become bishops in order to enrich themselves.[6]

1 See Roberts, *Manuscript, Society and Belief*, pp. 8–21, where his conclusion is: 'Behind this group of papyri it is not difficult to envisage the men familiar to us from the documentary papyri in the Arsenoite or Oxyrhynchus: tradesmen, farmers, minor government officials to whom knowledge of and writing in Greek was an essential skill, but who had few or no literary interests'. The recruitment of the Church is also discussed in detail in Martin, 'L'Église et la khôra égyptienne au IVe siècle', *REAug* 25 (1979), pp. 11–17, and the documentary evidence in van Haelst, *op.cit., passim.*

2 Roberts, *op.cit.*, p. 12, thinks that the best description of them are 'books published for a secret society', but there is no evidence that Christianity was a secret sect throughout the third century, nor that the books were always intended for a specific society.

3 Roberts, *op.cit.*, pp. 10–12.

4 See Ewa Wipszycka, *Les ressources et les activités économiques des églises en Égypte du IVe au VIIIe siècle* (*Papyrologica Bruxellensia* 10), Bruxelles 1972, p. 29. In a revealing document dated 5 February 304, a deacon complains about what his village church lacked (and obviously ought to have had): 'it had no money, no vestments, no cattle, no slaves, no boats, nothing except the bronze gate of the church now confiscated by the state'. See *P. Oxy.* 2673 quoted in Martin, 'L'Église et la khôra', p. 9, and van Haelst, 'Les sources papyrologiques', p. 498.

5 For the political part played by the Alexandrian bishop, see Bowman, *Egypt after the Pharaohs*, p. 78–80; Lallemand, *L'administration*, pp. 38–40; Rousseau, *Pachomius*, p. 6.

6 See *i.a.* Athanasius, *Historia Arianorum* 78.1.3 and the *Canons of Athanasius* 5. Even Origen speaks about the position of presbyter and bishop as something people boasted about (*Commenatrii in Mattheam* XV.26). Cf. Martin, 'L'Église et la khôra', p. 14f. and 24f.

On a smaller scale the presbyters and deacons, acting as representatives of the bishops, also took part in the accumulation of wealth and power, as shown by land registers and the emphasis on the ecclesiastical office in official correspondence. Obviously not only the bishops, but also the presbyters and deacons, were recruited largely from the urban elite.[1] With growing revenues the tasks that fell upon the Church and its bishops also increased. In addition to their prime duty, to care for the poor, especially widows, orphans and the sick, we find the bishops in the documents acting as arbitrators and official guarantors in financial conflicts, and as patrons and defenders of the oppressed against the authorities.[2]

Consequently we find around the bishop, not only his presbyters and deacons, ordained by him and subject to him by contract, but also crowds of followers from the urban lower classes and 'fugitives' from the villages.[3] From these we can expect the large fraternities that accompanied the bishops of the cities to have been recruited. They were the groups acting, sometimes violently, for the bishops against their adversaries, Christian as well as pagan. In the scholarly literature they are often called 'monks', but in the sources they are generally distinguished from these and designated as 'the ardent' or 'the zealous' (οἱ φιλόπονοι or οἱ σπουδαῖοι).[4] They do not seem to have caused enough problems to be mentioned in the ecclesiastical debate or at synods, and their regulations have not been preserved, although the existence and perhaps also character of these can be inferred from the pagan parallels.[5] They were zealous ascetics, who caried out their social and economic duties, but at the same time consecrated themselves to the service of the fraternity, the Christian

1 In a land register from Hermopolis in the 330's a presbyter is registered for 42 *arurae*, an amount giving him an economically much better position than a pagan priest; the bishop is registered for as much as 466 *arurae*, a proper fortune, enough to feed at least 50 families. See *P. Flor.* 71 + 81 quoted in van Haelst, *op.cit.*, p. 501, and Martin, *op.cit.*, p. 14, and in general A.K. Bowman, 'Landholding in the Hermopolite nome in the fourth century A.D.', *JRS* 75 (1985), pp. 137–163 with corrections in R.S. Bagnall, 'Landholding in late Roman Egypt: the distribution of wealth', *JRS* 89 (1992), pp. 128–149. The equation of 1 *arura* with the subsistence of one person during one year is given by Martin, 'L'Église et la khôra', p. 10. Bowman (*Egypt after the Pharaohs*, p. 17f.) comes to a similar result. In 351 a deacon in a small village in the Arsenoite nome writes a request to the authorities demanding his right, for as he puts it 'I am a deacon of the Catholic Church' (*P.Lond. 412* = *P. Abinn. 55*) as quoted by Martin, *op.cit.*, p. 17.

2 The social role of the Church is discussed in Martin, *op.cit.*, pp. 18–24 and the *audentia episcopalis* in Lallemand, *L'administration*, pp. 150–152.

3 Martin, *op.cit.*, p. 16., and Bowman, *Egypt after the Pharaohs*, p. 194.

4 For a study see Henri Leclerq, 'Confréries', in *DACL* III, and Ewa Wipzycka, 'Les confréries dans la vie religieuse de l'Égypte chrétienne', *Proceedings of the Twelfth International Congress of papyrologists*, Toronto 1970, pp. 511–525. The difference between them and the monks is clearly borne out by the reference in *Epistula Ammonis* 31–32, where monks, zealous and virgins are enumerated as separate groups.

5 Wipzycka, *op. cit.*, p. 511.

community and the poor. Celibacy, and for those married chastity in marriage, was recommended, but not demanded. Usually closely attached to the churches, where the members seem to have spent much of their time, they also had their own place, their φιλοπόνιον.

Literacy and Literature

In the earliest extensive report about the Church in Egypt we come across not only a bishop who was famous for his exegesis and writings, but also a group of teachers expounding his doctrine in the villages. As in Alexandria, the church in Arsinoë was a centre of teaching, a 'school', where a correct interpretation of the Scriptures was sought and taught, not as a mere intellectual exercise, but to gain true knowledge. Literacy and education were consequently of utmost importance. This is also substantiated by the traces in the papyri of the creation of a Christian scribal tradition, at first apparently independent but later influenced by the Alexandrian model, and by the emergence of Christian schools. With the introduction of Coptic, the Church extended school education to the Coptic-speaking majority. But even in these church schools classical tradition and Greek language were taught together with the Scriptures, as is indicated by a school text containing the Psalms on the *recto* and Isocrates' *Ad Demonicum* on the *verso.* A paraphrase of the opening lines of the *Iliad* in Greek together with eight verses of Psalm 46 in Coptic in another text shows the bilingual setting of the schools.[1] The Scriptures were not only studied and discussed in school, but also, and at a very early time, read publicly to the community, as is clearly shown by the recurring reading aids in the manuscripts. Thus, not only the bishops, responsible for the development of Christian interpretation of Scriptures, and the presbyters and teachers, responsible for the teaching, but also the readers in the local churches had to be literate.[2]

Among the early Christian manuscripts from Egypt the amount of scholarly texts is impressive. Codices such as the Coptos codex with Philo,

1 See *P. Lit. Lond.* 207, quoted by Roberts, *Manuscript, Society and Belief,* p. 10, and *Bodl. Gr. Inscr. 3019* edited in P. J. Parson, 'A School Book in the Sayce Collection', *ZPE* 6 (1970), pp. 133–149. Cf. Roberts, *op.cit.*, p. 67, who also mentions another school book in Coptic. At a much later date two exiled presbyters from Edessa are reported to have set up a school in Antinoopolis to counteract Arian propaganda. See Martin, 'L'Église et la khôra', p. 6, quoting Theodoret, *HE* IV.18.7–14.

2 See Roberts, *op.cit.*, p. 21f.. For the literacy of the clergy in general see Wipzycka, 'Le degré d'alphabétisation', p. 288f. with evidence also from texts like the *Canons of Hippolytus* and the *Canons of Athanasius.* In the case of the famous reader who did not sign his complaint himself, since he was ἀγράμματος (*P. Oxy.* 2673, dated 5 Febr. 304), the editors, followed by Roberts, *op.cit.*, p. 65, and Martin *op.cit.*, p. 15, suggest that he only was illiterate in Greek, but quite capable of writing in Coptic. Ewa Wipszycka, 'Un lecteur qui ne sait pas écrire ou un chrétien qui ne veut pas se souiller?', *ZPE* 50 (1983), pp. 117–121, instead convincingly argues that he avoided signing the letter for religious reasons.

the Deuteronomy codex with text-critical signs, as well as papyri with different versions of the Greek Old Testament testify to the existence of a Christian intellectual elite in Egypt already from the beginning of the third century. Within a decade after it had been written in the last decade of the second century, the profound attack on Gnosticism by Irenaeus, bishop of Lyon, at the other end of the empire, was read and copied in Upper Egypt. In the late third century there was at least one Christian scholar in Oxyrhynchus who knew both Latin and Greek, as is shown by a papyrus in which a Latin epitome of Livy and the Epistle to the Hebrews have been carefully preserved[1] On the back of a third century land register from Oxyrhynchus there is even a Hebrew–Greek onomasticon for the New Testament, possibly from a lost work by Origen.[2] In Leontopolis, in the decades around 300, a Christian scribe and scholar named Hieracas who had studied the writings of Origen, possibly in Alexandria, published learned books in Greek and in Coptic on the creation, on the interpretation of the Bible and on the ascetic life, and most probably there were many more who after studying in Alexandria lived as teachers of Christian philosophy and theology in the towns of Egypt.[3] That members of the Egyptian Church went as far as Rome, from where they corresponded with their communities, has already been noted.

This emphasis on literature is evident also in the emergence of Coptic as a written language as a result of the spread of Christianity, including its Gnostic and Manichaean forms. In order to reach larger parts of the population it was necessary to translate the religious literature into the vernacular. Thus the Church and the different sects also came to be the first to offer those who were uneducated, whether in classical Greek or classical Egyptian, the opportunities for cultural activities and the ensuing influence.[4] When the first texts were translated we do not know; of the manuscripts extant a few can be assigned to the late third century, but with little certainty. The existence of a Coptic version of the Gospels as early as 269 is often inferred from the statement in the *Vita Antonii* that Antony, reportedly ignorant of Greek, heard the Gospel read to him when he was eighteen years old. But the reliability of the date, and even of the

1 See Roberts, *op. cit.*, pp. 8–10, 24, quoting numerous other examples. The knowledge of Latin among Christians is also attested by the fragment of the Old Latin Genesis from fourth century Oxyrhynchus (*ibid.*, p. 17).

2 See Roberts, *op.cit.*, p. 9.

3 For Hieracas our main source is Epiphanius, who stresses his erudition and influence, but gives no details about his career and its dates. See Epiphanius, *Panarion* 67 and 69. See also Adolf von Harnack, *Geschichte der altchristlichen Literatur bis Eusebius. Zweite erweiterte Auflage,* I.1, Leipzig 1958, p. 467f., and Heussi, *Der Ursprung des Mönchtums,* pp. 58–65. The historicity of Epiphanius' own experiences in Egypt must, however, be questioned, and thus the suggested *terminus post quem* for Hieracas death given by Heussi as 335.

4 Wipzycka, 'Le degré d'alphabétisation', p. 286.

historicity of the account, is open to doubt, as is the notion that Antony should have been ignorant of Greek. Among the earliest documents in Coptic, the great majority are Biblical texts, canonical as well as apocryphal, translated from Greek. Some of these are bilingual, and are obviously some sort of school exercises. The evident dependence on Greek originals and the very strong influence of Greek on the first original Coptic texts suggest that not only the translators but also the first authors of Coptic texts were familiar with Greek.

The paucity of information about the Church in Egypt prior to the fourth century and the abundance of Gnostic material and references to Egyptian Gnostics have led scholars to regard Egyptian Christianity as thoroughly heterodox until the fourth century.[1] The denial of an orthodox tradition *ex silentio* is, however, precarious and the reliability of the heresiologists in this respect, especially Epiphanius, our major source, is highly questionable.[2] A more reliable source for the character of the traditions of the Church are the literary papyri. Although these are of course only glimpses randomly preserved, they still indicate which texts substituted the bulk of the reading of the Church. A survey of the early manuscripts gives an picture of third century Egyptian Christianity as strongly Biblical, and much less Gnostic than has been suggested. On the contrary it is evident that at least some were keen on refuting the Gnostics, as is shown by the papyrus preserving parts of Irenaeus *Adversus Haereses*. Even in the fourth century, from which most of the Gnostic papyri date, the non-Gnostic texts easily outnumber the Gnostic. The most frequent Biblical texts from the Old Testament are the Psalms and Genesis, and to a lesser degree Isaiah and Jeremiah; from the New Testament Matthew and John, but also Paul and Hebrews. Against a Gnostic reading of the last three one can infer the frequency of the Psalms, and that the Gospels are never found in mixed codices, *i.e.* with apocrypha. Besides the Scriptures, the most frequent texts are the *Shepherd of Hermas* and the *Paschal Homily* by Melito of Sardes, followed by the *Acts of Paul* and the homilies by Origen.[3]

1 This was first suggested by Bauer in his provoking *Rechtgläubigkeit und Ketzerei,* and has been reiterated since then, with the added evidence of the Nag Hammadi library.

2 A convincing refutation of Bauer's ideas is found in Roberts, *Manuscript, Society and Belief,* pp. 47–73. There is little support for Epiphanius' statement that his account of Egyptian heresies is based upon personal experience. Actually the evidence for his stay in Egypt is limited to a panegyric statement in Sozomenos, *HE* VI.32, and as pointed out by Jon Fredrick Dechow, *Dogma and Mysticism in Early Christianity. Epiphanius of Cyprus and the Legacy of Origen,* Ph.D. Diss. Univ. of Pennsylvania 1975, pp. 14–26, the account of his early life seems modelled upon the life of Hilarion, whose stay in Egypt as described by Jerome is far from trustworthy. See below, p. 176.

3 See Roberts, *op.cit.,* pp. 60–65.

Instead of a thoroughly Gnostic background scholars today emphasize a Jewish background for Egyptian Christianity, Gnostic as well as non-Gnostic. Until the virtual extermination of Egyptian Jewry as the result of the Jewish revolt in 115–117, the Jews had a very strong and influential position in Alexandria, and their deeply Hellenized character made them a natural setting for an emergent Christianity of which Philo was 'a Church Father' and the Jewish *therapeutae* the first Christian monks. The earliest Christians were, very likely, almost indistinguishable from the Jews, and their earliest places of worship were found in the Jewish quarters. A large and prominent enough community to attract 'teachers' of all kinds, the Jews also belonged to the Hellenized elite who were downgraded and alienated by the newly introduced Roman rule.[1] The breaking of the bonds between Jews and Christians came only with the severe persecutions of the Jews after their revolt in 115.

A Palestinian and Jewish background of Alexandrian Christianity is also attested both by the traditions associated with St. Mark, Apollos, Barnabas and Clement, and by the early and persistent use of *nomina sacra,* a Judeo–Christian invention originating in Jerusalem and strongly established in Alexandria.[2] The best evidence is, however, the Jewish character of the early literature associated with Alexandria and later frequently used in Egyptian Christianity. This includes texts such as the *Shepherd of Hermas,* which is constantly met with in the early papyri, the *Ascension of Isaiah,* quoted by the early monks, the *Apocalypse of Elijah,* and several of the Nag Hammadi texts.[3] That there was a Judeo–Christian tradition in a place like Arsinoë in the third century is evident both from what we hear about bishop Nepos and from the quotation of Aquila's literal translation of the Old Testament by a recipient of the famous letter from Rome to Arsinoë.[4] A persistent, strongly Jewish, current in Alexandrian Christianity is further attested by Clement and Origen who both wrote against *judaizers,* by Didymus who quotes the *Gospel According to the Hebrews*, and by Jerome who notes that the Alexandrian Christians are

1 See Green, 'The Socio–Economic Background of Christianity in Egypt'. In the first century A.D. ten to fifteen percent of the Egyptian population is estimated to have been Jewish.

2 See Birger A. Pearson, 'Earliest Christianity in Egypt: Some Observations', *The Roots of Egyptian Christianity,* pp. 132–156; A. F. J. Klijn, 'Jewish Christianity in Egypt', *ibid.*, pp. 161–175 and for the *nomina sacra* in the mss. Roberts, *Manuscript, Society and Belief,* pp. 26–48 and 54–58.

3 Other texts of this kind are the *Epistula Apostolorum,* the *Epistle of Barnabas,* the *Didache, 1* and *2 Clement,* the *Preaching of Peter,* and the *Sibylline Oracles.* See Klijn, *op.cit.*, pp. 166–168. The importance of the *Shepherd of Hermas* for monastic tradition is emphasized by Rousseau, *Pachomius,* pp. 136–138. The *Ascension of Isaiah* is quoted in *Epistula Ammonis* X and according to Epiphanius, *Panarion* 67, it was quoted by Hieracas.

4 For Nepos, see Eusebius, *HE* VII.24 , and for the Aquila quotation in *P. Amh.* 3(a) Musurillo, 'Early Christian Economy', *Chronique d'Égypte* 31 (1956), pp. 124–134.

still to some degree Jewish.[1] A Judeo–Christian background has also been suggested for the famous Alexandrian presbyter Arius.[2]

In this Judeo–Christian theological tradition we find an emphasis on knowledge by revelation and a Logos Christology based on Hellenistic Jewish ideas about Wisdom. The *locus* of this teaching, and thus of much of early Christianity in Egypt, was the group of students around an authorized teacher, the 'school', later put under the supervision of the bishop.[3] A good illustration of this setting, with roots both in Jewish wisdom schools and Greek philosophical schools, is the description of the *therapeutae* by Philo, which Eusebius took to refer to the first Christians, and Jerome and John Cassian to the first monks.[4] With their devotion to an ascetic life and to the study of the Scriptures, the *therapeutae* represent the ideals of a Hellenized Jew and mirror the type of communities we have to presuppose behind the Gnostic Christians collecting, transmitting and translating the Nag Hammadi texts. The educational setting and the emphasis on a philosophical life bring them close to the ideals met with in numerous papyri transmitting Greek and Late Egyptian wisdom texts: educational aphorisms and apophthegms with a focus on wisdom, silence, humility and restraint, and usually formalized as exhortations to 'the beloved son'.[5] In texts such as the *Sentences of Sextus* and the *Teachings of Silvanus* we can see how these traditions were Christianized and developed into an ascetic teaching later to be followed by monastic letters and the *apophthegmata*. Obviously both the Gnostic circles and the emerging monastic tradition owed a great deal to the wisdom schools, but while the former stressed esoteric knowledge and mythology, the latter preserved the apophthegmatic character and the emphasis on discipline.[6]

1 See Klijn, 'Jewish Christianity, p. 164f., and Hieronymus, *De viris illustribus* 8.

2 Lorenz, *Arius judaizans?*, pp. 141–179. Lorenz traces this Jewish influence to Lucian of Antioch, but this depends on Arius' being his disciple, a proposal which is today increasingly questioned; see Gregg & Groh, *Early Arianism*, p. 164f. and Williams, *Arius. Heresy & Tradition*, pp. 30–32.

3 The 'school' is characterized as an 'esoteric group' by Klijn, 'Jewish Christianity', p. 173, and as a 'conventcile' by Wilken, 'Wisdom and Philosophy', p. 162. For the Alexandrian school, see Robert M. Grant, 'Theological Education at Alexandria', *The Roots of Egyptian Christianity*, pp. 178–189.

4 Philo, *De Vita Contemplativa*, quoted by Eusebius, *HE* 2.16–17; Hieronymus, *De viris illustribus* 8 and 11; and Johannes Cassianus, *Institutiones* 2.5. For a refutation of the *therapeutae* as precursors of the monks, see Antoine Guillaumont, 'Philon et les origines du monachisme', *Philon d'Alexandrie*, Paris 1967, pp. 361–373 (repr. in *ibid., Aux origines du monachisme chrétien* (*Spiritualité Orientale* 30), Abbaye de Bellefontaine 1979, pp. 25–37. A more positive view is found in Rousseau, *Pachomius*, pp. 13–15.

5 See Lichtheim, *Late Egyptian Wisdom*, pp. 184–196.

6 The importance of the *Sentences of Sextus* and the *Teachings of Silvanus* for the study of early Christian ascetic teaching is discussed in Wilken 'Wisdom and Philosophy', pp. 143–167, and Schoedel, 'Jewish Wisdom and the Formation of the Christian Ascetic', pp. 169–199. For Sextus see also Henry Chadwick, *The Sentences of Sextus*, Cambridge 1959, and for

The Scriptures read in the early Egyptian Church were, however, not only wisdom literature, but also history and eschatology. The confusion resulting from the interpretation of these is borne out by the Nepos history, as well as by the various Gnostic texts. The literalism of the former and the mythologies of the latter were, however, increasingly challenged by the development of a Christian theology, which with the help of Platonic philosophy (in a wide sense) and allegorical exegesis reached its summit with Origen as head of the catechetical school of Alexandria. Although his subsequent condemnation worked against the preservation of evidence for Egyptian Origenism in the third and early fourth century, there is every reason to believe that Christian school tradition in Egypt was heavily Origenist until Athanasius made his impact and Theophilus destroyed the last strongholds among the monastic circles of Nitria. In the third century papyri from Upper Egypt, texts by Origen are among to the most frequent—one manuscript is even contemporary with the author—and in Coptos somebody had a Philo codex most likely derived from an archetype in Origen's library in Caesarea.[1]

In spite of the fact that Origen was condemned in Alexandria and later severely critized by bishops like Dionysius his tradition was preserved in the third and early fourth centuries by teachers such as Theognostus, Pierius and Stephen.[2] Outside Alexandria the most prominent Origenist was Hieracas, who had had a good education and who devoted his life to ascesis and exegetical work in Greek and Coptic, at least according to Epiphanius, who also claims an Origenist background for several of the heresies he describes as Egyptian.[3] Later in the century the monks of Nitria preserved an Origenist tradition and transmitted it to Evagrius.

The picture that emerges of third century Egyptian Christianity from the papyri and the texts attested in these is thus less spectacular than proposed by Bauer. Apparently different 'schools', more or less Jewish

---

the Coptic version, *NHC* XII.1. For Silvanus see Janssens, *Les leçons de Silvanos,* and *NHC* VII.4. Cf. above, p. 49f..

1 See Roberts, *Manuscript, Societ and Belief,* pp. 8 and 24. Another evidence for Origenist texts is the book list from before 312 (*P. Ash. Inv.* 3) published by Colin H. Roberts, 'Two Oxford Papyri', *ZNW* 37 (1938), pp. 184–188 with three texts of Origen mentioned.

2 See Wolfgang A. Bienert, *Dionysius von Alexandrien. Zur Frage des Origenismus im dritten Jahrhundert* (*PTS* 21), Berlin, 1978, p. 222f.. According to Bienert Dionysius was theologically independent of Origen and historically an anti-Origenist. The rehabilitation of Origen, plainly evident in late third century Alexandria, he regards as a result of pressure from abroad, but there is no proof that the pressure did not come from the school and the presbyters of Alexandria and from Egypt in general. For a more cautious view on possible anti-Origenism in Alexandria see Tim Vivian, *St. Peter of Alexandria,* pp. 110–126. See also Grant, 'Theological Education at Alexandria', p. 188f.. Stephen is named with Origen and Pierius as the authors cherished by the Origenist monks in Nitria and by Melania the elder, see *HL* 11 and 55.

3 See Epiphanius, *Panarion* 64, and Dechow, *Dogma and Mysticism,* pp. 79–82.

and more or less Gnostic, coexisted and preached the gospel, with or without the sanction of a bishop. Before the establishment of a fixed corpus of literature and a firm control of the Church by the bishops headed by the Alexandrian patriarch, *i.e.* before the mid-fourth century, it is rather meaningless to speak about orthodox and heretical Christians. A common Judeo–Christian heritage was handled differently by individuals and groups for whom the Alexandrian schools served as models and suppliers of ideas. The variety indicated by Epiphanius can actually be corroborated by papyri containing recommendations of the bearers as *bona fide* Christians; it is also echoed in the monastic accounts of inquiries concerning the affiliation of visiting brothers.

There is, moreover, little evidence for fierce theological conflicts within Egyptian Christianity before the Arian schism. At the outset the denouncement of Origen had most probably no theological ground, and the Meletian schism did not concern any theological issues. Even the Arian controversy seems to have originated, not so much in dogmatics as in a conflict about leadership and authority.[1] It can actually be doubted that the Meletian and Arian schisms were so radical in Egypt as Athanasius has made us believe. The three simultaneous bishops of Antinoopolis mentioned in a landlist apparently got along with each other, and as far as the monks are concerned, there is every reason to suspect that they were slow in their response to the condemnation of heretics propagated by Athanasius.[2]

1 The denouncement of Origen was allegedly based on his literal interpretation of the words about making oneself a eunuch for the sake of the kingdom of God, but it also seems clear that the real reason was jealousy and quarrels about the power and jurisdiction of the bishop. The Meletian schism started with questions about sincerity in the time of persecution, and a conflict about who was the true patriarch. According to Rowan Williams, *Arius,* pp. 41–47 and 82–91, even the Arian controversy originated not as much in a dogmatic controversy as in a conflict about leadership and authority. Even if the conflict between 'school theologians' and the hierarchy postulated by Williams, is not completely convincing, it seems clear that Arianism was a convenient label put upon the ideas combatted by Athanasius and not the theology of a presbyter of Alexandria dead even before he was first mentioned in Athanasius' writings.

2 See *P. Flor.* I 71 and *P. Giss.* II.7. There is strong evidence that the monks joined hands with the Meletians, but no early evidence that this led to bitter conflicts. Cf. Griggs, *Early Egyptian Christianity,* pp. 121–131, and *VP/SBo* 129 ([S^{5}16] Lefort, *S. Pachomii Vitae Sahidice Scriptae* (*CSCO* 99), Paris 1933, p. 180).

4. Monks and Monasteries

Anachoresis and Politeia

In the early fourth century papyri monks are referred to by the expressions μοναχός, ἀναχωρητής, and ἀποτακτικός. Of these only ἀποτακτικός is a new term; probably it derives from the usage of the verb ἀποτάσσω in Biblical texts about renunciation. Since it is the most frequent term in the papyri it seems to have been a kind of official designation of a special group of urban ascetics, apparently closely attached to church-life and imitation of the apostles. Towards the end of the century the term was, according to Epiphanius, used by certain heterodox monks.[1] The term used by Antony, as recorded in the *Vita Pachomii,* and the only one to refer to a well-known phenomenon in society, was ἀναχωρητής.[2] The noun ἀναχώρησις is common in literature and papyri since Ptolemaic time, both as a technical term for illegal absence from land in order to evade taxation, and as a more general term for withdrawal from social obligations. It has been argued that the Christian use of *anchorite* for a monk is due to the more restricted sense of illegal absence, understood as flight and even as revolt, but there is little evidence for this; the monastic *anchorites* did not hide from the authorities and only gradually retired into the mountains and deserts.[3]

The monastic ἀναχωρητής mentioned in fourth century papyri is primarily someone to whom one appeals for prayers—in spiritual as well as economic matters—and one of the *anchorites* is at the same time styled *apotactic.*[4] He is not cut off from society, but personally independent he acts from his retreat in much the same way as Antony does in the *Vita Antonii.* He is the holy man, the 'man of God', who by his prayers can influence worldly and heavenly powers. Apparently both *apotactic* and *anchorite* can be seen as more specialized terms than *monachos,* which

1 See 'Apotactite', *DACL* I, 2604–2606; For the references by Epiphanius see *Panarion* 47 and 61. *Apotactics* are also mentioned in contemporary legislation, see Per Beskow, 'The Theodosian Laws against Manichaeism', p. 3–11.

2 ⲉⲧⲃⲉⲡⲁⲓ̅ⲥ̅ ⲁⲛⲟⲕ ϩⲱ ⲁⲓ̅ⲥ̅ϣⲱⲡⲉ ϩⲛ̅ⲟⲩⲁⲛⲁⲭⲱⲣⲏⲥⲓⲥ *VP/SBo* 127 (S^5 16, Lefort, *S. Pachomii Vitae sahidice scriptae,* p. 178).

3 For the history of the term in Egypt and a critique of Bell and others see Henri Henne, 'Documents et travaux sur l'Anachôrèsis', *Akten des VIII. internationalen Kongresses für Papyrologie,* Wien 1955 (*MPER,* N.S. V), Wien 1956, pp. 59–66. This is not to say that no monks were tax fugitives; a likely candidate is a 'Paul from the Oxyrhynchite' mentioned in a certificate from 305/6 (*P. Oxy.* 2665). There is no evidence that his condemnation was part of the persecutions, nor is there any support for equating him with the Paul of Jerome's *Vita Pauli.* Cf. Judge, 'Fourth Century Monasticism', pp. 613–615.

4 See the examples given by Judge, *op.cit.,* p. 611.

rapidly grew to be *the* designation invariably used for all types of monks; probably it better suited the new traditions of monastic life that emerged with Antony, Pachomius and the first settlers in Nitria and Scetis.[1] In the texts we thus find both μοναχὸς ἀποτακτικός and μοναχὸς ἀναχωρητής. A frequent term in secular literature and juridical language for 'single', 'simple' or 'unique', μοναχός had as a translation of Aramaic *iḥīdayā* in the Judeo–Christian tradition represented by the *Gospel of Thomas* and the *Dialogue of the Saviour* come to designate an ascetic living a celibate life devoted to spiritual perfection.[2] The rapid spread of this term with emerging monasticism indicates that there was more of a Judeo–Christian tradition behind the movement than has usually been suggested.

The use of different terms should caution us against the idea that the monastic tradition in the early fourth century was something homogeneous. An *apotactic* was an ascetic of the town or village who had rejected marriage and lived in a separate place with other ascetics. Probably he had a kind of official position in the Church; he could still be a landholder, pay taxes and act as a trustee. An *anchorite* was someone who had withdrawn completely from society, who lived apart, but not necessarily in the desert, inaccessible to visitors. A *monk* was probably at the outset either of these, someone who for religious reasons lived a celibate life. With the monastic movement and the establishment of monasteries, however, the content of the word was determined by the examples of Antony, Pachomius and others. What the three terms have in common is the emphasis on renunciation of marriage and traditional social life. This emphasis seems to come from the search for liberation from the ties of family, society, and even bishop, in order to concentrate on spiritual progress, rather than

1 In their discussion of these terms the editors of the Nepheros archive seem to regard monks as a group different from *apotactics* and *anchorites,* but there is no evidence in the texts for this. That there were inhabitants in the monasteries who were not monks is obvious, but they can hardly have been designed as *apotactics* or *anchorites*. Cf. Kramer & Shelton, *Das Archiv des Nepheros,* p. 10.

2 Though absent in the LXX, μοναχός was used by Aquila in his translation of the Hebrew Bible, and apparently with a more restricted meaning, by Symmachus, who thus translates Hebrew *yeḥīdīm* in Ps. 68:7. According to Françoise-E. Morard, 'Monachos, Moine. Histoire du terme grec jusqu'au 4e siècle', *ZPT* 20 (1973), pp. 332–411, the restricted use has its roots in Essenic Judaism and Jewish Christianity. The term is missing completely in the writings of Philo, Clement and Origen, and except where Eusebius quotes Symmachus, it only reappears in the early fourth century as a technical term in papyri and in the writings of Athanasius and others. Its relations to the Syriac term *iḥīdayā* were first discussed by Alfred Adam, 'Grundbegriffe des Mönchtums in sprachlicher Sicht', *ZKG* 65 (1953–54), pp. 209–239, and Edmund Beck, 'Ein Beitrag zur Terminologie des ältesten syrischen Mönchtums', *Antonius Magnus Eremita 356–1956* (*SA* 38), Rome 1956, pp. 254–267. The first attestation in papyri is discussed by E. A. Judge, 'The Earliest Use of Monachos for 'monk' and the Origins of Monasticism', *JAC* 20 (1977), pp. 72–89, but his conclusions are rightly questioned by Morard, 'Encore quelques réflexions sur monachos', *VC* 34 (1980), pp. 395–401.

from a notion of celibacy as a prerequisite for salvation or an *a priori* devaluation of the body and sexuality.[1]

But for renunciation to be meaningful there must have been something to leave and a spiritual tradition to adhere to. A destitute and simple peasant is not likely to have established himself as an anchorite or founded a monastic community, even if he might have visited the holy man and eventually even joined a monastery. The background of the early ascetics and founders of monastic tradition must instead be sought among the same groups as the Christians and Gnostics in general, *i.e.* the demoted elite and the middle class of the growing towns, who were the ones burdened by heavy obligations and attracted by new social and religious ideas. What has been said about the egalitarian views of the Gnostics can be said also about the early monastic tradition.[2] The papyri reveal that a number of *apotactics* and *anchorites* came from the urban elite; and Antony himself is said to have been the heir of 300 *arourae,* a real fortune of land, while Amoun, the first monk in Nitria, is reported to have been of noble and wealthy descent. Though a hagiographic tendency to exaggerate the amount of wealth renounced by the monks cannot be excluded, the attention their breach with society received indicates that they did not come from the margins of society. The difficulty to break with family and tradition, as well as the awareness of the radical character of this breach which can be sensed in the sources also indicates a background of considerable social responsibility.[3] The attraction the monasteries had on less fortunate members of society presupposes that there already was an established tradition, and thus it belongs to a second stage. The activities of the Pachomian monasteries and the monastery of Hathor, moreover, clearly show that they had a well qualified leadership and probably rather high expectations on the monks accepted.

Instead of regarding the early monks as poor fugitives and the monastic communities as groups of antisocial 'hippies', we have to acknowledge that the sources depict the creation of new social and economic enterprises. The monks, whether called *apotactics, anchorites,* or simply *monks,* interacted with a society in which their 'profession' was officially

1 See Peter Brown, 'The Rise and Function of Holy Man', p. 95: 'He fled women and bishops, not because he might have found the society of either particularly agreeable, but because both threatened to rivet him to a distinct place in society'.

2 See Rudolph, 'Zur Soziologie, sozialen "Verortung" und Rolle der Gnosis', p. 22f. where we find the expressions 'Brüderethik', 'Aufhebung der gesellschaftlichen Unterschiede', und 'herrschaftskritische Auffassung'.

3 For a list of monks of noble and wealthy origin, see Martin, 'L'église et le khôra', p. 14f. with evidence from the sources. Rousseau, in his article 'The Formation of Early Ascetic Communities: Some Further Reflections', *JTS* 25 (1974), pp. 113–117, presents evidence for an emphasis in the sources on the complete breaks with family responsibilities. For the role of the family see Bowman, *Egypt after the Pharaohs,* pp. 130–136, pp. 113–117.

acknowledged, and in which they looked after their own economic interests. That they were successful in this we can infer from the protection and the alms they were able to offer.[1] Based on the cultivation of deserted or donated land and the work done by the well-organized work forces of the monks, the wealth of the Pachomian monasteries soon became a problem for the *koinonia*.[2] In the Nepheros archive we get a glimpse of the economic activities and the powers of a non-Pachomian monastery in the mid-fourth century, a very impressive picture of trade, industry and communication.[3] Even in the desert the monks were able, not only to make a living, but also to build cells and churches which were of equal standard to the houses in the villages.[4] The capacity to receive the very large numbers flocking to the deserts of Nitria and Scetis and to the monasteries in the Fayyūm and in the Nile valley in the latter half of the century is proof enough for what must be termed a prosperous and highly organized society of its own. Probably emerging monasticism is best described as an urbanization of the desert and deserted land, a description originating with the *Vita Antonii,* in which the author says: 'the desert was made a city (πόλις) by the monks; leaving their own they were registered for the citizenship (πολιτεία) of the heavens'.[5]

Grammata and Gnosis

It is usually assumed, not only that the majority of the monks were simple Coptic peasants, but also that they were completely illiterate. But all too often those with an insufficient command of Greek are regarded as

[1] See Rousseau, *Pachomius,* pp.10–13: 'To enroll oneself in the resurrected economy of Tabennesis (which was a deserted village, not a stretch of desert) was not to abandon society, but to transfer one's allegiance, as had many other "anchorite", from one rural community to another.' Judge, 'Fourth–century Monasticism', pp. 613–620, shows the same to be true about the monks mentioned officially in the papyri. On the distribution to the poor, see *VP/G* 6, 14, 28 and *VA* 3.

[2] See *VP/G* 127. The relations of the Pachomian monasteries with the world are dealt with in Rousseau, *Pachmoius,* pp. 153–158, and the question of poverty and riches is the theme of Bernward Büchler, *Die Armut der Armen. Über ursprunglichen Sinn der mönchischen Armut,* München 1980.

[3] See Kramer & Shelton, *Das Archiv des Nepheros,* pp. 3–34. Similar evidence is found in an earlier monastic archive, probably from the same monastery (*P. Jews.* 1913–1922). These letters report about orders of cloaks and shoes, apparently produced in the monastery (*P. Jews.* 1918, 1920 and 1922), see Bell, *Jews and Christians in Egypt,* pp. 86ff., 91ff. and 97ff..

[4] See Rousseau, *Pachomius,* p. 12 and the results of the excavations at Kellia. For publications see *Le Site Monastique des Kellia (Basse–Egypte), recherches des Années 1981–1983 (Mission Suisse d'Archéologie Copte de l'Université de Genève),* Louvain 1984.

[5] ἡ ἔρημος ἐπολίσθη μοναχῶν, ἐξελθόντων ἀπὸ τῶν ἰδίων, καὶ ἀπογραψαμένων τὴν ἐν τοῖς οὐρανοῖς πολιτείαν (*VA* 14). An interesting link with the people of Israel in the desert is suggested by Rousseau quoting a festal epistle by Athanasius where the people of Israel are said to have made the desert into inhabited land. See Athanasius, *Festal Letters* 10. According Brown, 'The Rise and Function', p. 83, this is the great difference between Syriac and Coptic monasticism.

ignorant and those without classical education (γράμματα) as illiterate (ἀγράμματος). Knowledge of texts by heart, usually seen as a sign of illiteracy, is more likely to be the result of repetitive reading than the result of memorization of oral tradition. With the growth of monasticism in the latter half of the fourth century there were, no doubt, illiterate monks. But even in late sources such as the *Historia Monachorum* and the *Historia Lausiaca* it is not unlikely that the few monks explicitly said to have been illiterate, like Antony's disciple Paul, who is nicknamed 'the simple' (ἁπλοῦς), are singled out because they were exceptional cases.[1] Education and literacy, moreover, are in these texts only mentioned in connection with monks who were either competent in several languages, or distinguished translators, teachers or scribes.[2] An ability to read the Scriptures is presupposed in most sources, and books are often mentioned in the texts, even in the *Apophthegmata Patrum.*[3] In the Pachomian monasteries the new monks were taught to read, and in their rules there are special regulations concerning literature and reading. The letters of Pachomius, Theodore and Horsiesius, as well as the rules and instructions they wrote, also show the community to have been highly literate; according to Palladius one of the tasks in a Pachomian monastery was to work in the *scriptorium* (καλλιγραφεῖον).[4]

The literate character of the earliest monastic society is most clearly brought out by the early documents themselves. In addition to the isolated papyri in which monks (*apotactic* and *anachoretic*) appear as recipients of letters and as trustees and a virgin (ἀειπάρθενος) is accused of appropriating 'Christian books', there are three major collections of monastic doc-

1 The cases are collected by Martin, 'L'Église et la khôra', p. 17f.. A main source for considering the majority of the monks illiterate is Socrates, *HE* VI.7 about the monks Theophilus called for support against the Origenists: ἀνθρώπους ἀκεραίους μέν, ἰδιώτας δὲ τῷ λόγῳ, τοὺς πολλοὺς δὲ ἀγραμμάτους ὄντας. But this is no proof of illiteracy, only of simplicity in speech and lack of education. By his allusion to 2 Cor. 11:6 Socrates most probably meant that the monks were not capable of understanding the niceties of the controversy about anthropomorphism and Origenism. In hagiographical texts one can always suspect that illiteracy is used as an argument for the holiness and solely divine inspiration of the saint, as is clearly the case in *VA*. See below, pp. 141–144.

2 *HM* VI.3, VIII.62 and *HL* XXI.3 refer to several monks knowing Greek, Coptic and Latin. A monastic copyist of Latin texts is noted by Johannes Cassianus, *Institutiones,* V.39.1–2. In this context it is worth noting that even in the archive of a monastery of Meletian affiliation Greek letters by far outnumber the Coptic. See Kramer & Shelton, *Das Archiv des Nepheros.*

3 See *i.a. AP/G* Abraham 3, Ammoes 5, Bessarion 12, Euprepios 7, Theodoros of Pherme 1, 29, Mark 1, Silvanos 5, and Serapion 2. Even Pachomius tells his disciples not to be impressed by the beauty of a book (*VP/G* 63).

4 The part played by books and libraries in the Pachomian monasteries has been analyzed by Clemens Scholten, 'Die Nag–Hammadi–Texte als Buchbesitz der Pachomianer', *JAC* 31 (1988), pp. 144–172. The *scriptorium* is referred to in *HL* 32.13 and Johannes Cassianus, *Institutiones* 4.12. For a general discussion see Wipzycka, 'Le degré d'alphabétisation', p. 293, citing *Historia Lausiaca, Apophthegmata Patrum* and the *Regula Pachomii.*

uments from the mid-fourth century. The first is the archive of a Meletian monastery called Hathor situated in the Kynopolite nome. On internal evidence they can be dated to the 330's. The main part of the archive consists of letters to Paieous, who is the head of the community and styled as presbyter and confessor (ὁμολογητής). This community was apparently bilingual and highly literate, even if some brothers were unable to sign their own names in Greek. The priest responsible for the administration of the monastery was even summoned by Constantine to the synod of Caesarea in 334.[1]

The second collection consists of letters to a respected and learned brother, designated 'Apa Paphnutius the anchorite'.[2] Unfortunately they give no hint as to their date and provenance, but on paleographical grounds they might be dated to the middle of the fourth century, and their origin must be somewhere in the Arsinoite/Fayyūm or in the lower Thebaid. In them Paphnutius is shown to have been a monk with a leading position in a community. He is appealed to for prayers for the well-being of his correspondents, who by their various greetings are shown to be familiar with his monastic community. The letters are written in good Greek apparently by people of education, some of them even with high-ranking titles. The third collection is the archive of Nepheros, a presbyter and head of a large monastic community in the 350's. This community is also called Hathor, but it is uncertain if it is identical with that of Paieous, and there is no proof that it was of Meletian affiliation. In the letters Nepheros is depicted as an eloquent spiritual teacher, competent in Greek and Coptic, a man who conducted an extensive official and private correspondence on financial as well as spiritual matters. Of his correspondents several were monks, most of them apparently also competent in Greek.[3]

If we can thus conclude that a large number of the first monks had a fairly high social background and some education, they cannot have been strangers to the philosophical and religious ideas around them.[4] Their close contacts with society, manifest in the sources, also prevented isolation from current debate. On the other hand, there is little evidence for conflicts between monks of different affiliation (Orthodox, Gnostic or Manichaean) before the late fourth century; the conflicts we hear about in the early monastic sources are within the communities, or with the Church. To the first monks the 'heresies' were apparently no clearcut

1 *P. Jews.* 1913–1922, see Bell, *op.cit.*, pp. 38–99.

2 *P. Jews* 1923–1929, see Bell, *Jews and Christians*, pp.100–120. His name is variously spelled as Παπνούθιος, Παφνούθιος, Παπνούτιος and Παφνούτιος.

3 See Kramer and Shelton, *op.cit.*, pp. 6–10 and 24–34.

4 For Pachomius attentiveness to current debates, see Rousseau, *Pachomius*, p. 26.

alternatives opposed to true Christianity; it was only when State and Church combined their efforts to define orthodoxy and stamp out everything else that the lines hardened. In a society with a confusing religious diversity, heterodox books can be suspected to be scrutinized for what could be edifying, not simply abhorred, and new ideas to be tested and modified, not rejected out of hand.[1] Pagan traditions were kept as long as they did not contradict the Christian faith or became forbidden, and pagan philosophers were partners in discussions, not chased away from their temples.[2]

The Manichaeans, once seen as the most important influence in the rise of monasticism, are conspicously absent in the earliest monastic sources, and in later ones they are merely condemned as the heretics *par excellence*. The presence of Manichaean missionaries and literature, indicated by the numerous refutations of Manichaeism, by the Manichaean sources and by the Manichaean texts preserved in Coptic, is no proof of a clearly defined and visible Manichaean movement. Their *mānistān* were no large monasteries of a Pachomian type—still less communities of anchorites—but most probably urban resthouses for wandering *electi*.[3] No doubt their ascetic lifestyle and strong emphasis on virginity and renunciation resembled the earliest monastic movement, and some of their literature could have been read by monks who were not professing Manichaeans.[4] The fact that various ascetic groups are singled out in the Theodosian decrees as Manichaeans in disguise and similar evidence from Egypt suggest not only that there were similarities, but probably also that the designation of a group as Manichaean was an suitable weapon against various ascetic oddities.[5] Probably the statements on Manichaeans disguised as Christians often

1 The existence of apocrypha and works by Origen in the Pachomian monasteries is evidenced by *VP/G* 31 and *VP/SBo* 189, quoting Athanasius, *Festal Epistles* 39. That heterodox ideas found their way into the monasteries is also shown by the note on the monk Patchelpius in *Ep. Amm.* 26.

2 A strong emphasis on the Egyptian character of early monasticism and the *AP* is found in Baumeister, 'Die Mentalität des frühen ägyptischen Mönchtums, pp. 145–160. Connections to Egyptian literature are suggested by H. Brunner, 'Ptahhotep bei den koptischen Mönchen', *ZÄS* 86 (1961), pp. 145–147, and M. Kaiser, 'Agathon und Amenemope', *ZÄS* 92 (1966), pp. 102–105.

3 See the thorough analysis of the meaning of the term *mānistān* given by Bo Utas, 'Mānistān and Xānaqāh', *Papers in Honour of Mary Boyce* (*Acta Iranica*, Ser. II, Vol. X), Leiden 1985, pp. 655–664. For this reference my thanks to Peter Bryder.

4 For examples see Eric Segelberg, 'Syncretism at work: On the Origin of some Coptic Manichaean Psalms', *Religious Syncretism in Antiquity (ed. P. Brown)*, Missoula 1975, pp. 191–203.

5 *Cod. Theod.* 16.5.7 and 16.5.9. The Manichaeans are called *solitarii* and are condemned together with groups such as Encratites, Hydroparastates, Saccophores, and Apotactics, primarily known from Asia Minor and Syria. See Beskow, 'The Theodosian Laws against Manichaeism', pp. 3–11. For other examples see Stroumsa, 'Monachisme et Marranisme', p 190–197.

have little to do with 'real' Manichaeism. There are no signs of success for explicitly Manichaean religious communities with rigid rules in Egypt in the same way as in Persia, and according to Augustine, also in Rome.[1]

In spite of much more material on Gnosticism there is as little evidence for Gnostic monks or monastic communities in the early fourth century as there is for Manichaean. What we have is a variety of ideas that can be called Gnostic and the fact that earlier Gnostic literature was still read and copied. But if and to what degree the proponents of these ideas and, more specifically, the keepers and readers of the Gnostic texts, could be distinguished from the 'orthodox' monks assembled around Antony and Pachomius or the members of Meletian and other monasteries, we do not know. The question 'Were the Nag Hammadi codices part of the library of a Pachomian monastery?' has generated a literature of its own.[2] The codices were found close to the site of a Pachomian monastery and had been bound in the mid-fourth century by Christian monks.[3] Since no convincing alternative has been put forward, and the impossibility of such an origin remains unproven, a Pachomian library remains the most plausible setting for the codices.[4] The fact that there is much in the texts that could have been regarded as edifying by intellectual monks is not disproved by the presence in the texts of speculation and mythology alien to the Pachomian tradition.[5] We should not today deny a fourth century monastic reader the capacity of selective reading and intelligent interpretation. The variety of ideas within the Nag Hammadi library plainly excludes the possibility of a group professing everything found in the texts.[6]

1 See Stroumsa, *op.cit.*, p. 311, for the evidence from Augustine.

2 The most recent contributions, with references to earlier publications are Scholten, 'Die Nag–Hammadi–Texte'; James E. Goehring, 'New Frontiers in Pachomian Studies', *The Roots of Egyptian Christianity*, pp. 236–257; Armand Veilleux, 'Monasticism and Gnosis in Egypt', *ibid.*, pp. 271–306 (=*idem.*, 'Monachisme et gnose', *LTP* 40 (1984), pp. 275–294 and 41 (1985), pp. 3–24). See also Rousseau, *op.cit.*, p. 27f. who is cautiously negative to any connection.

3 For details about the evidence from the bindings, see G. M. Browne and J. C. Shelton, *Nag Hammadi Codices; Greek, Coptic Papyri from the Cartonnage of the Covers* (*NHS* 16), Leiden 1981, pp. 5–11.

4 The doubts mainly come from Veilleux, who has collected the evidence for possible alternatives in his 'Monachisme et Gnose', p. 280. Rousseau, *op.cit.*, p. 27f. is also hesitant and refers to disputes with non-Pachomians. A more extensive but uncritical discussion on these is found in Büchler, *Die Armut der Armen*, pp. 138–145.

5 The most obvious examples are the *Teachings of Silvanus*, which has a parallel in the monastic *Teachings of Antony* (see above, p. 50 note 1), the *Sentences of Sextus*, the *Exegesis on the Soul*, the *Book of Thomas the Contender*, and the *Authoritative Teaching*. In his article Wincenty Myszor ('Antonius-Briefe und Nag-Hammadi-Texte') shows that there are numerous points of contact between monastic and 'Gnostic' reflection. But the monks also shared Plotinus' critical views on Gnosticism. See Rousseau, *op.cit.*, pp. 23–27.

6 This difficulty is evident in Tito Orlandi's attempt to place the Nag Hammadi texts within the context of the Origenist and Evagrian tradition attacked by Shenoute. The connections between the Nag Hammadi texts and Evagrian theology are no more convincing than those between them and Shenoute's antagonists. Cf. Orlandi, 'A Catechesis against Apocryphal

Since Gnostic ideas and literature are likely to have attracted the same groups in society as subsequently monasticism, and since ascetics joining the monasteries would have brought with them their cherished literature, there is nothing strange in apocryphal texts of a Gnostic character ending up in a Pachomian monastery.[1] That Gnostic ideas were increasingly filtered out in the theological process does not prove that Gnostic literature was always confined to distinct heretical sects and regarded as untouchable by all who did not adhere to the sect. Nor does the fact that Gnostic texts were read in a monastery prove that the monks shared all the ideas of the authors of the texts.[2]

As in the case of Egyptian Christianity in general, the presence of Gnostic texts in monastic libraries should not be given undue weight simply because we find Gnosticism exciting. The Nag Hammadi codices were perhaps only a minor part of the library, or probably libraries, they belonged to, and not likely to have been the books that were most frequently read. Unfortunately our evidence for the character of Egyptian monastic libraries does not go beyond the fifth century, and is thus of little value for what was kept and read in the early fourth century.[3] If the early collections of Christian manuscripts from Egypt (the Bodmer and Bala'izah papyri) have a monastic origin, they show that the libraries of the monasteries in addition to the Scriptures kept a wide variety of apocrypha, patristic texts and secular writings but only a few Gnostic

---

Texts by Shenute and the Gnostic Texts of Nag Hammadi', *HTR* 75 (1982), pp. 85–95. The only conclusion we can safely draw is 'that the reconstruction of the long work of Shenoute, *Contra Origenistas,* has shown that texts *such as* those from Nag Hammadi were widely read by the monks in Upper Egypt' (Orlandi, 'Coptic literature', *The Roots of Egyptian Christianity,* p. 56; italics mine).

1 Henry Chadwick, 'The Domestication of Gnosis', pp. 3–16, convincingly argues that Gnostic literature was less exotic and of less restricted usage than is generally believed.

2 The attempts to find evidence for Gnostic ideas in the Pachomian material or for conflicts in the monasteries that could have been caused by Gnostic teaching (*i.a.* by Charles Hedrick, 'Gnostic Proclivities in the Greek Life of Pachomius and the Sitz im Leben of the Nag Hammadi Library', *Nov. Test.* 22 (1980), pp. 78–94, and Fredrick Wisse, 'Gnosticism and Early Monasticism', *Gnosis. Festschrift für Hans Jonas,* Göttingen 1978, pp. 431–440) have not been successful. See Antoine Guillaumont, 'Gnose et monachisme: exposé introductif', *Gnosticisme et monde hellénistique. Actes du Colloque de Louvain-la-Neuve* (ed. Y. Janssens & J.-M. Sevrin), Louvain 1982, pp. 301–310. The process of defining orthodoxy within Pachomian tradition is demonstrated by James E. Goehring, 'Pachomius Vision of Heresy: The Development of a Pachomian Tradition', *Le Muséon* 95 (1982), pp. 241–262.

3 The monastic libraries of Egypt are discussed by Scholten, *op.cit.,* pp. 153–157. The only possible evidence from the fourth century is the book list published by Roberts, 'Two Oxford Papyri', pp. 184–188 (*P. Ash. Inv.* 3). It mentions three works by Origen, one by a Ἄπα Βαλ..., and one Ποιμήν. The last is likely to be the *Shepherd of Hermas,* frequently attested in the papyri, and Ἄπα Βαλ... could be Valentinus. Thus Klaus Koschorke, 'Zur spätgeschichte der Valentinianischen Gnosis', *Gnosis and Gnosticism (ed. M. Krause)* (*NHS* 17), Leiden 1981, p. 129f., and Chadwick, *op.cit.,* p. 15, but denied by Scholten, *op.cit.,* p. 156, n. 96, with reference to Helderman.

texts.[1] Probably it is no coincidence that in the earliest book list three works out of sixteen are by Origen. Another hint of the theological background available for an ardent ascetic in Egypt around 300 is given by the reports on Hieracas. In addition to a pagan education and a good knowledge of the Scriptures, he was acquainted with various apocrypha, quoting the *Ascension of Isaiah* and speculating on Melchisedek. His teaching shows several similarities with Gnostic texts and the Nag Hammadi library, but he was far from being an outright Gnostic. The greatest influence, moreover, came from Origen.[2] The strong Origenist tradition in Nitria and in Upper Egypt, evident in the writings of Palladius in the Pachomian texts and in Shenoute's polemic, was apparently of a long standing. There is actually no evidence for the oft-repeated statement that the majority of the monks were anti-Origenists even before the emergence of the controversy in the late fourth century.[3]

The legacy at hand for anyone who like Antony, at the turn of the third century, retreated from the duties of social life for the life of a philosopher, was not what, half a century later, a bishop like Athanasius wanted his flock to be fed with. It is not the strong Origenist flavour of Antony's letters that is strange, but the power of the traditional image of early monasticism produced by texts written and edited in the century after his death. It is thus to the question of how these texts transformed his image we now have to turn.

[1] See Scholten, *op.cit.*, p. 159f. for the Bodmer papyri (with reference to an unpublished work by J. M. Robinson: 'The First Christian Monastic Library'). For the Bala'izah papyri see Paul Kahle, *Bala'izah: Coptic Texts from Deir el–Bala'izah in Upper Egypt,* I–II, London 1954.

[2] Our only source for Hieracas is Epiphanius, *Panarion* 55.5, 67.1–7 and 69.7. See Harnack, *Geschichte der altchristlichen Literatur,* I, p. 467f., and Heussi, *Der Ursprung des Mönchtums,* p. 58–65.

[3] See *i.a.* Griggs, *Early Egyptian Christianity,* p. 83, in spite of his earlier appreciation of the varities within Egyptian Christianity. A more fruitful approach, which is, moreover, linked to Antony is Michael A. Williams, 'The *Life of Antony* and the Domestication of Charismatic Wisdom', *Charisma and Sacred Biography, JAAR* Thematic Studies XLVIII/3 & 4 (1982), pp. 23–40.

VI. THE *LIFE OF ANTONY*

1. THE *VITA ANTONII* – STATUS QUAESTIONIS

The most widely read text on early Egyptian monasticism is undoubtedly the *Vita Antonii.* Allegedly written by one of the most famous churchfathers it has formed not only the image of Antony but also largely that of monasticism in the Christian tradition. Although the verdict of scholars on the text has varied greatly, no one has ever denied the paramount importance of the *Vita.* Scorned by Adolf von Harnack as the 'probably most disastrous book that has ever been written', it is today hailed as 'next to the Gospel of St. Mark the most important biography of early Christianity' and as 'the most influential of Athanasius' writings'.[1] In spite of critical research and doubts about its authenticity and historical reliability it has preserved its position as the main source for the study of Antony and his monastic environment. While scholars have proposed widely different solutions to the question of the literary background and the purpose of the text, most have done so without reference to the historical situation, suggesting either that the text is simply a literary composition reflecting the theology of Athanasius, or that there was a fundamental conformity between Athanasius and Antony.[2]

As the first and most influential hagiographical text in the Christian tradition the *Vita Antonii* has been the subject of a very large and steadily growing number of studies. These have analysed the text from a wide range of different aspects, from questions such as textual criticism, the problem of the different versions, of the authorship, genre, and historical value, to sociological, psychological and theological interpretations of the

[1] See Adolf von Harnack, *Das Leben Cyprians von Pontus. Die erste christliche Biographie* (*TU* 39.3), Leipzig 1913, p. 81; Michael Williams, 'The *Life of Antony* and the Domestication of Charismatic Wisdom', p. 23f.; and Martin Tetz, 'Athanasius und die Vita Antonii. Literarische und theologische Relationen', *ZNW* 73 (1982), pp. 3–5.

[2] For the first, see Roldanus, *Le Christ et l'homme dans la théologie d'Athanase d'Alexandrie,* pp. 277–348; for the second see Louis Bouyer, *La vie de Saint Antoine. Essai sur la spiritualité du monachisme primitif,* Abbaye Saint Wandrille 1950 (2nd ed. in *Spiritualité Orientale,* 22, Abbaye de Bellefontaine 1977). An exception is Gregg & Groh *Early Arianism,* pp. 131–159.

text.[1] In addition to these studies of the *Vita* itself, the text is also increasingly drawn upon for general studies on early monasticism, on Athanasius, Arianism and hagiography, as well as on the spirituality of early Christianity and Late Antiquity in general.[2] In this wide field of research, there is, however, yet no growing consensus, and contradictory interpretations and opinions dominate the field. Three basic problems are still unsolved, and intensely discussed: the textual history and the relation of the different versions to each other; the question of authorship, sources and unity of the text; and the problem of defining the genre, purpose and value of the text as a historical source.

The Greek text, preserved in a vast number of manuscripts, has until recently been accepted as the original composition.[3] Of this Greek text two Latin versions, as well as a Coptic, an Armenian, a Georgian and an Old Slavonic version, are known and edited.[4] The Syriac version, however, differs substantially from the Greek. It is preserved in two recensions of which the shorter omits the sermons otherwise included in the *Vita*. It is characterized by being considerably longer than the Greek text, due to numerous pious elaborations and explanations which add little to the story itself. The importance of the Syriac version was pointed out as early as 1894 by Friedrich Schulthess, who suggested that it might depend on the source of the Greek text.[5] However, no further explanation of the differences was offered until Draguet, in his critical edition of 1980, claimed

1 The literature on the *VA* is large and rapidly growing, but no comprehensive bibliography is yet available. For earlier literature see Ludwig von Hertling, 'Studi storici antoniani negli ultimi trent'anni', *Antonius Magnus Eremita 356–1956* (*SA* 38), Rome 1958, pp. 13–34. For a recent bibliograpy see the new edition by G.J.M. Bartelink: *Athanase d'Alexandrie: Vie d'Antoine* (*SC* 400), Paris 1994.

2 The use of *VA* for studies of early monasticism and early Christian spirituality is too general to be listed. For the comparisons with classical biography see Patricia Cox, *Biography in Late Antiquity. A Quest for the Holy Man,* Berkeley 1983, and the titles quoted below.

3 Earlier editions and translations are listed in the recent edition by Bartelink (*SC* 400). An older survey of the Greek text is Gérard Garitte, 'Histoire du texte imprimé de la Vie grecque de S. Antoine', *BBR* 22 (1942–43), pp. 5–29.

4 For the versions, see Gérard Garitte, 'Le texte grec et les versions anciennes de la vie de saint Antoine', *Antonius Magnus Eremita 356–1956* (*SA* 38), Rome 1958, pp. 1–12 and the edition by Bartelink. The importance of the older Latin version for the establishemnt of the text is emphasized by G. J. M. Bartelink, 'Die älteste lateinische Übersetzung der Vita Antonii des Athanasius im Lichte der Lesarten einiger griechischen Handschriften', *RHT* 11 (1981), pp. 397–413. On the Coptic version see G. M. Browne, 'Coptico–Graeca. The Sahidic version of St. Athanasius' Vita Antonii', *GRBS* 12 (1971), pp. 59–64. On the Old Slavonic version see A. de Santos Otero, 'Die altslavische Überlieferung der Vita Antonii des Athanasius', *ZKG* 90 (1979), pp. 96–106, and C. Hannick, 'Maximos Holobolos in der kirchenslawischen homiletischen Literatur', *Wiener Byzantinische Studien,* XIV, Wien 1981, pp. 181–185.

5 F. Schulthess, *Probe einer syrischen Version der Vita Antonii* (*Diss. Strassburg*), Leipzig 1894. The Syriac text was subsequently published by P. Bedjan, *Acta Martyrum et Sanctorum* V, Paris–Leipzig 1895, pp. 1–121, and by E. A. W. Budge, *The Book of Paradise,* II, London 1904, pp. 1–93.

that the Syriac version does not depend on the Greek, but on its source, well preserved in the Syriac but completely reworked in the Greek. This conclusion was based on a linguistic analysis in which he claimed that the Syriac text ought to be regarded as a translation of a 'Coptizising' Greek text of a type characteristic of the early, bilingual monastic environment.[1]

Draguet was followed by Barnes, who on the basis of Draguet's edition claimed that the Syriac depends on a Coptic original written in the monastic community, and that the Greek is a revision made for a more educated Greek audience. A critical comparison of the Syriac and the Greek text shows, however, that the Greek cannot be a revised and abridged version of the text preserved in Syriac, but that the Syriac text must be explained as an elaboration of the Greek.[2] The linguistic arguments for the Syriac version must also be regarded as inconclusive.[3] Among the other oriental versions the Arabic and Ethiopic remain unedited. The Arabic tradition is very rich and to a large extent completely independent of the Greek text. It attributes, moreover, the *Vita* not only to Athanasius, but also to Serapion of Thmuis. Most probably it is based on lost Coptic versions. The Ethiopic text seems to have as its original source, probably transmitted via Coptic and Arabic, a Greek version slightly different from the preserved one, but also different from the one witnessed to by the Syriac text.[4] Of both these editions are sorely needed.

1 Renée Draguet, *La vie primitive de saint Antoine conservée en syriaque* (*CSCO* 417–418), Louvain 1980. The question of priority and authorship is discussed in the introduction to the French translation (*CSCO* 418), pp. 100*–112*, where he summarizes his linguistic observations.

2 T. Barnes, 'Angels of Light or Mystic Initiate. The Problem of the "Life of Antony"', *JTS* 37 (1986), pp. 353–368. His conclusions, however, are questionable. The linguistic arguments of Draguet, even if correct, do not actully prove that the 'copticizing' model of the Syriac version id prior to the Greek text. Nor is there anything implausible in Greek elements being filtered out and Egyptian elements added in a 'copticizing' Greek or a Coptic reworking of the Greek text. A direct translation from Coptic to Syriac is, moreover, not made more probable by Barnes's arguments. Unfortunately the priority of the Syriac version has been accepted as a *communis opinio* without further analysis. See Andrew Louth, 'St. Athanasius and the Greek *Life of Antony*', *JTS* 39 (1988), pp. 504–509, and Peter Brown, *The Body and Society*, p. 213. Convincing refutations of the arguments of Draguet and Barnes for the priority of the Syriac version are given by Louise Abramowski, 'Vertritt die syrische Fassung die ursprüngliche Gestalt der Vita Antonii?', *Mélanges Antoine Guillaumont. Contributions à l'étude des christianismes orientaux* (*CO* 20), Genève 1988, pp. 47–56 and Rudolf Lorenz, 'Die griechische Vita Antonii und ihre syrische Fassung', *ZKG* 100 (1989), pp. 77–84.

3 See David Brakke, 'The Greek and Syriac Versions of the *Life of Antony*', *AB* 112 (1994), pp. 29–53

4 For the Arabic mss., see *GCAL* I, p. 312 and 456, to which large numbers of mss. kept in Coptic monasteries, especially in the monastery of St. Antony, have to be added. For some of them see Rubenson, 'Arabic Sources'. For the Ethiopic version, of which he is preparing an edition, see Louis Leloir, 'Premiers renseignements sur la vie d'Antoine en éthiopien', *Antidoron. Hommages à Maurice Geerard*, Wetteren 1984, pp. 9–11, and *idem*, 'Le prophétisme ecclésial d'Antoine', *After Chalcedon. Studies in Theology and Church History offered to Professor Albert van Roey for his seventieth birthday*, Leuven 1985, pp. 217–231.

The *Vita Antonii* was already in its earliest stages of transmission attributed to Athanasius of Alexandria as indicated by Evagrius of Antioch, Gregory of Nazianzus, Rufinus, Jerome, John Chrysostom and the *Vita Pachomii*.[1] Athanasius' authorship of the *Vita* was also generally taken for granted until Helmut Weingarten published his famous thesis in 1877, in which he not only denied Athanasius' authorship, but also the historicity of the account and even the existence of monasticism before the 330's.[2] The reaction to Weingarten's proposals was strong and his refusal to accept Athanasius as author was rapidly and unanimously rejected.[3]

Subsequent research has taken for granted that the *Vita* is an authentic work of Athanasius and has concentrated on questions of the purpose and literary composition of the text, and on what it reveals about the theology of Athanasius himself.[4] Some of Weingarten's and subsequently Reitzenstein's observations on the tensions within the text have, however, been resuscitated by Martin Tetz, suggesting that the *Vita* is Athanasius' revision and augmentation of an earlier life written by Serapion of Thmuis.[5] Although there has been little response to the attribution of an earlier *Vita* to Serapion, the suggestion that Athanasius is responsible only for the reworking of an original *Vita* has been widely accepted, especially since it is congruous with the proposed priority of the version underlying the Syriac text. Still, there has been no attempt, neither in the case of the Greek nor of the Syriac version, at comprehensive textual criticism, in search of different layers indicating a variety of sources and authors.

Although Athanasius' authorship was quickly reestablished, Weingarten's attack on the *Vita* as an historical source has had a more favourable reception. Regarding the *Vita* as a literary composition (and as a

---

An edition of the Arabic version or versions, most likely based on Coptic texts, and their Ethiopic translation would add important knowledge to the process of reception and adaptation of the text in the Coptic monastic tradition.

1 See Evagrius Antiochenus, *S. Athanasii episcopi Alexandrini praefatio* (*PG* 26, 837f.); Gregorius Nazianzenus, *Oratio 21* (*PG* 35, 1081); Rufinus, *HE* I.8; Hieronymus, *De viris illustribus*, 87, 88, and 125; John Chrysostom, *In Mattheam homiliae* 8.5 (*PG* 57.89) and *VP/G* 99. A more complete list of all references until the eighth century is given in Bartelink's edition p. 37–42.

2 See Helmut Weingarten, *Der Ursprung des Mönchtums im nachkonstantinischen Zeitalter*, Gotha 1877.

3 Weingarten's thesis was convincingly refuted as early as 1886 by Julius Mayer and Albert Eichhorn. Athanasius' authorship is taken for granted by Karl Holl, Eduard Schwartz, Richard Reitzenstein, Guidio Müller, in his *Lexicon Athanasianum*, Karl Heussi, Hermann Dörries and the patrologies of Altaner, Quasten and the *CPG*.

4 Roldanus, *Le Christ et l'homme*, pp. 277–348; *idem*, 'Die Vita Antonii als Spiegel der Theologie des Athanasius und ihr Weiterwirken bis ins 5. Jahrhundert', *Theologie und Philosophie* 58 (1983), pp. 194–216; Gregg & Groh, *Early Arianism*, pp. 131–159.

5 Tetz, 'Athanasius und die Vita Antonii'. The attribution to Serapion is based on his role in the *Vita* and on his two letters to the monks. For these, see René Draguet, 'Une lettre de Sérapion de Thmuis', pp. 1–25, and *PG* 40, 925–942. It is worth noting that Serapion is cited as author of a *Vita* in some of the Arabic manuscripts, see *GCAL* I, p. 458.

model for later hagiography), a large number of scholars suggested that it was written according to the rules of classical biography or even directly modelled on earlier lives of philosophers.[1] Though none of the many different models suggested has been able to explain the entire structure of the *Vita* in a convincing manner, the literary study of the text has clearly shown that it is a carefully structured composition.[2] The only undisputable parallel to the text of the *Vita* that has been found is the famous description of how Antony came out from what had been his self-chosen prison for twenty years as a mystic initiate from a shrine. In this case Richard Reitzenstein could adduce a passage from the *Vita Pythagorae,* which is so close that a literary borrowing has to be presumed.[3] Although his conclusion, that the *Vita* is nothing but a model for ascetic life, a model for which Athanasius is completely dependent on Greek literature and philosophy, has not met with general approval, the *Vita* has since been regarded primarily as the presentation of an ideal in the form of a biography with little or no historical value.

In these early studies on the form of the *Vita,* its relationship to the historical setting was of little or no concern, since it was taken for granted that the text was written either in order to present pagans with a Christian as the ideal philosopher, or in order to give Christians an ideal to imitate. With growing interest in monastic studies and the publication of new sources, this has changed. Instead of comparing the *Vita* with other lives, Hermann Dörries in one of the most important contributions to research on the *Vita* used the sayings attributed to Antony as his source for a study of the historical reliability of the biography. His conclusion was that the ideal presented in the *Vita* is a profound theological reworking of the story of a simple monk whose authentic words are preserved in the sayings.[4] While Dörries on the one hand was able to demonstrate the Athanasian character of the theology presented in the *Vita* and the obvious intent of the author to present Antony as a hero of the Church and of orthodox faith, he on the other maintained that there was not only a

1 For the studies by Mertel, Priessnig, Holl, Reitzenstein, List, Cavallin, and Schütt, see the bibliography and the excellent critical evaluation of previous research in G. J. M. Bartelink, 'Die literarische Gattung der Vita Antonii', *VC* 36 (1982), pp. 38–62.

2 See Bartelink, 'Die literarische Gattung der Vita Antonii', p. 59, and A. Priessnig, 'Die biographische Form der Plotinvita des Porphyrios und des Antoniuslebens des Athanasius', *BZ* 64 (1971), pp. 1–5.

3 *VA* 14. Athanasius describes Antony's appearance and the result of his long enclosure with the same expressions used in *Vita Pythagorae* 34.35 to describe the effects of the way of living practised by Pythagoras. The two texts are quoted and compared in Reitzenstein, *Des Athanasius Werk,* p. 14, with the conclusion that the *VA* is dependent on a lost source used by Poprhyry. The attempt by Bartelink to find echoes of Platon in the *Vita* is not equally convincing, see G. J. M. Bartelink, 'Echos an Platon's Phaedrus in der Vita Antonii', *Mnemosyne* 37 (1984), pp. 145–147.

4 Dörries, 'Die Vita Antonii', pp. 193–199.

historical foundation for the *Vita,* but also a fundamental accord between the monk and the bishop. In the *Vita* the true history of Antony was not distorted, but transformed. Two fundamental presuppositions of Dörries are, however, open to doubt. Firstly the reliability of the sayings as a historical source is questionable; secondly it can be doubted if the *Vita* is as unpolemical as he suggests. In a number of recent articles it has been suggested that the aim of the *Vita* was less to propagate the ideals of the Egyptian monks, than to correct them and enlisten the support of the monks for the author's ecclesiastical policy.[1]

In summary, it is obvious that the intense research on the *Vita Antonii* in the last hundred years has led to a state of greater confusion than ever before. The originality of the Greek text is questioned, as well as Athanasius' authorship. To some the tensions in the text indicate a variety of influences; to others its unity indicates a careful composition. While some regard the text as an important primary source for early monastic thought and life, others see it as a literary creation shaped on classical models for polemical hagiographical purposes. While some suppose the *Vita* to be written to promote the ideals of simple monks, other see its purpose as a critic of charismatic heterodoxy. The only consensus that can be detected is that the *Vita* in its Greek version has an Athanasian imprint, most obvious in the sermons, the philosophical debate and the interpretations of the struggle, and the intensified retreat into the desert.[2] The reliability, as far the the general outline of Antony's life is concerned, is, moreover, not only generally accepted but presupposed. Due to the attempts to trace the text back to an original version with roots in the Coptic monastic setting the reliability of the *Vita* as a source for this environment is even in the ascendant.[3]

Behind this confusion in research lies not only the problem to what extent the *Vita* presents *one* or *several* ideals, but also different views on the character of early monastic tradition represented by Antony, and on the relationship between this tradition and Athanasius. More important than the mere statement that the *Vita* is written to present the story of an ideal monk is the answer to the questions about the purpose of this presentation and the character of the alternative ideals against which

1 See Brian Brennan, 'Athanasius' Vita Antonii. A Sociological Interpretation', *VC* 39 (1985), pp. 209–227; M. Williams, 'The *Life of Antony*', pp. 30–40; Gregg & Groh, *Early Arianism,* pp. 142–153.

2 See Dörries, 'Die Vita Antonii', pp. 177–188, and Roldanus, *Le Christ et l'homme,* pp. 286–294.

3 Not only the predilection for the Syriac version, but also the view that Athanasius used earlier sources, as proposed by Tetz, has strengthened the tendency to rely on the historical information of the *Vita.* A recent example of this is Peter Brown, *The Body and Society,* pp. 213–235, where the *Vita* and *i.a.* the *Letters of Antony* are used indiscriminately.

Athanasius contrasts his image of Antony.[1] Although the borrowing from the *Vita Pythagorae* and the debate with the philosophers indicate that the author also had pagan readers in mind, there is no reason to doubt the explicit statement that the text was written for a monastic audience, and that Antony was depicted as a saint in order that the readers should emulate his life.[2]

The problem is to what extent the ideal presented corresponded to actual monastic life in the Egyptian desert and actually incorporated earlier traditions. Is the *Vita* an encomium based on reliable sources or a bid for support for the author's theology or even a commended alternative to contemporary heterodox practices? In the previous chapter it has been established that there are good reasons to doubt that the early monks were as uneducated, as obedient to ecclesiastical office, and as stoutly orthodox as Athanasius depicts Antony. The following comparison with the letters will reveal if and to what extent Antony's theology as presented in his letters is reproduced in the *Vita* and to what extent the image of Antony gained from the letters is consistent with the image or images presented in the *Vita*.

2. THE *VITA* AND THE THEOLOGY OF THE LETTERS

The most striking contrast between the *Vita* and the letters is the contrast between the emphasis of the first on spiritual warfare and the second on knowledge, between ἄσκησις in the *Vita* and γνῶσις in the letters. In the *Vita* the author implores his readers to emulate the ideal presented, in the letters he implores them to understand the teaching presented. In the first Antony repeatedly stresses Christ's part in the struggle against the demons, in the latter he underlines that self-knowledge is the most essential spiritual weapon. This striking difference is, however, partly to be accounted for by the dissimilarity in genre, purpose and historical setting of the texts. The letters are the spiritual testament of a master written in order that his disciples might not be diverted from a sound understanding of spiritual things or from endurance in their ascesis. The *Vita* is a story about a saintly life and the superiority of Christianity probably intended for readers more impressed by Greek philosophy or charismatic heretics than by the theology of the Church. While Antony refers his disciples to self-knowledge as the path of salvation, Athanasius refers to the imitation of an example, of Antony himself.

[1] See the well founded methodological critique of Dörries in M. Williams, 'The *Life of Antony*', pp. 35–38.

[2] See *VA* Prologus.

Instead of *gnosis,* which is not a prominent term in the text, the *Vita* has a strong emphasis on the need for rational thinking. The long sermon to the monks repeatedly stresses the need to analyse and understand the temptations, or the manifold tricks of the demons, as they are called. It is by rational reasoning that demonic prophesy is ridiculed, in much the same way as, earlier in the text, Antony himself is reported to have unmasked the temptations in his way by means of sound logic.[1] Although references to self-knowledge are rare, also the *Vita* sees knowledge about one's own life as a precondition for a discipline (ἄσκησις) that overcomes the devil.[2] Moreover, it is not only by considering what Christ has granted him, but also by reflecting on 'the spiritual part of the soul' (τὸ νοερὸν τῆς ψυχῆς) that Antony is said to have extinguished the fire of the devil's deceptions.[3]

The debate with the philosophers, which is the only part of the *Vita* that really presents a theological argument, at first seems to contradict the image of Antony as a man of *gnosis.* Here Antony is presented as someone who sets faith against knowledge. A close reading, however, makes it clear that the conflict between the philosophers and Antony in the *Vita* is not a conflict between faith as irrational belief and knowledge as rational understanding, but a conflict on how to acquire true knowledge. It is the sound mind (νοῦς) and not blind belief that is opposed to the study of literature (γράμματα) and not to knowledge:

> 'What do you say? Which is first—mind or letters? And which is the cause of which—the mind of the letters, or the letters of the mind?' When they replied that the mind is first and invented the letters, Antony said: 'Now you see that in the person whose mind is sound there is no need for the letters'.[4]

In both the letters and the *Vita* the possibility of true knowledge lies in the direct relation between God and man through the spiritual part of his soul (τὸ νοερὸν τῆς ψυχῆς), *i.e.* the mind (ὁ νοῦς), which is the sign that man is created in the image of God. In his criticism of the philosophers Antony even implies that the mind is unchangeable. It is not the soul that is

1 In *VA* 21–38 Antony sets out to explain systematically the traits and methods of the demons, and in 39–41 he reports about his own experiences. In *VA* 11 he reacts to a temptation by a rational argument, and in 31–33 he reduces the demonic power to prophesy to a matter of capacity for fast running.

2 See also the emphasis on 'giving attention to one's own life', used as a description of what was the aim of the ascetics when Antony started his own ascetic life (*VA* 3), and the word used for what he achieved by his first ascetic training, συσφίγγω ἑαυτόν (*VA* 8).

3 *VA* 5: καὶ τὸ νοερὸν τῆς ψυχῆς λογιζόμενος, ἀπεσβέννυε τὸν ἄνθρακα τῆς πλάνης ἐκείνου. The importance of the spiritual part of the soul (τὸ νοερὸν τῆς ψυχῆς), *i.e.* the mind, is also stressed in *VA* 20 and 45.

4 *VA* 73: Ὑμεῖς δὲ τί λέγετε; Τί πρῶτόν ἐστι, νοῦς ἢ γράμματα; καὶ τί τίνος αἴτιον, ὁ νοῦς τῶν γραμμάτων, ἢ τὰ γράμματα τοῦ νοῦ; Τῶν δὲ εἰπόντων πρῶτον εἶναι τὸν νοῦν, καὶ τῶν γραμμάτων εὑρετήν· ἔφη ὁ Ἀντώνιος· Ὧ τοίνυν ὁ νοῦς ὑγιαίνει, τούτῳ οὐκ ἀναγκαῖα τὰ γράμματα (*VA* 73).

an image of the mind, but the mind that is an image of God.[1] The basic concept of knowledge in the *Vita* is not too different from that of the letters. 'Knowledge through an act of faith' is for Antony of the *Vita* rooted in the same natural disposition of man as is self-knowledge for the author of the letters.[2]

> Tell us first, how are things, and especially knowledge about God, accurately conceived—through verbal proof or through the power of faith? And which is prior, the power of faith or the verbal proof? When they replied that the power of faith is prior, and that this is accurate knowledge, Antony replied: 'Well said! Faith comes from the disposition of the soul, but arguments from the skill of him who constructs them. Thus for those who have the power of faith verbal proof is unnecessary or probably even useless.'[3]

It is thus not the concept of knowledge manifest in Antony's letters that is the target of the polemic of the *Vita.* When Antony is repeatedly presented as an 'unlettered' man the alternative is not the man of *gnosis,* but the man of letters.[4] The use of the concept 'faith' (πίστις) and the constant references to revelation are not signs of a confrontation with a theology such as Antony's, but part of the apologetic tradition in which Athanasius stood.

The emphasis in the letters on original creation as rational, and on the need to return to this original rational state, to the true nature of man, is also in accordance with central notions in the *Vita.* In the polemic against the philosophers it is very much the rational character of Christianity that Antony is said to have emphasized, while accusing his opponents of relying on inventions and logical somersaults. What is true is what is natural,

1 *VA* 74: καὶ λοιπὸν καὶ αὐτὸν τὸν νοῦν διὰ τὴν ψυχὴν τρεπτὸν εἰσάγετε. ʻΟποία γὰρ ἦν ἡ εἰκών, τοιοῦτον ἀνάγκη κἀκεῖνον εἶναι, οὗ ἐστιν ἡ εἰκών. Ὅταν δὲ περὶ τοῦ νοῦ τοιαῦτα νομίζετε, ἐνθυμεῖσθε, ὅτι καὶ εἰς αὐτὸν τὸν Πατέρα τοῦ νοῦ βλασφημεῖτε (Then you make even the mind changeable because of the soul. For, as the image is, so is by necessity that of which it is an image. But when you think that way about the mind, realize that you also blaspheme against the Father of the mind).

2 As has been emphasized repeatedly, it is in this speech to the philosophers that the theology of Athanasius is most explicitly present in the *Vita.* As noted above there are strong links between this theology and that of Antony's letters. In both man is created in the image and likeness of God primarily by being rational, endowed with an uncorruptible mind. For the anthropology of the *Vita Antonii* in relation to other writings of Athanasius, see J. Roldanus, *Le Christ et l'Homme dans la Théologie d'Athanase,* pp. 286–348. For the letters see above, Chapter IV.

3 *VA* 77: εἴπατέ μοι πρῶτον ὑμεῖς, τὰ πράγματα, καὶ μάλιστα ἡ περὶ τοῦ Θεοῦ γνῶσις, πῶς ἀκριβῶς διαγινώσκεται, δι' ἀποδείξεως λόγων, ἢ δι' ἐνεργείας πίστεως; καὶ τί πρεσβύτερόν ἐστιν, ἡ δι' ἐνεργείας πίστις, ἢ ἡ διὰ λόγων ἀπόδειξις; Τῶν δὲ ἀποκριναμένων, πρεσβυτέραν εἶναι τὴν δι ἐνεργείας πίστιν, καὶ ταύτην εἶναι τὴν ἀκριβῆ γνῶσις· ἔφη ὁ 'Αντώνιος· Καλῶς εἴπατε· ἡ μὲν γὰρ πίστις ἀπὸ διαθέσεως ψυχῆς γίνεται· ἡ δὲ διαλεκτικὴ ἀπὸ τέχνης συντιθέντων ἐστίν. Οὐκοῦν οἷς πάρεστιν ἡ διὰ πίστεως ἐνέργεια, τούτοις οὐκ ἀναγκαία, ἢ τάχα καὶ περιττὴ ἡ διὰ λόγων ἀπόδειξις.

4 See *VA* 1, 72–73 and below, p. 141–144. Cf. *VA* 33 where Antony states that no one is condemned for his lack of knowledge and study.

whereas the falsehood of paganism is evident in the perversity of its ideas and myths.[1] That Christian life is a return to what is natural is also the essence of the teaching about about virtue in Antony's sermon to the monks. Here, as in the polemic against the philosophers, what is Christian is set against what is pagan. But the difference is not between two sets of virtues, a Biblical and a non-Biblical, but between natural virtue as a gift of creation and the virtues of philosophical studies. It is simply by being as he was made that man is preserved for the Lord.[2]

> But do not be afraid to hear about virtue, and do not be a stranger to the term. It is not distant from us, nor does it arise outside us. It is an action in us, and the task is easy if only we want it... Thus, all virtue needs is our will, since it is in us, and arises from us. When the soul maintains what is spiritual, virtue arises. To maintain what is according to nature, is for it to remain as it was made—and it was made good and perfectly straight... That the soul is straight means that its spiritual [part] is in its natural state, as it was made.[3]

It is in this context the often discussed passage in chapter fourteen of the *VA*, where the author of the *Vita Antonii* clearly uses a description of Pythagoras taken from the source used by Porphyry in his *Vita Pythagorae*.[4] Again, the parallels between the views behind the *Vita* and the letters are evident. In the biography Antony is presented, when reappearing after twenty years of isolation, as preserved in his former condition, in perfect harmony, tranquillity, and purity, 'guided by reason and steadfast in what accords with nature'.[5] The ideal is the unchanged natural condition in which the mind governs soul and body in perfect harmony. In the first letter, describing this harmony between body and soul, it is even said about the body that it 'has taken on something of that other spiritual body, which will be taken on at the resurrection of the just', as it is stated in the first letter.[6] The concept of 'the peace of the soul', recurrent in the *Vita,* and the 'rest', the *anapausis,* of the letters are

1 See *VA* 74–76.

2 *VA* 20 Τηρήσωμεν τῷ Κυρίῳ τὴν ψυχήν· ἵν' αὐτὸς ἐπιγνῷ τὸ ποίημα αὐτοῦ, οὕτως οὖσαν τὴν ψυχήν ὥσπερ πεποίηκεν αὐτήν (Let us preserve the soul for the Lord, so that he may recognize his work, the soul being the same as he made it). After having ridiculed the prophecies of the demons Antony admits a divine foreknowledge, but preserves it for him whose 'soul is pure in every way and in its natural state' (ὅτι καθαρεύουσα ψυχὴ πανταχόθεν, καὶ κατὰ φύσιν ἑστῶσα) *VA* 34.

3 *VA* 20: Μὴ φοβεῖσθε δὲ ἀκούοντες περὶ ἀρετῆς, μηδὲ ξενίζεσθε περὶ τοῦ ὀνόματος· οὐ γὰρ μακρὰν ἀφ' ἡμῶν ἐστιν οὐδ' ἔξωθεν ἡμῶν συνίσταται, ἐν ἡμῖν δέ ἐστι τὸ ἔργον, καὶ εὔκολόν ἐστι τὸ πρᾶγμα, ἐὰν μόνον θελήσωμεν. ... Οὐκοῦν ἡ ἀρετὴ τοῦ θέλειν ἡμῶν μόνου χρείαν ἔχει· ἐπειδήπερ ἐν ἡμῖν ἐστι, καὶ ἐξ ἡμῶν συνίσταται. Τῆς γὰρ ψυχῆς τὸ νοερὸν κατὰ φύσιν ἐχούσης, ἡ ἀρετὴ συνίσταται. Κατὰ φύσιν δὲ ἔχει, ὅταν ὡς γέγονε μένῃ, γέγονε δὲ καλὴ καὶ εὐθὴς λίαν. ... Τὸ γὰρ εὐθεῖαν εἶναι τὴν ψυχήν, τοῦτό ἐστι τὸ κατὰ φύσιν νοερὸν αὐτῆς ὡς ἐκτίσθη.

4 See Reitzenstein, *Des Athanasius Werk,* p. 14, and above, p. 130, note 3.

5 *VA* 14: Τῆς δὲ ψυχῆς πάλιν καθαρὸν τὸ ἦθος. ... ἀλλ' ὅλος ἦν ἴσος, ὡς ὑπὸ τοῦ λόγου κυβερνώμενος, καὶ ἐν τῷ κατὰ φύσιν ἑστώς.

6 *Ep. Ant.* I.71. See also the description of Antony at the end of his life in *VA* 93.

undoubtedly related. But while Antony still longed for rest when he wrote his letters, Athanasius presents him as having achieved it in an early stage of his ascetic career.[1]

In the letters the most manifest sign of an Origenist background was the teaching on the cosmic fall from unity to diversity. Cosmology is not a theme in the *Vita,* but as in the letters the question of the nature of the demons prompts the author to discuss the origin of evil. In the beginning of the sermon on the demons, the same emphasis as in the letters is given to the demons as parts of God's creation. In words similar to what we find in the letters, Antony is said to have stated that the demons were not created as such, but that they fell from 'the heavenly mind'.[2] In his debate with the philosophers in the *Vita* Antony returns to the question of the fall. Here, however, he defends the incarnation by contrasting it with what he thinks is even more ridiculous, namely ideas akin to the Origenist teaching indicated in the letters. Most probably it is precisely the idea of the preexistence of the souls and their fall from the 'mind', the νοῦς, that is rejected.[3] Although not a direct conflict, the difference between the passages suggests tension between a more authentic Origenist tradition and the new emphases of theology at the time of the Arian controversy.[4]

As indicated by the expression 'the spiritual part of the soul', the *Vita* presupposes the same Platonic foundation for its anthropology as the letters. The ideal is the same in both, stability and peace as a result of the transformation of the soul and the body through purification in accordance with the spiritual in man, his *nous*. Although 'motion' (κίνησις) is not a central concept in the *Vita,* we find the same identification of evil with

1 See Roldanus, 'Die Vita Antonii als Spiegel', p. 196, and Louth, 'St. Athanasius and the Greek *Life of Antony'*, p. 505f..

2 VA 22: Πρῶτον τοίνυν τοῦτο γινώσκωμεν, ὅτι οἱ δαίμονες οὐ καθ' ὃ δαίμονες καλοῦνται, οὕτω γεγόνασιν· οὐδὲν γὰρ κακὸν ἐποίησεν ὁ Θεός· ἀλλὰ καλοὶ μὲν γεγόνασι καὶ αὐτοί, ἐκπεσόντες δὲ ἀπὸ τῆς οὐρανίου φρονήσεως, καὶ λοιπὸν περὶ τὴν γῆν καλινδούμενοι. That φρόνησις is used synonymously to νοῦς is not only substantiated by the early Latin version having *mens,* but also by the fact that νοῦς is rarely used in the *Vita,* and usually replaced by φρόνησις, or τὸ νοερὸν τῆς ψυχῆς.

3 *VA* 74: Πῶς δὲ χλευάζειν τολμᾶτε ἡμᾶς, λέγοντας τὸν Χριστὸν ἄνθρωπον πεφανερῶσθαι· ὅπου γε ὑμεῖς, ἐκ τοῦ νοῦ τὴν ψυχὴν ὁρίζοντες, φάσκετε πεπλανῆσθαι αὐτὴν καὶ πεπτωκέναι ἀπὸ τῆς ἀψῖδος τῶν οὐρανῶν εἰς σῶμα. The reading ἐκ τοῦ νοῦ of some of the mss. and accepted by Bartelink in contrast to ἐκ τοῦ οὐρανοῦ preferred by *PG* and most modern translations, is not only a *lectio difficilior,* where it is quite plausible that οὐρανοῦ in the standard text is taken from the second phrase, but is also substantiated by the early Latin version having 'quando vos mentem illam summam separatis de anima'. In the Syriac version the entire anti-Origenist passage is missing. The explanation for this omittance in the Syriac suggested by Abramowski, 'Vertritt die syrische Fassung', p. 55, is not completely convincing. It is as likely that the responsibility rests with the strong Origenistic current in Syriac monasticism in this period.

4 For this tension in Athanasius' writings, see Louth, *The Origins of Christian Mystical tradition,* pp. 77–80. For the Arian crisis as a conflict about the legacy of Origen see Rowen Williams, *Arius,* pp. 131–157, 175–178.

feelings of unrest as in the letters, and the same emphasis on bringing the body under control.[1] In contrast to the letters the emphasis of the *Vita* is, however, not on the passions of the soul, but on the passions of the body. The ascetic zeal, expressed in the contempt Antony felt for his body and the shame he felt for his need to eat, goes far beyond the views presented on repentance and purification of body and soul in the first letter.[2]

This different emphasis is caused by a completely different perspective on fallen man and the history of salvation. While the failure of God's acts for the salvation of man is a central theme in the letters, there is nothing comparable in the *Vita.* Instead of regarding the consequences of the fall as a 'growing wound', the *Vita,* in accordance with Athanasius' theological outlook, regards them as the state of mortality.[3] For Athanasius and the *Vita* the essence of salvation is Christ's victory over death, a victory which reestablishes immortality. Thus there is no place for the dynamic and mythological interpretation of man and his history which characterizes the letters. The Christian, represented by Antony, is in essence already restored; what must be conquered is something external. Certainly the demons are frightening and constantly surround Antony, but through the power of Christ and his cross they are easily dispersed. The Old Testament is in the *Vita* not a history of God's unsuccessful attempts to save man, the failure of which forced Him to send his Son, but a collection of examples for the zealous. Only once is the law of Moses mentioned, and the few references to commandments all refer to the commandments of the Lord in the New Testament.[4]

1 One of the very few Biblical quotations common to the *Vita* and the letters is 1 Cor. 9:27, 'I castigate my body, and bring it into subjection'. See *VA* 7 and *Ep. Ant.* I.32, 40. See also the parallel between *VA* 45 'that the body should be subservient to the soul' and *Ep. Ant.* I.27–32.

2 See *VA* 45: Καὶ γὰρ καὶ μέλλων ἐσθίειν καὶ κοιμᾶσθαι, καὶ ἐπὶ ταῖς ἄλλαις ἀνάγκαις τοῦ σώματος ᾐσχύνετο, λογιζόμενος τὸ τῆς ψυχῆς νοερόν (Also when he was about to eat or sleep or to attend the other bodily necessities, he was ashamed as he thought about the spiritual part of the soul). See also *VA* 47 stressing Antony's ascetic ardour in never washing himself, and the subsequent comment that nobody ever saw his naked body. The shame over the naked body is also manifest in the story about Amoun's visit to Antony in *VA*.60: Εἶτα ἀπελθόντος τοῦ Θεοδώρου, ᾐσχύνετο πάλιν καὶ ἑαυτὸν γυμνὸν ἰδεῖν (Then, even after Theodore had departed, he was ashamed over seeing himself naked). Commenting on the first passage quoted above Festugière, 'Sur une nouvelle édition du »De vita Pythagorica« de Jamblique', *REG* 50 (1937), p. 494, indicates the reason for this shame by contrasting it with what is said about the heroes of pagan hagiography. In the latter the saint is regarded as a god, and thus above any need for food; in consequence he must not be seen eating. In the Christian texts, the saint is a limited human being, suffering under the needs of the body, ashamed that he cannot overcome them completely. In his interpretation of the view of the body in the desert fathers, Peter Brown overlooks this side of the *Vita;* see his *Body and Society,* pp. 213–240.

3 See Dörries, 'Die Vita Antonii', pp. 182–184.

4 See *VA* 81 for the single reference to Moses and the written law. References to the commandments are found in *VA* 33 and 55.

The focus on Christ in the *Vita* has long been noted and used as the major argument for an Athanasian authorship and as an indication of the purpose of the entire text. Labeled as 'das christologische Korrektiv' this emphasis has even been regarded as the sign of a reworking of an older less Christocentric text.[1] According to the *Vita* it is not Antony who overcomes the demons, but Christ in him; it is not the power of the saint but the sign of the cross that expels the demons and performs miracles. Against this manifest Christocentric tendency of the *Vita* there are, especially in the Syriac version, passages which stress the image of Antony as a holy man to the extent of presenting him almost as a saviour in himself. These passages have consequently been regarded as proofs for the non-Athanasian and more original and authentic version.[2]

A comparison with the letters shows that this Christocentric perspective in the *Vita* is completely alien to them. This difference is indicated also by the preference for the name 'Jesus' in the letters, in contrast to the *Vita,* in which we usually find 'Christ'.[3] In the letters the emphasis is on the coming, the *parousia,* of Jesus and on the significance of his mission, while the emphasis in the *Vita* is on what Christ does in the Christian. It is the love of Christ, the mention of his name, the faith in him, the sign of his cross, and the zeal, virginity and martyrdom for his sake that are essential to the *Vita*. Even in the debate with the philosophers the Christological arguments are there to explain the presence of Christ in the Christian. It is because of the incarnation, of God and the Son of God appearing as a man, that the Christian has his power. In order to show what really matters, the debate, moreover, ends with Antony cleansing some of the bystanders from demons with the sign of the cross.[4]

If Christ plays an extremely important part in the *Vita,* the opposite must be said about the Holy Spirit—the term does not even occur in the text. The word spirit (πνεῦμα), which is also extremely rare, usually refers to the evil spirits, especially to the spirit of fornication (τὸ πνεῦμα

1 See Louth, 'St. Athanasius and the Greek *Life of Antony*', p. 504ff.; Tetz, 'Athanasius und die Vita Antonii', p. 20. Festugière, 'Sur une nouvelle édition du »De vita Pythagorica« de Jamblique', p. 491, speaks about an 'affirmation revient sans cesse comme un refrain', and Dörries writes ('Die Vita Antonii', p. 173): 'Es ist geradezu das Kennzeichen der Vita Antonii, an allen entscheidenden Stellen als den eigentlichen Handelnden und Wirkenden den Herrn und seine Gnade einzuführen'. In his summary, Roldanus, *Le Christ et l'Homme,* pp. 364–370, also emphasizes how the Athanasian interpretation of Christ has structured the *Vita.*

2 Tetz, *op.cit.,* pp. 20–27, and Barnes, 'Angel of Light or Mystic Initiate', pp. 353–368.

3 In the Georgian version of the letters *Jesus* occurs alone 12 times, *Christ Jesus* or *Jesus Christ* 12 times, and *Christ* alone 10 times. In the *Vita* the name *Jesus* never occurs alone, *Jesus Christ* and *Christ Jesus* only seven, but *Christ* alone 41 times. It is also worth mentioning that the term 'Christian' occurs frequently in the *Vita,* and once 'Christianity' is also mentioned, terms completely absent from the letters.

4 *VA* 80.

τῆς πορνείας). Only once in the entire *Vita* is there a reference to the Spirit as a giver of grace.[1] The contrast with the language of the letters could not be greater. To a certain extent it is Christ who, in the *Vita*, plays the part which is given to the Spirit in the letters. The main reason for the discrepancy lies, however, in different understandings of ascesis and of what the Christian himself achieves in his salvation.

In the letters ascesis is mainly the method of purification of body and soul in order to bring them into harmony and regain man's natural condition. Because of the weakness of the body and the soul, and their susceptibility to the influence of the evil spirits, ascesis has to be practised constantly, with endurance and discrimination. It is a struggle and a suffering in which man has to pray for the compassion of God, who grants his spirit as a consoler and guide without, however, liberating man from his responsibility for his salvation.[2] In the *Vita* ascesis is above all seen as *the* preparation for the warfare against the demons, it makes man strong and invincible, it frightens the demons and pleases God. While the letters speak about penance and purity, the *Vita* speaks about power and perfection. While Antony of the letters is greatly troubled and vexed in his spirit, Antony of the *Vita* is calm, filled with joy and peace. His ascesis and piety have made him righteous, and he has nothing to fear, in contrast to the author of the letters who trembles with fear, knowing that he has nothing 'to render the Lord for the love he receives'.

This difference is also evident in how the demons are described in the two texts. Though the letters and the *Vita* agree on the origin of the demons, and on their multitude and cunning, their parts in the spiritual struggle are quite different. In the letters the demons are primarily responsible for hatred and contempt, for weariness and despair. They are bodiless and invisible and manifest themselves only in the deeds of men. They fill men with deceit, and when man feeds on them they become his food and tie down his 'heavy' body, making it a vessel of death.[3] In the *Vita* the demons can, on the contrary, be seen and heard, they smite and run, they speak and prophecy. They appear and transform themselves, they discuss and plan, they are hurt and frightened. Nowhere else is the creative hand of the author as visible as here. In his piece of writing the demons have become actors playing against Christ in a cosmic drama visualized in Antony's struggle.[4] Their warfare is described in three

1 *VA* 22: Διὸ καὶ πολλῆς εὐχῆς, καὶ ἀσκήσεώς ἐστι χρεία· ἵνα τις, λαβὼν διὰ τοῦ πνεύματος χάρισμα διακρίσεως πνευμάτων, γνῶναι δυνηθῇ τὰ κατ' αὐτούς.

2 See *Ep. Ant.* I and above p. 85f..

3 *Ep. Ant.* VI. 27–55. Cf. above, pp. 86–88 on the demonology of the letters.

4 See Jean Daniélou, 'Les démons de l'air dans la "Vie d'Antoine"', *Antonius Magnus Eremita 356–1956* (*SA* 38), Rome 1958, pp. 136–147, and Plácido Alvarez, 'Demon Stories in the *Life of Antony* by Athanasius', *CS* 23 (1988), pp. 101–118.

stages: their evil suggestions and seductions, their phantasms and terrors, and finally their claims to work for us.[1] Of these three, the first is mentioned but not emphasized in the letters. The second, very prominent in the *Vita,* especially in the description of Antony's own life, is not only absent, but foreign to the letters. It is only the third that is really parallel in both texts. The attitude of Antony towards the demons is also very different in the two texts. In the *Vita* the demons are ridiculed and treated with contempt since they have no power; they can easily be chased away with the sign of the cross and a phrase from the Bible. In the letters they are omnipresent; making the bodies of man their dwelling, they condemn him to lifelong warfare within himself. His hope for deliverance rests with his prayers for God's compassion.

In spite of the apparent difficulties in comparing a complex text such as the *Vita* with a corpus of unsystematic letters such as Antony's, some general conclusions and suggestions for further study can be made. On the one hand it is obvious that much of the philosophical and theological background that is presupposed in the presentation of the hero of the *Vita* is shared by the author of the letters.[2] On the other there are important differences, which reveal a tendency in the *Vita* that is alien to the letters. The most obvious sign of this difference in perspective is the emphasis in the *Vita* on Christ and his victorious cross as the active force of the Christian. This emphasis is firmly rooted in Athanasius' theology and part of the Nicene tradition that developed during the Arian controversy.[3] Although Antony shared Athanasius' dislike of Arian Christology, the letters show that he did not draw the same conclusions as his biographer on what this implied for the doctrine of salvation. While Athanasius rightly depicted Antony as an anti-Arian he, nevertheless, transformed his theology.

This transformation, reflected in some of the tensions of the *Vita,* is not without parallels in the tension between the *Contra Gentes* and the *De Incarnatione Verbi* and represents the shift of perspective from the turn of the third to the middle of the fourth century. This theological shift is linked to a historical development that is behind the other major difference between the letters and the *Vita,* the victory of Christianity over paganism. To Antony of the letters pagan philosophy and Christian faith do not seem

1 A summary of these stages is given in *VA* 23. The description of Antony's own struggle against the demons is structured according to the same stages.

2 Athanasius' dependence on Origen is well established; see *i.a.* Dörries, 'Die Vita Antonii', p. 188f., Louth, *The Origins,* p. 77f., and Meijering, *Athanasius,* pp. 9–29. For parallels between the letters and *Contra Gentes,* see Chapter IV.

3 The arguments by Gregg and Groh that the *Vita* is a part of Athanasius' polemic against the Arians are convincing. But their conclusion that the monks in Egypt were the target for this polemic is less well founded. See Gregg & Groh, *Early Arianism,* pp. 131–159.

to have been contradictory, they were both a quest for the ultimate. Antony of the *Vita*, however, was an ardent antagonist of philosophical reasoning, a man to whom precise knowledge (ἡ ἀκριβῆ γνῶσις) depends on the power of faith (ἡ δι' ἐνέργεια πίστις) and not logical reasoning (ἡ διὰ λογῶν ἀπόδειξις).[1]

3. THE *VITA ANTONII* AND THE AUTHOR OF THE LETTERS

The main purpose of the *Vita* is, however, not to present a theology, but the life of Antony, the author of the letters. The question is to what extent the letters can be adduced to support or reject that presentation. Although they contain almost nothing biographical, it is still possible to draw some important conclusions about Antony from them. The letters reveal that he must not only have been literate but also possessed of some education. His theology shows that he must have had a fairly good knowledge about contemporary philosophical ideas and a fair acquaintance with Origenist tradition and exegesis. The common structure of several of the letters and the way he refers to his correspondents shows that he had probably enjoyed a leadership in several monastic communities for quite some time. References in the letters indicate that he was an ardent anti-Arian and that he lived in the vicinity of Arsinoë. His theological background, his emphasis on self-knowledge and the lack of references to authoritative writings or to ecclesiastical leaders suggest that he was what could be called a charismatic teacher of spiritual *gnosis*.

In contrast to this image gained from the letters the *Vita* allegedly presents Antony as an illiterate monk not knowing Greek. This view is based on the statement in the first chapter that he did not attend school, and on his presentation as a 'simple' man (ἰδιώτης) who had not studied letters (γράμματα μὴ μαθών), as well as on the fact that an interpreter is mentioned in the debates with the Greek philosophers.[2] But if these isolated statements are confronted with other parts of the *Vita*, it is clear that the crucial term *grammata* cannot in the *Vita* refer to elementary education in how to read and write.[3] On the contrary, there is ample evidence in the *Vita* for literary activity in connection with Antony. When

1 See *VA* 77.

2 See *VA* 1: γράμματα μὲν μαθεῖν οὐκ ἠνέσχετο; *VA* 72 καὶ φρόνιμος δὲ ἦν λίαν· καὶ τὸ θαυμαστὸν ὅτι, γράμματα μὴ μαθών, ἀγχίνους ἦν καὶ συνετὸς ἄνθρωπος, *VA* 73 ἄλλων δὲ πάλιν τοιούτων ἀπαντησάντων πρὸς αὐτὸν ἐν τῷ ὄρει τῷ ἔξω, καὶ νομιζόντων χλευάζειν, ὅτι μὴ μεμάθηκε γράμματα. For the interpreter *VA* 74: ἔλεγε δι' ἑρμηνέως, τοῦ καλῶς τὰ ἐκείνου διερμηνεύοντος. The interpreter is also mentioned in chapter 72 and 77. Significantly, Antony is never called ἀγράμματος, which is the common term for illiterate.

3 This was pointed out already in 1939 in the unfortunately overlooked article 'A propos des Letters de S. Antoine l'Ermite' by Gérard Garitte. The article is not even mentioned in von Hertling's comprehensive study 'Studi storici Antoniani'.

emulating the ascetics around him he paid special attention to one of them in his studies;[1] when teaching his disciples self-control he recommended them to write down their acts and thoughts;[2] when describing the acts of the demons he relates how they interfere with the reading of the ascetic;[3] when receiving a letter from the emperor he finally agrees to respond;[4] and when hearing about the persecutions by the Arians he is reported to have sent a letter to a military commander.[5]

It is, moreover, evident that the use of the expression 'to learn letters' (γράμματα μαθεῖν) in the *Vita* is connected with the important dichotomy throughout the text between Hellenistic philosophy and mythology on the one hand and the Christian faith on the other. The Greeks are reported to travel widely to gain knowledge (ἵνα γράμματα μάθωσιν) while there is no need for the Christian to go abroad on account of the kingdom of heaven since it is within himself.[6] The philosophers depend on their own learning, the letters, whereas Antony depends on the mind given to him by God.[7] It is thus evident that the phrase is used in the *Vita* not to emphasize that Antony was illiterate, but simply as a way to express the difference between pagan philosophy and Christian faith as the means to obtain true knowledge. Most probably the real background for Antony's alleged illiteracy is the description of Jesus in John 7:15.[8]

The same is *mutatis mutandis* true about the question of language. For the author of the *Vita* it is important to present Antony as the opposite of a learned Greek philosopher. He must have been unlettered, since he was, as it is written, only taught by God (θεοδίδακτος).[9] He was not someone who knew pagan culture, and he did not care about it; his was another city, another citizenship.[10] His fame did not depend on his profound knowledge

1 *VA* 4.

2 *VA* 55.

3 *VA* 25.

4 *VA* 81.

5 *VA* 86.

6 See *VA* 20.

7 *VA* 72. Cf. *VA* 77 quoted above, p. 134. With a quotation from 1 Cor. 2:4, this contrast is again expressed at the end of the debate as a contrast between syllogisms and faith: εἰ ἀκμὴν ὑμεῖς ἀπιστεῖτε ζητοῦντες τοὺς ἐκ τῶν λόγων συλλογισμούς. ἡμεῖς μὲν οὐκ. ἐν πειθοῖ σοφίας ἑλληνικῆς λόγοις, ὡς εἶπεν ὁ διδάσκαλος ἡμῶν, ἀποδείκνυμεν· τῇ δὲ πίστει πείθομεν ἐναργῶς προλαμβανούσῃ τὴν ἐκ τῶν λόγων κατασκευήν (*VA* 80).

8 πῶς οὗτος γράμματα οἶδεν μὴ μεμαθηκώς;

9 *VA* 66, quoting John 6:45. See also *VA* 85 where the intelligence of Antony is a sign of God's presence precisely because he is a common man: ἀκούσας δὲ ὁ στρατηλάτης ταῦτα καὶ ἕτερα πολλα παρ' αὐτοῦ, θαυμάσας, ἔλεγεν, ἀληθῶς εἶναι τοῦτον δοῦλον τοῦ θεοῦ· πόθεν γὰρ ἰδιώτῃ τοιοῦτος καὶ τοσοῦτος νοῦς, εἰ μὴ ἦν ἀγαπώμενος ὑπὸ τοῦ θεοῦ.

10 See *VA* 14 for the expression 'making the desert a city' and 'the citizenship of the heavens'. In *VA* 44 this new society created by his example and word is described. The worthlessness of culture and possession is emphasized in *VA* 17, and exemplified by his

of pagan wisdom or a particular skill, only on his God-given piety.[1] Thus it is natural to find that an interpreter is mentioned precisely in his debates with the philosophers. Elsewhere in the *Vita,* however, there is no mention of any interpreter: not in connection with the letter of the emperor, nor in his dealings with governors and judges, nor during his visits to Alexandria. Moreover, the philosophical and theological language of his sermons and arguments in the *Vita* definitely presupposes a knowledge of Greek at least as much as the letters do.[2]

Due to the tendency of the *Vita* to regard Antony as unlettered his education is of no importance in the text. That he did not attend school is simply a *topos* fitting into the purpose of the *Vita.* Of greater interest are the reports about a long period of ascetic training before Antony leaves the neighbourhood of the village and shuts himself up in the deserted fortress. He is said to have spent no less than seventeen years learning from a number of ascetic teachers, each with his particular ascetic speciality.[3] Though the *Vita* later on plays down the importance of this education, it is not denied that Antony had a long period of ascetic training. What we know about the religious movements in general, and Christianity in particular, in Egypt of the late third century makes it quite likely that his teachers were less orthodox than his later biographer. No doubt, the theological background of the letters would have been easily accessible to Antony if he had been a disciple of wandering ascetics teaching a philosophically speculative theology following the various schools of Alexandria, including the Origenist tradition.[4]

Except for this tendency to regard Antony as unlettered, and the emphasis on his piety, not on any writings of his, as the basis for his fame, there is little in the *Vita* that contradicts the image of Antony as a monastic leader in correspondence with his communities of disciples. Even when emerging from his first ascetic training he has numerous disciples, whom he is said to have visited from time to time, including a group in the

---

aversion towards bathing in *VA* 47, and by his lack of interest in the letter of the emperors in *VA* 81. In spite of this he shows himself to be well acquainted with Egyptian and Greek mythology in the debates with the philosophers! See *VA* 75–76.

1 VA 93: οὐ γὰρ ἐκ συγγραμμάτων, οὐδὲ ἐκ τῆς ἔξωθεν σοφίας, οὐδὲ διά τινα τέχνην, διὰ δὲ μόνην θεοσέβειαν ὁ Ἀντώνιος ἐγνωρίσθη· τοῦτο δὲ ὡς Θεοῦ δῶρον οὐκ ἂν τις ἀρνήσαιτο.

2 The only other sources mentioning interpreters in connection with Antony are Hieronymus, *Vita Hilarionis* 30, and the *HL* 21.15. In the latter a certain Kronios is mentioned as Antony's interpreter and Antony is explicitly said to have been ignorant of Greek. Since both these texts were written much later, well into the fifth century, and the authors both knew the *Vita,* they cannot be regarded as decisive. Cf. above p. 41f. where the passage from *HL* 21 is quoted.

3 *VA* 3–10. Although he reportedly enclosed himself in a tomb for some time, it is not until he entered the desert in *VA* 11 that his seclusion is a major theme.

4 See above, pp. 119–125 for this kind of setting.

Arsinoë area.[1] After his retreat to the interior desert he keeps in close touch with the monks near the Nile valley and is actively engaged in debates with heretics and pagans, as well as in solving social conflicts and healing the sick and the possessed. Even if the *Vita* in the earlier parts and in the first sermon stresses the need for *anachoresis* and silence, Antony is at the same time presented as an active leader who feels responsible for his children, as he calls them in the *Vita* as well as in the letters.[2]

But even if the *Vita* has preserved a more authentic image of Antony than has been generally admitted, there is a major shift from the image produced by the letters. The teacher of *gnosis* has become a saint. In this process the major feature is not the rejection of anything authentic, but the transformation of it for a new purpose. Even if Antony was a less staunch supporter of ecclesiastical authority than the *Vita* suggests, there is no evidence that he opposed bishops or priests. He was by no means a Gnostic, but simply adhered to the traditional teaching of the catechetical school of Alexandria. In the same way as the theology of Antony, implicit in his letters, is preserved in the *Vita,* but developed along the lines of Athanasius' own theology, the historical Antony is not eradicated in the biography, but made to serve the needs of the Church. In the *Vita* Antony is still the charismatic teacher, 'taught by God alone', but he has also become the defender of the Church and the adversary of the heretics.

1 *VA* 14.

2 See *i.a. Ep. Ant.* V.1, 5, 11, VI.3, 14, 17, VII.1, 4, 49, and *VA* 22, and 66.

VII. THE *SAYINGS OF THE DESERT FATHERS*

1. THE APOPHTHEGMATA PATRUM AS HISTORICAL SOURCES

With growing suspicion against the trustworthiness of the *Vita Antonii* as a source, the sayings, *apophthegmata*, attributed to Antony in the various collections, have been increasingly drawn upon for an authentic image of him.[1] In his attempt to delineate the historical value of the *Vita,* Dörries made the sayings attributed to Antony his criterion for historical trustworthiness. Supported by the prevailing tradition which regards the sayings as the more or less authentic voices from the desert, and combining his comparison with a profound analysis of the tendencies and Athanasian imprints on the *Vita,* he could reach but one conclusion: The sayings attributed to Antony give us a true and vivid picture of a good representative of the anchoritic tradition, a man speaking the language of the desert, while the *Vita* presents an image transformed by the theology of Athanasius, an Antony in the public eye, but deprived of his own charisma.[2] Before we discuss Dörries' conclusions and confront the sayings attributed to Antony with the letters, it is important to examine the question of the historical reliability of the *apophthegmata* in general.

The sayings are preserved in various collections in all the languages of the Christian tradition. These collections are evidently the result of a long development during which single sayings and minor collections were incorporated into what became, in each language, one or sometimes two comprehensive standard types of collections. In addition to these, of which the edited texts are only examples, there are a great number of smaller collections derived from various stages of the transmission. Numerous collections are still unedited, and especially in the case of the large Arabic *apophthegmata* tradition research is sorely needed. Even if we limit ourselves to the printed collections of sayings, we are still dealing with about 2.500 different sayings, preserved in seven major and five minor

1 The term is used for the sententiae, short dialogues, parables or anecdotes connected with the early monastic movement, primarily in Lower Egypt, and preserved in collections without any story linking them to each other.

2 See Dörries, 'Die Vita Antonii', p. 198f.

collections.[1] Of the sayings most are found in several collections; some 600 are even found in almost all the major collections, while some hundred are attested in a single collection. Thus there is no doubt that the collections for most of their material all derive from a common origin.

In research on the sayings there are two different approaches. The first is the study of the collections and their relationships. Here, the early attempts to cover all the collections in comprehensive comparative studies have been replaced by more modest attempts to analyse and edit single collections or collections closely related to each other. The second approach is the study of the individual saying, its form, content, and historical setting. Here a number of different methods are used: formal, sociological, theological and historical. Whatever the approach, the search for the most original and authentic collections or individual sayings has been central, and there has been little discussion on the possibility of later influences on the compilation of the collections, influences which may have distorted the picture presented of the origins of the monastic movement.

The first scholar to compare the collections was Theodor Hopfner. In a study of the fragmentarily preserved Sahidic collection (Sa) he discussed its relation to the Latin, the Greek and the Syriac collections. On the basis of a note in Photios he concluded that the systematic Greek collection (GS), of which he knew only the chapter headings, probably derived from a lost collection of hagiographies. A comparison of the titles of the chapters, as given by Photios, convinced him that the Latin version attributed to Pelagius and John (PJ) was a translation of that collection (GS). Moreover, he considered GS closely related to the source of the Greek alphabetical and anonymous collections (G and GN). His examination of

[1] The collections are quoted as follows:

[AP] G	=	Collectio Graeca Alphabetica (*CPG* 5560)
[AP] GN	=	Collectio Graeca Anonyma (*CPG* 5561) [incl. mss. *K* and *J*)
[AP] GS	=	Collectio Graeca Systematica (*CPG* 5562) [incl. mss. *QRT*)
[AP] PJ	=	Collectio Latina Systematica (*CPG* 5570)
[AP] PA	=	Collectio a Paschasio Dumiensi (*CPG* 5571) (the short recension in *PL* 73 = *Pa*)
[AP] M	=	Collectio a Martino Dumiensi (*CPG* 5572)
[AP] CSP	=	Collectio Commonitiones Sanctorum Patrum (*CPG* 5573)
[AP] R	=	Collectio a Pseudo-Rufino (*CPG* 5574)
[AP] S	=	Collectio Syriaca, recensio Enaniesu (*CPG* 5577)
[AP] A	=	Collectio Armeniaca, recensiones A & B (*CPG* 5582+5583)
[AP] Sa	=	Collectio Sahidica (*CPG* 5588)
[AP] Bo	=	Collectio Bohairica (*CPG* 5589
[AP] *E*	=	Collectiones Aethiopicae (*CPG* 5597 et 5598)

For editions, see the bibliography under *Apophthegmata Patrum.* The numbers are those of the editions according to the tables in *Les Sentences des Pères du désert. Troisième recueil & tables,* Solesmes 1976, pp. 202–289. Thus *G* is quoted according the names of the fathers, while *GN, GS* and *PJ* are quoted according to the system of Guy, *Recherches sur la tradition grecque des* Apophthegmata Patrum (*Subs. Hag.* 36), Bruxelles 1962, and S according to the edition of Budge.

the Sahidic version (Sa) showed this to be another translation of the source of PJ, *i.e.* GS.[1]

At the same time as Hopfner, but completely independent of him, Wilhelm Bousset made a much more comprehensive and detailed comparison of the various collections. In his research he also covered the history, form and significance of the *apophthegmata.* His study, published after his death, still remains the standard work on the sayings. From the contents of the collections, and the order of the sayings within them, he concluded that PJ and Sa were translations of G+GN organized systematically, but that G+GN, as preserved in the manuscripts, particularly in the anonymous section, is a later, expanded version which served as the model for the Armenian translations (A). In contrast to these he regarded the large Syriac collection (S), as well as the minor Latin versions attributed to Rufinus (R), Paschasius (of which he only knew the short recension (Pa)), and Martinus Dumiensis (M) as translations of the sources for G+GN. But, as he admitted himself, these conclusions were only tentative, since they were based on non-scholarly editions of single and often late manuscripts. Although his impressive and very useful tables clearly show the close relationship existing between the various collections, they also prove that, except for PJ and G, their history is extremely complicated.[2]

Because of the complex nature of the collections of sayings, and the need for more stringent research on the sources, later scholars have devoted themselves to studies and editions of single collections, primarily the Greek and the Latin. The most important work is the study on the manuscripts of the Greek collections, G+GN as well as GS by Jean-Claude Guy. After identifying the significant differences between the manuscripts of each collection, and the existence of manuscripts with collections of mixed types, he reconstituted and analysed a standard form of both types of collections. He concluded that both represented independent results of a long history of redactions, thus rejecting Bousset's conclusion that the systematical collection, in this case GS, derived from G (the so called *Alphabetikon*).[3]

As for the Latin tradition some of the smaller collections have been edited, including Paschasius. A number of studies on the textual history of

1 Th. Hopfner, *Über die koptisch-sa'idischen Apophthegmata Patrum Aegyptiorum* (*Denkschriften der Kaiserlichen Akademie der Wissenschaften in Wien,* Phil.-Hist. Klasse 61:2), Wien 1918, pp. 1–11, 17–21. The larger number of sayings and the divergent structure of *Sa* as compared with *PJ* made him suggest that it depended on an earlier stage of the transmission of the text than *PJ.*

2 W. Bousset, *Apophthegmata,* see especially pp. 1–13, 18–53.

3 J.-C. Guy, *Recherches,* pp. 190–200. To his reconstitution of *GS* should be added the earlier, but to Guy apparently unknown work by N. van Wijk, 'Das gegenseitige Verhältnis einiger Redaktionen der 'Ανδρῶν ἁγίων βίβλος...' (see, Michel van Esbroeck, 'Les Apophthegmes dans les versions orientales', *AB* 93 (1975), p. 382).

these collections, but without comparisons with collections in other languages or inquiries into their sources, have also been produced.[1] Of the oriental collections the Armenian and Syriac were edited in previous centuries, the Arabic and Georgian printed from single manuscripts and only the Ethiopic critically edited.[2]

This is not the place to examine the results of previous research on the relations between the collections of *apophthegmata* in general, or to answer the remaining questions about their growth. But before discussing the other approach to the trustworthiness of the sayings, a few observations are appropriate. First of all, it is essential in comparing collections to distinguish between dependence in structure and dependence in text. Thus, a collection can be dependent on one source for its structure, but have the material from another source. Different systems of organization of the material can also be combined and material added to already existing collections. As for the two types of organization, systematic or alphabetical, they are clearly independent of each other as far as their structure is concerned. Since there are alphabetical collections without signs of any systematical principle, and systematical collections without any alphabetical order, both types must be original creations. A combination of both, *i.e.* an alphabetic structure within each chapter of the systematic structure, as in the Greek and Latin systematical collections (GS and PJ), obviously derives from both these traditions. Thus they cannot be regarded as simply derived from the *alphabetico–anonyma* (G+GN), as proposed by Bousset on the basis of PJ, or as fully independent, as suggested by Guy. The close relationship Bousset established, through his analysis of PJ, between the systematical collection on the one hand, and the *alphabetikon* (G) plus the fourth part of the anonymous collection GN on the other, cannot be denied. But at the same time the almost complete correspondence, in the distribution of the sayings in the chapters, between the Greek systematical

[1] See the editions of *PA* and *CSP* by J. Geraldes Freire. The editions are discussed by G. Philippart, 'Vitae Patrum. Trois travaux récents sur d'anciennes traductions latines', *AB* 92 (1974), pp. 353–365. For *PJ*, see also C. M. Battle, *Die «Adhortationes sanctorum Patrum» im lateinischen Mittelalter. Überlieferung, Fortleben und Wirkung* (*Beiträge zur Geschichte des alten Mönchtums und des Benidiktinerordens* 31), Münster 1972.

[2] Little has yet been done on the relations between these and the Greek and Latin versions. Exceptions are van Esbroeck, 'Les Apophthegmes dans les versions orientales', pp. 381–389, and Bernard Outtier, 'Le modèle grec de la traduction géorgienne des Apophthegmes par Euthyme', *AB* 95 (1977), pp. 119–131 on the Georgian versions (*CPG* 5593 and 5594), and the studies of single mss of the rich and very complex transmission in Arabic by Joseph-Marie Sauget (see his *Une traduction arabe de la collection d'Apophthegmata Patrum de ʿEnānīšōʿ. Étude du ms. Par. ar. 253* (*CSCO* 495), Louvain 1987 and the articles listed in *CPG* 5602–5604). The Ethiopic version has attracted special attention since it records many sayings in first person. This is accepted as a sign of authenticity by Regnault, 'Aux origines des collections d'Apophthegmes', *Les Pères du désert à travers leurs Apophthegmes*, Solesmes 1987, pp. 19–36 followed by Burton-Christie, *The Word in the Desert*, pp. 79f. and Graham Gould *The Desert Fathers on Monastic Community*, pp. 20–24.

GS and the Armenian versions, which have no alphabetical order, proves that for its arrangement in chapters, GS depends on a tradition independent of the *alphabetico–anonyma* G+GN. This does not, however, prove anything about a dependence of GS on G+GN in the matter of text.[1]

Secondly, it can be taken for granted that the general tendency was to augment the collections, and to improve the organization. For the systematic types of collections this means that, as far as structure is concerned, the Syriac version (S) (part one, Enaniesu book IV, chs. I-XIV) and the Armenian (A) represent an earlier stage than the Greek systematical (GS) and the Sahidic (Sa), which are both systematic and alphabetical. It can also be supposed that the organization in 14 chapters, preserved in the first part of S and in the fourth part of GN, is prior to the one in 19, as in A, 20 or 21, as in GS, or even 23 chapters, as suggested for the original Latin version. The divergences, in some of the chapters, between S and GN suggest that in the original systematic form the chapters were still fewer.[2] Two observations indicate that the systematic division is older than the alphabetical. Firstly, there is the evidence of Evagrius and Cassian, who both used collections of sayings as sources treating them thematically.[3] Secondly, an arrangement according to the themes of monastic virtues and dangerous thoughts (λογισμοί) seems more in conformity with the early monastic setting than an alphabetical arrangement according to the names of the fathers. The secondary nature of alphabetical arrangement is also indicated by the fact that often the sayings listed under the father who reported the sayings, not the one who supplied the essence of the word.

Thirdly, the fact that the sayings depend on a fluid and perhaps partly oral tradition, which not only antedated the first major collections but also lived on alongside the growth of the literary compositions, prevents us

1 Even if the objections to what Bousset regarded as evidence for the dependance of *PJ* on *G* raised by Guy are accepted, they only show that it is not *G* as represented by the preserved manuscripts, but an earlier model that has influenced *GS*. The alphabetical arrangement in *GS* and in *G* is so similar that there has to be a connection, and as Bousset has shown for *PJ*, it is impossible to regard the *Alphabetikon* as dependent on *GS*. Guy also admits that *PJ* and hence *GS* depends upon a common source with *G*, a source probably arranged alphabetically. Here the limitation of Guy's study to the Greek tradition is unfortunate. The fact that the first 19 chapters in *A* and *GS* are identical (chapter 20 in *GS* is found mainly in ch. 19 in A, and ch. 21 in *GS* is found in the later part of ch. 10 in *A*) suggests that *GS* was also an unorganized systematical collection before it was arranged alphabetically under the influence of *G*.

2 A comparison of the relations between the different chapters in *GS*, the fourth part of *GN*, and the first part of *S* gives the following result:

GS	1	2	3	4	5	6	7	8	9	10	11	12	13	14	15	16	17	18	19–21
GN IV	–	1	1	2	3	7	4	7	6	5	8	–	9	10	11	12	13	14	-------
S 1	–	1	4	2	11	5	6	8	–	8	8	3	9	7	10	6	9	13	------

3 See Bousset, *op.cit.*, p. 71–76. For Cassian see also Hans-Oskar Weber, *Die Stellung des Johannes Cassianus zur ausserpachomianischen Mönchstradition* (*Beiträge zur Geschichte des alten Mönctums und des Benediktinordens* 24), Münster 1961.

from regarding the relations between the collections as simply a question of literary dependence on a first and original redaction. Not only is it likely that there were a number of original and unrelated redactions, differing in some respects but similar to each other in others, but it is also evident that the collections are the result of a long process of growth, in which individual sayings were added, independently of each other, at various stages in the various collections. As Guy has shown, each redactor and each scribe regarded himself at liberty to include new sayings from other collections, to reject sayings from the collection he used as a source, or simply to reorganize his source.[1] It is not even certain that structural affinities between two collections always prove dependence; the content of a saying, the names mentioned, or other aspects, may explain the inclusion of a saying in the same place in two different collections. What remains strikingly constant is the individual saying, and usually its attribution, not the collection as such. Thus, the historical reliability must be related to the saying, and not to the collection in general.[2]

In summary, the comparisons of the five major collections (G, GS, PA, S, and A) which have so far been edited and analyzed show a closer relationship between G, GS and A, and a greater degree of independence for S and PA, which were accordingly given preference by Bousset. The priority of PJ among the various recensions of the Greek systematical collection (GS), and the fourth part within the anonymous collection (GN), suggested by Guy, must also be considered as an established fact. For a judgement on the historical trustworthiness of the sayings, however, criteria other than the inclusion in a collection are necessary. The inclusion of a saying in a number of otherwise different and unrelated collections can only support its authenticity, while the absence of a saying in a collection does not prove its unauthenticity, as exclusions may have been made for various reasons.[3]

In his monumental work Bousset combined the comparative analysis of the collections with the second approach, analyzing the historical setting

[1] See Guy, *Recherches*, pp. 52, 63. Especially illuminating are his discussions on the various mixed and derived forms, see pp. 111–115, 189–190, and 201–230. The unity in content and concern in a collection like G demonstrated in the recent studies by Burton–Christie and Gould, referred to above (p. 148, n. 2), is rather a sign of conscious redaction than historical trustworthiness. One cannot at the same time argue that the collection is a source authentically documenting the early fathers and that it is a source documenting a special view of the past. See Gould, *op.cit.*, pp. 4f., 14 and 17–25.

[2] The stability in attribution, and the fact that almost half of the sayings are anonymous seems to indicate that sayings should not be thought of as randomly attributed to celebrated fathers. On the question of priority for attribution over anonymity, see René Draguet, 'Les apophthegmes des moines d'Égypte. Problèmes litteraires', *Bulletin de l'Académie de Belgique. Classe des lettres et des sciences morales et politiques*, V, 47 (1961), p. 144.

[3] An important fact to remember is that between the first fathers and the redaction of the sayings the monastic tradition of Egypt suffered greatly by the Origenist controversy.

and the internal development of the sayings. In order to establish a chronology he relied on the attributions of the sayings in the alphabetical collection and the names mentioned in them. The value of this chronology for the question of the reliability of the sayings rests, however, with the authenticity and correctness of the attribution. False attributions are, however, evident not only in the comparatively few cases where the attributions differ in the collections, but also in other cases. To Bousset, the main criteria for the reliability of a saying was its form and to some extent its content. Only forms compatible with oral tradition, *i.e. sententiae*, parables and short poignant anecdotes, could belong to the original tradition, and the only authentic sayings were those that could be reconciled with the general image created on the basis of these criteria.[1]

Later research on the sayings has generally followed Bousset and refined the analysis of the forms with particular interest in the development of individual sayings from a simple to a more elaborate form, or from oral to written form The short poignant answer to the request for a word of spiritual guidance is generally regarded to be the authentic saying, while the anecdotes, dialogues, and exhortations are thought to be later developments. This view of the development of the sayings is supported by the analyses of a number of cases in which different versions represent clearly distinguishable stages in the process.[2]

It is, however, methodologically unsound to rely on formal criteria based upon what is typical for the genre as a whole. An individual saying cannot be assessed on the basis of what is typical of the sayings regarded as trustworthy because they are typical for what sayings ought to look like. With this method the diversity is reduced to a minimum through rejection of untypical sayings, and what we get is an idealized picture of what was later seen as the common ground of early monasticism.[3] To reject sayings that are longer or more complex or those that are dogmatic or philosophical only strengthens the prejudice against the early monks as simple, uneducated peasants. What is preserved in the sayings is certainly only part of the truth about these monks, and there is no guarantee that the compilation and transmission of the sayings was not intentionally selective.

1 See Bousset, *Apophthegmata,* pp. 76–93. Bousset is here influenced by his background in the 'religionsgeschichtliche Schule' and its approach to the Gospel tradition.

2 In two articles Guy argues for the existence of three stages in the development of the sayings, the primitive and authentic *logos,* the generalized saying, and the narrative or sermon, concluding that the collections generally give only the third stage. See Jean-Claude Guy, 'Remarques sur le texte des *Apophthegmata Patrum* ', *RScR* 43 (1959), pp. 252–258, and *idem,* 'Note sur l'évolution du genre apophthegmatique', *RAM* 32 (1956), pp. 63–68.

3 In a short but important note on the sayings Graham Gould warns against this use of a 'theory that is too simple for the material', and argues for the existence of authentic narratives, Biblical interpretations and exhortations among the sayings. See Gould, 'A Note on the *Apophthegmata Patrum* ', *JTS* 37 (1986), pp. 133–138.

What is typical for the collection as a whole—especially when the odd sayings are rejected—reveals more about the collections *per se*, and *their* historical background, than about the society in which the sayings originated.[1] In accordance with traditional criteria for historical research it is not what agrees with the general tendency of the text that is likely to be most reliable, but rather what does not fit in with the purpose of the compiler.

That the authenticity of a saying, or the spuriousness of another, cannot be established by the analysis of the form, or the historical situation of the saying, is amply demonstrated by the numerous borrowings from other sources in the sayings. These are often regarded as later interpolations, of no interest for the study of the sayings. As we will see in the case of Antony, there is no indication that the inclusion of passages from contemporary writings was a later practice, foreign to the early collectors and copyists. As shown above, the concept of the movement as illiterate is questionable and actually finds little support in the sayings themselves.[2]

2. THE *APOPHTHEGMATA PATRUM* AND ANTONY

Of the names most often mentioned in the collections of *apophthegmata,* Antony's is second only to that of Abba Poimen, whose position in the growth of the tradition of sayings is central. Regardless of the authenticity of the individual sayings attributed to Antony, this fact supports his image as a major figure in the earliest monastic tradition. This image is emphasized also by the wide distribution of the sayings referring to him. Of the 119 sayings referring to Antony, only 38 are under his name in the alphabetical collection: 18 are found under other names in the alphabetical collection, and another 16 in the anonymous part.[3] Of these 72, 66 occur in A, 49 in S, 45 in GS (35 in PJ), 30 in PA, 21 in Bo, 21 in E, and 6 in Sa. Of the additional 47 sayings 32 appear in Bo, ten in the smaller Latin collections, two in S, two in QRT and one in A.

1 The important fact that the collections depend on a kind of monastic school tradition, centered around the person of Abba Poimen and that they were not made in Egypt in the fourth century but most probably in Palestine in the earlier part of the fifth century, *i.e.* after the expulsion of the Origenist intellectuals, has generally not been taken into account. An exception is Jean Gribomont, ' Les Apophthegmes du désert', *Rivista di storia e letteratura religiosa,* 13 (1977), pp. 534–541.

2 In the sayings statements about literature abound, and a number of fathers are even designated as scribes. See *i.a. AP/G* Abraham 3, Ammoes 5, Bessarion 12, Euprepios 7, Theodoros of Pherme 1, 29, Mark 1, Silvanus 5, and Serapion 2. See also the analysis of Scripture in the desert by Douglas Burton-Christie in his *The Word in the Desert.*

3 See table of sayings in the appendix, pp. 193–195. I have not included the sayings attributed to Antony in the Armenian or Bohairic collection only, but in all other sources to other fathers (*i.e.* Joseph of Thebais, Poimen 1, Poimen 19, and Poimen 168). I have also excluded Poimen 125, which is a doublet of Antony 4, and *CSP* V.2 (=R 31), which is an elaborated version of *HL* 39.1 and only later attributed to Antony.

If we are to place these Antonian sayings into groups according to their respective support in the most important collections, we arrive at the following result:

> 18 sayings are found in G, GS, PA, S and A;
> 4 sayings are found in all these except GS;
> 20 sayings are found in all these except PA;
> 8 sayings are found in G, S and A, but not in GS and PA;
> 8 sayings are found in G, PA and A, but not in GS and S;
> 11 sayings are found only in G and GS or A.

If one should accept the reliability of the sayings on the basis of their occurrences in the collections least likely to be dependent of each other, the first 22 should be considered genuine, and the next 36 probably genuine, whereas the rest should be considered in all probability spurious.[1] This division fits rather well with the sayings considered genuine by Heussi and Dörries, except that Heussi rejected some with the help of historical and formal criteria, while Dörries kept them in and included others, with the help of the same criteria![2]

However, when other sources on Antony are included in our analysis of the authenticity of the sayings, the results are somewhat different. Of the 119 sayings, eight have parallels in the *Vita,* three in Antony's letters, two in the letters of Ammonas, two in the *Historia Lausiaca,* one in the *Historia Monachorum,* two in Socrates, two in Sozomenus, and one each in Jerome and Rufinus.[3] In principle, these parallels can be explained in three

1 The first 22 are: *AP/G* Antony 1, 3, 7, 10, 11, 12, 15, 17, 18, 19, 20, 21, 29, Ammonas 1, Isidorus 6, Poimen 119, Sisoës 14, *GN* 202, 298, 321, 322, 490. The second group consists of: *AP/G* Antony 2, 4, 6, 8, 9, 13, 14, 16, 23, 24, 25, 26, 27, 28, 30, 32, 33, 37, 38, Amoun 1, Ammonas 7, John the Eunuch 2, Hilarion, Macarius the Egyptian 4, Nisteroos 2, Poimen 75, Paul the Simple, Sisoës 7, 9, 28, *GN* 206, 417, 444, 603, J 759, 760.

2 Heussi rejected *AP/G* Antony 6, 18, 24, 25, 26, 27, 28, 30, 33, 37, 38 and John Eunochos 2. Dörries included *AP/G* Antony 5, 31, 35, and PA 76,4 (Pa 26,4). See Heussi, *Der Ursprung,* p. 107f., and Dörries, 'Die Vita Antonii', pp. 147–163.

3

G Antony 5	*Epistula Ammonis* IX
G Antony 9	*Epistula Antonii* VI.53, cf. VI.105
G Antony 10	*Vita Antonii* 85
G Antony 22	*Epistula Antonii* I.35–41
G Antony 30	*Vita Antonii* 59–60
G Antony 31	*Vita Antonii* 81, Sozomenus *HE* I.13 (cf. II.31)
G Poimen 87	*Epistula Antonii* VII,60
G Pityrion	*Historia Monachorum* 15
QRT 12	*Vita Antonii* 3
QRT 13	*Vita Antonii* 3–5
PA 84,3	Socrates *HE* IV.23
Pa 19,3	*Historia Lausiaca* 21,1–15
Pa 19,4	*Vita Antonii* 66 and *Historia Lausiaca* 21.16
CSP V,1	*Vita Antonii* 16ff.
R 218	Jerome, *Epistula ad Castricianum,* Socrates *HE* IV.25, Sozomenus *HE* III.15, and Rufinus *HE* II.7
Bo 21	*Epistula Ammonis* II
Bo 51	*Vita Antonii* 16.

different ways: the dependence of the parallel text on the saying, the reverse dependence, or a common source. Only in the first case is the parallel of no value as a historical source, but for such a dependence there is no evidence in any of these cases. In the second case the value of the saying as a source for an independent oral tradition is of course nil, but this does not prove that it is unreliable as a source for Antony. In the third case the saying and the parallel text strongly support the historical authenticity of each other.

The problem is that the existing parallels do not support the criteria applied for the *apophthegmata, i.e.* good attestation in the collections or adherence to a primitive form. Two of those sayings attributed to Antony which have the poorest attestation in the collections are actually those best attested outside the collections.[1] This indicates that it is impossible to reject sayings as unauthentic simply by referring to their occurence in only one or two collections, or to their different literary form.

In addition to the difficulties in judging which sayings should be considered genuine, there is the further problem of different versions of the same saying. In his analysis of the sayings attributed to Antony, Dörries confined himself to an examination of the alphabetical sayings as they are found in the printed Greek text, mentioning some of the others in an appendix only.[2] The reliability of this Greek text is, however, questionable.[3] Since there are no critical editions of the various collections of sayings, except the Ethiopic version, *PA* and *M*, it is impossible to examine the precise relationships of the different versions of individual sayings. But even a cursory comparison of the different versions of some of the sayings attributed to Antony clearly shows how complex the situation is, and how dangerous it is to assume that one and the same collection always gives the best text.

1 The first of them, *G* Antony 22, which is an extract from the letters is of course not typical for the sayings, but the rejection of it on this criteria by Heussi and Dörries is obviously wrong. The second, Antony 31, is attested both in *VA* and in Sozomenos *HE*. Heussi rightly argues that the version given by Sozomenus is likely to be the most faithful. In the saying and in the *VA* the purpose of the passage is obviously to prove Antony's fame and his disinterest in the authorities. See Heussi, *Der Ursprung*, pp. 90–93. Dörries prefers to leave the question of Sozomenus' trustworthiness aside, but maintains that the saying is prior to the version in the *Vita* (Dörries, 'Die Vita Antonii', p. 158f.). This is, however, unlikely, since a development from a polite letter to an invitation is far more plausible than the opposite. Cf. below, p. 183.

2 Dörries, 'Die Vita Antonii', pp. 215–218.

3 In his work Bousset thus refrained from making comparisons of the texts, with one exception in which he thought he could prove the primacy of S over G and the Latin collections. See Bousset, *Apophthegmata*, pp. 53–57. For the deficiencies of the printed text of *G*, see also Guy, *Recherches*, pp. 36–41, 57, and R. Draguet, 'Les apophthegmes des moines d'Égypte', pp. 134–149. As shown already by Hopfner, this Greek text is very close to the Latin text of *PJ* and to *Sa*, whereas *Pa*, *R* and *M* usually provide a secondary and elaborated text.

In a saying (*AP/G* Ant. 9) which is strikingly similar to a passage in letter VI, Antony says, according to the Greek and Latin versions: 'From the neighbour comes life and death. If we gain our brother, we have gained God, but if we scandalize our brother, we have sinned against Christ'. The Syriac version instead has: 'If we benefit our brother, we benefit ourselves'. A comparison with the letters make it likely that S has the more original saying, while G and PJ have an elaborated version, probably intended to sound more orthodox. In another saying (*AP/G* Ant. 11) only the Greek text gives 'fornication' as the remaining temptation for the monk, whereas PJ, A, S and Bo give the temptations 'of the heart'. Since the other temptations all refer to members of the body it can be surmised that also this did. Most likely it is not the heart that was originally intended —why should it be changed to 'fornication'?—but the genitals. The tendency to avoid any mentioning of the sexual organs is obvious in a similar passage in the letters. When writing about the purification of the members of the body in his first letter, Antony lists the purification of the eyes, the ears, the tongue, the hand, the stomach, and then, with a euphemism, what is 'below the belly'. For the Syriac and Arabic translators of the letters even this paraphrase was, however, too provocative.[1]

A third example is the saying about Antony testing some visiting fathers (*AP/G* Ant. 17). According to the Greek, Latin and Armenian texts the younger visitors tried to interpret the presented text; only Abba Joseph, the eldest, confessed his inability. In the Syriac version also the younger visitors said they were unable to interpret the words. Here it is evident that S is secondary in character, since it makes the anecdote pointless. Finally there is a saying (*AP/G* Macarius the Egyptian 26) in which the Armenian text seems to have preserved the original rendering in contrast to G, which is the only other attestation of this saying. Here Macarius returns from a visit to Antony and relates the discussion he has had with the famous father to some brothers. In A he reports that he asked Antony why he had no offering (προσφορά) where he stayed. In G he tells Antony instead that the fathers of Scetis did not have any. Since the point of the anecdote, in both versions, is that Macarius did not tell the brothers what Antony replied, because it was not essential for them to know, only the version in A makes sense. Here it is easy to conclude that the redactor

1 See *Ep. Ant.* I.66. The tendency to avoid speaking about sexuality is borne out by a similar revision of this text in the versions. While the Latin and the Georgian versions agree speaking about the thoughts of fornication coming from below the belly (L: 'quae per cogitationem coitus sub alvo metitur', G: მუცლისა მიერ აღძრულთა სიძვისა გან გულისტყუათა), the Syriac text has a vague reference to the heart, and the Arabic simply omits the reference all together.

of G felt that the text had to be changed, and that the other versions preferred to drop it altogether.[1]

But the decisive difficulty in Dörries' attempt to make the sayings the main source for our knowledge about Antony is the problem of the interpretation of the sayings. Even Dörries' own conclusion that the sayings present us with an image of Antony which differs little from the image of the early desert fathers in general, should caution us against relying on them for an authentic image of the individual father.[2] As already mentioned, the sayings present us with what is typical, especially if we use the traditional criteria in deciding which sayings ought to be considered as genuine. The purpose of collecting sayings is clearly not an interest in the individual, but in the spiritual instruction and the ideal presented, regardless of whether it could be attributed to a certain father or only referred to an anonymous *abba*. This is evident not only in the preference for a systematic organization of the material, but also in the way the collections are still used for monastic education.[3] It is also illustrated by the cases where we have parallels between the *Vita* and the sayings. With the possible exception of *AP/G* Antony 31, it is evident that it is not the sayings which have contributed anything to hagiography, but hagiography that has been used to make up the sayings.[4] This does not mean that the sayings are of no historical value, or generally unauthentic. But an analysis of the collections of sayings and their common core only reveals what was considered worth transmitting on the basis of the purpose of the spiritual words, the λόγια, and the collection, the *Apophthegmata Patrum*. The historical value of each individual saying must therefore be measured against other sources.[5]

Moreover, even if a large number of the sayings attributed to Antony could be considered genuine, they still give us a very limited image of the

[1] See above, pp. 75, 79–81, for the problems connected with an understanding of Antony's views on the Church.

[2] See Dörries, 'Die Vita Antonii', p. 162f. He even maintains that the 'Grundgedanken' of the 'Eremitentum' can be reconstructed from the sayings attributed to Antony. How this is to be combined with their use in the quest of a historical person is a riddle.

[3] See Jean-Claude Guy, 'Educational innovation in the Desert Fathers', *Eastern Churches Review* 6 (1974), pp. 44–51.

[4] This does not mean that the sayings in general are fragments of hagiographical texts, as suggested by Hopfner, *Über die koptisch-sa'idischen Apophthegmata,* p. 2f.. For the majority of sayings, there is no evidence for this. But on the other hand, the case of the *Life of John Kolobos* where sayings have been used to form a *Vita* is singular (cf. Bousset, *Apophthegmata,* p. 88f.

[5] For Bousset the assignment of a saying to oral tradition, based on an analysis of the form, was enough to guarantee the authenticity, whereas the fact that a saying had parallels in historical writings or was culled from such made it historically suspect. But even if this is true for research on what was typical for the tradition, it does not make the sayings of a certain father a reliable historical source for the individual. See M. Williams, 'The *Life of Antony*', p. 36f. for a succinct critique of Dörries' methodology.

saint, shaped by what the tradition considered to be of permanent edificatory value. If we want to know something about the historical person, we have to look for what is untypical of the fathers in general. Instead of rejecting sayings that have parallels in other texts and sayings which do not have the character of an *apophthegma,* we must find out if there is anything in the Antony image of the sayings that sets him apart from tradition, if there are traces of things that tradition might have had reasons to try to obliterate.

The first thing that emerges from even a cursory reading of the 119 sayings that refer to Antony is his use as an ideal and as the principal authority for the monastic tradition. Repeatedly, the sayings record visits by monks to Antony for spiritual advice or fathers citing Antony as an example, and often Antony is drawn on for the support of other prominent monks.[1] To this group of sayings could be added the numerous instances in which Antony is cited to authorize a monastic principle.[2] Thus there is no doubt that the sayings support an image of Antony as the leading figure in the early anchoritic tradition of Lower Egypt. If we are to draw any other conclusions from the sayings, two themes might be more prominent in the sayings attributed to him than in the collections in general: the profound interpretation of the Scripture, and the emphasis on spiritual insight.[3] On the other hand, the emphasis on rigidity in ascetic practice and despair over one's own sins, seem less prominent than in the sayings at large. Among the Antonian sayings, two stand out as strange, both on the question of the Church and its sacraments. In the first (Macarius the Egyptian 26) it is said that there was no eucharist where Antony stayed, and in the second Antony speaks about the 'true Church' as something purely spiritual (Bo 84). Both sayings are poorly attested, but this can be due to their somewhat unorthodox contents. If they reveal anything historically authentic, they further support the image of Antony as a philosopher and ascetic teacher of a kind of Christian *gnosis*.[4]

1 See *G* Ant 12, 17, 18, 19, 26, 27, Ammonas 7, 8, Amoun 1, Isidorus 6, Hilarion, Macarius the Egyptian 4, 26, Nisteroos 2, Poimen 75, 87, Pityrion, Paul the Simple, Sisoës 9; *GN* 630; *Pa* 19.3; *CSP* V.2; *R* 218; *S* II.103; *Bo* 16, 26, 27, and 58. A special case are the sayings refering to Antony in heaven: *G* Antony 28, Sisoës 14; *GN* 202 and 520.

2 See *i.a.* *G* Antony 1, 13, 20, 21, 29, 34, 38; *Pa* 15.2, and 35.2. It is obviously not possible to define precisely which sayings attributed to Antony have this character of establishing rules. To make Antony a reformer of a an older more austere tradition on the basis of these, as Dörries does, seems to me to overinterprete the sayings (see Dörries, 'Die Vita Antonii', p. 162).

3 For references to scriptural interpretation, see *G* Antony 3, 17, 19; *K* 295; *QRT* 12; *Bo* 38, and 48; for sayings about spiritual insight *AP/G* Antony 2, 8, 10, 22, 30, 40; *J* 760; *PA* 84.3; *Pa* 19.4; R 218; *A* XVIII.77; *Bo* 21, 34, and 51. A possible connection to the teaching later expounded by Evagrius can be found in *G* Pityrion (=*HM* 15), who links each demon to a passion.

4 For this interpretation of *G* Macarius the Egyptian 26 see above p. 155.

3. THE ANTONIAN *APOPHTHEGMATA* AND THE LETTERS OF ANTONY

The problems involved in an analysis of the sayings and their authenticity make it rather difficult to compare them with the letters. The fact that most topics in the letters have no parallels in the sayings only confirms that the latter have a strongly non-dogmatic character, and that the transmission and compilation of the collections was governed by interests which wanted to avoid theological issues. What is significant is that there are a number of close correspondences between the sayings and the letters. These range from a long excerpt from one of the letters to short identical passages and similarities in thought and expression. If some of the latter are independent of the text of the letters, they give us an important confirmation of Antony's teaching as presented in the letters. The fact that at least some of the sayings are dependent upon the letters confirm their attribution to Antony and prove their reception in the monastic environment.[1]

Though a detailed comparison of the teaching of the letters with that of the sayings is not possible, some of the major features that emerge from the analysis of the letters can be compared. The image of Antony obtained from the letters attributed to him is primarily that of a teacher of *gnosis* who emphasizes a more profound understanding of the Scriptures and of the inner man, the image of a master, confident in his position as a leader and a counsellor of his disciples, whom he sees as his beloved spiritual children. For this image there is actually some support in the sayings. Not only is Antony repeatedly called upon for advice and spiritual teaching, he is also in demand as a refuge and a father for those who are not accepted elsewhere. The number of sayings referring to Antony, and their wide dissemination in the collections, as well as the prevailing use of Antony as the ideal which defines the rule, also confirm the image provided by the letters. And though there is no systematic treatment of his teaching in the sayings, a number of sayings are not only close to the teaching of the letters; they are also easier to understand in the light of the letters.

The importance of the concept of knowledge about the nature of created things as the first step in true γνῶσις, developed by Evagrius, but visible already in the letters of Antony, is actually confirmed in a saying

[1] See below for a full discussion of the parallels. In the case of *G* Antony 22 = *Ep. Ant.* I.35–41, the character of the saying and the verbal correspondence proves a textual dependence. The poor attestation of the saying is often used as an argument for the late character of the borrowing. But it is quite possible that the saying is omitted in many collections on account of its content. As for the others, *G* Poimen 87 = *Ep. Ant.* VII.60 does not make much sense as a single saying, and is clearly an extract from the context given to it in Letter VII. Also here the attestation is poor. In the case of *G* Antony 9 = *Ep. Ant.* VI.53, it is impossible to determine if the saying is dependent on the text of the letters or on a common oral tradition.

which Evagrius, in one of his very rare references to a source, attributed to Antony:

> A certain philosopher came to Antony, the righteous, and said to him, 'How can you endure, father, being deprived of the comfort of books?' 'My book, o philosopher,' replied Antony, 'is the nature of things created, and it is present whenever I want to read the words of God'.[1]

This saying even seems to presuppose that Antony was regarded as one of the philosophers and, moreover, that he had an influence on Evagrius, who otherwise usually refers to Macarius the Egyptian as his teacher. Self-knowledge, the second step in the hierarchy of knowledge and the one most strongly emphasized in the letters, is explicitly mentioned as essential in a saying in the Bohairic collection,[2] and in a saying in the anonymous Greek collection we find a kind of summary of what the first letter teaches on the motions of the body, the teaching to which the excerpt in the alphabetical saying belongs.[3]

The teaching of the letters on the history of salvation is absent in the sayings attributed to Antony, and there is very little on the law, or on Jesus Christ in Antony's sayings as in the *apophthegmata* generally.[4] As mentioned above there is, however, an emphasis on the correct interpretation of the Scriptures, and on God's judgments. In one saying Antony is even rebuked for his inquiries into the divine secrets.[5] In another Antony himself rebukes the young monks who think they understand the meaning of the Scriptures.[6] Antony is, more significantly, even depicted as the father to whom Moses is wont to reveal the deeper interpretation of the

1 Τῷ δικαίῳ 'Αντωνίῳ προσῆλθέ τις τῶν τότε σοφῶν καὶ πῶς διακαρτερεῖς, εἶπεν, ὦ πάτερ, τῆς ἐκ τῶν βιβλίων παραμυθίας ἐστερημένος; 'Ο δέ φησι· τὸ ἐμὸν βιβλίον, φιλόσοφε, ἡ φύσις τῶν γεγονότων ἐστί, καὶ πάρεστιν ὅτε βούλομαι τοὺς λόγους ἀναγινώσκειν τοὺς τοῦ θεοῦ. Evagrius, *Praktikos* 92 quoted *verbatim* in Socrates *HE* IV.23. The saying is also found in *PL* 73,108C (*Verba Seniorum* VI.4.16), and *PA* 84.3.

2 *Bo* 38 (*AMG* XXV, p. 35): ⲁϥϫⲟⲥ ⲟⲛ ⲛϫⲉ ⲁⲃⲃⲁ ⲁⲛⲧⲱⲛⲓⲟⲥ ϫⲉ ⲥⲉⲣ ⲛⲟϥⲣⲓ ⲛⲁⲛ ⲉⲙⲁϣⲱ ⲉⲑⲣⲉⲛⲫⲱⲧ ⲉϩⲟⲩⲛ ⲉⲧⲉⲛⲣⲓ ⲟⲩⲟϩ ⲛⲧⲉⲛϯ ϩⲑⲏⲛ ⲉⲣⲟⲛ ⲉⲙⲁϣⲱ ϩⲉⲛ ⲡⲉⲛⲃⲓⲟⲥ ⲧⲏⲣϥ ϣⲁⲧⲉⲛⲉⲙⲓ ⲉⲣⲟⲛ ϫⲉ ⲛⲟⲓ ⲛⲁϣ ⲛⲣⲏϯ ⲉϣⲱⲡ. 'Abba Antony also said: "It is very profitable for us that we flee into our cells and meditate intensely on ourselves during all our life until we know ourselves, of what kind we are."' In another Bohairic saying, *Bo* 34 (*AMG* XXV, p. 32), knowledge is mentioned without any object in one of the—for early monastic literature—typical series of virtues begetting other virtues.

3 *AP/GN K* 295. The saying is only preserved in mss. Coislin 283, f. 129v–130v, which is not yet published. See Guy, *Recherches*, pp. 99–101. A French translation based on the mss. is published in *Les sentences des pères du désert. Nouveau Recueil*, Solesmes 1970, p. 171.

4 In one saying (*Bo* 39 =*AMG* XXV, p. 36) Antony, however, refers to the law in words close to what we find in the letters: ⲁϥϫⲟⲥ ⲟⲛ ⲛϫⲉ ⲁⲃⲃⲁ ⲁⲛⲧⲱⲛⲓⲟⲥ ϫⲉ ⲡⲓⲅⲣⲁⲡⲧⲟⲛ ⲛⲛⲟⲙⲟⲥ ⲁⲛ ⲡⲉ ϯⲙⲉⲑⲙⲏⲓ ⲁⲗⲗⲁ ⲡⲓϩⲏⲧ ⲉⲧⲧⲟⲩⲃⲏⲟⲩⲧ ⲑⲁⲓ ⲧⲉ ϯⲙⲉⲑⲙⲏⲓ ⲛⲧⲉ ⲡⲓⲣⲱⲙⲓ. (Abba Antony also said: 'It is not the letter of the law that is righteousness, but it is the pure heart which is the righteousness of man').

5 *G* Antony 2. Here again the need for keeping attention on oneself (προσέχειν σεαυτῷ) is stressed.

6 *G* Antony 17.

Bible, and the father who knows the Scriptures by heart.[1] He is even depicted as the man who teaches Didymus of Alexandria, the celebrated blind exegete of allegory, to concentrate on what can be seen in the spirit.[2] There are, moreover, two interesting sayings in which Antony himself gives instances of allegorical interpretation. In the first Antony interprets the meaning of the loaves in the parable of the man who in the middle of the night asks his friend for three loaves of bread (Luke 11:5-8). According to him, the three loaves are hospitality, poverty, and abstinence.[3] In the second he interprets the furnace of Babylon and the cloud from which God spoke to Moses as the cell of the monk.[4]

The dangers that threaten even the most zealous monks, described in the pleas in the letters, are found also in the sayings, as is the emphasis on the need for discernment (διάκρισις). One of the sayings (*Antony* 8) can actually be seen as a summary of what is repeatedly said in the letters:[5]

> He also said: 'There are some who wore down their bodies through *ascesis*, but since they had no discernment, they were far from God'.

In several sayings Antony is depicted as a man of discernment. In one he has foreknowledge of the fall of a monk famous for the gift of working miracles.[6] He is able to determine whether visions come from the demons or not, and warns against demons appearing to be angels of light.[7]

The need for a monk to preserve his inner vigilance, a theme in complete accord with the letters, is found also in a saying which has a close parallel in the *Vita:* [8]

1 In *G* Antony 26 he thus is given the interpretation of a difficult passage in Leviticus by going out alone in the desert, as was his habit (συνήθεια). *QRT* 12 (for the common collection of the three mss. designed by these *sigla*, see Guy, *Recherches*, pp. 121–124) is an excerpt of *VA* 3, where it is said that his memory replaced the books: Καὶ γὰρ προσεῖχεν οὕτως τῇ ἀναγνώσει, ὡς μηδὲν τῶν γεγραμμένων ἀπ' αὐτοῦ πίπτειν χαμαί, πάντα δὲ κατέχειν, καὶ λοιπὸν αὐτῷ τὴν μνήμην ἀντὶ βιβλίων γίνεσθαι.

2 The story about Antony and Didymus (*R* 218) is also found in Rufinus *HE* II.7; Jerome, *Epistula ad Castricianum* (ep. 68); Socrates *HE* IV.25; and Sozomenus *HE* III.15. The historicity of the story is propounded by Butler (*The Lausiac History of Palladius,* I, p. 221), who sees the accounts of Rufinus and Jerome as independant of each other, and thus both originating with Didymus himself, whom both visited. For a discussion, see below, p. 173f.

3 *Bo* 48.

4 *GN* 206. In *S* I.54 the saying is attributed to Antony, and there is no need to reject this attribution.

5 Εἶπε πάλιν, ὅτι εἰσί τινες κατατρίψαντες τὰ ἑαυτῶν σώματα ἐν ἀσκήσει, καὶ διὰ τὸ μὴ ἐσχηκέναι αὐτοὺς διάκρισιν, μακρὰν τοῦ Θεοῦ γεγόνασιν. *AP/G* Antony 8. Cf. *Ep. Ant.* VI.106.

6 *G* Antony 14.

7 *G* Antony 12, *A* XVIII,77. The relation to what the *Vita* says about him is here obvious. Another saying could even be regarded as dependent on the text of the *Vita. See AP/G* Antony 30 and *VA* 29–30.

8 *G* Antony 10 and *VA* 85.

G Antony 10

Εἶπε πάλιν· Ὥσπερ οἱ ἰχθύες
ἐγχρονίζοντες τῇ ξηρᾷ τελευτῶσιν, οὕτως καὶ οἱ μοναχοὶ,
βραδύνοντες ἔξω τοῦ κελλίου, ἢ
μετὰ κοσμικῶν διατρίβοντες,
πρὸς τὸν τῆς ἡσυχίας τόνον
ἐκλύονται. Δεῖ οὖν, ὥσπερ τὸν
ἰχθὺν εἰς τὴν θάλασσαν, οὕτως
καὶ ἡμᾶς εἰς τὸ κελλίον ἐπει-
'γεσθαι, μήποτε βραδύνοντες ἔξω
ἐπιλαθώμεθα τῆς ἔνδον φυλακῆς.

Vita Antonii 85

Ὥσπερ οἱ ἰχθύες ἐγχρονίζοντες
τῇ ξηρᾷ γῇ τελευτῶσιν, οὕτως οἱ
μοναχοὶ βραδύνοντες μεθ' ὑμῶν,
καὶ παρ' ὑμῖν ἐνδιατρίβοντες
ἐκλύονται. Δεῖ οὖν, ὥσπερ τὸν
ἰχθὺν εἰς τὴν θάλασσαν, οὕτως
ἡμᾶς εἰς τὸ ὄρος ἐπείγεσθαι·
μήποτε ἐμβραδύνοντες, ἐπιλαθώμεθα τῶν ἔνδον.

In this case it is obvious that one of the texts is directly dependent on the other. While Heussi regarded the version in the *Vita* as the origin of the saying, Dörries argued for the opposite view.[1] In the *Vita* the saying is inserted into an actual situation: it is a reply to a military commander who asked Antony to stay at the 'outer' monastery. Two expressions (the ἡσυχία and the φυλακή) found in the saying are, moreover, lacking, and for κελλίον in the saying we have ὄρος in the *Vita*. To Dörries the omission in the *Vita* of the concepts common to the tradition of the sayings, ἡσυχία, φυλακή and κελλίον, was sufficient proof that its version was secondary. This conclusion is, however, based on a presupposed priority and reliability of the sayings tradition. Nothing prevents us from assuming that they were included precisely because they are typical of that tradition. A comparison of the different versions of the saying, moreover, shows clearly that these expressions are not generally used even in the various collections of *apophthegmata*.[2] A decisive argument for the priority of the text of the *Vita* is that the word ὄρος for a monastic site is attested in early fourth century documents, while κελλίον with this meaning is first attested in texts from the late fourth century. The priority of ὄρος is also supported by the fact that it corresponds to Coptic ⲧⲟⲟⲩ, which also has both the meaning 'a monastic site' and 'a mountain'.[3] In the *Vita,* ὄρος is, moreover, the word generally used for Antony's place, the

1 See Heussi, *Der Ursprung,* p. 107, and Dörries, 'Die Vita Antonii', p. 151f..

2 The Latin text in *PJ* II.2 is a literal translation of the Greek, while *R* 109 and *S* I.20, which are identical, only give the first part of the saying, both having the equivalent of 'cell'. In *S* II.472 we have a more complete form of the saying, but here it is not the cell, but the mountain that is mentioned. The Coptic version (*Bo* 12) is very close to the Greek, but it has no equivalent to ἡσυχία and the equivalent for κελλίον (ϯⲣⲓ) is used only once, in the second place we find the equivalent of ὄρος (ⲡⲓⲧⲟⲟⲩ).

3 For the meaning and use of ὄρος in Egypt, see H. Cadell & R. Rémondon, 'Sens et emplois de τὸ ὄρος dans les documents papyrologiques', *REG* 80 (1967), pp. 343–349. The earliest attestation with the meaning monastery is *P. Jews* 1913 dated 334. The Coptic equivalent ⲧⲟⲟⲩ referring to a monastic settlement is even found in a letter dated to the late third or early fourth century, see *Coptic Texts in the University of Michigan Collection (ed. by William H. Worrell),* Ann Arbor 1942, pp. 171–173. The first evidences for κελλίον as referring to a monastic site are in a fragment attributed to Antony's disciple Ammonas, in Evagrius, and in the *apophthegmata.* See Lampe, *A Patristic Lexicon*, p. 741.

Vita, ὄρος is, moreover, the word generally used for Antony's place, the 'outer' as well as the 'inner' monastery. The fact that the version in the *Vita* is shorter and inserted into an actual situation clearly speaks for the priority of the *Vita* and the subsequent generalization of the passage into a saying.[1]

A final aspect of the letters that is reflected in the sayings is Antony's emphasis on love. In the letters he repeatedly urges his correspondents to understand his love for them, and our need to love our neighbour. A saying about the importance of loving our neighbour is one of those sayings which has close parallels in the letters:

G Antony 9	Ep.Ant. VI.53
Εἶπε πάλιν, ὅτι ἐκ πλησίον ἐστὶν ἡ ζωὴ καὶ ὁ θάνατος. Ἐὰν γὰρ κερδήσωμεν τὸν ἀδελφόν, τὸν Θεὸν κερδαίνομεν· ἐὰν δὲ σκανδαλίσωμεν τὸν ἀδελφόν, εἰς Χριστὸν ἁμαρτάνομεν.	For they know that our perdition is from our neighbour, and our life is also from our neighbour.

Obviously neither the saying nor the letter can be said to be directly dependent on the other; the similarities must go back to a common origin in Antony's own teaching. In another saying of much the same meaning, Antony stresses that he has never put his own good before the benefit of a brother.[2] In the sayings not only the love of the neighbour, but also Antony's love of God is emphasized. His fame is even said to rest on his greater love of God, a love that has chased away his fear of God.[3] With this Biblical allusion, Antony of the sayings expresses the longing for unity and communion so characteristic of Antony's letters.

As in the case of the *Vita Antonii,* the comparison of the sayings with the letters reveals that the choice between their complete rejection and an uncritical reliance on them as sources is an all too simplistic view of the problem. When confronted with the letters and the image of Antony gained through them, the sayings appear in new light. As a collection they show us the image of Antony which later monastic tradition called for, but as single pictures they are still glimpses of a man of cherished memory. Through his incorporation into tradition, the teacher of *gnosis* became the star of the desert. In this process the main criteria for preservation was apparently the identification of the image of Antony with the ideals of later generations of his disciples. The *apophthegmata* are no nostalgic recollections of randomly preserved pieces of history but didactic sayings of a living tradition.

1 In fact there is no evidence for the use of a kind of Q source (a collection of sayings) in the *VA*. If Athanasius had access to one, it is strange that no other saying is quoted.

2 *G* John the Eunuch 2.

3 *G* Antony 32 and Amoun 1.

VIII. REFERENCES TO ANTONY IN OTHER SOURCES

It is hardly surprising, considering Antony's fame and authority in the early monasticism, that numerous references to him are found scattered in the historical and monastic texts of the early Church. The dependence of a great many of these on the *Vita Antonii* testifies to the popularity and rapid dissemination of the biography, and eventually it becomes almost impossible to find Antonian traditions that did not grow out of the *Vita*, occasionally supplemented with information drawn from some other early text. It seems as if independent traditions on Antony ran dry within the first hundred years after his death. This does not mean that the later texts are irrelevant for the study of how the image of Antony developed. There are *i.a.* three important homilies on Antony, by Hesychius of Jerusalem, by Severus of Antioch, and by John of Hermopolis.[1] These homilies testify not only to the continuous recollection and transformation of his image, but also to its propagation, since Hesychius wrote in Greek, Severus was only preserved in Syriac, and John a Copt. In Arabic we find a number of Antonian legends, probably based on lost Coptic texts. The Arabic texts are, however, all unedited, but at least one was in late mediaeval times translated into Latin and subsequently became of some importance for the image of Antony in the West.[2] But since these homilies and legends contain nothing that can be traced back beyond the early texts, and show no influence from the letters, they are of no importance for this study.

In addition to the *Vita* and the *apophthegmata,* references to Antony in the early literature are found primarily in a letter by Serapion of Thmuis, in the Pachomian literature, in the writings of Jerome and Rufinus, in the

[1] For the homliy by Hesychius of Jerusalem (385–460) see M. Aubineau, *Les homélies festales d'Hesychius de Jérusalem,* I (*Subs.Hag.* 59), Bruxelles 1978, pp. 262–288. For the Syriac homily by the anti-chalcedonian patriarch of Antioch, Severus (465–538), see M. Brière, *Les homélies cathedrales du Sévère d'Antioche* (*PO* 23.1), Paris 1932, homily 86, pp. 39–71. For the Coptic homily by the late sixth century bishop of Hermopolis Magna (ϣмоүн, al-Ašmūnayn), see Gérard Garitte, 'Panégyrique de Saint Antoine par Jean, évêque d'Hermopolis', *OCP* 9 (1943), pp. 100–134 and 330–365.

[2] The text was translated in Cyprus by the famous Spanish dominican Alphonse Bonhomme in 1341. It is characterized by a mass of legendary material and a manifold use of Old and New Testament apocrypha as models for the stories about Antony. It is evident that the author was familiar with the *VA*, but by and large the text is typical for the hagiographical development of the images of famous saints. The Latin text is edited by François Halkin, 'La légende de S. Antoine traduite de l'Arabe par Alphonse Bonhomme', *AB* 60 (1942), pp. 143–212. A similar work is also found in the Latin translation of Arabic Antoniana in Echellensis, *Sapientissimi Patris nostri Antonii,* pp. 108–118.

Historia Monachorum, in Palladius, and in the histories of Socrates, Sozomenus and Theodoret. Besides these, there are some less significant references to Antony or to the *Vita* in other texts, and an increasing use of his sayings. In Athanasius there is, apart from the *Vita*, a single reference, in which Antony is said to have written several letters to Gregory, the Arian intruder on the patriarchal throne.[1] There is also a mention of his visit to Alexandria in the index to Athanasius' festal letters.[2] The strangest reference is by Synesius of Cyrene, the pagan philosopher who was made a bishop of Ptolemais by Theophilus of Alexandria in 412. In one of his pre-Christian writings he lists Antony with Hermes and Zoroaster as a man renowned for his wisdom.[3] The earliest explicit mention of the *Vita* is found in Gregory of Nazianzus, and the first use of one of his sayings is attested in Evagrius. The occupation of Antony's two monasteries by his disciples is also mentioned in Sulpicius Severus.[4]

In addition to their historical value, the references to Antony are important for what they show about the growth of Antonian traditions and the image of Antony before the *Vita* suppressed almost all other evidence. By analysing these references in conjunction with the Antony image gained from the letters and the *Vita,* we can hopefully trace some further sources for the various images, and gain insight into how the image developed. At the same time we must keep in mind that what we have are only glimpses from his life and teaching, glimpses filtered through the memories of his disciples and friends and recorded by people who never met him, people who were motivated by other interests than historical truth.

1. The Letter from Serapion of Thmuis

Serapion, bishop of Thmuis from *c.* 339 to 365 (except when deposed by pro-Arians), and a friend and collaborator of Athanasius, is mentioned in the *Vita* as Antony's disciple and intimate companion. It has even been suggested that the *Vita* is a revision of an earlier text by Serapion himself.[5] Two letters addressed to monastic communities are preserved among his writings. The first is a Greek letter to the monks in general, without any specific mention of Antony,[6] but the second (preserved only in Syriac and Armenian, but originally written in Greek) is a letter of consolation

1 Athanasius, *Historia Arianorum* II.14.

2 Index to Letter X (337–338). See R. Lorenz, Lorenz, *Der Zehnte Osterfestbrief des Athanasius von Alexandrien,* pp. 3–6.

3 Synesius, *Dion* 10. See Garth Fowden, *The Egyptian Hermes,* p. 179.

4 Evagrius, *Praktikos* 92; Gregory of Nazianzus, *Oratio* 21; Sulpicius Severus, *Dialogi,* XVII.

5 For references to Serapion, see *VA* 82 and 91. A detailed discussion on the relation between Serapion and Antony is given in Tetz, 'Athanasius und die Vita Antonii', pp. 8–11.

6 *CPG* 2487; *PG* 40, 925–941.

written to the disciples of Antony soon after his death.[1] The explicit reference in the text to the sad state of the Orthodox camp caused by the triumph of the Arians fits the date given by Jerome for Antony's death, *i.e.* 356, which must also be the date of the letter.[2] The Syriac and Armenian texts appear to be independent translations of the Greek original, the Armenian representing a later and more elaborate version of the text.

The letter is a lamentation over Antony's death and an exhortation to follow his example. Serapion describes Antony as the *abba* (γέρων), whose prayers upheld the world and averted the wrath of God. He entreats his disciples to unite in order to preserve the power (δύναμις) Antony had exercised, and so obtain peace for the Church plagued by the Arian persecutions. Unfortunately, there is no historical information about Antony, and the rhetorical style and panegyrical vocabulary make the interpretation difficult.[3] But the text makes clear that Antony was seen as a main proponent of the Athanasian party and thus it supports the statements of the *Vita* and the letters that he was firmly anti-Arian. It furthermore shows the importance attached to Antony beyond the monastic setting, and emphasizes his role as that of an intercessor and a mediator. Independently of the *Vita* and the sayings, he is here exalted as the greatest of the monks.

2. The Pachomian Literature

The anonymous *Vita Pachomii* is preserved in a number of Coptic, Greek and Arabic versions, as well as translations that can be shown to derive from one or another of these.[4] Since the first publication of Coptic and Arabic texts of the *Vita* there has been a lively debate among scholars on

1 *CPG* 2493; Edited by R. Draguet ('Une lettre de Sérapion de Thmuis', pp. 4–17) with detailed arguments for the attribution to Serapion.

2 See Hieronymus, *Chronicon* ad annum 356. The reference in the letter to the occupation of the churches of Alexandria and the flight of the orthodox to the desert is corroborated by the fact that the church of Theonas was seized by the duke on Febr. 8, 356, at which occasion Athanasius went into the desert for his third exile (356–362). See Athanasius, *Apologia de fuga sua* 24–25. Later the same year all churches were handed over to the Arians.

3 Tetz ('Athanasius und die Vita Antonii', pp. 13–16), sees in the letter and its lack of Christology a radically different theology than Athanasius' and the clearly Athanasian parts of the *Vita*. This is, however, to overinterpret a short letter written in affection and according to rhetorical tradition by a highly literate bishop to the disciples of an outstanding teacher and ascetic when hearing about his death. The confidence put in the intercessions of the monk and the rhetorical pomposity in the letter is actually paralleled in some of the letters to Paphnutius (*P. Jews* 1923–1929, see Bell, *Jews and Christians*, pp. 100–120) and to Nepheros (Kramer & Shelton, *Das Archiv des Nepheros*, p. 8, see *i.a.* letter 10, pp. 65–69). One of the letters (*P. Jews* 1929) is possibly even from Athanasius himself!

4 A complete list of editions with the various translations is given by Armand Veilleux, *The Pachomian Koinonia, I, The Life of Pachomius* (*CS* 45), Kalmazoo 1980, pp. 477–480. The text of the *Vita* is quoted according to the editions of Halkin and Lefort, but the references to the Coptic are according to Veilleux, *op.cit.* and introduced as *VP/SBo*.

the priority of the various versions.[1] For a long time the debate focused on whether the Greek or the Coptic version takes priority, but recent studies tend to see both as independent witnesses to a common source. It has been suggested that the Arabic version is a translation of this source.[2] From the versions it is evident that behind the various Lives there are orally transmitted stories and probably also short written accounts, and that the versions, where they differ, have redactional purposes of their own. Though the final redaction of the Greek and Coptic versions known to us cannot have been made before the last decades of the fourth century, and the first reference to written Lives is given at about this time by Evagrius, a careful analysis of the individual passages shows that the majority have a nucleus that can be considered contemporary with the accounts.[3]

Antony is in the introduction to *Vita Pachomii* mentioned as a precursor of Pachomius, and in the Greek text his war with the demons is used to mirror Pachomius' own struggle. Since the Greek *Life* explicitly mentions the *Vita Antonii* as a model, it must have been known to the final redactor of this version.[4] Praise for Antony and Athanasius is also found in an interesting passage where Theodore quotes Pachomius as having referred to them and the Pachomian *koinonia* as 'the three great things flourishing in Egypt by God's favour'.[5] The quotation is, however, used so that it gives the impression that it is an attempt to enhance the reputation of the *koinonia.* A similar saying attributed to Antony is found in Coptic and Arabic collections of sayings. In the Coptic saying it is Athanasius, Macarius and Pambo who are praised, while the Arabic gives us Pachomius instead of Pambo.[6] While it is evident that the Arabic version of the saying is secondary, and probably influenced by the *Vita Pachomii,* it is harder to

1 The debate is summarized by Rousseau, *Pachomius,* pp. 37–48, and James E. Goehring, *The Letter of Ammon and Pachomian Monasticism* (*PTS* 27), Berlin 1986, pp. 3–23.

2 See Veilleux, *The Pachomian Koinonia,* pp. 1–18. It is the penetrating analysis and the stemma of Veilleux which is today most widely accepted. For other opinions by de Vogüé and Chitty, see Goehring, *op.cit.,* pp. 22–23, and Rousseau, *op.cit.,* p. 40.

3 The literature on the *Vita Pachomii* is vast; a good bibliography is found in Veilleux, *op.cit.* pp. 481–488. The character of the text and its redactional motives are discussed in Goehring, 'New Frontiers in Pachomian Studies', pp. 236–257, and Rousseau, *Pachomius,* pp. 37–55 and *passim.* See also Friedrich Ruppert, *Das Pachomianische Mönchtum und die Anfänge klösterlichen Gehorsams, Münsterschwarzacher Studien 20,* Münsterschwarzach 1971, and Büchler, *Die Armut der Armen,* for discussion on main traits in the *Vita.*

4 See the introduction in *VP/G* 2 and *VP/SBo* 2. The reference to Antony and the demons in *VP/G* 22 seems to depend on the *Vita Antonii,* as probably the entire chapters 17–19. Another explicit mention of the *Vita Antonii* is found in *VP/G* 99. The relation between the two *vitae* is discussed in Rousseau, *Pachomius,* pp. 45–48 and 60 n. 17.

5 *VP/G* 136, *VP/SBo* 134 (S^5 16, Lefort, p. 185).

6 For the Coptic see *AP/Bo* 26 (*AMG* XXV, p. 27). The Arabic saying is not edited, but found *i.a.* in the mss. *Vat. ar.* 398, f. 90v and *St. Ant. Theol.* 177, f. 109r. A Latin translation is found Ecchellensis, *Sanctissimi Patris Nostri Antonii Magni,* p. 107, reprinted in *PG* 40,1100.

decide the priority between the Coptic saying and the passage in the *Vita*. The fact that in the latter the passage is connected with the visit of the Pachomians to Antony, discussed below, supports the priority of the Antonian version.

The most important account involving Antony in the *Vita Pachomii* is the long passage on the visit paid to Antony by Theodore and a number of brothers.[1] Here the *Vita* is independent of other sources, since the version incorporated in the Arabic corpus of Antonian writings is clearly secondary.[2] Even if the different versions of the story vary greatly, the account in the Greek *Vita* being much shorter than the one found in the Coptic, the story is essentially the same, and there seems to be no reason to doubt its historicity. The visit is reported to have taken place in 346, at the time of Athanasius' return from his second exile and the death of Petronius, Pachomius' successor, shortly after Pachomius' own death.[3] On their way to Alexandria the Pachomian monks learn that Antony is weak and ill, staying at Pispir, his 'outer' monastery close to the Nile. They interrupt their voyage and visit him. Antony rejoices and regains his strength. When he learns of Pachomius' death he comforts them and praises the founder of the *koinonia,* thereby provoking a debate in which he extols the cenobitic life even above the anchoritic. Hearing about the subsequent death of Petronius, he praises Horsiesius, the appointed successor, and writes to Athanasius in support of him and the Pachomians. In the Greek text the death of Petronius was already known at the time of the visit, and Antony hands his letter to the brothers. In the Coptic version he hears about Petronius' death only after their departure, and sends the letter to Athanasius together with a letter of consolation to them; both are included in the Coptic text.[4]

1 *VP/G* 120, *VP/SBo* 124–134 (S^5 16, Lefort, pp. 174–185). The relations between the two accounts is discussed by Rousseau, *Pachomius,* p. 179 n. 15.

2 The text is not found in *Vat. ar.* 398 nor in the Latin translations, but in *i.a. St. Ant. Theol.* 177 and *St. Mac. Hom.* 23 and 24. This text is not the same as the sermon published in *Kitāb rauḍat al-nufūs fī rasā'il al-qiddīs Anṭūniyūs,* pp. 180–184, quoted in *GCAL* I, 458, l. 3, as suggested by Zanetti, *Catalogue,* p. 50. It corresponds to *VP/SBo* 126–129 (S^5 16, Lefort, p. 177–180).

3 According to the *Vita Pachomii,* Pachomius died on May 9, 346 and Petronius on July 19 the same year. Athanasius returned to Alexandria on Oct. 21 (Athanasius, *Festal Index* 18). In the Greek version of the story, the visit takes place after the Pachomian monks got the news about Petronius' death, but it is unclear if they were still in Upper Egypt or already in Alexandria. In the Coptic version the visit takes place on the way to Alexandria, where they get the news.

4 *VP/SBo* 133 (S^5 16, Lefort, p.183f.). In the first letter Antony refers to a revelation for his praise of Horsiesius and in the second he urges the bishop to encourage the Pachomians and instill loyalty in them to their newly elected leader. As later developments showed, this loyalty was not very strong and Horsiesius soon had to abdicate (see *VP/G* 129, *VP/SBo* 139).

The debate between Zacchaeus, a young Pachomian, and Antony, as well as the importance attached to Antony's letter of recommendation sent to Athanasius, shows that the purpose of the story is to prove that Antony supported the Pachomians. The importance of Antony's and Athanasius' support is also evident at the end of the story in the Coptic version, where the Pachomian brothers are astonished at the interest the famous monk and the great patriarch took in them. It is here that Theodore reports Pachomius' words in praise of Athanasius, Antony and the *koinonia.* In the debate with Zacchaeus, Antony's support for Pachomius and the *koinonia* meets with distrust, since Antony does not himself live a cenobitic life. Antony replies by referring to his age and lack of cenobitic training, extolling Pachomius' achievement. To support this he refers to the importance he himself attaches to the task of leading souls to God by constantly visiting the monks and receiving visitors. In the Coptic version this is further illustrated by a second debate, in which some angry dignitaries questioned him about the attention he had showed the Pachomians and the praise he had given them. To defend himself Antony refers to a revelation received through an angel of God. In a final debate he must defend his praise against his own disciples, who complain about the suspicion they meet with when they visit Pachomian monasteries. Antony replies by referring to the need to beware of false prophets. The impression the text gives is that it is intended to support a stricter attitude on orthodoxy than generally connected with the Antonian tradition.[1]

The story about the visit is of interest for the understanding of the Antonian as well as the Pachomian tradition. Firstly, it gives strong support for Antony's predominant position in early monastic Egypt. Antony is called upon both to support the Pachomian tradition in general and the election of Horsiesius as the successor of Petronius. He is further brought forward to recommend the Pachomians to Athanasius, and it is at least implied by the story that Antony had a considerable influence in Alexandria. The story also refers to his correspondence with the emperors, adding support to the historicity of that account, and to the reports about the constant flow of dignitaries visiting him. It furthermore shows how his name was in general use as a password for refuge in monasteries. Secondly, it supports the image of Antony as a diligent letter-writer, engaged in the spiritual education of his monks as well as in counselling and mediation. Thirdly, there is an implication that the Antonian tradition was regarded as less strictly orthodox than the Pachomian monasteries.

[1] The Pachomians are said to have replied to the complaints of the Antonian monks by stating that many come and assert that they are the disciples of Antony but then it turns out that they are heretics. Antony's comment is recorded as: 'Do you want the brothers of the holy *koinonia* to act as you do and not test anyone?' (ⲉⲧⲉⲧⲛ̄ⲟⲩⲱϣ ⲉⲧⲣⲉⲛⲉⲥⲛⲏⲩ ⲛ̄ⲧⲕⲟⲓⲛⲱⲛⲓⲁ ⲉⲧⲟⲩⲁⲁⲃ ⲣ̄ⲧⲉⲧⲛ̄ϩⲉ ⲛ̄ϭⲉⲧⲙ̄ϣⲱⲡⲉ ⲛ̄ⲣⲉϥⲇⲟⲕⲓⲙⲁⲍⲉ ⲛ̄ⲗⲁⲁⲩ) *VP/SBo* 129 (S[5] 16, Lefort, p. 180).

There is no manifest sign in this story of any dependence on earlier literature on Antony. The parallels with the *Vita Antonii* and the *apophthegmata* in the references to the emperors, dignitaries, etc., are too commonplace to be conclusive. There is, however, one important parallel to Antony's letters, the use of 'Israelite' and the interpretation given. According to the Coptic versions of the *Vita Pachomii*, Antony writes about Horsiesius, the new head of the *koinonia,* in a letter of consolation to the Pachomians:

> Now, then, holy brothers, we should not call him Horsiesios, but rather the 'Israelite', that is, the one who sees God with interior as well as exterior eyes. You, brothers, are blessed because God has made you worthy of a father strengthened with the Spirit of God.[1]

The only other case where the term 'Israelite' occurs in Pachomian writings as an honorary title for a monk is in the preceding chapter in the Coptic Life, but this passage, unparalleled in the Greek Lives, seems to be a later addition modelled on the story about the visit to Antony and Alexandria. Actually 'Israelite' is a very rare term in early monastic sources, and the copious use of it in Antony's letters is unparalleled elsewhere.[2] The interpretation above—in contrast to the reference to John 1:47 'a true Israelite in whom there is no guile'—presupposes the etymology of the name as 'a man (or a soul) who sees God' based on Gen 32:28. This interpretation is characteristic of Origen, and the only parallel in early monastic literature outside Antony's letters is in the *Conlationes* of Cassian.[3] The most plausible explanation for the occurence of the term and the interpretation of it in the Pachomian Lives is that Antony is the actual source. A direct dependence upon a letter is also more likely than a preserved oral tradition.

The other Pachomian text containing a reference to Antony is the *Epistula Ammonis.*[4] It purports to be a letter to Theophilus from a certain Ammon, who in his youth in 352 had become a monk in a Pachomian

1 ⲧⲉⲛⲟⲩϭⲉ ⲛⲉⲥⲛⲏⲩ ⲉⲧⲟⲩⲁⲁⲃ ⲙ̄ⲡⲣ̄ⲧⲣⲉⲛⲙⲟⲩⲧⲉ ⲉⲣⲟϥ ϫⲉϩⲱⲣⲥⲓⲏⲥⲓⲟⲥ, ⲁⲗⲗⲁ ⲡⲓⲥⲣⲁⲏⲗⲓⲧⲏⲥ ⲉⲧⲉⲡⲉⲧⲛⲁⲩ ⲉⲡⲛⲟⲩⲧⲉⲡⲉ ϩⲛ̄ⲛⲃⲁⲗ ⲉⲧϩⲓϩⲟⲩⲛ ⲙⲛ̄ⲛⲉⲧϩⲓⲃⲟⲗ ⲛ̄ⲧⲱⲧⲛ̄ϭⲉ (*VP/SBo* 133, Lefort, p. 182). In the Greek Life, where the Pachomians are present when Antony hears about Horsiesius' appointment, and there thus is no need of a letter, Antony tells them to call Horsiesius the 'Israelite', but the interpretation of the word is omitted (*VP/G* 120). The omission could be a deliberate avoidance of Origenist language.

2 In the *apophthegmata* the term is found only once in the alphabetical collection *G*—with a reference to John 1:47, not to Gen 32:28—and not at all in the Latin, Coptic or Syriac versions. The term is also absent from *VA*, *HL*, *HM* and the documentary archives of Paieous, Paphnutius and Nepheros (Bell, *Jews and Christians,* and Kramer & Shelton, *Das Archiv des Nepheros*).

3 See *Ep. Ant.* III.5–6 and, without the explicit interpretation, V.1, VI.2, 78, 93 and VII.5. For Cassian, see his *Conlationes,* Praefatio, and V.25 and XII.11. Cf. above, p. 41 and 69, where the references to Origen and previous literature are given.

4 *CPG* 2378. Edited by J. Goehring, *The Letter of Ammon and Pachomian Monasticism* (*PTS* 27), Berlin 1986.

monastery, in which he stayed for three years. He then moved to Nitria, and was later called to a bishopric. The letter is more of an encomium on Theodore than a personal letter. Theodore was Pachomius' favourite disciple and headed the *koinonia* from 351 to 368. The letter was probably written about 400 to Theophilus, archbishop of Alexandria (385-412). The literary character of the *Epistula Ammonis* is obvious, as is the fact that the incidents it relates took place when the author was young, some forty or fifty years earlier. But even if it differs in important respects from more original Pachomian material, it reveals a detailed knowledge about the Pachomian tradition independently from the *vitae,* and its historical information is remarkably accurate.[1]

In this letter Antony is mentioned twice, first as the writer of a short letter, quoted in extenso, and subsequently as the famous monk at whom the assembled bishops, including Athanasius, marvelled.[2] While the second instance refers to Antony's fame, the significance of the first is greater. Here Ammon relates how Theodore speaks about a revelation on post-baptismal sins, and shortly afterwards receives a letter by Antony containing exactly the same teaching. The letter is generally accepted as genuine, and Ammon is supposed to have relied on a copy of it when he wrote his encomium.[3] The letter is in Greek, but is said to have been written in Coptic and translated for the Greek brothers. It contains a greeting and a reference to a revelation as the reason for the letter, followed by the assurance of forgiveness for those who have repented their post-baptismal sins. It runs as follows:

> Antony, to [his] beloved son Theodore, greetings in the Lord. I knew that *the Lord will do nothing without first revealing a teaching to his servants, the prophets* (Amos 3:7). I [first] thought that there was no need for me to disclose to you what God had revealed to me long ago, but when I saw your brothers, those who were with Theophilus and Kopres, He [God] enjoined me to write to you, disclosing that almost everywhere there are many who, although they worship Christ in truth, have sinned after being baptized and [then] weep and mourn. Since He has heard their weeping and mourning, God has wiped out the sins of all those who have acted so, until the day in which this letter is given to you. Read it to your brothers, so that they too

1 A detailed analysis of the letter and its relation to the other Pachomian sources is given in Goehring, *The Letter of Ammonas,* pp. 103–122. Goehring takes his stand between Lefort's opinion of the letter as an apocryphal work of little historical value and Chitty's appreciation of its value as a historical source. Goehring regards it as authentic, but due to its late date and obvious encomiastic purpose not reliable in detail. The author's use of accurate sources is particularly important, see *ibid.,* pp. 110–111.

2 *Epistula Ammonis* 29 and 34.

3 See *CPG* 2332; Quasten, *Patrology,* III, p. 152; and Dörries, 'Die Vita Antonii', p. 221. The only argument given is, however, the reference to *AP/G* Antony 25 and 30, made by Dörries, and these sayings are too general to be of any value for the authenticity of this letter. With some hesitancy Goehring, *The Letter of Ammon,* p. 111, 277f., accepts the genuineness, offering a fresh argument discussed below. The power of the myth about Antony's illiteracy created by *VA* 1 and 72 is strikingly attested by the note on p. 278.

> might hear it and rejoice. Give greetings to the brothers. The brothers send you greetings. I pray that you may have good health in the Lord.[1]

The letter, and Theodore's revelation preceding it, has striking parallels with the teaching in the *Shepherd of Hermas.* Here we find the same assurance of post-baptismal forgiveness until this day, on the condition of true repentance. Like Hermas, the revelation and the subsequent confirmation given by the letter, represent an attempt to relax a very strict view on post-baptismal sin. As noted above the *Shepherd of Hermas* is well represented in the early papyri, and seems to have been a popular text in Egyptian Christianity. Though it cannot be proved that Pachomius used it, his teaching as presented in the *Vita Pachomii* has striking parallels with it.[2] The obvious allusion to Hermas in Ammon's text gives further proof of the importance of the *Shepherd* for early monastic tradition. At the same time the allusion should caution us against interpreting the reference to the day the letter is received as an absolute limit for forgiveness, and consequently to a doctrine of a single possibility of post-baptismal forgiveness. Neither in Pachomian nor in Antonian material is there any support for such a doctrine.[3] The letter, as the revelation before, wants to emphasize the need for repentence and to comfort repentent monks with an assurance of forgiveness, supported by the reference to God's revelation.

In a wider context the purpose of the insertion of Antony's letter is to verify Theodore's gift of foreknowledge and his divine revelations. The expressions 'until the day this letter is given to you' and 'read it to your

1 Τῷ ἀγαπητῷ υἱῷ Θεοδώρῳ 'Αντώνιος ἐν κυρίῳ χαίρειν. ᾔδειν μὲν ὅτι *οὐ μὴ ποιήσει κύριος ὁ θεὸς πρᾶγμα, ἐὰν μὴ ἀποκαλύψῃ παιδείαν πρὸς τοὺς δούλους αὐτοῦ τοὺς προφήτας·* καὶ ἐνόμιζον μὴ δεῖν με δηλῶσαι σοι ἅπερ μοι ὁ θεὸς πρὸ πολλοῦ ἀποκαλύψας ἦν. ἐπειδὴ δὲ ἑωρακότι μοι τοὺς ἀδελφούς σου τοὺς περὶ Θεόφιλον καὶ Κόπρην προσέταξεν γράψαι σοι, δηλῶν ὅτι πολλοὶ τῶν μετὰ ἀληθείας τὸν Χριστὸν προσκυνούντων, μετὰ τὸ βαπτισθῆναι ἡμαρτηκότων σχεδὸν ἐν ὅλῳ τῷ κόσμῳ, κλαυσάντων καὶ πενθησάντων, ὁ θεὸς τὸν κλαυθμὸν καὶ τὸ πένθος ἀποδεξάμενος, τὰς ἁμαρτίας ἐξήλειψεν πάντων τῶν οὕτως πορευσαμένων ἕως ἐκείνης τῆς ἡμέρας ἐν ᾗ ἂν ἡ ἐπιστολὴ ταύτη (*sic.* αὕτη?) ἐπιδοθῇ σοι. ἀνάγνωθι οὖν αὐτὴν τοῖς ἀδελφοῖς σου, ἵνα καὶ αὐτοὶ ἀκούσαντες χαρῶσιν. ἄσπασαι τοὺς ἀδελφούς. ἀσπάζονται σε οἱ ἀδελφοί. εὔχομαί σε ὑγιαίνειν ἐν κυρίῳ. The somewhat awkward constructions in the Greek text could indicate a translation from Coptic. In this case it is probably one of the first texts translated from Coptic to Greek. The translation is my revision of that of James Goehring.

2 Rousseau, *Pachomius,* pp. 136–138, convincingly argues for regarding the *Shepherd* as a part of Pachomius' background. Probably the *Shepherd* was read in the churches of Upper Egypt as a canonical writing far into the fourth century; it was included as such in the fourth century *Codex Sinaiticus,* which is likely to be of Egyptian origin.

3 Here I find it difficult to agree with Goehring, *The Letter of Ammon,* pp. 275–278, who sees a reference to such a doctrine and regards it—more plausible in the anchoritic tradition of Antony, than in a Pachomian setting—as an argument for the authenticity of the letter. Even if the words in the letter and in the preceding sermon, are taken to mean that God will forgive sins committed until the day mentioned, they do not exclude a future forgiveness for future sins. The stress is on the assurance for forgiveness certified by the authority of Antony, not on any doctrine.

brothers, so that they too might hear it and rejoice', are so well integrated into the situation and the sermon preached before, that the story either must be be composed around the letter, or the letter revised in accordance with the story. The content of the letter and Theodore's sermon are not only of minor importance in the larger context, but even somewhat strange. Nowhere else in the *Epistula Ammonis* or in other Pachomian material is there any reference to a limit for forgiveness. That there was a tradition with a very harsh view stressing the uncertainty of forgiveness in the early anchoritic tradition is evident from the sayings, and a similar anxiety is palpable in Antony's letters.[1] Moreover, there is nothing in this letter to contradict an attribution to Antony; on the contrary, its emphasis on repentance and mercy and the author's wish to comfort his brother monks fit very well with the seven Antonian letters. If genuine, the letter not only supports Antony's position in relation to the Pachomians, but also the view of him as literate.

3. Jerome and Rufinus

Jerome and Rufinus, intimate friends to become bitter enemies, both visited the Egyptian monastic scene in the late fourth century, and both referred to the monks of Egypt as the great masters of the desert.[2] Although Antony had died some eighteen years before Rufinus' first visit, which probably took place in 373, and almost thirty years before Jerome's visit in 385 or 386, the visitors were able to meet with his friends and disciples and to collect reliable information about him. Both of them stayed with Didymus—Rufinus for some six years—and were told about his contacts with Antony. Rufinus, who spent almost ten years in Egypt, also visited Antony's monastery at Pispir. While Jerome had read the *Vita Antonii* some ten years earlier— he even wrote a companion to it, the *Vita Pauli*— there is nothing in Rufinus that shows a dependence on Antony's *Vita*.

Unfortunately Rufinus does not say much about Antony. His greatest interest during his stay in Egypt was the theology of Origen, as taught by

[1] In Antony's letters forgiveness is in fact only mentioned twice, and in both cases as part of what Jesus accomplished by his *parousia*, and impending judgement is a constant theme. See above p. 77f, 81–85, and *i.a. Ep. Ant.* I.77, II.34–35, III.32–37, V.30–34, VI.106–107. But there is nothing to indicate that Antony had a strict doctrine on the limits of post-baptismal sin.

[2] For Rufinus, see Françoise Thelamon, 'Rufin d'Aquilée', *DSp* 13, 1988, pp. 1107–1117 and Francis X. Murphy, *Rufinus of Aquileia (345–411). His Life and Works,* Washington 1945, especially pp. 28–58. For Jerome, see J.N.D. Kelly, *Jerome. His Life, Writings and Controversies,* London 1975.

Didymus. But he mentions that he was also taught by the monks when he visited Nitria, Kellia, Scetis, and that he even went down to Antony's monastery at Pispir and saw two of his disciples there.[1] His stay in Egypt is first mentioned in a letter Jerome wrote to him when he heard about his old friend visiting the monks in Scetis. Rufinus himself refers to his stay in Egypt both in his expanded and revised translation of Eusebius' *Historia Ecclesiastica* and in his *Apologia*. His interest in the monks of Egypt is evident by the fact that he later greatly contributed to the literature on the desert fathers by revising and translating the *Historia Monachorum.*

In his *Historia Ecclesiastica* Rufinus refers to Antony on three occasions. In the first reference he simply mentions Antony as the first hermit, and in the second he enumerates his disciples: Macarius (the Egyptian), Isidorus, the other Macarius, Heraclides, and Pambo.[2] The list is interesting, since it does not agree with the names given in the *Historia Monachorum,* which Rufinus himself translated, not even with the variants that are found only in his Latin version. There is, however, little reason to doubt the accuracy of the list; the *alius* Macarius is probably the Macarius mentioned both by Palladius and Jerome, not the famous Macarius of Alexandria.

The third reference to Antony in Rufinus is of greater interest. Here Rufinus speaks about Didymus, his teacher, whom Antony once consoled on his blindness. Antony is said to have come from the Thebaid to Alexandria to stand up for the faith of Athanasius against the Arians.[3] While in Alexandria he meets with Didymus and tells him not to be saddened by the loss of his carnal eyes, which he shares with rats and mice; he should instead rejoice at having the eyes of the angels, through which God can be seen and through which the great light of knowledge has been revealed to him. The same story is told by Jerome in a letter to a blind monk, and by Socrates and Sozomenus in their Church histories. It is also handed down in a saying in the Pseudo-Rufinian collection R.[4] While Socrates and Sozomenus follow Rufinus closely, Jerome and the saying, which must be considered a literal extract from his letter, tell the story quite differently. For the sake of comparison the texts of Rufinus and Jerome are given here.

1 Rufinus' stay with the monks is mentioned first by Jerome in his letter to Rufinus in Egypt, dated 374, see Hieronymus, *Epistula ad Rufinum* (ep. 3). It is also referred to by Rufinus, both in his *HE* and in his *Apologia* II,15. In *HE* II.4 he emphasizes the need for a special book on the monks, and in *HE* II.8 he relates the names of those he met.

2 Rufinus, *HE* I.8 and II.4. In *HE* II.8 he says that the monks he met at Pispir 'qui appellabatur mons Antonii' were Poimen and Joseph.

3 Rufinus, *HE* II.7.

4 Hieronymus, *Epistula ad Castricianum* (ep. 68); Socrates, *HE* IV.25; Sozomenus, *HE* III.15; *AP/R* 218.

Rufinus, *HE* II.7:

Hunc etiam beatus Antonius cum fidei Athanasii testimonium laturus adversum Arrianos de Thebaide Alexandriam descendisset, magnificis consolatus est verbis: nihil te, inquit, offendat, o Didyme, quod carnalibus oculis videris orbatus, desunt enim tibi illi oculi, quos mures et muscae et lacertae habent; sed laetare, quia habes oculos, quos angeli habent, e quibus deus videtur, per quos tibi magnum scientiae lumen accenditur.

Jerome, *Epistula ad Castricianum:*

Beatus Antonius, cum a sancto Athanasio, Alexandriae episcopo, propter confutationem haereticorum in urbem esset accitus et isset ad eum Didymus, vir eruditissimus, captus oculis, inter ceteras sermonicationes, quas de scripturis sanctis habebant, cum eius admiraretur ingenium et acumen animi conlaudaret, sciscitans, ait: 'num tristis es, quod oculis carnis careas?' Cum ille pudore reticeret, secundo tertioque interrogans tandem elicuit ut moerorem animi simpliciter fateretur. Cui Antonius: 'Miror,' ait, 'prudentem virum ejus rei dolere damnum, quam formicae, et muscae, et culices habeant, et non laetari illius possessione, quam soli sancti et apostoli meruerunt'. Ex quo pervides, quod multo melius sit spiritu videre quam carne et illos oculos possidere, in quos festuca peccati non possit incidere.

Since Jerome's letter was written before Rufinus' account, and it is extremely unlikely that Rufinus is dependent on his text, even that he could have had the opportunity to read it, both authors must rely on earlier tradition. A comparison of the texts gives the impression that Jerome expanded the original short saying by Antony with a frame story in which Didymus is praised. He substituted the comparison with rats, mice and lizards for the even smaller ants and flies as well as the saints and apostles for the angels and concluded with a Biblical allusion. Even if it is possible that both Jerome and Rufinus heard the story from Didymus, it is more likely that Jerome heard the story from Rufinus, with whom he was in close contact until their strife began in the early 390's.[1] Since Socrates is known to have used Rufinus, and Sozomenus both Socrates and Rufinus, their accounts are less valuable.[2]

The value of Rufinus' account is that it was written by someone who had come to know the Egyptian scene from within before the dissemination of texts such as the *Vita Antonii,* the *Vita Pauli,* the *Historia Monachorum* and the *Historia Lausiaca.* From his report it is evident that he regarded the monks as learned men with deep spiritual insight. He also supplies us with the names of the important monks of the generation after

1 Against C. Butler, *The Lausiac History of Palladius,* I (*Texts and Studies* 6.1), Cambridge 1898., p. 221, who seems to put more trust in Jerome than in Rufinus, something modern research has little reason to do. Even if very unlikely it cannot, however, be excluded that Jerome has preserved the original story, of which Rufinus has only kept the pointed saying.

2 Jerome wrote his letter in A.D. 397, and Rufinus wrote in A.D. 402–403 (Thélamon, 'Rufin d'Aquilée', p. 1111). Socrates explicitly mentions his use of Rufinus (see *HE* II.1). For Sozomenus, see the introduction to the edition by Bidez, pp. xliv–xlviii, and G. Schoo, *Die Quellen des Kirchenhistorikers Sozomenos,* p. 25f.. Socrates differs from Rufinus only in a reference to Didymus' learning, and Sozomenus only drops the reference to the Arians.

Antony. His story about the visit of Antony to Didymus gives evidence for Antony's ties with the Origenist party in Alexandria. If the visit is the same as the one recalled in the *Vita,* which seems most likely, Rufinus' account supports dating the visit to 337 A.D. before and in preparation for Athanasius' return from his first exile.[1] .

Besides the above-mentioned reference to Antony in Jerome's letter to Castricianus, Antony is referred to in two other letters by Jerome, first as the man who made monasticism famous, secondly in connection with the translation Evagrius of Antioch made of the *Vita Antonii.*[2] In his *De viris illustribus* Jerome has the important entry on Antony, referring to his seven letters, and he also mentions him in the entry on Serapion of Thmuis, of whom Antony is said to have been a friend, and in the entry on Evagrius of Antioch, where the translation of the *Vita* is mentioned.[3] More significant for Jerome's views on Antony, however, are the references to him in his hagiographical writings, the *Vita Pauli* and the *Vita Hilarionis.*

In the first, the *Vita Pauli,* he sets up a rival to Antony, proclaiming Paul to be the first hermit.[4] Generally this Life has been regarded as a work of fiction by Jerome, and as an attempt to emulate the *Vita Antonii,* already famous and known to Jerome in the Latin translation his host had made a few years earlier.[5] The date for its composition has been put at 375, which makes it Jerome's first major work. Nevertheless, there are

1 See *VA* 69–71 and Athanasius, *Epistulae festales* (Index for Letter X, 338 A.D., see Lorenz, *Der Zehnte Osterfestbrief des Athanasius von Alexandrien,* p. 3–6). Since the Index relates what happened in the Coptic year (Sept. 337–Aug. 338) it does not solve the problem of the date of the visit, 337 or 338, or the related question of whether Athanasius was in Alexandria and responsible for the summons of Antony. Athanasius' presence, as postulated by Jerome and *R* and at least indicated by the *VA* requires 338, but the lack of reference to Athanasius in Rufinus and the ambiguity in the *VA* makes 337 quite likely. For a discussion see Tetz, 'Athanasius und Die Vita Antonii', pp. 23–24 and Lorenz, *op.cit.*, pp. 3–5.

2 Hieronymus, *Epistula* 22 and 57.

3 Hieronymus, *De viris illustribus,* 88, 99, and 125.

4 The text is preserved in Latin, Coptic, Greek and Syriac, but the relationship between the versions is still a matter of dispute, as also the question of authorship. Of the four versions the three first have all been declared the original. Amélineau, who edited the Coptic text, regarded it as the original (E. Amélineau, *Histoire des monastères de la Basse-Égypte* (*AMG* XXV), Paris 1894, pp. 1–14), while a more well founded preference for the Greek version (ed. by J. Bidez, *Deux versions grecques inédites de la Vie de Paul de Thèbes,* Gand 1900) was propounded by F. Nau, 'Le texte grec original de la Vie de S. Paul de Thèbes', *AB* 20 (1901), pp. 121–157, and *idem,* ' Le chapitre ΠΕΡΙ ΑΝΑΧΩΡΗΤΩΝ ΑΓΙΩΝ', *ROC* 10 (1905), pp. 395–408. The Latin version (*PL* 23,17–28, cf. A. Oldfather, *Studies in the Text Tradition of St. Jerome's Vitae Patrum,* Urbana 1943) has been known as a work of Jerome since his own days. It is, if not an original work by Jerome, at least a substantial elaboration of the source used. See P. Rousseau, *Ascetics, Authority and the Church,* pp. 133–134.

5 See Dörries, 'Die Vita Antonii', pp. 205–206, and M. Fuhrmann, 'Die Mönchsgeschichten des Hieronymus. Formexperimente in erzählender Literatur', *Christianisme et formes littéraires de l'antiquité tardive en occident,* Geneva 1976. Even his contemporaries regarded Paul as an invented figure; see *Vita Hilarionis* 1, where Jerome defends himself.

passages in this *Vita* that seem to be authentic, and the structure of the text is not that of a well-composed literary unit. In all probability Jerome compiled his version on the basis of some, probably written, sources.[1] The text is not a complete *vita,* but an account of how Paul and Antony first met, introduced by a reference to the debate on who was the first monk, and an account of the persecution which caused Paul to become a hermit. The emphasis is on Paul's precedence, and by elaborating the connection with Elijah and Elisha, present already in the *Vita Antonii,* it is indicated that Antony should be seen as his disciple.

The *Vita Hilarionis* is a complete *Vita*, which describes the life and character of Hilarion, including his short period as a disciple of Antony's. Jerome's authorship has never been questioned, and the date for its composition is generally given as c. 390.[2] Antony is depicted as the teacher of Hilarion, later to become the father of Palestinian monasticism. The purpose is clearly to provide the Palestinian monasticism with a history, and to trace its origins back to Egypt; Jerome supports his writing by referring to Epiphanius of Salamis, who, he says, had been close to Hilarion and had written a letter about him.[3] The text is clearly dependent on the *Vita Antonii*, and adds little to the Antonian image. It relates how Hilarion, at the age of fifteen, stayed with Antony for two weeks to study his discipline; unable to endure the crowds around him he decided to leave for Palestine and take up the life of a hermit.[4] At the age of 65, after hearing about Antony's death, he is said to have fled fame and crowds in Palestine and returned to Egypt. His goal was the 'inner' monastery of Antony, and arriving there he moved in as his successor. By his prayers he is reported to have procured rain after three years of drought caused by the mourning of the elements due to Antony's death. After some time he moved on to Sicily, and finally to Cyprus.[5]

[1] It is suggested that a source used by the compiler of the *Vita Pauli* is found in a small collection of sayings, later integrated into the Latin *Vitae Patrum* as book VI, ch. III. See Nau, ' Le chapitre ΠΕΡΙ ΑΝΑΧΩΡΗΤΩΝ ΑΓΙΩΝ', pp. 405–407.

[2] The text is printed in *PL* 23, 29–54. For studies of style and motives see Fuhrmann, *op.cit.*, pp. 41–58, Rousseau, *Ascetics, Authority and the Church*, pp. 136–139.

[3] There is no evidence for Hilarion preserved besides Jerome, Sozomenus, who is deeply indebted to him, and two rather unreliable sayings. The sources about Epiphanius' early life, his monastic education in Egypt and his relations with Hilarion, are extremely poor, confined to the reference in Jerome's *Vita,* and a single note in Sozomenus (*HE* VI.32), the reliability of which is highly suspect taking Sozomenus' predilection for Epiphanius into account.

[4] *Vita Hilarionis* 3. Besides the lack of any independent support, and the obvious attempt to link Hilarion to Antony, the historicity of the account is hard to upheld. Since Hilarion is said to have been 65 years old in 356, he must have been born in 291, which puts the stay with Antony in 306, a time when Antony's name can hardly have been 'in the mouth of all the peoples of Egypt', and he himself visited by crowds of afflicted.

[5] *Vita Hilarionis* 29–32. The obvious desire to emphasize Hilarion's discipleship to Antony and almost outbid him, makes also this account suspect. The use of Antony as a model for the *Vita Hilarionis* is stressed by Rousseau, *Ascetics, Authority and the Church,* pp. 136–139.

Jerome's references to Antony thus reveal more about Jerome and the impact of the *Vita Antonii* than about Antony himself. His eagerness to be associated with Athanasius' famous work, and his attempt first to outdo it and then to imitate it, are obvious—to him even the Latin translation by Evagrius of Antioch is authoritative as *the* model for translation.[1] It is with the hero of Egypt that he wants to connect the monastic tradition in Palestine and his own literary production. His interest in Antony has, however, supplied one of the most important leads in the literature on Antony—the note about his seven letters in *De viris illustribus.*

4. THE *HISTORIA MONACHORUM IN AEGYPTO*

A report on the monks of Egypt, the *Historia Monachorum in Aegypto,* was allegedly written after a visit to Egypt in 394 by seven monks from Jerusalem.[2] The work was long known in Latin only—which led Jerome to regard it as a work by Rufinus—while the Greek text was preserved only as a part of the Palladian corpus. Preuschen and Butler identified it as a separate text, written in Greek but revised and translated by Rufinus, who added some passages of his own.[3] The text has been regarded as rather untrustworthy, and the journey as fictitious, but recent research awards it more credibility.[4] Like the *Historia Lausiaca* it consists of a number of short biographical sketches, here combined with reports of encounters between the group and the Egyptian monastic fathers. To a large extent its information can be checked against other material, and the monks mentioned are no doubt historical. The emphasis of the text is, however, not on biographical data but on visions, miracles and austere ascetic practices.

1 Repeatedly he stresses that this translation is the ideal he tries to emulate in his work as a translator. See Hieronymus, *De viris illustribus* 125.

2 The Greek text was first edited by E. Preuschen, *Palladius und Rufinus: ein Beitrag zur Quellenkunde des ältesten Mönchtums,* Giessen 1897; a new edition was made by A-J. Festugière, *Historia Monachorum in Aegypto* (*Subs. Hag.* 34), Bruxelles 1961 (revised reprint with French translation and commentary in *Subs. Hag.* 53, Bruxelles 1971).

3 Preuschen, *op.cit.,* and C. Butler, *The Lausiac History of Palladius,* pp. 13–15. The opposite view was taken by R. Reitzenstein, *Historia Monachorum und Historia Lausiaca. Eine Studie zur Geschichte des Mönchtums und der frühchristlichen Begriffe Gnostiker und Pneumatiker* (*Forschungen zur Religion und Literatur des Alten und Neuen Testaments* 7), Göttingen 1916, but the evidence in André-Jean Festugière, 'La problème littéraire de l'Historia Monachorum', *Hermes* 83 (1955), pp. 257–284, is convincing. A new edition of the Latin text (*PL* 21, 387–462) is published by Eva Schultz-Flügel, *Tyrannius Rufinus Historia Monachorum sive de Vita Sanctorum Patrum* (*Patristische Texte und Studien* 34), Berlin 1990. For the Oriental versions, see *CPG* 5620.

4 The authenticity of the journey was claimed by Butler, and a summary of the arguments is given by Ward in *The Lives of the Desert Father (intr. by B. Ward, tr. by N. Russell),* London 1980, pp. 4–7. Schultz-Flügel regards it likely that the text is based on a report from an actual journey which has then been embellished with numerous other stories. For a very critical view, see Owen Chadwick, *John Cassian,* London 1950, pp. 7–8.

The Historia Monachorum has no separate entry on Antony, but refers to several monks as his disciples, and relates a few anecdotes about him. The disciples mentioned are Pityrion, Ammonas, Macarius the Egyptian, Kronides, Paul the Simple, and in the Latin version of Rufinus Origen the Nitriote.[1] There are also accounts of Amoun's visit to Antony, and of how Antony saw Amoun's soul ascend to heaven; both incidents mentioned in the *Vita Antonii.*[2] Pityrion is reported to have been Antony's second successor as superior at Pispir after Ammonas, and famous for exorcising demons. He is also said to have delivered many discourses, speaking with particular authority on the discernment of spirits (διάκρισις); relating each passion to a corresponding demon, he anticipated Evagrius' systematic treatment of the passions and the demons, and linked his teaching with Antony's.[3] Kronides is reported to have been 110 years old and one of Antony's original disciples. The author(s) remembers him as a teacher who delivered many admonitions and spiritual discourses.[4] On Macarius the Egyptian there are six anecdotes, typical of the *apophthegmata* tradition where some have close parallels. In one of them Antony declares Macarius to have received his spirit and to be the heir to his virtues, and in another Macarius is tempted by the devil to use the privilege of having received 'the grace of Antony'.[5] In the story about Paul, Antony receives him, an aged man, and puts him severely to the test before accepting him as a disciple; Paul then becomes a paragon of obedience and humility.[6] Finally, Origen the Nitriote is said to have been a great teacher and a man of the highest prudence, excelling in stories about the virtues of his master, *i.e.* Antony.[7]

1 *HM* 15; 20.13; 21; 24; and for Origen of Nitria, Rufinus' version of *HM* 20. In order not to confound him with his great namesake, I refer to him as 'the Nitriote'.

2 *HM* 22. Cf. *VA* 60 and *HL* 7. While the *HL* explicitly refers to the *VA* as its source, the account in *HM* can hardly be directly dependent on the text in *VA,* even though the latter is clearly the more original form.

3 *HM* 15. Pityrion and his teaching about the demons and passions are also found in *AP/G* Pityrion. For the demonology, cf. above, pp. 86–88.

4 *HM* 20.13. He (Κρονίδης or in Rufinus' Latin version *Cronius*) is otherwise unknown, if he is not to be identified with Kronion (Κρονίων), said to be 110 years old in Sozomenus' *HE* VI.30, and/or Kronios (Κρόνιος) mentioned in *ibid.* III.14 and in *HL* 7, 21 and 22 as one of the early monks in Nitria, a presbyter and an acquaintance of Antony, perhaps identical with Chronius (Χρόνιος) in *HL* 47 It is, however, possible that there were several monks with similar names.

5 *HM* 21.2: 'Ιδοὺ ἐπαναπέπαυται τὸ πνεῦμά μου ἐπὶ σέ, καὶ ἔσῃ λοιπὸν τῶν ἐμῶν ἀρετῶν κληρονόμος, and 21.3: 'Ιδοὺ τὴν χάριν εἴληφας 'Αντωνίου. The connection between Macarius the Egyptian and Antony is particularly important, since Macarius became the great authority after Antony within the anchoritic tradition and the teacher of Evagrius.

6 The account is quite different from the one found in *HL* 22, summarized in Sozomenus, *HE* I.13. Paul is also attested as a disciple of Antony in *AP/G* Paul the Simple.

7 Origen the Nitriote is mentioned in *HL* 10 as a disciple of Pambo, a priest and *oikonomos,* and member of the Origenist group in Nitria. He is also mentioned in Sozomenus *HE* VI.30.

The references to Antony in the *Historia Monachorum* are important as evidence of traditions independent of the *Vita*. Here Antony emerges as the great master of the past, the teacher of men now famous. Moreover, almost all of them are linked not only to Antony but also to the roots of the Origenist tradition among the monks, and they are known as intellectuals. Two of them, Macarius the Egyptian and Origen the Nitriote, are directly related to the group of Origenists described by Palladius. If identical with Chronius, Kronides, the third, was one of Palladius' instructors, and one of his disciples later became a leader of the Origenist monks when they were expelled by Theophilus. The fourth, Pityrion, was an outstanding teacher on discernment whose teaching resembles what we find in the writings of Evagrius. Only the fifth, Paul the Simple, does not fit into the picture. In his simplicity he almost seems to be conceived as a counterbalance, to show that spiritual strength is independent of intellectual capacity.

5. PALLADIUS AND THE *HISTORIA LAUSIACA*

The *Historia Lausiaca* is one of the most intensely discussed texts on early monasticism. It was written in Greek by Palladius (c. 365-425), bishop of Helenopolis in Asia Minor from around 420. He had been a disciple of Evagrius, and had stayed with him for nine years in the desert of Nitria until, in 399, the group of Origenists to which he belonged was thrown out.[1] The Greek version, which has an extremely complicated text history, was edited by Butler in 1904 according to one of the three known recensions, but his edition has been heavily criticized.[2] The Latin and the Syriac versions differ substantially from the Greek, and the question of the composition and transmission of the text is far from resolved.[3] The work

[1] A recent summary of the research on Palladius is found in E. D. Hunt, 'Palladius of Helenopolis: A Party and its Supporters in the Church of the Late Fourth Century', *JTS* 24 (1973), pp. 456–480.

[2] Butler, *The Lausiac History*, II. Of the other recensions one was printed twice in the 17th century, the other never edited. A Latin translation is found in *PG* 34, 995–1260. For the debate see Butler, 'Palladiana', *JTS* 22 (1921), pp. 138–155; R. Draguet, 'Butler et sa "Lausiac History" face à un Ms. de l'édition, le Wake 67', *Le Muséon* 63 (1950), pp. 205–230; and Derwas Chitty, 'Dom Cuthbert Butler, Professor Draguet and the "Lausiac History"', *JTS* 6 (1955), pp. 102–110.

[3] In Latin two different versions are known (*PL* 74, 243–342, and *PL* 74, 343–382), but a critical edition is still wanting. The Syriac version is printed in P. Bedjan, *Acta martyrum et sanctorum*, VII, Paris 1897, pp. 1–192; and E. A. W. Budge, *The Book of Paradise*, II, London 1904, pp. 93–242. For other Oriental versions, see *CPG* 6036. In Coptic a number of fragments are known, and it has been argued that a Coptic source is used by Palladius for parts of the text. See E. Amélineau, *De 'Historia Lausiaca' quaenam sit huius ad monachorum Aegyptiorum historiam scribendam utilitas*, Paris 1887, pp. 73–124; M. Chaine, 'La double recension de l'*Histoire Lausiaque*' dans la version copte', *ROC* 25 (1925–26), pp. 232–275; P. Peeters, 'Une vie copte de S. Jean de Lycopolis', *AB* 54 (1936), pp. 359–381; R. Draguet, 'Le chapitre de l'*Histoire Lausiaque* sur les Tabennésiotes dérive-t-il d'une source copte?', *Le Muséon* 57 (1944), pp. 53–145 et 58 (1945), pp. 15–96, *idem*,

is a collection of portraits of the famous monks of the second half of the fourth century and has many affinities with the *apophthegmata*, the Pachomian texts and the *Historia Monachorum*. From its structure and its relationship to the other texts it seems evident that Palladius used written sources. He was, however, less interested in miracles and edifying stories, and his work has a strong flavour of Origenism, of the tradition of Evagrius.[1]

There is no entry on Antony in the text, but several of his disciples are presented, and stories of their encounters with him are included. The story of Amoun's visit to Antony and the revelation of his death, is told in accordance with the *Vita*. Of Pambo, who was a central figure among the Origenists, it is said that he surpassed even Antony in accuracy of speech (ἀκριβὴς τοῦ λόγου), which indicates that he was a profound theologian.[2] Explicitly mentioned as Antony's disciples are only Macarius and Amatas, who are said to have buried him, and Paul the Simple.[3] More important, however, are the other monks connected with Antony in the text: Isidorus, Didymus, Kronios, Hierax, and Stephen of Libya. Isidorus, who is mentioned as someone who had met Antony, had been a monk at Nitria; he became an ambassador of the patriarch Theophilus, but was later denounced by the same as an Origenist.[4]

Didymus, whom Palladius met now and then during his stay in Egypt, is said to have told him about a visit by Antony to his cell, on which occasion Antony gave an example of obedience. The point of the story is: if even Antony obeyed me, you should not hesitate to do so.[5] Kronios is said to have sought refuge with Antony after he had fled from his monastery. He later reports how he once acted as Antony's interpreter when a learned

---

'Une nouvelle source copte de Pallade: le ch. VIII (Amoun)', *Le Muséon* 60 (1947), pp. 227–255.

1 A penetrating study is given in Reitzenstein, *Historia Monachorum und Historia Lausiaca*, pp. 143–184, who also compares the character of the *HM* and *HL* on the basis of three stories met with in both, *ibid.* pp. 11–77. See also D. F. Buck, 'The structure of the Lausiac History', *Byzantion* 46 (1976), pp. 292–307. The Evagrian connection is emphasized by R. Draguet, 'L'*Histoire Lausiaque*, une œuvre dans l'esprit d'Évagre', *RHE* 41 (1946), pp. 321–364 and 42 (1947), pp. 5–49.

2 *HL* 8 gives the account of Amoun's visit to Antony, evidently dependent on the *VA*, and *HL* 10 deals with Pambo and his excellence.

3 Macarius and Amatas are mentioned in this connection also in the *Vita Pauli*, and are also listed in Jerome's chronicle for A.D. 356. While Amatas is otherwise unknown, there are, besides Macarius the Egyptian and Macarius of Alexandria, a number of different Macarii, one of whom is mentioned by Rufinus (*HE* II,4). Nau, however, suggests that the names Amatas and Macarius are the result of erroneous reading by a copist already in the sources of the *Vita Paulii*, see Nau, 'Le texte grec original de la Vie de S. Paul de Thèbes', *AB* 20 (1901), p. 136.

4 *HL* 3. For the career of this Isidorus, see Chitty, *The Desert a City*, pp. 50, 54, 57–59 and 67. He is not to be confounded with the other Isidorus, presbyter of Scetis.

5 *HL* 4.

Alexandrian practicing a solitary life (μονάζων) sought his advice. In this story Antony acts as an arbitrator, and it is here that we find the first reference to Antony as the 'Great One' (ὁ μέγας).[1] Kronios is also the one who in the *Historia Lausiaca* relates Antony's vision on the ascension of the souls, a story originally told in the *Vita Antonii.* He is furthermore the informant for the story about Paul the Simple.[2] Hierax is in the *Historia Lausiaca* only mentioned as the other authority for the story about Paul the Simple.[3] Stephen of Libya is said to have been a friend of Antony's, and a master of discernment (διάκρισις). He is otherwise unknown, but may be identical either with the theologian mentioned in connection with Origen and Pierius, or with the monk who once fell into shameful libertinism.[4]

In another text by Palladius, the *Dialogue on the Life of John Chrysostom*, the same connection between Antony and the Origenist monks of Nitria is also made. When Palladius relates what he knows about the monks who were expelled from Egypt for their Origenism and later received by John in Constantinople, he mentions Antony thrice. First he states that Hierax, the senior among the Origenists and 90 years old at the time of writing (in 408), had once lived with Antony.[5] In connection with Isaac, another famous Origenist, he states that his master, Macarius, had been the disciple of Antony.[6] Later on he refers to another Isaac who was the disciple of Kronios, here called a disciple of Antony. About this second Isaac, Palladius says that he had the most profound knowledge of the Scriptures.[7]

The importance for the study of Antony of the accounts of Palladius lies not so much in what is said about Antony himself. That he was known to have been the 'Great One', a famous arbitrator and one who could hardly be surpassed, does not add much to the image created by the *Vita Antonii* or the *apophthegmata*. Far more important is what we are told

1 *HL* 21.

2 *HL* 21 and 22. Antony's vision is taken from *VA* 66 and is paralleled in *AP/Pa* 19.4 and *AP/Bo* 33 (Amélineau (*AMG* XXV), p. 31). Kronios is also known as an elder father in Nitria in HL 7, and as a priest of Nitria suceeded by the Origenist Isaac in the *Apophthegmata.* He could be the same as the famous Chronius mentioned in connection with Paphnutius, Evagrius and Palladius in *HL* 47, and possibly also as the disciple of Antony named Kronides in *HM* 20. Cf. above p. 178.

3 *HL* 22.

4 *HL* 24. In *HL* 11 an otherwise unknown writer by name of Stephen is mentioned as a famous theologian together with Origen, Didymus and Pierius, and in *HL* 55 together with Origen, Gregory (of Nazianzus ?), Pierius and Basil. The story of the libertine in *HL* 47 is one discussed by the Origenistic group consisting of Chronius, James the Halt, Paphnutius—all three known friends of Antony—and Evagrius, Albanius and Palladius himself.

5 Palladius, *Dialogus de vita Iohannis Chrysostomi* 17 (*SC* 341, p. 332).

6 *Ibid.*, 17 (*SC* 341, p. 340). Macarius is probably Macarius the Egyptain.

7 *Ibid.*, 17 (*SC* 341, p. 340).

about the interest the leading monks in Nitria and Scetis took in Origen and in speculative theology; and that these monks were, moreover, closely related to Antony and his disciples. There is no reason to distrust the information given by Palladius, who knew the monks well and was an eye-witness to the controversy. His account about Origenism in Nitria and the expulsion of the monks is, moreover, supported by other sources. It is thus evident that behind Evagrius, and the Origenist monks exiled in 400, there was a tradition connected with such names as Didymus, Macarius the Egyptian, Macarius the Alexandrian, Paphnutius, Hierax, Isidorus, Origen the Nitriote, Kronios, Isaac, and possibly also Pityrion. Of these most are in one way or other described as heirs of Antony.

6. SOCRATES, SOZOMENUS AND THEODORET

It was the lack of any reference to monks in general and to Antony in particular in Eusebius' *Historia Ecclesiastica* which made Weingarten doubt that there were any monks before the late 320's, and to regard Antony as an invented figure. There is, however, nothing in the sources on Antony which makes it likely that he became famous before the late 320's, much less that he was known abroad. As we have seen, Rufinus included Antony into his continuation of Eusebius, and so did Socrates, Sozomenus and Theodoret. All three dealt extensively with the monastic movement in fourth-century Egypt; they used literary sources known to us, but also traditions otherwise unknown.[1]

Socrates makes three references to Antony. First he includes a very short chapter on Antony in his account of the 330's. He simply refers to the *vita* Athanasius had written, and gives a hint about its content.[2] Secondly, Antony is mentioned twice in connection with his account of how the monks were persecuted by the Arians during the reign of Valens in 374. Here he tells the story about how Amoun became a monk and how Antony saw his soul ascend to heaven, and relates what he knows about Didymus, Arsenius, Pior, Isidorus, Pambo, Piteros, the two Macarii and Evagrius. He then enumerates the works of Evagrius, quotes the *Praktikos* and the *Gnostikos* at length, and ends with the story of how Ammonius, one of the famous 'tall brothers', cut off his ear to avoid ordination as

1 Socrates is edited by R. Hussey, *The Church History of Socrates Scholasticus,* I–III, Oxford 1853, an earlier edition is reprinted in *PG* 67, 29–872; Sozomenus is edited by J. Bidez & G. C. Hansen, *Sozomenus, Historia Ecclesiastica, GCS* 1, Berlin 1960, an earlier print is reprinted in *PG* 67, 844–1630. Theodoret is edited by L. Parmentier and F. Scheidweiler (*GCS* 44), Berlin [2]1954. For the sources of Sozomenus see G. Schoo, *Die Quellen des kirchenhistorikers Sozomemos, Neue Studien zur Geschichte der Theologie und Kirche,* 11, Berlin 1911. For those of Socrates and Theodoret, see the editions listed in my bibliography.

2 Socrates *HE* I.18.

bishop. Besides Evagrius he mentions the *Vita Antonii* and Palladius as his sources, but it is clear that he must have had other sources as well, probably a collection of sayings, since some of his stories are closely related to these. When quoting Evagrius he incorporates literally the story about Antony's reply to the philosopher: 'My book, o Philosopher, is the nature of things that are made, and it is present whenever I wish to read the words of God'.[1] After describing the persecutions of the monks and the exile of the two Macarii, he inserts a chapter on Didymus, in which he tells the story of Antony consoling him on his blindness, translated almost word by word from Rufinus.[2]

In Sozomenus, Antony is first mentioned in the chapters dealing with his meeting with Amoun. Here Sozomenus is heavily dependent on the *Vita Antonii,* and probably also on the *Historia Lausiaca.* A few details are, however, his own: Coma is mentioned as Antony's birthplace, and he is said to have had disciples of great renown in Egypt and Libya, Palestine, Syria and Arabia.[3] On three occasions Sozomenus then relates how Antony supported Athanasius and his Nicene position.[4] It is here the statement is found that Antony frequently wrote to the emperor on the reinstatement of Athanasius from his first exile. It seems likely that this could be the historical source behind the two independent accounts of a correspondence with the emperors, one in the *Vita* and the other in the *apophthegmata.*[5] When, in his long chapter on the monks in Egypt, Sozomenus mentions Hilarion's stay with Antony, he follows Jerome's account closely, and in the following chapter on Didymus he retells the story as he found it in Rufinus and Socrates.[6] Finally he relates from the *Vita Antonii* the story of Antony's vision of the Arian insurrection, adding that it happened before the Arians, during the reign of Constantius, took possession of the churches.[7]

Theodoret has only two references to Antony. In both cases he is obviously dependent on his predecessors. Writing about how Peter, who succeeded Athanasius, was overthrown and replaced by the Arian intruder Lucius, he mentions the renowned Antony, who made the desert a training place for virtue. The monks persecuted and exiled by Lucius, 'the famous

1 *HE* IV.23. Cf. above, p. 159.

2 Socrates, *HE* IV.25.

3 Sozomenus *HE* I.13–14. For Syria this is the earliest evidence, in the next century Philoxenus refers to an Adelphius of Edessa as Antony's disciple and originator of the Messalian heresy. See his *Epistula ad Patricium* 108-110 (*PO* 30.5, pp. 851–855)

4 Sozomenus *HE* II.17, 31, and III.13.

5 Sozomenus *HE* II.31. The fact that a correspondence is mentioned in so many different ways, in the *Vita,* in the *Vita Pachomii,* in the sayings and here makes it unlikely that it was something invented. See above p. 154, n. 1.

6 Sozomenus *HE* III.14 and 15.

7 Sozomenus *HE* VI.5.

Macarius, his namesake, Isidorus and the rest' are subsequently referred to as Antony' disciples.[1] Later on, in his chapters on Julian of Saba, the hero of Syrian monasticism, who is said to have once visited Egypt, Theodoret compares Julian's visit to Antioch—in order to oppose the Arians—with Antony's visit to Alexandria which had the same purpose.[2]

Obviously, the validity of these accounts varies, depending on which sources were used, how closely they were followed, and the purpose of inserting the references. However, all of them give evidence to Antony's fame and to the pre-eminent influence of the *Vita* in the making of his image in the fifth century. But the *Vita* is not the only source; there are also passages derived from Rufinus, Jerome, Palladius and, more significantly, Evagrius. The only original and important historical notices are those on Antony's correspondence, and on the exile his disciples suffered because of the Arians. As in the *Vita,* the emphasis is heavily on Antony as an anti-Arian supporter of Athanasius, and as a teacher of ascesis. But at least in Socrates the philosophical and Origenist character of the tradition initiated by Antony is still remembered.

1 Theodoret *HE* IV.18. This is the same exile as the one mentioned in Socrates *HE* IV.24 and Sozomenus *HE* VI.20, but whereas Socrates only mentions the two Macarii, Sozomenus also mentions Pambo, Heraclides and other disciples.

2 Theodoret *HE* IV.24.

CONCLUSION

In his *Life,* the *Vita Antonii,* Antony is described as an unlettered monk. In this study he is shown to have been a *man of letters.* The authenticity of his seven letters, mentioned by Jerome and quoted by fifth century Coptic authors, is as firmly attested as that of any other ancient writings. The only arguments against an attribution of the letters to Antony are based on a view of the early monks that does not stand up to the evidence of contemporary documents. An analysis of the historical setting and the sources used to support the notion of Antony and his companions as ignorant and illiterate shows that this view mirrors modern prejudice rather than historical reality. But though the contents of the letters indicate that Antony knew some Greek, a comparative analysis of all the versions preserved shows that the letters were composed in Coptic. Since they can be dated to the third or fourth decade of the fourth century, they must be regarded as one of the first examples of original Coptic literature that have been preserved. Antony is thus not only a father of the monastic tradition, but quite possibly 'the first real Coptic author'.

A comparison of the complete Arabic, Georgian and Latin versions, the Syriac version of Letter I, and the Coptic fragments shows that the loss of most of the original and of the early Greek translation does not prevent the analysis of their content and the major concepts used. The comparison reveals that the Georgian text is by far the most reliable, and that it can, when checked against the Latin and the Arabic, be used as a trustworthy witness to what Antony wrote. Though no exact reconstruction of the original text is possible, and a great deal of uncertainty remains, the main features of Antony's thinking are manifest in the preserved texts.

The key to the understanding of the letters is the repeated exhortation 'know thyself', and the view that salvation is the return of man to his original and spiritual nature. Throughout the letters it is knowledge, *gnosis,* and man's 'spiritual essence', his οὐσία νοερά, that are emphasized. Although Antony presents no systematic teaching, it is evident that his theology must be understood against the background of contemporary Platonic traditions. Antony shared the Platonic concepts of knowledge and being and the emphasis on original unity of all that is spiritual and rational (νοερός and λογικός). With the Platonists of his time he regarded stability as an essential attribute of truth and saw diversity and motion as signs of transience and lack of true reality. But he was no philosopher, and was probably not aware of all the implications of his presuppositions. Apparently the Platonic framework was to him a self-evident setting for his Christian *gnosis.* In spite of the importance to Antony of knowledge and a spiritual understanding of the Scriptures he was no Gnostic, but shared Plotinus' criticism of the dualism and secrecy characteristic of Gnostic teaching.

In addition to the Platonic background, the letters reveal that Antony was clearly influenced by Origenist theological tradition. He held the same views as Origen not only on the Creation, the Fall and the salvation of man, but also on the interpretation of the Scriptures. Most probably, several of the Biblical quotations and their interpretation depend on an Origenist school tradition. Antony's links with Didymus, the best known Origenist of the fourth century, are also well attested in other sources.

But although Origen's writings are found to be the most fruitful instruments for the interpretation of Antony's letters, these lack important traits of the Alexandrian synthesis between Platonism and Christianity such as *e. g.* the *Logos* Christology. There is, moreover, no manifest quotation in the letters of any text outside the Bible, and it seems as though Antony developed his own theological synthesis on the basis of an acquaintance with Platonic tradition and the legacy of Origen. A comparison with contemporary texts shows striking similarities with the Alexandrian theology of the early fourth century, the theology of texts such as the *Teachings of Silvanus* and to some degree Athanasius' *Contra Gentes.* Probably Antony's teaching was not too different from that of the lost writings of Alexandrian theologians like Theognostus, Pierius, and Hieracas.[1]

It is thus impossible, as has often been done in the past, to accept the authenticity of the letters and still preserve the traditional image of Antony as unlettered. On the contrary, the content of the letters proves that Antony's theology was not the product of a native and naïve Coptic Biblicism unaffected by Greek thought. A critical examination of the documentary sources for early fourth century Egypt shows that Antony was certainly not unique among the first monks in his acquaintance with Greek philosophy and Origenist theology. The economic and social crisis of the third century and the high level of cultural exchange caution us against a view according to which the Egyptian monks were 'simple and uneducated people' who fled society because of poverty and fear of punishment, or fanatic monks who went into the desert in order to fight

1 It is thus no longer possible to maintain that 'Antony the Great is unlikely to have been familiar with Origenized Platonism' (R. Williams, *Arius. Heresy and Tradition*, p. 89).

the demons on their own ground.[1] In the Egypt of the late third century, a country where new leaders and new social structures were in high demand and traditional religion was in decline, new religious movements such as monasticism were not the products of people on the margin of society, but of intellectuals dissatisfied with what tradition had to offer. An analysis of contemporary papyri indicates precisely the kind of historical and theological background that is revealed by Antony's letters. The close affinities between Antony's letters and the *Teachings of Silvanus* are a warning against any simplistic view suggesting a clear border between orthodoxy and heresy in Antony's time.

The authenticity of Antony's letters and the analysis of their content make them an important contribution to the study of the *Vita Antonii,* a field of study characterized by a confused state of research. The basic accord between the theology of the letters and that of the *Vita,* and the shared heritage of Antony and Athanasius, strongly support the Athanasian authorship of the *Vita* and the primacy of the Greek version. The suggestions that the *Vita* is marked by tensions between Athanasian theology, monastic tradition and hagiographical style are shown by a comparison with the letters to be the result of three main tendencies which have governed the transformation of the image of Antony.

Firstly, the *Vita* is marked by the Arian conflict, a conflict decisive for Athanasius' entire life and literary production. An anti-Arian emphasis on Christ as the divine actor in man is superimposed on the Origenist theology of Antony. Secondly, the *Vita* presupposes the complete victory of Christianity over paganism and the subsequent rejection of the Greek philosophical heritage. While the Antony of the letters sees the quest of the philosophers and that of the Christian monks as almost identical, the Antony of the *Vita* is taught by God alone, stubbornly opposed to the philosophers and their education and teaching. Thirdly, the *Vita* is a political text; it has the express purpose to present *the* model for Christian living. While the author of the letters exhorts his disciples to strive towards a deeper understanding of his words, the author of the *Vita* exhorts them to emulate the ideal presented. The letters show that the purpose of the *Vita* was neither to 'humanize' a charismatic teacher nor to 'elevate' a simple monk, but to use the influence of Antony to depict the victory of Orthodoxy over pagans and heretics, the victory of the cross over the demons, of *gnosis* by faith over *gnosis* by education, of the 'man taught by God', the *theodidaktos,* over the philosophers.[2]

1 See R. P. C. Hanson, *The Search for the Christian Doctrine of God,* Edinburgh 1988, p. 268, for the quotation.

2 The contrast between the *Vita* as written to 'humanize or elevate' is from M. Williams, 'The *Life of Antony* and the Domestication of Charismatic Wisdom', p. 36.

The analysis of the letters and of the socio-economic and cultural situation in Egypt in the late third and early fourth century presents an image of the historical setting for the rise of the monastic tradition which is difficult to reconcile with the sayings of the desert fathers, the *apophthegmata.* Their reliability as historical sources for the first generations of monks is, however, open to doubt. Firstly, the complex nature of the tradition and the small amount of research done is a warning against any use of the *apophthegmata* as historical sources. Secondly, it is possible to show how inadequate many of the earlier approaches to the question of the trustworthiness of the sayings are. Since the collections are late and repeatedly revised compilations, the historicity of the *apophthegmata* does not rest with the collections but with the single sayings. There is little evidence that the most reliable sayings are those which fit a theory of oral tradition. The level of literacy and the cultural background of the first monks suggest that written tradition was of greater importance than has earlier been admitted, and probably the excerpts from monastic literature are not late additions but original contributions to the growth of the *apophthegmata.* Thirdly, the collections preserved all date after the Origenist controversy which deeply affected Egyptian monastic tradition, and there is no proof that the bulk of the sayings go back half a century before Theophilus expelled many of the most prominent fathers in the *Apophthegmata Patrum.*

Since the purpose of the sayings is not historical recollection but ascetical education, there is no guarantee that they give a well-balanced image of earlier generations. Although a number of the sayings attributed to Antony can be reconciled with what the letters reveal about him, their historical value is very restricted, and in all cases where sayings are directly paralleled in other texts, the sayings are dependent on the texts, not vice versa. Even if they are not necessarily inaccurate, the sayings reveal only the principles by which the image of Antony was transformed according to the needs of the monastic tradition. The evident tendency is to adduce Antony as an authority for the most important principles of monastic life.[1]

Due to his fame Antony is mentioned in a number of other sources besides the *Vita Antonii* and the *Apophthegmata Patrum.* These testify to his predominant position in early monastic tradition. Independently of the *Vita Antonii* the letter of Serapion of Thmuis shows how Antony was regarded as an important supporter of the Athanasian party, while the *Vita*

[1] The development of the Antonian tradition from the letters to the *apophthegmata* and the *Vita* is paralleled by the process of transformation within the tradition that made the *apophthegmata,* a transformation excellently described by Rousseau in his *Ascetics, Authority and the Church,* pp. 68–76.

Pachomii illustrates that he was a man of influence in Alexandria and his name a most useful label of orthodoxy. The most important evidence, however, is the way Antony is linked to the well-known names of the Origenist group of late fourth century monks in Nitria and Scetis in sources such as the *Historia Monachorum* and the writings of Palladius, Rufinus, Socrates and Sozomenus. When combined with what the letters reveal about Antony's theology, this evidence makes it safe to conclude that Antony played an important role in the making of the Origenist tradition which formed an essential background for Evagrius' theology.[1]

The confrontation of the letters and the theology implicit in them with the historical context of the rise of monasticism and with the other sources on Antony thus has repercussions far beyond the narrow limits of Antonian studies. Against the attempts to play down the importance of Alexandrian theology for the early monastic tradition, the letters strongly support the predominant role of Origen and his legacy.[2] Probably the most important theological documents preserved from the founders of the tradition, the letters imply a setting radically different from what is often suggested, a setting which in fact conforms with what the papyri reveal about Egypt at the turn of the third century. Although the letters differ considerably from the Pachomian material, they support the trends in Pachomian studies that emphasize Pachomius' acquaintance with contemporary theological discussion and the possibility of a Pachomian origin for the Nag Hammadi codices. The letters, moreover, show how inadequate the *Vita Antonii* and the *apophthegmata* are for studies of the attitudes of the first monks. The importance of these sources lies instead in what they reveal about the changes in the Egyptian Church and in the monastic tradition during the fourth century, and about the process by which the image of the teacher of *gnosis* was transformed to that of a saint.

Although it is as the saint depicted by the *Vita* and the *apophthegmata* that Antony has been remembered throughout the centuries, there is another legacy of his, a legacy related to the teacher of the letters. As shown by the manuscripts it is primarily in Egypt and in Arabic that the letters have remained part of living tradition. In this tradition the seven letters belong to a large corpus of text attributed to St. Antony. In the

1 The importance of the Origenist monastic tradition for Evagrius' theology is generally acknowledged, but no connection to Antony has previously been suggested. See Antoine Guillaumont, *Les 'Kephalaia Gnostica' d'Évagre le Pontique*, Paris 1962, pp. 55–59, 81–87. A comparison of Antony's letters and the extent works of Evagrius will no doubt reveal a large number of affinities.

2 Though he correctly stresses the influence of Origen on the later monastic tradition, William Seston's attempt ('Remarques sur le rôle de la pensée d'Origène dans les origines du monachisme, *RHE* 108 (1933), pp. 197–213) to reject an Origenist influence on Antony on the basis of the *Vita Antonii* is manifestly inadequate.

Arabic corpus it is not the Antony image of the *Vita* that one meets, but an image similar to the one gained from his letters. The attribution in this corpus of the letters of Ammonas to Antony is, although false, a sign of a continuity in what could be termed a 'school of St. Antony'. A comparison of these letters with Antony's reveals how the theological tradition he represented was developed in the decades after his death. In the *Teachings of Antony,* a text which includes a passage also found in the *Teachings of Silvanus,* the Arabic corpus presents another piece of evidence for the close relationship between Alexandrian theology and Antonian tradition.[1] Together with the pseudo-Antonian texts preserved in Greek, the most important being the chapters which introduce the famous *Philocalia,* the corpus testifies to an Antonian tradition with roots in the letters.[2]

The fact that the letters were not widely diffused outside Egypt is probably best explained by their Origenist content. But before the Origenist controversy and the condemnation of Origen and Evagrius in the sixth century they were undoubtedly read by the monks also outside Egypt. A comparison of the letters with Evagrius' extant works reveals numerous very close parallels which support the connection between Antony and Evagrius suggested by Palladius and others.[3] This connection is furthermore strengthened by the discovery that John Cassian is ultimately dependent on the description of God's summonses in Antony's first letter.[4] The most important link between Antony and the later Origenist monks was undoubtedly Macarius of Egypt. It is quite possible that a comparison of Antony's letters with the letters attributed to Macarius can reveal a significant literary tradition quite independent of the question of the authenticity of the texts. Perhaps the early connection made between Messalianism and Antony has some historical background.[5] The parallels between Antony's letters and some passages in the writings of Dorotheus of Gaza also indicates that there was an early diffusion of the letters.[6]

1 The Arabic corpus has not been properly edited, still less analyzed. See my 'Arabic Sources' and the editions of Ammonas, the *Teachings of Antony* and the *Rule of Antony* listed in the bibliography.

2 For the chapters in the Philocalia, see the articles by Irenée Hausherr and Endré von Ivanka in the bibliography. Two other Greek texts attributed to Antony are discussed by Gérard Garitte in two articles also listed in the bibliography.

3 See Samuel Rubenson, 'Evagrios Pontikos und die Theologie der Wüste...

4 See above, p. 85, n. 5.

5 For the Macarian letters, see André Wilmart, 'La lettre spirituelle de l'abbé Macaire', *RAM* 1 (1920), pp. 58–83, and Ugo Zanetii, 'Deux lettres de Macaire conservées en arabe et en géorgien', *Le Muséon* 99 (1986), pp. 319–333. For Theodoret's and Philoxenus' statements about Adelphius as a disciple of Antony, see Antoine Guillaumont, 'Messaliens', *DSp* X, Paris 1980, pp. 1074–1083.

6 Dorotheus repeatedly quotes Antonian sayings but nowhere explicitly refers to the letters. In the first discourse there are, however, two manifest parallels to the letters: Abraham is

Although the *Vita Antonii* can be said to have created *the* image of Antony that has made him the best known of the fathers of monasticism, the *Vita* did not invent Antony, nor did it rescue him from obscurity. His letters reveal that quite independently of Athanasius' biography, the historical figure behind it was a spiritual teacher of great significance. Against the background of contemporary philosophy and with the help of an Origenist legacy he struggled to understand the Scriptures and the essence of man's quest for salvation. With burning love for his monastic brothers he wrote to them about God's compassion for man, about repentance and demonic assault, but above all about the joy and peace that can be gained by true self-knowledge and by the return to the Creator through the coming of Jesus and the granting of the 'Spirit of adoption'.

described as moved by the law of nature (= *Ep. Ant.* I.3–8) and the same quotation from Jer. 28:9 (LXX) about the healing of Babylon appears as in *Ep. Ant.* II.16–17 and III.21–22. See Dorothée de Gaza, *Oeuvres spirituelles* (*SC* 92), Paris 1963.

APPENDIX

APOPHTHEGMATA MENTIONING ANTONY

Italics indicate similar passages without attribution to Antony.

	G & QRT	GS (PJ)	PA, R, M & CSP	Syriac	Armenian	Coptic	Eth.	Parallels
1	Ant 1	VII.1	32.1	I.131	II.29	Bo 32	II.51	R 105
2	Ant 2	XV.1		II.218	XV.1		II.87	
3	Ant 3	I.1	32.8	II.35+202	I.1	Bo 44	I.16.1	R 108
4	Ant 4	XV.2		II.368	XV.2a+121	Bo 25		
5	Ant 5							*Ep.Amm* IX
6	Ant 6	I.2	M 54	II.197	I.1R	Bo 3		
7	Ant 7	XV.3	39.2	I.453	XV.2b	Bo 43	II.109	R 129
8	Ant 8	X.1		I.296	X.1		II.447	*Ep.Ant* VI.106
9	Ant 9	XVII.2		II.33	XVII.13			*Ep.Ant* VI.53
10	Ant 10	II.1	32.7	I.20, II.472	II.2R	Bo 12	II.1	R 109b; *VA* 85
11	Ant 11	II.2	93.1	I.46	II.11	Bo 40	II.2	cf. *VA* 49
12	Ant 12	X.2	70.2	II.56	X.48			
13	Ant 13	X.3			X.49	Bo 7		
14	Ant 14	VIII.1		II.415-416	VIII.1+X.47	Bo 15	II.64	
15	Ant 15	VIII.2	25.1	I.229	VIII.19			R 88
16	Ant 16	X.4		II.114	X.1R			
17	Ant 17	XV.4	100.5	I.551	XV.73			
18	Ant 18	IV.1	88.8	I.10	IV.1			
19	Ant 19	XVI.1	21.1	I.202	VII.46		II.94	Pa 6.2
20	Ant 20	VI.1	14.2	I.178	VI.1	Bo 23	II.43	R 68
21	Ant 21	IX.1	41.8	I.606	IX.1	Bo 13		
22	Ant 22	V.1			V.1	Bo 22	II.33	*Ep.Ant* I.35-41
23	Ant 23	X.5		II.246	X.108B	Bo 8	I.28.1	
24	Ant 24	XVIII.1		II.3	XVIII. 93	Bo11, Sa 172	I.18.6	
25	Ant 25			II.179	X.108	Bo 2		cited in Bo 124
26	Ant 26			II.39	XII.1			Amm 12 in mss.
27	Ant 27	XVII.5		II.161	XV.74	Bo 14		
28	Ant 28			II.43	XVII.22(23)	Bo 54		John Moschos 28.
29	Ant 29		41.9	I.406	V.68	Bo 10		
30	Ant 30			II.473	XVIII.13	Bo 1		cf. *VA* 59-60
31	Ant 31				X.162			*VA* 81, Soz *HE* I.13
32	Ant 32	XVII.1		II.403b	XVII.27		I.37.11	
33	Ant 33	III.1		II.208	III.1		II.3	
34	Ant 34				X.63			
35	Ant 35	XI.3			XI.24			
36	Ant 36	XIV.1			XIV.18			

G	GS & QRT	PA, R, (PJ)	Syriac M & CSP	Armenian	Coptic	Eth.	Parallels	
37	Ant 37	XI.1	73.1b		XI.1a			
38	Ant 38	XI.2	73.1a		XI.1b		II.310	R 176
39	Amm 7			I.449a	XVIII.89			cf. A XVIII.84a
40	Amm 8		24.5	I.449b	IX.28			cf. -"- and Pa 9.3
41	Amo 1	XVII.3		II.180	XVII.31			
42	Isid 6		31.4	II.348a	XV.93			
43	Joh. E 2			*I.404*				
44	Hilar	XVII.4		II.112	XVII.11	Bo 5		
45	Mak. 4	VII.14		II.221	VII.63	Bo 164, Sa 38		
46	Mak 26				XV.6			
47	Nist 2	I.18		II.21a	I.3		I.16.8	
48	Poi 75			II.135	XIX.12a			
49	Poi 87				XII.21			*Ep.Ant* VII.60
50	Poi 119	III.29-30	*Pa 38.1*	I.154	*III.8a(A)*			also in M 33
51	Pityrion						*HM* 15	
52	Paul	XVIII 26	56.3		Sa 191	I.38		
53	Sis 7	XX.5		I.8	XIX.33	Sa 265		
54	Sis 9	XV.62		II.307	XV.44	Sa 117		
55	Sis 14	XX.7	52.4	II.109	XVIII.9			
56	Sis 28			I.11	II.49			
57	N 202	VII.41	32.2	I.9	VII.22	Sa 49		
58	N 206	VII.46		*I.54*	VII.22			cf. CSP VI.3c
59	N 298	XV.71	36.2	*II.511*	XV.139	Sa 127		R 125
60	N 321	XV.99	*88.6*	I.45	XV.152		II.410	*Pa 32.1*
61	N 322	XV.100	39.1	*II.239*	XV.153			*Pa 15.1; R 128*
62	N 417		*App. 13*		IX.20; X.221			
63	N 444		*77.1*					*Pa 27.1*
64	N 490(=N 67)		39.3	II.2	XIX.1+41			Pa 15.2; R 130
65	*K 295*							
66	*N 518*				X.91		I.13.29	
67	N 520	XV.129b			III.43b			
68	N 592/1-2				III.78b			
69	*N 603*		*95.2*		*I.48*			*Pa 35.2*
70	N 630				XI.6			
71	*J 759*		39.1b		X.83R			
72	*J 760*		20.1c		X.244			Pa 6.1c; R 76c
73	*QRT 12*						VA 3	
74	*QRT 23*						VA 3-5	
75			76.4					*Pa 26.4*
76			76.5					cf. G 896 m.fl.
77			84.3					Evagr. *Prakt.* 92
		(VS VI.4.16)						Socr. *HE* IV.23
78			Pa 19.3			Bo 33		*HL* 21.1-15
79			Pa 19.4					*VA* 66, *HL* 21.16
80			Pa 19.5					
81			Pa 40.1	(II.46)				also in M 29+53
82			CSP V.1					cf. *VA* 16ff.
83			CSP V.2					R 31, *HL* 39

	G & QRT	GS (PJ)	PA, R, M & CSP	Syriac	Armenian	Coptic	Eth.	Parallels
84			R 218					Rufinus *HE* II.7 Hieron. *ep.* 68 Socr.*HE* IV.25; Soz. *HE* III.15
85				I.607				
86				II.103				
87					XVIII.77			
88						Bo 4		
89						Bo 9		
90						Bo 16		
91						Bo 17		
92						Bo 18		
93						Bo 19		
94						Bo 20		
95						Bo 21		*Ep.Amm.* II
96						Bo 26		
97						Bo 27		
98						Bo 28		
99						Bo 29		
100		cf. X.79				Bo 30		cf. *Ep.Amm. I*
101						Bo 31		
102						Bo 34		
103						Bo 35		
104						Bo 36		
105						Bo 37		
106						Bo 38		
107						Bo 39		cf.*Ep.Ant.* IV.5
108						Bo 41		
109						Bo 42		
110						Bo 45		
111						Bo 46		
112						Bo 47		
113						Bo 48		
114						Bo 49		
115						Bo 50		
116						Bo 51		*VA* 16
117						Bo 52+53		
118						Bo 58		
119						Bo 84		

NOTE ON TRANSLATION

The following translation of the letters of St. Antony into English has been made on the basis of all the extant versions. The general principle has been to make a comparative analysis of all the versions of each verse and draw a conclusion about what the author could originally have written. The result is thus a tentative text, which does not pretend to be neither exact, nor the final. Except for the fourth letter, and for the passages of the sixth which are preserved in Coptic, and the first, preserved in Syriac, the Georgian and the Latin texts have been the most important. The Arabic version has turned out to be less useful, since it very often either summarizes or elaborates on the text. But in the very frequent cases where the Georgian and the Latin text disagree, and it has been impossible from the meaning and the context to choose which one to follow, I have accepted the one closest to the Arabic. As for the first letter I have usually followed the versions agreeing with the Syriac text, but I have not, as most other translators, relied completely on the Syriac, since it is poorly edited, and since it tends to avoid some of the most characteristic ideas. For all passages preserved in Coptic, in which the letters were originally written, I have kept as close as possible to the Coptic text.

The notes are mainly linguistical, giving the Georgian, Latin, Arabic and sometimes Coptic and Syriac terms translated in the body of the text, as well as all important variations. I have not, however, noted all the cases where the Arabic version, especially of letter six, summarizes or elaborates on the text without changing its meaning. Since the letters were written in a language heavily influenced by Greek, and since the theological concepts of the letters are all Greek I have retranslated some of the most important concepts into Greek. Unfortunately it has not been possible to give a full commentary of the text in the notes, but for the most important ideas and concepts I refer the reader to similar passages and back to the analysis of Antony's theology in chapter four.

The abbreviations used in the notes to the translation are:

A: the Arabic version
C: the Coptic version
Gr: the tentatively reconstructed Greek version
G: the Georgian version
L: the Latin version
S: the Syriac version

LETTER ONE

[1]First of all, I greet you in the Lord.[1]

I believe that the souls, whether male or female, whom God in his mercy has assembled by his own Word,[2] are of three kinds[3].

[2]Some were reached by the Word of God through the law of promise[4] and the discernment of the good inherent in them from their first formation.[5] [3]They did not hesitate but followed it readily as did Abraham, our father. Since he offered himself in love[6] through law of promise, God appeared to him, saying: [4]*Go from your country and your kindred and from your father's house to the land that I will show you.*[7] [5]And he went without hesitating at all, but being ready for his calling. [6]This is the model for the beginning of this way of life. It still persists in those who follow this pattern. [7]Wherever and whenever souls endure and bow to it[8] they easily attain the virtues,[9] since their hearts are ready to be guided by the Spirit of God. [8]This is the first kind.

[9]The second kind we find in those who hear the written law testify of all pain and punishment prepared for the wicked [10]and announce the blessed promises for those who progress.[10] [11]Through the testimonies of the written law their thoughts are aroused, and they try to enter into their calling. [12]David, too, testifies of this, saying: *The law of the Lord is without blemish*

---

1 G missing until the end of verse 11.

2 L adds: *vocantis ad praedicationem suam;* S: *have come close to the mercy of God;* A: *by the gospel of the Spirit of God.*

3 L: *modos;* S: ܦܘܪ̈ܫܢܐ (*manner*); A: رتب (*division*).

4 S: ܢܡܘܣܐ ܕܚܘܒܐ ܕܩܐܡ ܒܟܝܢܗܘܢ (*law of love which is in their nature*); A: ناموس الطبيعة والحرية (*law of nature and of freedom*); L: *testamentariam legem;* G is missing. This term occurs throughout the letters. In the many parallels the Georgian version has, აღთქუმაჲ რჩული or აღთქუმისა რჩული. The Latin invariably has *testamentaria lex.* The Greek expression behind was most probably ὁ νόμος τῆς ἐπαγγελίας (or ἡ διαθήκη τῆς ἐπαγγελίας, *cf.* Eph. 2:12). For the varying expressions in the Syriac and Arabic, and for Antony's understanding of the place of the law, see above, p. 73f. with notes.

5 L: *a prima sui conditione;* S: *derīš berīṯehōn* (*from the beginning of their creation*); A: *awalan* (*from the beginning*). A similar expression occurs also in I:30; II:10 and V:40, where the Georgian version has: პირველი დაბადებული (or დასაბამაჲ). For Antony's understanding of the *original condition,* see above, pp. 60–67.

6 Thus S. L: *quia porrexit indaginem* (?); A: —.

7 Gen. 12:1.

8 Thus L and S. A: *and all who do so.*

9 Thus L and A. S: *receive the honour of an ascetic life*

10 S: *flourish in the fear of God,* A: *strive justly.*

and vivifies the soul.[1] [13]and elsewhere he says: *The revelation of thy words gives light and makes children wise,*[2] [14]and of the same more than we are able to recount.

[15]The third kind we find in those whose hearts are hard from the beginning[3] and who persist in the works of sin. God the merciful sends afflictions and chastisment upon them, [16]until through their afflictions they are made aware and repent and return. And if they repent with all their heart they enter into the calling and attain the virtues, like the others about whom I have already written.

[17]These are the three gates for the souls who come to repent until they obtain grace, and the calling[4] of the Son of God.

[18]But I believe that those who have entered[5] with all their heart, and have prepared themselves to[6] endure all the trials of the enemy until they prevail, [19]are first called by the Spirit,[7] who alleviates everything for them so that the work of repentance becomes sweet for them.[20]He sets for them a rule for how to repent in their bodies and souls [21]until he has taught them the way to return to God, their own Creator. [22]He also gives them control over[8] their souls and bodies in order that both may be sanctified and inherit together:

[23]First the body through many fasts and vigils, through the exertion and the exercises of the body,[9] [24]cutting of all the fruits of the flesh.[10] [25]In this the Spirit of repentance[11] is his guide, testing him through them, so that the enmity[12] does not bring him back again.[13] [26]Then the guiding Spirit begins to open the eyes of the soul, to show it the way of repentance that it, too, may be purified.[14]

---

1 Ps. 18:8 LXX (= Ps. 19:8 Vulgata). S adds the second part of the same verse: *The testimony of the Lord is sure, making wise the simple,* instead of the following quotation from Ps. 118:130.

2 Ps. 118:130 LXX (= Ps. 119:130 Vulgata).

3 Thus G and S. L: *saepe inter vitia;* A:—.

4 A omits.

5 L adds *the struggle.*

6 S adds: *despise all afflictions of the flesh and.*

7 G and A as well as some of the mss of S have *Holy Spirit.*

8 G: იძოლებაჲ; L: *violentiae compulsionem;* S: *the way to force;* A: *strength until they subdue.*

9 L seems to have misunderstood its source, adding: *anima vero in spiritu atque solertia*

10 Instead of *fruits* in G and L, S says *desires.* The phrase is missing in A. Except for a few cases with გუამაჲ, G has throughout the letters ჴორცი for both σῶμα and σάρξ. I have, as far as possible, followed the Latin version making a distinction between *corpus* and *carnis.*

11 For a discussion of the various designations of the Spirit, see above, p. 79–81.

12 Thus L and G (*inimicitia*); S: *the enemy;* A: *anything of the matters of the world.*

13 A avoids the theme of testing by saying: *For this reason the Spirit of Repentance consoles this man and teaches him that he shall not return to what is behind him, and not adhere to anything of the matters of the world.*

14 For a comparison of the different versions of verses 26–27 see above, p. 31f.

[27]The mind[1] also starts to discriminate between them and begins to learn from the Spirit how to purify the body and the soul through repentance. [28]The mind is taught by the Spirit and guides us in the actions of the body and soul, purifying both of them, [29]separating the fruits of the flesh from what is natural to the body,[2] in which they were mingled, and through which the transgression came to be,[3] [30]and leads each member of the body back to its original condition, [31]free from everything alien that belongs to the spirit of the enemy.

[32]The body is thus brought under the authority of the mind and is taught by the Spirit, as the words of Paul testify: *I castigate my body and bring it into subjection.*[4] [33]Then mind sanctifies it in food and drink and sleep, and, in one word, in all its movements[5], [34]even separating itself from the natural union through its own sanctity.[6]

[35]I believe that there are three movements in the body.[7] [36]There is a natural, inherent movement[8], which does not operate unless the soul consents, otherwise it remains still. [37]Then there is another movement as a result of stuffing the body with a multitude of food and drink. The heat of the blood, caused by excessive eating, stirs up the body, which is now moved by gluttony. [38]Because of this the apostle says: *Be not drunk with wine, wherein is excess.*[9] [39]And the Lord enjoined his disciples in the Gospel saying: *Take heed lest at anytime your hearts be overcharged with surfeiting and drunkenness*[10] and pleasures. [40]Especially since they seek the level of sanctity[11] they should say: *I castigate my body and bring it into subjection.*[12] [41]The third movement comes from the evil spirits, tempting us out of envy and seeking to divert those who attempt to sanctify themselves.

---

1 G: გონებაჲ (throughout the letters); L: *sensus* (except for III:6, *mens;* and VII:31, *habitudo);* S: ܗܘܢܐ, ܪܥܝܢܐ; A: — (otherwise عقل). The use of the terms *mind, heart* and *soul* in the letters of St. Antony is discussed above, p. 69, note 1, and p. 70, note 1.

2 G: ყოველი კორცისა ბონებაჲ; L: *universa corporis naturalia;* S: *members of the body;* A: *the body.* For a discussion of the concepts of separation and mingling, see above p. 70.

3 Thus G (adding *of the law*) and L. S: *already from the first movement;* A omits the passage.

4 1 Cor. 9:27.

5 G: აღძრვაჲ; L: *motus;* S: ܙܘܥܐ; A: حركة From the Greek text of the verses 35–41 it is clear that the Greek version had κίνησις. For the Origenist background of the use of this expression in Antony's letters, see above, pp. 64–67.

6 S: ܡܫܘܬܦܘܬܐ, ܟܝܢܝܬܐ, ܕܪܥܝܢܐ (*the sexual intercourse of the imagination*); G: ბონებაჲ ტანაშერთვისა; L: *naturalem copulam;* The entire verse is missing in A.

7 This passage until the end of verse 41 is also preserved in Greek in a saying in the alphabetical collection of the Apophthegmata Patrum (*Antony* 22).

8 Gr: κίνησιν φυσικὴν συναναφυρεῖσαν αὐτῷ.

9 Eph. 5:18.

10 Luk 21:34.

11 A: *put on the habit of monasticism* (*sic. !*)

12 1 Cor. 9:27. This verse is missing in the preserved Greek saying.

[42]If the soul perseveres in these three ways and keeps to what the Spirit has taught the mind, it purifies both from the three types of affliction. [43]But if the mind spurns the testimonies which the Spirit has given it, then evil spirits override the [natural] constitution of the body[1] and stir up these movements,[2] [44]until the soul grows weary and asks from where it can receive help and converts and adheres to the testimony of the Spirit and is healed. [45]Then it believes that this is its rest[3]: to abide with God, who is its peace.

[46]This I have said about repentance in the body and the soul, and how they are sanctified. [47]And when the mind accepts this struggle,[4] then it prays in the Spirit and begins to expel the afflictions of the soul[5] which have come upon it through its own greed. [48]The soul is then in communion with the Spirit, since it keeps the commandmends it has received. [49]And the Spirit teaches it how to heal all its afflictions, and how to expel them one by one, from head to foot, those mingled with what is natural to the body as well as those which are independent of the body, but have been mingled with it through the will.

[50]It sets a rule for the eyes that they may see rightly and purely and never again have anything alien in them, [51]and for the ears that they may hear in peace, and never again wish to hear anything evil or any slandering of men, [52]but rather all kinds of benevolence and mercy towards all creation; for in [both of] them it was once sick.

[53]It also teaches the tongue its own purity, since its affliction is great. For the one who speaks is sick and gives to the tongue his own works. Thus the afflictions are made abundant through this member, which is the tongue. [54]This is confirmed by James, the apostle, who says: *If someone thinks that he serves God and does not control his tongue, but deceives his own heart; his worship is vain.*[6] [55]Somewhere else he says that, *the tongue is a small member, but it defiles the whole body.*[7] And there is more like this than we can quote. [56]But if the mind is strengthened by the Spirit, it is first purified itself, then it examines the words and gives them to the tongue, so that they are free from hypocrisy and self-will. [57]Thus the words of Solomon are

---

1 Thus L. G: *then evil spirits sow in the constitution of the body;* S: *the evil spirits take dominon over it and sow in the mass of the body all passions;* A: *the evil spirits prevail over him and defiles his body.*

2 For a comparison of the different versions of this verse, see above, p. 32f.

3 G: განსვენება (ἀνάπαυσις, ἀνάψυξις); L: *requies;* S: ܢܝܚܐ; A: راحة. See also V:9 with note and above, pp. 84–85.

4 Thus G (adding *kind of*) and L. S: *If the heart conquers in this contest;* A: *when the mind grants* (*sic.* should be *is granted*) *this blessing.*

5 S adds *from the body.*

6 James 1:26.

7 James 3:5. Here G and A both add what is missing in L and S from the text of the NT: *but it utters great things.*

fulfilled: *My words are spoken by God. There is nothing twisted or perverse in them,*[1] [58]and somewhere else he says, *The tongue of the wise heals,*[2] and so on.

[59]And also the movements of the hand, if they were moved disorderly by the will of the soul, are now made firm by the Spirit and destined to move towards purity by prayers and acts of mercy.[3] [60]And on them the word about prayer is fulfilled, stating, *Let the lifting up of my hands be as the evening sacrifice,*[4] and also, *The hands of the diligent makes rich.*[5]

[61]Also the belly is purified in its eating and drinking, although it used to be insatiable in these matters, once it had been moved towards them by the will of the soul. Through desire and greed for food and drink [62]not a few have fallen in with the demons, and of them it is said by David, *I do not dine with one who has a high look and an insatiable heart.*[6]

[63]To those, however, who seek purity[7] the Spirit assigns this rule of purification: moderation after the power of the body, [64]devoid of any greed or desire. [65]On them this word of Paul is fulfilled saying: *Whether you eat or drink, or whatever you do, do all to the glory of God.*[8]

[66]Then, in regard to the sexual thoughts moved from below the belly,[9] the mind is again taught by the Spirit how to distinguish between the three types of movements mentioned above, and how to strive for purification [67]having the help of the Spirit. All the movements are then quenched by the power of the Spirit, pacifying the entire body and extinguishing the movements. [68]This is the word given by Paul: *Mortify your members which are upon the earth; fornication, uncleanness, and evil desires*[10] and so forth.

[69]And then also the feet, which formerly did not walk soundly according to the will of God; the mind, being united under the authority of the Spirit,[11] makes them walk according to the will of the Spirit, [70]that they may minister in good works so that the whole body may be changed and placed under the authority of the Spirit. [71]And I think that [even] now this dwelling[12] has

---

1 Prov. 8:8.

2 Prov. 12:18.

3 G and S add: *that these acts may be fufilled by them,* possibly influenced by the next sentence.

4 Ps. 140:2 LXX (= Ps. 141:2 Vulgata).

5 Prov. 10:4.

6 Ps. 100:5 LXX (= Ps. 101:5).

7 L adds *through the Lord*

8 1 Cor. 10:31. The entire passage is missing in S.

9 G: *from the belly;* S and A avoid all reference to sexuality and refer instead generally to the three motions mentioned earlier in the letter.

10 Col. 3:5. G and S also mention *passion.*

11 S deviates greatly from the other versions by additional explanations and smoothening of what must have been a very condensed and rough paragraph in the original. L: *The mind which is placed under the will of the Spirit...;* A: *The heart, which has been filled with grace.*

12 Thus S; G: *this;* A: *this body;* S: —.

taken on something of that other spiritual body which will be taken on at the resurrection of the just.[1]

72This I have said concerning the afflictions of the soul which have become mingled with what is natural to the body, in which the soul moves, so that it has become a guide to the evil spirits working in its members

73But I also say that the soul has some [movements] proper to it alone, which we will now examine: 74Pride is an affliction apart from the body, self-glorification another, as well as insolence, hatred, envy, wrath, pusill-animity, impatience and the rest[2] 75But if it gives itself to God whole-heartedly, God the merciful gives to it the Spirit of repentance and shows it how to repent in the case of each affliction, 76and also how the enemies prevent her and try to possess her, not allowing her to repent.

77If the soul endures and obeys what the Spirit has taught it about repentance, then the Creator has mercy on the weariness of its repentance through the labours of the body, such as prolonged fasts, vigils, much study of the Word of God and many prayers, as well as the renunciation of the world and human things, humility, and contrition.[3] 78And if it endures in all this, then God the merciful sees its patience in the temptations and has mercy and helps it.[4]

---

1 S: *...that when the whole body is purified and has accepted the fulness of the Spirit, it has all it will receive at the resurrection of the just;* A: *so that it will rise at the resurrection of the faithful*

2 The list is the same in G and L. S has *contempt* instead of pusillanimity and *laxity* instead of impatience. A deletes *self-glorification* and *insolence*.

3 S: *humility and tears and endurance of penitence;* A: *service to all men with purity of heart and humility of the spirit.*

4 A adding: *since He is a lover of mankind, who deserves glorification.*

LETTER TWO

*1*Beloved and honoured brothers, Antony greets you in the Lord!

*2*Truly, my beloved in the Lord, God did not visit his creatures only once, *3*but since the beginning of the world, as soon as anyone has turned through the law of promise[1] to the Creator of all, God embraces him in his benevolence, grace and Spirit. *4*As for those rational beings[2] in whom the law of promise grew cold[3] and whose faculties of the mind[4] thus died, so that they can no longer know themselves after their first formation, *5*they have all become irrational and serve the creatures instead of the Creator. *6*But in his great benevolence[5] the Creator of all visited us through the law of promise, for our essence[6] is immortal.

*7*Those who have become worthy of grace and have been fortified with the law of promise and taught by the Holy Spirit and accepted the Spirit of adoption,[7] *8*they have become able to worship the Creator as is proper.[8] As Paul says, *for our sake they have not yet received the promise.*[9]

*9*In his irrevocable love the Creator of all desired to visit our afflictions and confusion. *10*He thus raised up Moses, the Lawgiver, who gave us the written law and founded for us the house of truth, the spiritual[10] Church, which creates unity,[11] since it is God's will that we turn back to the first formation.[12] *11*Moses built the house, yet did not finish it, but left and died.

---

1 See I:2 with note and above, pp. 73–74.

2 G: მეტყოელი ბონებაჲ; L: *rationalis natura;* A: ناطقين .

3 Thus L: *refriguit.* G: *the souls and faculties of their minds died through the covenant of promise.* A: *have become weak and have been corrupted by the movements of the soul and have died...* The parallels in III:10, V:16, and VII:7 support L. In these G has განქმობაჲ which can be used for ξηραίνομαι as well as ψύχομαι. The idea of the cooling down of the minds and its background in Origen is discussed above, p. 74, note 3.

4 G: საცნობელნი გულთა; L: *officia animorum.* For the same expression see below, III:10, 44 (without *the mind*), VII:7 and 31.

5 G: სახიევრებაჲ; L: *bonitas;* A: صلاح; Gr*: ἐπιεικία or ἀγαθωσύνη.

6 G: არსებაჲ; L: *substantia* (in some of the subsequent cases *exstantia and essentia*); A: — (in the subsequent cases usually جوهر).

7 For the various designations of the Spirit, see above, pp. 79–81.

8 *Cf.* John 4:20 and above, p. 84. See also III, 9, 12, 31; IV:15; V:34 and VII:58*s.*

9 Hebr. 11:39–40.

10 Thus A: كنيسة الناطقة; A and L both have *Catholic.* I consider it much more likely that an original expression, probably ΕΚΚΛΗϹΙΑ ΝΟΕΡΑ, has been changed into *Catholic Church,* than the other way round. For this verse and Antony's understanding of the Church, see above, p. 75 and 78–81.

11 Thus G; L: *which he created;* A: —.

12 *Cf.* I:2, 30; V:40.

[12]Then God by his Spirit raised up the council[1] of the prophets, and they built upon the foundation laid by Moses, but could not complete it and likewise they left and died. [13]Invested with the Spirit, they all saw that the wound was incurable and that none of the creatures was able to heal it, [14]but only the Only-begotten, who is the very mind and image of the Father, who made every rational creature in the image of his image. [15]Knowing that the Saviour is a great physician, they all assembled and offered prayers for their members, that is for us, [16]crying out and saying: *Is there no balm in Gilead? Is there no physician there? Why then is not the health of the daughter of my people recovered?* [17]*We would have healed her, but she is not healed: now therefore let us forsake her.*[2] [18]But God in his abundant love came to us and said through his saints, *Son of man, make to thyself vessels of captivity.*[3]

[19]And he, *being in the form of God, counted it not a prize to be equal with God: but emptied himself, and took upon him the form of a servant, and became obedient unto death, even the death of the cross. Wherefore God also has highly exalted him, and given him a name which is above every name, that at the name of Jesus Christ every knee should bow, of things in heaven and things in earth and things under earth, and that every tongue should confess that Jesus Christ is Lord, to the glory of God the Father.*[4]

[20]Now then, beloved, let this word be manifest to you, that for our sake the Father in his benevolence *did not spare his Only-begotten, but delivered him up for the salvation of us all.* He gave himself for our sins, [21]and *our iniquities humbled him, and by his stripes we were healed,*[5] [22]and by the word of his power he gathered us from all lands, from one end of the earth to the other,[6] [23]resurrecting our minds, giving us remission of our sins, and teaching us that we are members of one another.

[24]My brothers, I beseech you in the name of our Lord Jesus Christ, understand this great dispensation that *he was made like unto us, yet without sin.*[7] [25]Every rational being, for whom the Saviour came, ought to examine his way of life and know himself and discern between evil and good, so that he may be freed through his coming.[8] [26]For those who are freed by his

---

1 G: კრებული (*concilum*); L: *chorus;* A: *all the prophets.*

2 Jer. 8:22 and 51:9 (28:9 LXX). See also V:21ff. Antony's use of this quotation and the following from Ezek. 12:3 and their parallels are discussed above, p. 76.

3 Ezek. 12:3, *cf.* Jer. 46:19.

4 Phil. 2:6–11.

5 Rom. 8:32 combined with Is. 53:5.

6 G: ყოველთა გან სოფელთა კიდით გან ქუეყანისაჲთა ვიდრე კიდედმდე სოფლისა; L: *ex omnibus regionibus ab extremo terrae usque ad ultimum orbis;* A: *min aqṭār al-arḍ wa kull al-maskūnah* (in III:24: *min kull al-ʿālam min aqṭār al-arḍ ilā aqṭārihā*).

7 Hebr. 4:15.

8 G: მოსლვაჲ; L: *adventus;* A: مجيء. See also III:1, 27, 29, 34, 37; V:9; VI:16, 83; VII, 32–35, 45, 58*h* and 58*t*. For a discussion of the concept of the *parousia* of Christ, see above, pp. 82–85.

dispensation are called the servants of God. But this is not yet perfection,
rather it is the time of righteousness, and it leads to adoption. [27]Jesus, our
Saviour, knew that they were about to receive the Spirit of adoption, and
that they knew him, since they were taught by the Holy Spirit, and thus he
said, *Henceforth I call you not servants, but brothers and friends, for all
things that the Father has taught me, I have made known unto you and
taught you.*[1]

[28]Grown bold in their minds, knowing themselves and their spiritual
essence[2], they gave voice and said: *Even though we have known Thee after
the flesh, yet now henceforth know we Thee so no more.*[3] [29]And they
received the Spirit of adoption, and cried out saying, *We have not received
the Spirit of bondage again to fear; but we have received the Spirit of
adoption, whereby we cry, Abba, Father.*[4] [30]Now, therefore, O God, we
know what Thou hast given us: *that we are the children and heirs of God,
and joint heirs with Christ.*[5]

[31]Let this word be manifest to you: Whosoever has not prepared his own
betterment, nor struggled with all his strength, let him know that for him the
coming of the Saviour will be unto judgement, [32]*for to some it is the savour
of death unto death, and to some the savour of life unto life.*[6] [33]*For he is set
for the fall and rising again of many in Israel, and for a sign which shall be
spoken against.*[7]

[34]I beseech you, beloved, in the name of Jesus Christ, do not neglect
your salvation, but *let each one rend his heart and not his garment,*[8] lest we
wear this garment in vain, preparing ourselves for judgement. [35]For the time
is near in which the work of each one of us shall be examined. [36]As for the
all too few words: there are many others, which could be written to you. But
it is said, *Give occasion to a wise man, and he will be yet wiser.*[9] [37]I salute
you *from the least to the greatest.*[10] And may the God of peace keep you all,
my beloved.

---

1 Joh. 15:15.

2 G: გონიერი არსებაჲ; L: *sensualis substantia* (in some of the parallels *exstantia*); A: جوهر العقلي ; The Coptic version of the parallel in IV:10 has ⲟⲩⲥⲓⲁ ⲛⲟⲉⲣⲁ. Gr*: οὐσία νοέρα. See also III, 1, 13; IV, 10; V, 1, 15f.; VI, 2, 5, 56, 69; VII, 5, 8, 11, 58*b*, *c*, *n*, 59. For a discussion of this expression, see above, p. 61f (note 7) and 68–71.

3 2 Cor. 5:16.

4 Rom. 8:15.

5 Rom 8:17.

6 2 Cor. 2:16.

7 Luk. 2:34.

8 Joel 2:13.

9 Prov. 9:9.

10 Acts 8:10.

Letter Three

*1*A sensible[1] man who has prepared himself to be freed at the coming of Jesus[2] knows himself in his spiritual essence[3], *2*for he who knows himself also knows the dispensations of his Creator, and what he does for his creatures.

*3*Beloved in the Lord, our members and joint heirs with the saints, I beseech you in the name of Jesus Christ to act so[4] that he gives you all the Spirit of discernment[5] *4*to perceive and understand that the love I have for you is not the love of the flesh, but the love of godlinessh.[6]. *5*About your[7] names in the flesh there is nothing to say; they will vanis But if a man knows his true name he will also perceive the name of Truth.[8] *6*As long as he was struggling with the angel through the night Jacob was called Jacob, but when it dawned he was called Israel, which means "a mind[9] that sees God".[10]

*7*I believe that you are not unaware that the enemy of virtue always plots against truth. *8*Therefore God has not visited his creatures only once, *9*but from the creation of the world some have prepared themselves to come to the Creator through the law of his promise, learning from that how to worship their Creator as is proper. *10*But through much weakness, the heaviness of the body and the concern for evil the law of promise has grown cold and the faculties of the mind have been worned out. *11*Thus they have not been able to discover themselves as they were created, *12*namely as an eternal substance[11], which is not dissolved with the body but still cannot be freed through its own righteousness.[12] Therefore God in his benevolence

---

1 G: პირმეტყუელი; L: *rationabilis;* A: ناطق.

2 The concept of the *parousia* of Christ is central to the letters. See also II:31; III:27, 29, 34, 37; V:9; VI:16, 83; VII, 32–35, 45, 58*h* and 58*t*, and the discussion above, pp. 82–85.

3 See II:28 with note.

4 G omits; A adds: *strive for that which is your duty towards the Lord*

5 *Cf.* Ef. 1:17. G: სული მეცნიერებისა; L: *discretionis spiritus;* A: روح الافراز; Gr*: τὸ πνεῦμα τῆς διάκρισις (?).

6 See the note to IV:2.

7 L: *our.*

8 L: *But a man should know the true name.*

9 G: გონებაჲ (νοῦς); L: *mens;* A: عقل.

10 *Cf.* Gen. 32:24–28.

11 G: არსებაჲ; L: *substantia;* A: جوهر

12 L: *nec praevaluit semetipsam liberare injustitia* (??)

turned to it[1] with the law of Scripture to teach them to worship the Father as is proper, [13]for God is one and the spiritual essence also exists through oneness.[2] [14]Let this word be manifest to you, my beloved, that all who are not at peace draw battles upon themselves and are a judgement to themselves.[3]

[15]But the Creator saw that their wound was great and needed care. [16]He, who is himself their Creator and healer, Jesus, thus sent forerunners before himself. [17]I do not hesitate to say that Moses, who gave us the law, is one of them[4] [18]and that the same Spirit which was in Moses acted in the assembly of the saints when they all prayed for the Only-begotten Son of God. [19]John, too, is one of his forerunners, *for the prophets and the law were until John and the kingdom of God suffers violence and the violent take it by force.*[5]

[20]Those invested with the Spirit saw that no one among the creatures could heal this great wound, but only the goodness[6] of God[7], his Only-begotten, whom he sent as salvation of the entire world. [21]He is the great healer who is able to heal this great wound.[8] [22]In his benevolence, and for the salvation of us all, *the Father of creation did not spare his Only-begotten, but delivered him up for our sins.* [23]*He was humbled by our iniquities and by his stripes we were healed.*[9] [24]Through the word of his power he gathered us from all lands, from one end of the earth to the other, [25]resurrecting our hearts from the earth and teaching us that we are members of one another.

[26]I beseech you, my beloved in the Lord, to understand this writing, since it is the commandment of the Lord. It is really great for us to meditate on the form Jesus accepted for our sake, *he was made like unto us in everything, yet without sin.*[10] [27]Thus we have to free ourselves at his coming,[11] [28]so that he can make us wise through his ignorance, enrich us through his poverty[12] and strengthen us through his weakness, and resurrect

---

1 L and A: *them.*

2 G: გონიერი იგი არსებაჲ არს ერთობითა; L: *secundum sensualem essentiam in idipsum est unitas;* A: *al-jawhar al-ᶜaqlī aydān kā'in fi-l-waḥadānīyah.* See also above, p. 64.

3 Thus L and A. G omits any reference to judgement.

4 G : *his prophets;* and A: *the greatest of the prophets.*

5 Matt. 11:12–13; Luke 16:16.

6 This is the only place where L has *beatitudo* instead of *bonitas,* which is the usual term in L for სახიერებაჲ in G, the equivalent of ἐπιεικία or ἀγαθωσύνη.

7 A: *of the Son* !

8 G: *Since he is the great healer able to heal this great wound, they prayed to God.*

9 Rom. 8:32 and Is. 53:5. The Arabic version instead quotes Gal. 1:4: *He laid down his life for us, and by this he healed us all.*

10 Hebr. 4:15.

11 A: *to rejoice at his coming.*

12 *Cf.* 2 Cor. 8:9.

us all when *he destroys him who has the power of death.*[1] [29]Therefore we may cease to call for Jesus in the flesh[2], for the coming of Jesus [already] assists us in the service of the good until we have expelled all evil. [30]Then Jesus will say to us[3]: *Henceforth I call you not servants, but brothers.*[4] [31]When the apostles were about to receive the Spirit of adoption,[5] the Holy Spirit taught them to worship the Father as is proper.

[32]But as for me, miserable prisoner in Christ, this time which we have reached is a time of joy, as well as grief and tears, [33]for they are many of our generation who *have put on the habit of godliness*[6] *but denied its power.*[7] [34]I rejoice over those who have prepared themselves to be freed through the coming of Jesus, [35]but I lament over those who speak in the name of Jesus but act according to the will of their own hearts and bodies. [36]Over those who have considered the lengthy time, their hearts failing them, and who have laid off the habit of godliness and become like beasts, I cry. [37]Remember that for them the coming of Jesus is a judgement.

[38]But you, my beloved in the Lord, know yourselves, so that you may know this time[8] and be prepared to *offer yourselves to God as a pleasing sacrifice.*[9] [39]Truly, my beloved, I write to you *as to wise men,* who are able to know themselves.[10] [40]I know that he who knows himself knows God and his dispensations for his creatures.

[41]Let this word be manifest to you, that I do not have the love of the flesh for you, but the love of godliness, [42]for *God is glorified in the communion of the saints.*[11]

[43]Be prepared, yourselves, while we still have some who pray for us,[12] that *the fire, which Jesus came to send on the earth,*[13] may be kindled also into your hearts, [44]so that you may strain your hearts[14] and your faculties to discriminate between good and evil, right and left, the eternal and the

---

1 Hebr. 2:14.

2 L: *we may cease to care for the flesh;* A: *we can find rest and do not need Jesus any longer in the flesh.*

3 A: *said to his disciples.*

4 John 15:15.

5 For a discussion of the various designations of the Spirit in the letters of St. Antony, see above, pp. 79–81.

6 G: სამოსელი ღმრთისმსახურებისაჲ; L: *indumenta pietatis;* A: شكل العبادة.

7 2 Tim. 3:5.

8 *Cf.* II:35, III:32, 48, IV:16; VI:28, 39–40, 81 and 115. For the role of the concept of time in Antony's letters, see above, pp. 81–86.

9 *Cf.* Rom. 12:1.

10 1 Cor. 10:15. A: *able to understand what is written.*

11 Ps. 88:8 LXX (= Ps. 89:8 Vulgata).

12 L adds: *and for your salvation*

13 Luke 12:49

14 L: *habitudines;* A: *will.*

passing.[1] 45 Since Jesus knew that the power of the devil lies in the matter of
this world,[2] he advised his disciples: 46 *Lay not up for yourselves treasures
on earth* and *Take no thought for the morrow, for the morrow will take
thought for the things of itself.* [3]

47 Truly, my beloved, when it is calm all captains boast, but in high winds
the true skill of the captain becomes manifest. 48 Therefore, know the time in
which we are.[4] 49 As for the all too few words of freedom, there is much to
be told to you, but 50 *if one gives occasion to a wise man he will be yet
wiser.*[5] 51 I greet you all *from the least to the greatest.*[6]

1 G: სიმთკიცჱ და უძლორებაჲ (Gr*: κράτος καὶ ἀσθένια ?); L: *a substantia insubstantiam;* A: *the lasting from the non-lasting.* For a more full discussion of these terms, see above p. 63.

2 A: *that satan rages.*

3 Matt. 6:19, 34.

4 For a discussion of these two verses and the metaphor of the captain, the κυβερνήτης, see above, p. 82.

5 Prov. 9:9.

6 Acts 8:10.

LETTER FOUR

[1]Antony writes to all his dear brothers in Christ: Greetings!

Members of the Church[1], I never fail in remembering you. [2]I want you to know the love I have for you, that it is not the love of the flesh, but the love of godliness.[2] [3]For the friendship of the body is not stable nor lasting—it is moved about by alien winds. [4]Everyone who fears God, and keeps his commandments is a servant of God. [5]But in this service there is no fulfillment, although it is just, and a guide to adoption. [6]Even the prophets and apostles, the holy choir[3], those elected by God to be entrusted with the apostolic message, were thus made prisoners in Christ through the benevolence of God the Father. [7]For Paul says: *Paul, the prisoner of Christ Jesus, called to be an apostle.*[4] [8]And so the written law works with us[5] in a good service until we are able to restrain all passions[6] and to fulfill[7] the good ministry of virtue through this apostolic [life ?][8].

[9]When they[9] had come close to the[10] grace Jesus said to them[11]: *Henceforth I call you not my servants, but my brothers and my friends, for all that the Father has taught me, I have made known unto you and taught you.*[12] [10]Those who had come close, by being taught by the Holy Spirit, came to know themselves in their spiritual essence[13]. [11]And in their self-knowledge they called and said: *We have not received the spirit of bondage again to fear, but the spirit of adoption whereby we cry: Abba, Father,* that

---

1 L has *Catholic* instead of *Church.*

2 C: ⲘⲘⲚⲦⲢⲈϤϢⲘϢⲚⲞⲨⲦⲈ; G: სიყვარული ღმრთისმსახურებისაჲ; L: *spiritus culturae Dei*; A: *spiritual love.* The Greek was probably θεοσέβεια. *Cf.* III:4, 41; V:2, and Rom 12:1. The different versions of the verses 2–3 are discussed above, p. 24f.

3 C: ⲬⲞⲢⲞⲤ; G: კრებული; L: *chorus;* A: —. The different versions of verse 6 are discussed above, p. 25f.

4 This is not a real quotation, since Paul never uses the words *prisoner* and *called* together. But see Eph. 3:1 and Philem. 1:1.

5 L and G: *you.* The different versions of verse 8 are discussed above, p. 26f.

6 G adds *of the body.*

7 L and G: *accept the fulfillment of.*

8 Or *according to this apostolic saying.* C has *apostolic* without any reference. L: *apostolic mandate;* G: *apostolic life;* A: *apostolic saying.*

9 C: *he* (probably a confusion in the mss. of ϥ and ⲩ). G: *someone,* L: *we;* A: *we.*

10 L and G: *to accept the.*

11 C: *them;* G: *them* (ms. B)/*him* (ms. A); L: *us;* A: *us.*

12 John 15:15. The word *my,* repeated three times in the C, twice in the A, once in L, is not in G and not in the text of the NT.

13 ⲞⲨⲤⲒⲀ ⲚⲞⲈⲢⲀ (οὐσία νοέρα), *cf.* II:28 with note.

we shall know what God has granted us. [12]*If we are children we are heirs, the heirs of God and joint heirs with the saints.*[1]

[13]My dear brothers, joint heirs with the saints, no virtues are alien to you; they are all yours, for when you have become revealed to God, you have no obligations[2] towards this bodily life.[3] [14]*The Spirit does not enter a soul that has an unclean heart, nor a body that sins. It is a holy power, far from any deceit.*[4] [15]Truly, my beloved, *I write to you as to wise men,*[5] who are able to know themselves. He who knows himself knows God, he who knows God must worship him as is proper.

[16]My beloved in the Lord, know yourselves! Those who know themselves know their time,[6] and those who know their time are able to stand upright without being moved by shifty tongues.

[17]As for Arius, who stood up in Alexandria, he spoke strange words about the Only-begotten: to him who has no beginning[7], he gave a beginning, to him who is ineffable[8] among men he gave an end, and to the immovable he gave movement.[9] [18]*If one man sins against another man, one prays for him to God. But if someone sins against God, to whom should one pray for him?*[10] That man has begun a great task, an unhealable wound. If he had known himself, his tongue would not have spoken about what he did not know. It is, however, manifest, that he did not know himself.

---

1 Rom. 8:15–17. G adds: *with Christ.*

2 G and L: *you are not guilty.*

3 C: ⲃⲓⲟⲥ ⲥⲁⲣⲕⲓⲕⲟⲛ (*sic.*); G: ჴორციელი ცხორებისა; L: *a mala vita;* A: العالم الوقتى.

4 Sap. 1:4–5. The different versions of verse 14 are discussed above, p. 28.

5 *Cf.* 1 Cor. 10:15.

6 For the concept of time see also II:35; III:32, 38, 48; VI:28, 39–40, 81 and 115, and above, pp. 81–86.

7 G and L: *time.*

8 G: *eternal.*

9 The reference to Arius and is discussed above, pp. 43–45 (for the dating of the letters) and 76–78 (for the Christology). For the concept of immobility, see above, p. 66, note 8.

10 1 Sam. 2:25.

LETTER FIVE

*1*Antony greets his beloved children, holy Israelite children, in their spiritual essence[1]. I do not need to call you by your names in the flesh,[2] which are passing away, for you are Israelite children. *2*Truly, my sons, the love I have for you is not the love of the flesh, but the love of godliness.[3] *3*Therefore I do not tire of praying for you day and night that you may come to know the grace he has granted you, *4*that God did not visit his creatures just once, but from the beginning of the world God looks after his creatures and he raises up the generations one by one through occasions and gifts of grace.[4]

*5*Now, my children, do not neglect to cry out day and night to God, entreating by the benevolence of the Father, to grant you help from above,[5] and teach you what befits you.[6] *6*Truly, my children, we dwell in our death and stay in the house of the robber, bound by the fetters of death. *7*Therefore, *do not give sleep to your eyes, nor slumber to your eyelids,*[7] that you may in all sanctity *offer yourselves as a sacrifice to God,*[8] whom no one can inherit[9] without sanctity.

*8*Truly, my beloved in the Lord, let this word be manifest to you, that you may do good, *9*and so give rest[10] to all the saints and readiness[11] to the ministry of the angels, and rejoice at the coming of Jesus, for because of us none of them has yet found rest.[12] *10*Even to my miserable self, dwelling in this house of clay, you will thus bring happiness to my soul.

---

1 *Cf.* II:28 with note.

2 L omits.

3 *Cf.* IV:2 with note.

4 G: მიზეზითა და მადლითა (Gr*: αἰτίαι καὶ χαρίσματα); L: *occasionibus et gratia.* A summarizes the entire sentence: *For God, in his mercy, raises up all by his grace.*

5 G (ms. A) omits *help from above.*

6 G: კეთილ არს თქუენდა (*quod bonum est vobis*); L: *quid in se habeat;* A: ما يجيب (*that which is proper*).

7 Ps. 131:4 LXX (= Ps. 132:4 Vulgata).

8 *Cf.* Rom. 12:1.

9 G: დამკჳიდრებაჲ (Gr*: ἐνοικέω, κληρονομέω); L: *haereditare;* A: *see.* It is impossible to know of the original meant *see God, inherit God* or *live with God.* (Chitty and Cremaschi: translate, *inherit;* Louf and Wagenaar, *see*).

10 G: განსუენებაჲ (ἀναπαύω, ἀναψύχω); L: *reficere;* A: نيح, نياح. See also I:45, VI:16, 83 (not L), 84, 98 and 99 (not G). *Cf.* Matt. 11:28, and above, pp. 84–85 with notes.

11 G: გულსმოდგინებაჲ (προθυμία); L: *alacritas;* A: سرور (*joy*)!

12 *Cf.* Hebr. 11:39–40.

[11]Truly, my children, this affliction and humiliation of ours gives distress to all the saints. For our sake they weep and moan before the Creator of all. [12]Thus, because of the moaning of the saints, the God of all is angry with all our evil deeds.[1] [13]But our progress and justification stirs up the assembly[2] of the saints, and they pray devoutly and make joyful exultation before our Creator, [14]and he himself, the Creator of all, rejoices in our good[3] deeds on the testimony of his saints and so he grants us great gifts of grace.

[15]That you may know that God always loves his creatures,[4] their essence[5] being immortal, not to be dissolved with the body: [16]Having seen that the spiritual essence had descended into the abyss,[6] being completely dead, and that the law of promise had grown cold[7], [17]God in his benevolence visited them through Moses. [18]Mose truly founded the house of truth, and wanted to heal the great wound and bring them back to their original unity, but he could not, and left them. [19]Then, too, the council[8] of the prophets built upon the foundation of Moses, but they were unable to heal the great wound of their members, and realized that their power ceased. [20]Thus the communion of all the saints assembled in unity and offered prayers before their Creator, saying: [21]*Is there no balm in Gilead? Is there no physician there? Why then is not the health of the daughter of my people recovered?* [22]*O Lord, we would have healed Babylon, and she is not healed. Now let us forsake her and flee from her.*[9]

[23]And all[10] prayed by the benevolence of the Father for his Only-begotten, because unless he himself would come, none of the creatures would be able to heal the great wound[11]. [24]For this reason the Father in his benevolence spoke and said: *Son of man, make to thyself vessels of captivity.*[12] [25]For the salvation of us all, the Father *did not spare his Only-begotten, but delivered him up for our sins.*[13] [26]*Our iniquities humbled him and by his stripes we were healed,*[14] [27]and he gathered us from all lands,

---

1 A: ... *becomes angry with the evil spirits and destroys for us their evil works.*

2 G: ერსა (Gr*: ὄχλος, σπεῖρα, στράτευμα); L: *chorus.*

3 G (ms. A) and L omit.

4 A omits the entire passage until verse 30 with a refrence to what has been said in the previous letters.

5 G: არსებაჲ (οὐσία); L: *exstantia.*

6 G: უფსკრულად; L: *abyssum;* A: —.

7 *Cf.* II:4 and III:10.

8 G: კრებული (*congregatio, concilum*); L: *chorus.*

9 Jer. 28:8–9 (LXX) *Cf.* 8:22 and 51:9 (Vulgata). *Cf.* II:16–17. Antony's use of this quotation and the following from Ezek. 12:3 and their parallels are discussed above, p. 76.

10 G adds *the saints.*

11 G adds: *of men.*

12 Ezek. 12:3 LXX, *cf.* Jer. 46:19. G adds: , *and go into captivity willingly.*

13 Rom 8:32.

14 Is. 53:5.

from one end of the earth to the other, [28]resurrecting our minds from the earth and teaching us that we are members of one another.

[29]Take heed, children, that the word of Paul may not be accomplished upon us, that: *We have the form of godliness, but deny its power.*[1] [30]Let each one of you[2] rend his heart and weep before him and say: *What shall I render unto the Lord for all his benefits towards me?*[3] [31]But I tremble, my children, lest the word be accomplished upon us: *What profit is there in my blood, when I go down to corruption?*[4]

[32]Truly, my children, I talk to you *as to wise men,*[5] so that you understand what I tell you: [33]Unless each one of you hates all earthly possessions[6], and renounces them and all their workings by all his heart and stretches out the hands of his heart[7] to heaven and to the Father of all, he cannot be saved.[8] [34]But if he does this God will have mercy because of his labour, and grant him the invisible fire which burns up all impurity from him and purifies his[9] mind[10]. [35]Then the Holy Spirit will dwell in us,[11] and Jesus will stay with us and thus we will be able to worship God as is proper.[12] [36]But as long as we have peace[13] with the natures of this world[14] we remain enemies of God[15] and of his angels and all[16] his saints.

[37]Now therefore, I beseech you, my beloved, in the name of our Lord Jesus Christ, not to neglect your true life[17], and not to confound the brevity of this time with time eternal, nor mistake the skin of the corruptible flesh with the reign of ineffable light, and not to let this place of damnation squander the angelic thrones of judgement .

---

1 2 Tim. 3:5.

2 L: *us.*

3 Ps. 115: 3 LXX (= Ps. 116:12 Vulgata).

4 Ps. 29:10 LXX (= Ps. 30:10 Vulgata).

5 *Cf.* 1 Cor. 10:15.

6 G: ყოველი ბუნებაჲ განისაჲ მის მონაგებისაჲ (*omnem naturam terrenae possessionis*); L: *omnem pulverem naturae hujuscemodi materiae;* A: الطبيعة الهيولانية الارضية (*earthly material nature*).

7 A: *out his mind.*

8 The last four words and the beginning of next sentence are missing in L.

9 G: *our*

10 G: სული იგი მთავრობისა; L: *principalem ipsum;* A: عقله *(his mind)*; Gr*: ἡγημονικός (τῆς ψυχῆς) ?. Except for VI:62, where G, too, drops *of the soul,* this is the only instance in the letters where the mind is called *hegemonikos* and not *nous.*

11 A: *him.* In L the following line has disappeared and the text reads: *et sic possimus habitare apud Patrem sicut oportet.*

12 *Cf.* II:8; III, 9, 12, 31 an IV:15.

13 L: *succumb to (fatiscimus);* A: *persist in being reconciled with.*

14 G: სოფლისათა ამათ ბუნებაჲ (Gr*: αἱ φύσεις τοῦ κόσμου); L: *naturali materiae;* A: *this material nature.*

15 L omits *of God.*

16 L omits *all.*

17 G: *your salvation;* A: *your life and your salvation.*

38Truly, my children, my heart wonders and my soul is terrified that we are all engolfed as if by a flood[1] and carried away as if drunk by wine. 39Each one of us has sold himself by his own will and we are dominated by it.[2] We do not want to lift our eyes[3] to seek the glory of heaven and the works of all the saints and to walk in their footsteps.[4]

40Now, therefore, understand that, whether it be the holy heavens or angels or archangels[5] or thrones or dominions or cherubim or seraphim or sun or moon or stars, or patriarchs or prophets or apostles, or devil or satan or evil spirits or the powers of the air, or (to say no more) whether it be man or woman, in the beginning of their formation they all derive from one, except the perfect and blessed Trinity: Father, Son and Holy Spirit.[6] 41Because of the evil conduct[7] of some it was necessary that God should set names upon them after their works. 42And those who made the best progress, he gave more abundant glory.[8]

---

1 Missing in G. A combines the two references: *we are drunk by the passions like a people drunk from the pleasures of wine.*

2 The entire sentence is missing in A.

3 G adds *to heaven,* probably because of diplography.

4 A expands the sentence by *in order to inherit with them the eternal inheritance.*

5 Missing in L

6 A has avoided the Origenist content by stating first that the spiritual beings have all been created for one purpose alone, the glorification of God, and then that all the enumerated have been created by the Trinity.

7 L: *because of the good movement of some;* A: *because of the sensual movements.*

8 Apparently the end of the letter is missing.

LETTER SIX

[1]Antony greets all his dear brothers, who are at Arsinoë and its neighbourhood, and those who are with you, in the Lord. [2]All of you who have prepared yourselves to come to God, I greet you in the Lord, my beloved, the young and the old, men and women, Israelite children, saints in your spiritual essence.

[3]Truly, my beloved, you are greatly blessed,[1] for great gifts of grace[2] have been given to your generation. [4]Thus, for the sake of him who has visited you, you should not weary in the struggle until you have offered yourselves as a sacrifice to God in all sanctity, without which none can inherit God.

[5]Truly, my beloved, it is great for you to attempt to understand the spiritual essence, in which there is neither man nor woman; rather it is an immortal essence, which has a beginning but no end. [6]You ought to know how it is utterly fallen into this humiliation and great confusion, which has come upon all of us. But since it is an immortal essence which is not destroyed with the body, [7]God, seeing this incurable wound, and seeing that it had become grave, [8]visited them in his mercy, and after a time he, in his benevolence, granted them the law as an assistance[3] through Moses, who gave the law. [9]And Moses founded the house of truth and wanted to heal the great wound, but could not complete the building of the house. [10]Then all the host of the saints assembled in unity and prayed by the benevolence of God for our salvation, that he would come to us[4] to save us all, [11]He, who is the great and true high priest and true physician, who is able to heal the great wound. [12]For this reason he, following the will of the Father, divested himself of his glory; *being God, he took the form of a servant,* [13]*and gave himself for our sins, and our iniquities humbled him and through his stripes we were all healed.*[5]

[14]Therefore, my beloved in the Lord, I want you to know that it was for our foolishness that he choose to become a fool, for our weakness he accepted the form of weakness, for our poverty he became poor and for our death he assumed death,[6] and that he endured all this for our sake. [15]Truly,

---

1 Missing in L.

2 Thus G and A. L: *promissio.*

3 G: შეწევნაჲ (ἐπιχορηγία); L: *unde et operatus est.*

4 L: *to the earth*

5 *Cf.* Phil 2:6–7, Gal. 1:4 and Is. 53:5.

6 *Cf.* 1 Cor. 1:18–28, 3:18–19, 4:10; 2 Cor. 8:19.

my beloved in the Lor d, we ought not *to give sleep to our eyes, nor slumber to our eyelids,*[1] *16*but pray and beseech the benevolence of the Father until he comes to our help[2] and we thus may find rest[3] at the coming of Jesus and strength so that we are able to follow the saints,[4] who are eager to support us in the time of our negligence, making them zealous so that they may help us in the time of our tribulations. Then *he that sowes and he that reapes rejoice together.*[5]

*17*I want you to know, my children, the great distress which I have for you, for I see the great disgrace that comes upon us[6] all, *18*and contemplate the struggle of the saints and their tears, which they shed at all times before God for our sake,[7] *19*when they see[8] all the labour of their Creator[9] and the evil devices of the devils and their disciples, which they always plan for our perdition, *20*since their part is in the hell to come. Therefore they want us to be lost with them, so that we shall be with the multitude.[10]

*21*Truly, my beloved, *as to wise men I talk to you,*[11] that you may know all the dispensations of our Creator, which he made for us, that he has payed visits to us[12] through manifest and secret revelations[13]. Yes, we are called sensible, but have put on an irrational mind, *23*so that we are ignorant of how the secret contrivances and manifold crafts of the devil work, and how they might be known.[14] *24*For they know that we have tried to know our disgrace[15] and sought for a way to escape their acts, which they effect in us. *25*And not only do we not obey the evil counsels which they sow in our hearts, but many of us even laugh at their contrivances.[16] *26*They know the

---

1 Ps. 131:4 LXX (= Ps. 132:4 Vulgata).

2 G: თანაგამოვიდეს (Gr*: συνέρχομαι ?); L: *egrediatur.*

3 G: განსუენებაჲ (ἀνάπαυσις); L: *requiem. Cf.* Acts 3:19–20 and above, V:9 with note and pp. 84–85.

4 G: *and strength to the ministry of the saints,...* Apparnetly either G or L has misunderstood the Greek source, and since the passage is completely reworked in A it is impossible to decide which version one should prefer. It is quite possible that L has elaborated on the text and that we originally had more or less the same text as in V:9.

5 John 4:36.

6 A: *you.*

7 A adds: *they yearn for you to be like them.*

8 A adds: *the dispensations of their creator in his wonderful incarnation and.*

9 A adds: *for our salvation.*

10 A: *in this great destruction.*

11 *Cf.* 1 Cor. 10:15; A: *I ask you.*

12 A adds: *through the incarnation.*

13 G: ქადაგებაჲ (Gr*: κήρυγμα, *praedicatio*); L: *praeconia;* A omits.

14 Translated according to L. G: *Or do you not know the many contrivances and crafts of the devil, how they are, since they hate us.*

15 G: სირცხჳლი; L: *confusionem;* A: *wijāᶜanā wafaḍīḥatanā.*

16 A: *they began to do their work with scorn.*

indulgence of our Creator, that he died because of them[1] in this world, and
prepared for them to inherit Gehenna as a result of their own negligence.
[27]I want you to know, my children, that I do not cease to pray to God for
you, day and night, [28]that he may open the eyes of your hearts that you may
see all the secret evils which they pour upon us every day in this present
time. [29]I ask God to give you a heart of knowledge and a spirit of discernment, that you may be able to lift you hearts before the Father as a pure
sacrifice in all sanctity, without blemish.

[30]Truly,[2] my children, they are jealous[3] of us at all times with their evil
counsel, their secret persecution, their subtle malice, their spirits of
seduction, [31]their fraudulent thoughts, their faithlessness which they sow in
our hearts every day, their hardness of heart and their numbness,[4] [32]the many
sufferings they bring upon us at every hour, the weariness which causes our
hearts to be weary at all times, [33]all their wrath, the mutual slander which
they teach us, [34]our self-justifications in our deeds,[5] and the condemnations[6]
which they sow in our hearts [35]so that we, when we are alone, condemn our
fellows, though they are not with us, [36]the contempt they send into our
hearts through pride so that we become hard-hearted[7] and despise one
another, becoming bitter against each other with hard words, and troubled
every hour accusing each other and not ourselves, [37]thinking that our
struggle comes from our fellows,[8] judging what is outside while the robbers
are all inside our house, [38]and [furthermore, with] the disputes and divisions
we have with each other until we have established our own words so that
they seem justified in the face of the other, [39]and they incite us to do things
which we are unable to do (and whose time it is not)[9], and makes us weary
of things we do and which are good for us.

[40]Therefore they make us laugh when it is time for weeping, and weep
when it is time for laughter, simply turning us aside every time from the
straight way. Through many other deceits they make us their slaves, but
there is no time now to reveal all of them. [41]But when they fill our hearts
with all these and we feed on them and they become our food, then God is

1 Missing in G.

2 The verses 30–44 are quoted in Coptic in Besa, *Epistula ad Heraï*. See above p. 16.

3 C: ⲥⲉϥⲑⲟⲛⲉⲓ (Gr: φθονέω); G: გუეშურებაჲ (*sic*); L: *invidere.*

4 Thus C and A: C: ⲛⲉⲩⲧⲟⲙ ⲛϩⲧ ⲙⲛⲛⲉⲩⲟⲛϣⲥ; A: *qillat al-amāna wa sahr al-qalb*; G: განკუირვებაჲ და განკრთომაჲ; L missing.

5 From here until the end of verse 37 A has summarized the contents in a few sentences.

6 G adds: *of envy*

7 C: ⲛⲁϣⲧϩⲏⲧ ; G: გულფიცხელ (Gr*: σκληροτράχηλος, σκληροκαρδία); L: *duri cordis.*

8 L has misundersttod its model: *opinantes laborem nostrum et* (*sic* Sarasio, Migne: *ex*) *propria constare virtute.*

9 C: ⲁⲩⲱ ⲉⲙⲡⲥⲏⲩ ⲣⲱ ⲁⲛⲡⲉ ; G and L missing.

wroth with us.[1] ([42]And he visits us by resolving[2] us from the heaviness of this body, that we may leave it. [43]Then our evil works which we wrongly commited will be revealed to us in the body for the last (?) punishment[3], and we will wear it again by the mercy of the Creator and thus *our end will be worse than our beginning.*[4])

[44]Therefore, do not fail to beseech the goodness of the Father that perchance a helper will come to you so that you may teach yourselves to know what is truly right. [45]Truly, I tell you, my children, that this our vessel in which we dwell is our destruction, and a house full of war. [46]In truth, my children, I tell you that every man who delights in his own desires, and who is subdued to his own thoughts and sticks to what is sown in his own heart and rejoices in it and thinks in his heart that it is some great chosen mystery[5], and through it justifies himself in what he does, [47]the soul of such a man is the breath[6] of evil spirits and his counsel towards evil, and his body a store of evil mysteries which it hides in itself: [48]and over such a one the demons have great power, because he has not dishonored them before all men.

[49]Do you to know that they have not one single method of hunting, that we should know it and escape it? [50]And if you seek, you will not find their sins and iniquities revealed bodily, for they are not visible bodily.[7] [51]But you should know that we are their bodies, and that our soul receives their wickedness;[8] and when it has received them, then it reveals them through the body in which we dwell. [52]Now, then, my children, let us not give them any place; otherwise we shall stir up the wrath of God against us, [53]and they will move freely[9] [as if] in their[10] home and laugh at us, since they know that our destruction is of our neighbour, and also our life is of our neighbour.[11] [54]For, who has ever seen God, and rejoiced with him and kept

---

1 G and L: *then God has mercy upon us until our evil has ceased.* The following two verses are not found in the Coptic quotation of Besa, nor in the Arabic version. It is impossible to exclude that they could be original, but as they stand they are barely intelligible.

2 G: ქცევაჲ (*se-vertere*); L: *resolutio.*

3 G: ტანჯვად შეურაცხად (*torqueatur contemptim;* Gr*: βάσανος ἔσχατος ?); L: *poena expositio.*

4 Matt. 12:45; Luke 11:26. The quotation does not make sense.

5 G: რჩეულ საიდუმლოჲ; L: *exsistentia* (?) *sacramenta;* A: *asrār.*

6 G: აერ (*aer,* ἀὴρ); L omit; A: *residence.*

7 L omits.

8 L: *their bodies are the souls which receive their wickedness.*

9 G: წარვიდენ; L: *permiscentur;* Gr*: περιπατέω (?).

10 L: *our.*

11 The meaning of the verse is obscure at several points. In particular the word translated with *neighbour* poses a problem. G has: მოყუასი (πλήσιος, ἑταῖρος, ἕτερος; *proximus*); L has: *proximo* in the first place and *prope* in the second; and A only says: *that we have our lives from one another.* The second part of the verse is quoted as a saying in the *Apophthegmata Patrum* (*AP/G* Antony 9), in a way which presupposes the translation I have choosen. See above, p. 158 and 162. Chitty translates: *and they will go away home and laugh at us. For they know that our perdition is from our neighbour, and our life also is from our neighbour.* Louf sticks to the

him within himself, so that he would not leave him, but help him while he dwells in this heaviness? 55 Or, who ever saw a demon fighting against us and preventing us from doing good, or opposing us, standing somewhere in the body, so that we should become afraid and flee from him? No, they are all hidden, and we reveal them by our deeds. 56 They are, moreover, all from one (source)[1] in their spiritual essence; but through their flight from God great diversity has arisen between them since their deeds are varying.[2]

57 Therefore all these names have been imposed on them after the deeds of each one. 58 Some of them are called archangels, some thrones and dominions, principalities, powers and cherubim.[3] 59 These names were given to them since they kept the will of their Creator. 60 But due to the wickedness of the conduct[4] of others it was necessary to name them devil and satan, after their own evil conduct. Others are called demons, evil and impure spirits, spirits of seduction[5] and powers of this world, and there are many other varities among them. 61 But there are also those who have opposed them in this heavy body in which we dwell—some of them are called patriarchs, and some prophets and kings and priests and judges and apostles, and there are many other chosen after their good conduct. 62 All these names are given to them, whether male or female, for the sake of the variety of their deeds and in conformity with their own minds[6], but they are all from one (source).

63 Therefore, whoever sins against his neighbour sins against himself, and whoever does evil to his neighbour does evil to himself. Likewise, whoever does good to his neighbour does good to himself. 64 For truly, who would there be who could do evil to God, or who exists who can hurt him, or who is there who can give him rest, or who can ever serve him, 65 or who exists who could ever bless him, as if he would need his blessing, or who could

---

Arabic version and translates: *et ils reviendront dans leur nouvelle demeure se moquer de nous, sûrs de l'imminence de notre perte. Ne négligez pas mes paroles, car les démons savent que notre vie dépend de ces échanges entre nous.* Wagenaar translates: *Dan trekken zij zich in hun huis terug en lachen ons uit, want zij weten dat onze ondergang evenzeer veroorzaakt wordt door onze naaste als ons (geestelijk) leven.*

1 L: *Creator*

2 The following passage is the most obvious sign of a direct influence from Origen. see above, pp. 64–68.

3 A: *archangels, thrones, lords, rulers, cherubim and seraphim.* For these expressions and the following *cf.* Eph. 1:21; 6:12; Col. 1:16 *etc.*

4 Or *movement.* G: სლვისა (ἀναστροφὴ); L: *motus.*

5 L. *flatus* (!!) *erroris* for πνεῦμα τῆς πλάνης.

6 G: მთავრობაჲ (ἀρχὴ, ἡγημονικὸς, κεφαλὴ); L: *principatus.* The sentence is somewhat obscure. In both G and L the word translated *mind* is added to the adverbial expression *in accordance with the variety of their deeds;* in G as a simple genitive, in L as *juxta principatum ipsorum.* A has paraphrased the original, avoiding the difficult expression. The same Georgian and Latin words are used in V:34.

honour him so that he [really] is honoured, or who could exalt him so that he [really] is elevated? [66]Therefore, let us raise up God in ourselves by spurring one another, [67]and deliver ourselves to death for our [own] souls and for one another, and doing this we shall reveal the essence of our own mercy.[1] [68]Not that we should become self-lovers, lest we come under the power of inconstancy[2] [69]For he who knows himself knows all, and thus it is written: *who called everything into being out of nothingness.*[3] [70]Saying this, they speak about their spiritual essence, which is hidden in this corruptible body, which it did not have from the beginning, and which it will be called away from. [71]But he who is able to love himself, loves all.

[72]My dear children, I pray that this will not be a burden to you, nor that you should tire of loving one another. [73]Lift up your body in which you are clothed and make it an altar and lay upon it all your thoughts and leave all evil counsels before God, [74]and lift up the hands of your heart to him, that is to the Creator of the mind[4], and pray to God that he gives you the great invisible fire, [75]that it may descend[5] from above and consume the altar and all upon it, as well as all the priests of Baal, who are the hostile works of the enemy, that they may fear and flee before you as before the prophet Elijah.[6] [77]Then you will see as it were the track of a man[7] over the sea, who will bring you the spiritual[8] rain, which is the comfort of the Spirit of comfort.

[78]My dear children in the Lord,[9] Israelite children, there is no need to bless, nor to mention, your[10] transient, names in the flesh, [79]for you are not ignorant of the love I have for you, that it is not the love of the flesh, but the love of godliness. [80]Therefore I am confident that it is[11] for you a great blessing that you have tried to know your own shame and to make firm the invisible essence, which does not pass away with the body. [81]Thus I think that your blessing has begun (even) in our time. [82]Let this word be manifest to you[12], that you should not regard your progress and entry into the service

---

1 L has summarized: *ut hoc agentes commendemus illam circa nos bonorum viscerum essentiam.*

2 G: დაუდგრომელისა მის ძალისა მათისა ნაწილ (*inconstantis potentiae eorum pars*); L: *illorum inconstantis portionis;* A: *naṣīb al-šarīr.*

3 2 Mack. 7:28; *cf.* Sap. 1:14.

4 G: გონებაჲ მოქმედი (νοῦς ποιῶν ?); L: *sensus agendorum;* A:—.

5 G adds: *upon you*

6 *Cf.* 1 Kings 18:38–40.

7 *Cf.* 1 Kings 18:44: καὶ ἰδοὺ ʹεφέλη μικρὰ ὡς ἴχνος ανδρὸς ἀνάγουσα ὕδωρ. The words *cloud, small as* are missing in all three versions.

8 L: *specialem* !

9 The verses 78–81 are missing in A.

10 L: *our*

11 The following lines are missing in L, probably due to haplography caused by the repetition of the word *blessing*, μακάριος.

12 A omits the exhortation.

of God[1] as your own work; rather a divine power supports you always. 83 Be eager *to offer yourselves as a sacrifice to God always*[2] and arouse the power that supports you and give rest to the coming of God,[3] and to all the host of the saints[4] and to my miserable self, which dwells in this house of dust and darkness.[5]

84 This is why I speak to you, and give you rest, and pray:[6] We are all created from one invisible[7] essence, having a beginning but no end;[8] thus, they who know themselves know that the essence of unity is immortal.

85 I want you to know that our Lord Jesus Christ is the true mind of the Father, by whom all the fulness of every rational nature[9] is made to the likeness of his image, he himself being the head of all creatures and the body of the Church.[10] 86 *Therefore we are all members of one another and the body of Christ. The head cannot say to the feet, 'I do not need you'; and if a member suffers the whole body is moved and suffers.*[11] 87 But if a member is estranged from the body, having no contact with the head, but delighting in the passions of the flesh, it has contracted an incurable wound and has forgotten its beginning and its end.

88 For this reason the Father of creation had mercy upon us for the sake this wound which none of the creatures[12] could heal, but only the goodness of the Father.[13] 89 And he sent us his Only-begotten, who for the sake of our servitude *accepted the form of a servant,*[14] 90 and *gave himself up for our sins, and our iniquities humbled him, but through his stripes we were all healed.*[15] 91 And he gathered us from all lands, until he resurrected our hearts from the earth, and taught us that we are of one essence and members of one another. 92 Therefore we ought to love one another warmly, for he who loves his neighbour loves God, and he who loves God[16] loves his own soul.[17]

---

1 *Cf.* Rom. 12:1. The last words missing in L; A: *gain these excellent gifts.*

2 The exhortation is missing in A.

3 For this expression see above VI:16 with note and Acts 3:19–20.

4 The entire verse is rather obscure. The translation above is based on G. L: *praebete cooperanti unita est universo sanctorum choro;* A: *struggle and persist in your good works, so that the saints and my poor spirit may rejoice with you.*

5 Thus L. G has a strange plural: *these bodies of clay and darkness.*

6 Thus G; L: *Why should I speak to you, if not to give you rest? And why do I pray,*

7 A: *spiritual and invisible.*

8 L adds *only that we should love one another*

9 G: მეტყველი ბონებაჲ; L: *natura rationabilis;* A: الطبيعة الناطقة .

10 *Cf.* Col. 1:18. A adds: *as the apostle Paul says.*

11 *Cf.* 1 Cor. 12:21, 26–27. A adds: *as the apostle also has said.*

12 Missing in L.

13 *Cf.* III:20.

14 Phil. 2:7.

15 Rom.: 8:32; Gal. 1:4; Is. 53:5.

16 Missing in L.

17 A adds: *as the apostle John says.*

[93]Let this word be manifest to you,[1] my dear children in the Lord, holy Israelite children, and prepare yourselves to go and *offer yourselves as a sacrifice unto God*[2] in all sanctity, for no one can inherit him without sanctity. [94]Do you not know, my dear, that the enemy of virtue always contemplates evil against the truth? [95]Therefore, my dear, take heed, and *do not give sleep to your eyes, nor slumber to your eyelids,*[3] [96]but cry out to you Creator day and night that he may send you a helper from above, who may encompass your hearts and thoughts in Christ.

[97]Truly, my children,[4] we dwell in a house of robbers and are bound by the bonds of death. [98]Truly, I tell you that this our negligence, humiliation and outward confusion[5] is not only harmful for us, but it is also labour to the angels and all the holy of Christ, since for our sake they have not yet found peace.[6] [99]Truly, my beloved, our humiliation gives pain to all of them, as our salvation and pride[7] gives joy and rest[8] to all of them.

[100]And you should know that the goodness of the Father does not cease to do good to us always, from when it was first moved until this day, so as not[9] to make us guilty of our own death,[10] [101]for we are created with a free will, and thus the demons watch out for us always. But for that reason it is written, *the angel of the Lord encamps around those who fear him and delivers them.*[11]

[102]Now, my children, I want you to know that, from the first movement[12] until now, all who have become estranged from virtue and fulfilled their wickedness are counted as children of the devil, [103]and those who are of them, know it, and so they try to fashion each one of us after his own will. [104]Knowing that the devil has fallen from above because of [his] pride,[13] they, cunning as they are, attack through pride[14] and contempt for one another, first those who have attained a high level. [105]They know that thus

---

1 The verses 93–100 are missing in A

2 *Cf.* Rom. 12:1.

3 Ps. 131:4 LXX (= Ps. 132:4 Vulgata).

4 The verses 98–101 are also preserved in Coptic in a quotation in the same letter of Besa, *Epistula ad Heraï*. See above p. 16.

5 Thus C and L: ⲙⲛⲧϭⲓⲛⲣⲓⲕⲉ ⲉⲃⲟⲗ, *extranea commotio*. G: *estrangement from virtue*. A is missing.

6 The last sentence is missing in the Coptic quotation. *Cf.* above II:8 quoting from Hebr. 11:39–40.

7 C: ϣⲟⲩϣⲟⲩ (καύχημα); G: სიქადული; L: *gloriatio*.

8 Thus C and L. G omits.

9 The negation is missing in L. Wagenaar follows L and translates: *zodat wij zelf de schuld dragen als we sterven moeten.*

10 The entire verse is missing in the quotation from Besa.

11 Ps. 33:8 LXX (= Ps. 34:8 Vulgata).

12 L: *from the creation;* A omits.

13 L adds: *et inanem gloriam.*

14 L and A add *and vainglory.*

they can cut us off from God, knowing that he who loves his neigbour loves God. For this reason the enemies of virtue sow the seed of division[1] in our hearts, so that we become great adversaries of one another, and do not at all, even from a distance, speak with our neighbour. [106]Truly, my children, I also want you to know that there are many who have endured great struggle in this way of life[2], but have been killed by lack of discernment. [107]Truly, my children, I consider it not strange at all that, if you neglect yourselves and do not discern your works, you fall into the hands[3] of the devil, and while you think you are close to God, and while you are expecting light, darkness overtakes you.

[108]Why did Jesus gird himself with a towel[4] and wash the feet of his disciples[5], [109]if not to make this an example and teach those who turn back to their first beginning[6], since pride is the origin of that movement which was in the beginning. [110]Therefore, if you do not have great humility throughout your heart and in all your mind,[7] in all your soul and in all your body, you cannot inherit the kingdom of God.[8] [111]Truly, my children in the Lord, I pray day and night to my Creator, who has entrusted me with his spirit, to open for you the eyes of your hearts that you may know this my love which I have for you, [112]and open the ears of you hearts that you may perceive your disgrace. [113]For he who knows his disgrace seeks again his chosen glory, and he who knows his death also knows his eternal life.

[114]*As to wise men I write to you,*[9] my children, for truly I fear that hunger may overtake you on the way, and in the place where we need to be made rich. [115]I wanted to see you face to face in the body, but I now look forward to the time, which is near, in which we will be able to see for ourselves the faces of one another, when distress and pain and tears shall have passed away, when joy will be among all.[10] [116]There is much more I would have liked to tell, but *if one gives occasion to a wise man he will be yet wiser.*[11] [117]I greet you all by name, my beloved children.

---

1 G: წყაროჲ განწვალებისაჲ (*fons divisionis*); L: *fomitem simulationum* (??)

2 L: *in conversatione sanctissima.*

3 G: ზომსა (μέτρον); L: *mensura.* The same word is translated *level* in I:40 and VI:104.

4 *Cf.* John 13:4–5. L adds: *ac ponens pelvim;* A adds: *undressed, poured water into the waterbowl.*

5 G and L: *inferiorum.*

6 G: დასაბამსა პირველსა; L: *principium.*

7 A adds *in all spirit.*

8 A adds *as it is written.*

9 1 Cor. 10:15.

10 A adds *who are worthy of it.*

11 Prov. 9:9.

LETTER SEVEN

[1]Know, my children, *the grace of our Lord Jesus Christ, that, though he was rich, he was made poor for our sake, so that we may be made rich through his poverty.*[1] [2]Through his submission he freed us, through his weakness he strengthened us and through his foolishness he made us wise. [3]Through his death he will resurrect us, and thus we will be able to raise up our voices highly and say, *though we have known Christ after the flesh, yet now henceforth know we him so no more, but in Christ each one is a new creature.*[2]

[4]Truly, my beloved in the Lord, I tell you that as for the all too few words of freedom, through which we are all freed, I have much to tell you,[3] but it is not now the time. [5]Now I greet you all, my dear children in the Lord, holy Israelite children in your spiritual essence.[4] [6]Truly it was right for you, who have come close to your Creator, to search for the salvation of your souls through the law of promise, [7]but through the multitude of wickedness, the evil of confusion and the cupidity of the passions this promise grew cold and the faculties[5] of our[6] mind perished, [8]and therefore they will not be able to perceive our glorious spiritual essence because of the death into which we have fallen. [9]For this reason it is written in the holy books that, *as in Adam all die, even so in Christ shall all be made alive.*[7]

[10]Now, therefore, he is the life of every rational being[8] created by him in his own image, for he is the true mind[9] of the Father and the immutable image of the Father.[10] [11]But the essence[11] present in the creatures made in his image is mutable, and thus[12] the evil, in which we all are dead, has come

---

1 2 Cor. 8:9.

2 *Cf.* 2 Cor. 5:16–17.

3 A: *I tell you that this word is subtle in its meaning, and that I have a lot to say about it, but...*

4 The last sentence is missing in A.

5 G: საცნობელი (αἰσθητήριον ?); L: *sensus;* A: حركة

6 L: *your.*

7 1 Cor. 15:22.

8 G: მეტყოელი გონებაჲ (νοῦς λογικός); L: *rationabilis natura;* A: ناطقين .

9 G: გონებაჲ; L: *sensus;* A: عقل .

10 L adds *quae assumpta est* and omits the next sentence.

11 G: არსებაჲ (οὐσία); L: *sensus;* A: *visible image.*

12 My conjecture follows A and is midway between G and L. L has: *Praeter illam ... accidit malitia* (*through it...*), whereas G has a simple instrumental form: *Through the occurence of evil in us...* .

upon us, and we are [now] alien to the nature[1] of the spiritual essence.
12Therefore, as I have said, through all that is alien to nature[2], we have
acquired a dark house full of war.[3] 13And I tell you, that the knowledge of
all virtues has vanished from us. 14For this reason the Father, our God, saw
our weakness, that we thus were not able to invest ourselves with truth,[4]
15therefore he, in his benevolence, came to visit his creatures through the
ministry of the saints.

16I pray to you all in the Lord, my beloved, that you understand what I
write to you, for I do not have the love of the flesh for you, but the love of
godliness. 17Prepare yourselves to come to your Creator, *rending your hearts
and not your garments,*[5] 18and bear this in mind: *What shall we render to the
Lord for all the benefits that he has done to us;*[6] 19in his great benevolence
and his incomprehensible love, he remembered us, even in this our dwelling
and humiliation. He did not *do unto us according to our sins,*[7] 20but had the
sun serve us in this house of darkness; and the moon and all the stars he
made serve what is vain and transient[8] for the sake of the consolidation of
the bodies,[9] 21and the other hidden powers, which serve us, though we do
not see them with our bodily eyes.

22Now, then, what shall we say to him on the day of judgement, or what
good has he held back from us, that he has not done to us? 23Did not the
patriarchs suffer for us,[10] did not the priests teach us, did not the judges and
the kings fight for us,[11] did not the prophets die for us,[12] 24or were not the
apostles persecuted for us, and did not his own son die for all of us? 25We
must therefore prepare ourselves to come to our Creator in all[13] sanctity.

---

1 G: გონებაჲ (*mind;* for ბონებაჲ, *nature,* as in the next verse ?); L and A: *nature.*

2 G: ბონებისა; L: natura.

3 A has reshaped the sentence completely: *It is alien to the spiritual nature, and by it we are born in the flesh and have become a house full of war.*

4 A: *and that He could not appear in us as He is, in righteousness and truth.*

5 Joel 2:13.

6 Ps. 115: 3 LXX (= Ps. 116:12 Vulgata).

7 Ps. 102:10 LXX (= Ps. 103:10 Vulgata).

8 G: ამაუებიტა წარწყმედელი; L: *vanitas et periturus;* A: *which is the world.*

9 G: კორცი შემტკიცებისა; L: *coprporum constabilitionis;* A: *in order to raise up the flesh* (!) The meaning of the verse is obscure, and I have kept as close as possible to the Latin text. The Georgian translator has obviously had great difficulties with the passage, which does not make much sense as it now stands. The Arabic translator has, as is so often the case, summarized the meaning, avoiding all difficulties or references to ideas not accepted at the time of translation. Antony here most probably refers to the common belief in the influence of the stars upon the character of the bodies.

10 Missing in L

11 Missing in L

12 Missing in A

13 Missing in G

26 The Creator[1] saw that not even the holy [among the] creatures could
heal the great wound which was in their own members;[2] 27 and since the
Father of the creatures knew the weakness of[3] their minds[4], he had mercy on
them in his great love, 28 and *did not spare his own Son,* but for the sake of
our salvation *he delivered him up for our sins.*[5] 29 *He was humbled by our
iniquities* and *by his stripes we were healed,*[6] 30 and by the power of his word
he gathered us from all lands, until he resurrected our minds from the earth
and taught us that we are members of one another.

31 Therefore we all, who approach our Creator, have to strain our minds[7]
and faculties, 32 in order to know the manifold distinctions between good and
evil. Thus you can come to know all the dispensations of Jesus which he has
done through his coming, for *he was made like unto us in everything yet
without sin.*[8] 33 But because the multitude of our wickedness and evil turmoil
and because of the heaviness of our own inconstancy, 34 the coming of Jesus
was unto some foolishness,[9] *to others a stumblingblock, and to others gain
and wisdom and power,*[10] and to some resurrection and life. 35 Let this be
manifest to you that his coming is the judgement for all the world, 36 for it is
said: *Days will come, says the Lord, when they shall all know me, from the
least of them unto the greatest of them, and they shall teach no more every
man his neighbour and every man his brother, saying, Know the Lord.*[11] and
I will make my name heard unto the ends of the earth, 37 *that every mouth
may be stopped, and all the world be brought under the judgement of God,*
for *when they knew God, they glorified him not as their*[12] *Creator.*[13]
Because of their lack of understanding they could not grasp his wisdom,
38 but each one of us sold himself to evil by his own will and has become its
servant.

39 Therefore Jesus divested himself of his glory *and took upon him the
form of a servant,*[14] that we might be freed through his servitude.[15] 40 We

---

1 The verses 26–32 are missing in the Arabic translation

2 L adds *by the Jews* !!

3 G adds *all*

4 Here and in the following: G: გონებაჲ; L: *sensus.*

5 Rom 8:32.

6 Is. 53:5.

7 G: გონებაჲ and საწნობელი; L: *habitudinis* and *sensus officia.*

8 Hebr. 4:15.

9 Missing in G.

10 *Cf.* 1 Cor. 1:23–24.

11 Jer. 31:34. L has only the first half of the quotation, while A has completed the quotation with the end of the verse: *for I will forgive them their iniquity, and I will remember their sin no more.*

12 G: *his*

13 A combination of Rom. 3:19 and 1:21

14 Phil. 2:7

15 The verses 40–42 are missing in A.

were fools and through our foolishness we did all evil, but he took the form of foolishness, that through his foolishness he might make us wise.[1] 41 We were poor and through our poverty all virtues vanished from us. But he took the form of poverty, that *through his poverty he might enrich us*[2] with all knowledge and understanding. 42 Not only this, he even took the form of our weakness, that through his weakness he might strengthen us. 43 *He became obedient to the Father in everything unto death, even the death of the cross,*[3] 44 that he might resurrect us all through his death[4] and *destroy him that had the power of death, that is, the devil.*[5] 45 And if we truly set ourselves free through his coming, we shall become disciples of Jesus and receive the divine inheritance through him.

46 Truly, my beloved in the Lord, I am greatly troubled and vexed in my spirit, for wearing the habit and having the name of saints we are glorified in front of unbelievers; 47 but I fear lest the word of Paul be fulfilled upon us, that says, *having the form of godliness, but denying the power thereof.*[6] 48 Because of the love I have for you, I pray to God for you that you may meditate on your own life and inherit what cannot be seen.

49 Truly, my children, even if we offer ourselves with all power and seek the Lord, we deserve no thanks. For we are only seeking what befits us, that which is after the nature[7] of our own essence. 50 For everyone who seeks God or serves him,[8] does so after the nature of his essence. 51 As for every sin, however, of which we are guilty; it is alien to us and far from the nature of our essence.

52 Truly, my beloved children in the Lord, who have prepared to *offer yourselves to the Lord as a sacrifice*[9] in all sanctity,[10] we have hid nothing that is to your benefit from you, but *what we have seen we declare unto you,*[11] that the enemy of virtue always meditates evil against the truth. 53 Also know, *that what is of the flesh always persecutes that which is of the Spirit,*[12] *and that all who want to live godly with Christ suffer persecution.*[13] 54 Therefore Jesus, knowing all the tribulations and temptations coming upon

---

1 *Cf.* 1 Cor. 1:25–28; 3:18–19 and 4:10.

2 *Cf.* 2 Cor. 8:9.

3 Phil. 2:8.

4 A adds *and resurrection.*

5 Hebr. 2:14.

6 2 Tim. 3:5.

7 Here and in the following verses: G: ბუნებაჲ არსებისა; L: *naturale substantiae;* A: جوهر الطبيعي.

8 The verses 50 and 51 are missing in L.

9 *Cf.* Rom. 12:1.

10 The sentence is missing in A.

11 *Cf.* 1 John 1:3. A adds at the end of the sentece: *that in it is your salvation.*

12 *Cf.* Gal. 4:29.

13 2 Tim. 3:12.

the apostles in this world,[1] [55]and knowing that by their temperance[2] they would destroy all the power of the enemy, which is idolatry, [56]comforted them and said, *In the world you shall have tribulation, but be of good cheer; I have overcome the world;*[3] [57]and he taught them, saying, *Do not fear the world, for all the malignity of the world are not worthy the glory that is to come. If the prophets, which were before you, were persecuted, you will also be persecuted. If they hate me, they will also hate you, but do not fear, through your temperance*[4] *all the power of the enemy will be destroyed.*[5]

[58]As for the all too few words, I have much to tell you, but it is written, *Give occasion to a wise man and he will be wiser.*[6]

([a]7 Let us comfort one another with some few words, for if the mind has discerned [everything], it no longer needs the fraud of bodily speech. [b]But I rejoice over all of you, my dear in the Lord, holy Israelite men in your spiritual essence. [c]A wise man has first to know himself, so that he may then know what is of God, [d]and all his grace which he has always bestowed upon us and then to know that every sin and every accusation is alien to the nature of our spiritual essence;[8] [e]and finally that our Creator saw that, through our free will we possess what is unnatural, by which our will has died; moved by his mercy, he, in his benevolence, wished to bring us back to that beginning without end. [f]He visited his creatures, *not sparing himself for the salvation of us all, he gave himself for our sins and our iniquities humbled him, but by his stripes we were all healed,*[9] [g]and by the word of his power he gathered us from all lands, from the one end of the earth to the other, teaching us that we are members of one another.[10]

[h]Therefore, if indeed we have prepared to make ourselves free at his coming, let each sensible man ask himself what he can render to God for all the gifts he has given us. [i]I too, the miserable one, who writes this letter,

---

1 A has elaborated greatly on this verse stating: *Those who want to consider the ascetical life in Jesus Christ are obliged to expel from themselves the bodily desires through the prayers to the Lord Jesus Christ, and He in his mercy and affection will abolish from them all difficulties and temptations, which originate in the body as it was with our fathers the apostles.*

2 L: *He by His chastity;* A: *their endurance*

3 John 16:33.

4 L: *sapientia.*

5 The quotation attributed to Jesus is made up from several different verses in the NT. *Cf.* Rom. 8:18, Matt. 5:12, John 15:20 and Luke 21:19. The Arabic version gives the two first quotations in a fuller form after the last two.

6 Prov. 9:9.

7 The passage in brackets (58*a*–58*t*) is missing in G, but is extant in both L, and less fully in A. It is either a separate letter, or, more probably, a summary of the preceding letter. The language and contents show beyond any doubt that it is by the same author and belongs to the same collection.

8 The verses *c* and *d* are summarized in the Arabic.

9 Rom. 8:32 and Is. 53:5.

10 58*e*–*g* are missing in A.

have, roused from the sleep of death, been mourning and weeping for most of the time that I have had upon the earth,[1] crying, *What can I render unto the Lord for what he has done to me?*[2] For in nothing are we betrayed, which he has not done for us in our humiliation. [k]He made his angels serve us, he appointed his prophets to prophesy, and bade his apostles to preach to us, and, truly, above all these the dispensation that his Only-begotten *took the form of a servant for our sake.*[3]

[l]I beseech you, my beloved in the Lord, who are joint heirs with the saints, to raise up your minds in the fear of God. [m]May this word be manifest to you, that John, the forerunner of Jesus, baptized[4] for our sake, for the remission of sins, but that we were sanctified in Christ by the Spirit.[5] [n]Let us now prepare ourselves in all sanctity to cleanse our spiritual essence, that we may be clean through the baptism of Jesus, so that we may *offer ourselves as a sacrifice to God.*[6] [o]Truly this Spirit of comfort, which comforts us,[7] [p]will bring us back to our beginning, so that we may gain again our own inheritance [q]and the teachings of that Spirit of comfort, the grace that,[8] *as many of you as have been baptized into Christ have put on Christ. There is neither male nor female, neither bond nor free.*[9] [r]Hence, all bodily speech fails them, when they receive the teaching of the Holy Spirit, at the time when they assume the holy inheritance [s]and *worship the Father as is proper, in Spirit and truth.*[10] [t]Let this word be manifest to you, not to wait for a future judgement in the coming of Jesus, for his coming is already a judgement for all of us.)

[59]Know then, that all[11] who have been invested with the Spirit always pray for us, that we may be reconciled with God and again receive our honour and put on the habit we had laid off, [since it] belongs to our spiritual essence.[12] [60]For often the voice has come from God the Father to

---

1 The Arabic version, followed by Wagenaar, has interpreted the reference to the time differently: *and that which remains for me of this short time on earth, has become mourning and weeping.*

2 Ps. 115:13 LXX (= Ps. 116:12 Vulgata).

3 Phil 2:7.

4 A adds *in water.*

5 A: *to the baptism of our Lord Jesus, who baptized in the Holy Spirit and the fire, which is the fire of good deeds.*

6 *Cf.* Rom 12:1.

7 A, instead of *who comforts us,* has the following: *received at baptism, gives us the works of repentence, that he may....*

8 The text is obscure: *et magisteria eiusdem Spiritus consolantis, huius rei gratia quotquot in Christo...*

9 Gal. 3:27–28.

10 John 4:24.

11 G: *the saints and the righteous.*

12 Thus G and A. L: *respicientur et vestientur vestimento illo, quo sumus exuti juxta sensualem nostram exstantiam.*

all invested with the Spirit, saying to them, *Comfort ye, comfort ye my people,* says the Lord to the priests, *speak ye comfortably to Jerusalem.*[1]
61God always visits his creatures and bestows upon them his benevolence.
62Truly, I tell you, my beloved, as for the all too few of the words of freedom, through which we are freed, there is much else to tell you, but it is said, *Give occasion to a wise man, and he will be yet wiser.*[2]

63May the God of peace give you grace, and the spirit of discernment[3], that you may understand that what I write to you is the commandment of God, 64and may the God of all grace keep you holy in the Lord until the last breath. 65I pray always to God for the salvation of you all, my beloved in the Lord. 66May the grace of our Lord Jesus Christ be with you all.[4]

---

1 Is. 40:1–2.

2 Prov. 9:9.

3 G: *wisdom.*

4 The four last verses are probably not original, but added to conclude the entire collection of seven letters.

BIBLIOGRAPHY

1. ABBREVIATIONS

MANUSCRIPTS AND PAPYRI.

Berlin syr.	Sachau, *Katalog der syrischen Handschriften in Berlin.*
BL	Wright, *Catalogue of the Syriac Manuscripts in thge British Library.*
Copt. Mus.	Mss. in the library of the Coptic Museum, Cairo (see Samir, *Tables de concordance des manuscrits arabes chrétiens.*)
Copt. Patr.	Mss. in the library of the Coptic Patriarchate, Ezbakiah, Cairo (see Samir, *op. cit.*)
Ming. syr.	Mingana, *Catalogue of the Mingana Collection of Manuscripts.*
P. Amh.	Grenfell & Hunt, *The Amherst Papyri.*
P. Ash. Inv.	Roberts, 'Two Oxford Papyri'.
P. Flor.	Comparetti and Viletti, *Papiri greco-egizii.*
P. Jews.	Bell, *Jews and Christians in Egypt.*
P. Lips.	*Griechische Urkunden der Papyrussammlung zu Leipzig.*
P. Lit. Lond.	Milne, *Catalogue of the Literary Papyri in the BM.*
P. Lond.	Kenyon & Bell, *Greek Papyri in the British Museum.*
P. Oxy.	*The Oxyrhynchus Papyri.*
P. Ryl.	*Catalogue of the Greek Papyri in the John Rylands library.*
Par. syr.	Zotenberg, *Catalogues des manuscrits syriaques et sabéens.*
Sbath	*Bibliothèque de manuscrits Paul Sbath. Catalogue.*
Sin. geo.	Garitte, *Catalogue des manuscrits géorgiens.*
St. Ant.	Mss. in the library of the Monastery of St. Antony at the Red Sea.
St. Mac.	Mss. in the library of the Monastery of St. Macarius, Wadi Natrun. (see Zanetti, *Les manuscrits de Dair Abû Maqâr.*)
Vat. ar.	Mai, *Scriptorum veterum nova collectio.*
Vat. lat.	*Index inventarii, codices mss. lat., Bibliotheca Apostolica Vaticana.*
Vat. syr.	Assemani, *Bibliothecae Apostolicae Vaticanae Codicum Manuscriptorum Catalogus.*

TEXTS AND COLLECTIONS.

AB	*Analecta Bollandiana.*
AMG	*Annales du Musée Guimet.*
AP	*Apophthegmata Patrum.*
AP/A	*Apophthegmata Patrum,* Collectio Armeniaca.
AP/Bo	*Apophthegmata Patrum,* Collectio Bohairica.
AP/CSP	*Apophthegmata Patrum,* Commonitiones Sanctorum Patrum.
AP/E	*Apophthegmata Patrum,* Collectio Aethiopica.
AP/G	*Apophthegmata Patrum,* Collectio Graeca alphabetica.

AP/GN	*Apophthegmata Patrum*, Collectio Graeca anonyma.
AP/GS	*Apophthegmata Patrum*, Collectio Graeca systematica (non edita).
AP/M	*Apophthegmata Patrum*, Collectio a Martino Dumiensi.
AP/PA	*Apophthegmata Patrum*, Collectio a Paschasio Dumiensi.
AP/PJ	*Apophthegmata Patrum*, Collectio Latina systematica (*Vitae Patrum* V–VI).
AP/QRT	*Apophthegmata Patrum*, Collectio minor (Mss. Q, R and T (§ 1) in Guy, *Recherches sur la tradition grecque* (*Subs. hag.* 36), Bruxelles 1962.
AP/R	*Apophthegmata Patrum*, Collectio a Pseudo–Rufino.
AP/S	*Apophthegmata Patrum*, Collectio Syriaca.
AP/Sa	*Apophthegmata patrum*, Collectio Sahidica.
BBR	*Bulletin de l'institut historique belge de Rome.*
BCNH	*Bibliothèque Copte de Nag Hammadi.*
BIFAO	*Bulletin de l'Institut Français d'Archéologie Orientale du Caire.*
BZ	*Byzantinische Zeitschrift.*
CC	*Corpus Christianorum.*
CO	*Cahiers d'Orientalisme.*
CS	*Cistercian Studies.*
CSCO	*Corpus Scriptorum Christianorum Orientalium.*
CSEL	*Corpus Scriptorum Ecclesiasticorum Latinorum.*
CPG	*Clavis Patrum Graecorum.*
DACL	*Dictionnaire d'archéologie chrétienne et de liturgie.*
DSp	*Dictionnaire de la Spiritualité.*
Ep. Amm.	Ammonas, *Epistolae.*
Ep. Ant.	Antonius, *Epistolae.*
GCAL	Georg Graf, *Geschichte der Christlichen Arabischen Literatur.*
GCS	*Die griechischen christlichen Schriftsteller der ersten drei Jahrhunderte.*
GRBS	*Greek, Roman and Byzantine Studies.*
HE	*Historia Ecclesiastica.*
HL	Palladius Helenopolitanus, *Historia Lausiaca.*
HM	*Historia Monachorum in Aegypto.*
HTR	*Harvard Theological Review.*
JAAR	*Journal of the American Academy of Religion.*
JAC	*Jahrbuch für Antike und Christentum.*
JEA	*Journal of Egyptian Archaeology.*
JRS	*Journal of Roman Studies.*
JTS	*Journal of Theological Studies.*
LÄ	*Lexikon der Ägyptologie.*
LTP	*Laval théologique et philosophique.*
LXX	The Septuagint.
MPER	*Mitteilungen aus der Papyrussammlung der österreichischen Nationalbibliothek (Papyrus Erzherzog Rainer).*
NAWG	*Nachrichten der Akademie der Wissenschaften zu Göttingen.*
NHC	*Nag Hammadi Codices.*
NHS	*Nag Hammadi Studies.*
Nov. Test.	*Novum Testamentum.*
OC	*Oriens Christianus.*
OCA	*Orientalia Christiana Analecta.*
OCP	*Orientalia Christiana Periodica.*
OLA	*Orientalia Lovaniensia Analecta.*
PG	*Patrologia Graeca.*
PL	*Patrologia Latina.*
PO	*Patrologia Orientalis.*

PTS	*Patristische Texte und Studien.*
RAC	*Realenzyklopaedie für Antike und Christentum.*
RAM	*Revue d'ascétique et de mystique.*
RB	*Revue Bénédictine.*
REAnc	*Revue des études anciennes.*
REAug	*Revue des études augustiniennes.*
REB	*The Revised English Bible.*
REG	*Revue des études grecques.*
RHE	*Revue d'histoire ecclésiastique.*
RHR	*Revue d'histoire des religions.*
RHT	*Revue d'histoire des textes.*
ROC	*Revue d'Orient Chrétien.*
RScR	*Recherches de science religieuse.*
RT	*Revue Thomiste.*
SA	*Studia Anselmiana.*
SAOC	*Studies in Ancient Oriental Civilizations.*
SC	*Sources Chrétiennes*
SHAW	*Sitzungsberichte der Heidelberger Akademie der Wissenschaften.*
Subs. Hag.	*Subsidia Hagiographica.*
TU	*Texte und Untersuchungen zur Geschichte der altchristlichen Literatur.*
VA	*Vita Antonii.*
VC	*Vigiliae Christianae.*
VP/G	*Vita Pachomii,* versio Graeca.
VP/SBo	*Vita Pachomii,* versiones Copticae.
ZÄS	*Zeitschrift für Ägyptische Sprache und Altertumskunde.*
ZKG	*Zeitschrift für Kirchengeschichte.*
ZKT	*Zeitschrift für Katholische Theologie.*
ZNW	*Zeitschrift für Neutestamentliche Wissenschaft.*
ZPE	*Zeitschrift für Papyrologie und Epigraphik.*
ZPT	*Freiburger Zeitschrift für Philosophie und Theologie.*
ZRG	*Zeitschrift für Religions- und Geistesgeschichte.*

2. Sources

Abū-l-Barakāt Ibn Kabar, *Miṣbāḥ al-ẓulmah fī īḍāḥ al-ḫidmah.* Wilhelm Riedel, *Der Katalog der Christlichen Schriftstellern in arabischer Sprache von Abu'l-Barakat* (*NAWG*, Phil.–Hist. Klasse), Göttingen 1902;
Khalil Samir, *Miṣbāḥ al-ẓulmah fī īḍāḥ al-khidmah,* I, Cairo 1971.

Acts of the Pagan Martyrs. H. A. Musurillo, *The Acts of the Pagan Martyrs,* Oxford 1954.

Alexander Lycopolitanus, *Contra Manichaei opiniones disputatio.* A. Brinkmann, *Alexander Lycopolitanus, 'Contra Manichaei opiniones disputatio',* Leipzig 1895.

Ammon, *Epistula ad Theophilum de Pachomio et Theodoro.* James E. Goehring, *The Letter of Ammon and Pachomian Monasticism* (*PTS* 27), Berlin 1986.

Ammonas, *Epistulae*

Arabic: Anbā Murqus al-Anṭūnī, *Kitāb rauḍat al-nufūs fī rasa'il al-qiddīs Anṭūniyūs,* Cairo 1899 (attributed to Antony).

Armenian: *Vitae Patrum,* II, Venice 1855.

Ethiopic: V. Arras, *Collectio Monastica* (*CSCO* 238–239), Louvain 1963.

Georgian: Gérard Garitte, 'De unius ex Ammonae epistulis versione iberica', *Le Muséon* 89 (1976).

Greek: F. Nau, *Ammonas, successeur de saint Antoine* (*PO* 11), Paris 1915.

Syriac: M. Kmosko, *Ammonii eremitae epistulae* (*PO* 10), Paris 1914.

Antonius, *Epistulae I–VII*

Arabic: Anbā Murqus al-Anṭūnī, *Kitāb rauḍat al-nufūs fī rasā'il al-qiddīs Anṭūniyūs*, Cairo 1899.

Rasā'il al-qiddīs Anṭūniyūs, Dayr al-qiddīs Anbā Maqār, 1979.

Coptic: E. O. Winstedt, 'The Original Text of One of St. Antony's Letters', *JTS* 7 (1906); Gérard Garitte, *Lettres de Saint Antoine* (see Georgian).

Georgian: Gérard Garitte, *Lettres de Saint Antoine. Version géorgienne et fragments coptes* (*CSCO* 148–149), Louvain 1955.

Latin: Symphorianus Champerius, *Epistolae Sanctissimorum*, Paris 1516; *PG* 40, 977–1000.

Syriac: F. Nau, 'La version syriaque de la première lettre de Saint Antoine', *ROC* 14 (1906).

Modern translations:

The Letters of St. Antony (tr. by Derwas Chitty), Fairacres 1974.

Saint Antoine: Lettres (tr. by André Louf), *Spiritualité orientale* 19, Abbaye de Bellefontaine 1978.

Leven, getuignissen, brieven van de heilige Antonius abt (tr. by Christofoor Wagenaar), *Monastieke cahiers* 17, Bonheiden 1984.

Vita di Antonio, Apoftegmi, Lettere (tr. by Lisa Cremaschi), Rome 1985.

The Apocalypse of Elijah. Steindorff, *Die Apokalypse des Elias* (*TU*, N.F. II, 3a), Leipzig 1899. *Cf. L'apocalypse d'Elie. Introduction, traduction et notes* (par J–M Rosenstiehl), Paris 1972.

Apophthegmata Patrum

Collectio Aethiopica: V. Arras, *Collectio Monastica* (*CSCO* 238–239), Louvain 1963; *idem., Patericon Aethiopice* (*CSCO* 277–278), Louvain 1967.

Collectio Armeniaca: *Liber qui dicitur Patrum Vitae, ed. Gregorius Hierosolymorum patriarcha et Iohannes eparchus*, Constantinople 1721; *Vitae Patrum*, I, Venice 1855. (cf. Leloir, *Paterica Armeniaca*)

Collectio Bohairica: E. Amélineau, *Histoire des monastères de la Basse-Égypte* (*AMG* 25), Paris 1894.

Collectio Graeca alphabetica: J.-B. Cotelier, *Ecclesiae graecae monumenta*, I, Paris 1677; *PG* 65.

Collectio Graeca Anonyma (pars): F. Nau, 'Le chapitre περὶ τῶν ἀναχωρητῶν ἁγίων et les sources de la vie de S. Paul de Thèbes', *ROC* 10 (1905); *idem*, 'Histoires des solitaires égyptiens', *ROC* 12 (1907), 13 (1908), 14 (1909), 17 (1912), 18 (1913).

Collectio a Martino Dumiensi: C. W. Barlow, *Martini episcopi Bracarensis opera omnia*, New Haven 1950; *PL* 74.

Collectio a Paschasio Dumiensi: J. Geraldes Freire, *A versão latina por Pascásio de Dume dos Apophthegmata Patrum*, I, Coimbra 1971; *PL* 73.

Collectio a Pseudo–Rufino: Rosweyde, *Vitae Patrum* III, Antwerpen 1615; *PL* 73.

Collectio Sahidica: M. Chaine, *Le Manuscrit de la version copte en dialecte sahidique des "Apophthegmata Patrum"* (*Bibliothèque d'études coptes,* VI), Cairo 1960.

Collectio Syriaca: P. Bedjan, *Acta Martyrum et Sanctorum,* VII, Paris 1897;

E. A. W. Budge, *The Book of Paradise,* I–II, London 1904.

Collectio Systematica Latina: Rosweyde, *Vitae Patrum* V–VI, Antwerpen 1615; *PL* 73.

Commonitiones Sanctorum Patrum: J. Geraldes Freire, *Commonitiones sanctorum Patrum,* Coimbra 1974.

The Arabic Life of St. Antony. Ed. F. Halkin, 'La légende de S. Antoine traduite de l'Arabe par Alphonse Bonhomme', *AB* 60 (1942).

Ascensio Isaie, see *The Old Testament Pseudepigrapha,* vol. II (ed. by James H. Charlesworth), London 1985.

Athanasius, *Apologia de fuga sua.* H. G. Opitz, *Athanasius Werke,* II, Berlin 1935–1941.

Contra gentes. Robert W. Thomson, *Athanasius: Contra Gentes and De Incarnatione,* Oxford 1971.

De Incarnatione Verbi. R. W. Thomson, *Athanasius: Contra Gentes and De Incarnatione,* Oxford 1971.

De Synodis. H.–G. Opitz, *Athanasius Werke,* II, Berlin 1935–1941.

Epistulae festales Coptic: L-Th. Lefort, *S. Athanase, lettres festales et pastorales en copte* (*CSCO* 150), Louvain 1955.

Syriac: *The Festal Letters of Athanasius, discovered in an ancient Syriac Version and edited by W. Cureton,* London 1848 (facsimile of Letter X in R. Lorenz, *Der zehnte Osterfestbrief des Athanasius von Alexandrien*).

Latin: *PG* 26.

Historia Arianorum. H.–G. Opitz, *Athanasius Werke,* II, Berlin 1935–1941.

Augustinus, *Confessiones.* P. Knöll (*CSEL* 33), 1896.

De Doctrina Christiana. G. M. Green (*CSEL* 80), 1963.

De resurrectione mortuorum (Sermo 361). *PL* 39.

Besa, *Letters and Sermons of Besa.* K. H. Kuhn (*CSCO* 158), Louvain 1956.

Canons of Athanasius. Wilhelm Riedel & Walter E. Crum (*Texts and Translation Society* 9), London 1904, repr. 1973.

Dorotheus, *Doctrinae.* L. Regnault & J. de Préville (*SC* 92), Paris 1963.

Johannes Cassianus, *Conlationes.* E. Pichery (*SC* 42, 54, 64), Paris 1955–1959.

De institutis coenobiorum et de octo principalium vitiorum remediis. Jean-Claude Guy (*SC* 109), Paris 1965.

Clemens Alexandrinus, *Stromata.* O. Stählin et L. Früchtel (*GCS* 52), Berlin 1952, (*GCS* 17^2), Berlin 1970.

Didymus, *Contra Manichaeos. PG* 39.

De Spiritu Sancto. PG 39.

Epiphanius, *Panarion.* Karl Holl (*GCS* 25, 31, 37), Leipzig 1915–1933.

Eusebius, *Historia Ecclesiastica.* E. Schwartz, *Eusebius Werke,* II.1–3 (*GCS* 9.1–3), Leipzig 1903–1909.

Evagrius Antiochenus, *S. Athanasii episcopi Alexandrini praefatio. PG* 26.

Gregorius Nazianzenus, *Oratio 21. PG* 35.

Hesychius Hierosolymitanus, *Homiliae paschales.* M. Aubineau, *Les homélies festales d'Hésychius de Jérusalem,* Vol. I (*Subs. Hag.* 59), Brussels 1978.

Hieronymus, *Chronicon.* R. Helm, *Eusebius Werke,* VII (*Die Chronik des Hieronymus*), (*GCS* 47), Berlin 1956.

De viris illustribus. E. C. Richardson (*TU* 14.1), Leipzig 1896.

Epistulae. Ed. J. Hillberg (*CSEL* 54, 56), Vienna & Leipzig 1910–1918.

Vita Hilarionis. PL 23.

Vita Pauli. PL 23.

Historia Monachorum in Aegypto.

Coptic: P. Devos, 'Fragments coptes de l'Historia Monachorum', *AB* 87 (1969).

Greek: A.-J. Festugière, *Subs. Hag.* 34 (1961), revised reprint with French translation in *Subs. Hag.* 53 (1971).

Latin: Eva Schulz-Flügel, *Tyrannius Rufinus Historia Monachorum sive De Vita Sanctorum Patrum* (*Patristische Texte und Studien* 34), Berlin 1990; *PL* 21, 387–462.

Syriac: P. Bedjan, *Acta Martyrum et Sanctorum,* VII, Rome 1897; E. A. W. Budge, *The Book of Paradise,* London 1904.

Johannes of Hermopolis, *A Homily on St. Antony.* Gérard Garitte, 'Panégyrique de saint Antoine par Jean, évêque d'Hermopolis', *OCP* 9 (1943).

Methodius Olympius, *De Resurrectione.* G. N. Bonwetsch (*GCS* 27), Leipzig 1917.

On the Origins of the World. The Facsimile Edition of the Nag Hammadi Codices: Codex II, Leiden 1974.

Origenes, *Commentarii in Canticum canticorum.* W. A. Baehrens (*GCS* 33), Leipzig 1925.

Commentarii in Matthaeum. E. Klostermann & E. Benz (*GCS* 40), Leipzig 1935.

Commentarii in Ioannem. E. Preuschen (*GCS* 10), Leipzig 1903).

Contra Celsum. M. Bonet (*SC* 132, 136, 147, 150), Paris 1967–1969.

De Principiis, H. Görgemanns & H. Karpp, *Origenes vier Bücher von den Prinzipien* (*Texte zur Forschung* 24), Darmstadt [2]1985.

Homiliae in Genesim. W. A. Baehrens (*GCS* 29), Leipzig 1920.

Homiliae in Ieremiam. P. Hunt & P. Nautin (*SC* 232, 238), Paris 1976–1977.

Homiliae in Leviticum. W. A. Baehrens (*GCS* 29), Leipzig 1920.

Homiliae in Numeros. W. A. Baehrens (*GCS* 30), Leipzig 1921.

Pachomius, *Regula.* A. Boon, *Pachomiana Latina. Règles et épîtres de S. Pachôme, épître de S. Théodore et 'Liber' de S. Orsiesius. Texte latin de S. Jérome* (*Bibliothèque de la revue d'histoire ecclésiastique* 7), Louvain 1932.

Epistula. H. Quecke, *Die Briefe Pachoms* (*Textus Patristici et Liturgici* 11), Regensburg 1975.

Palladius, *Dialogus de vita Iohanni Chrysostomi.* Anne-Marie Malingrey (*SC 341*), Paris 1988

Historia Lausiaca

Coptic: E. Amélineau, *De 'Historia Lausiaca' quaenam sit huius ad monachorum Aegyptiorum historiam scribendam utilitas,* Paris 1887.

Greek: C. Butler, *The Lausiac History of Palladius, I–II* (*Texts and Studies 6, 1–2*), Cambridge 1898–1904.

Latin: *PL* 74, 243–382.

Syriac: P. Bedjan, *Acta martyrum et sanctorum*, VII, Paris 1897; E. A. W. Budge, *The Book of Paradise*, London 1904.

Philo, *De ebrietate*. J. Gorez (*Les Œuvres de Philon d'Alexandrie* 11), Paris 1962.

De vita contemplativa. F. Daumas & P. Miquel (*Les Œuvres de Philon d'Alexandrie* 29), Paris 1963.

Philoxenus Mabbugensis, *Epistula ad Patricium*. R. Lavenant (*PO* 30.5), Paris 1963.

Plato, *Phaedrus*. C. F. Hermann (*Platonis Dialogi* II), Leipzig 1914.

Theaetetus. M. Wohlraab (*Platonis Dialogi* I), Leipzig 1902.

Plotinus, *Enneades*. R. Volkmann, *Plotini Enneades*, I–II, Leipzig 1883–1884.

Regula Antonii. Arabic: A. Mokbel, 'La règle de Saint Antoine le Grand', *Melto* 2 (1966).

Rufinus, *Apologia contra Hieronymum*. M. Simonetti in *Tyrannii Rufini Opera* (*CC* 20), Turnhout 1961.

Historia Ecclesiastica. Th. Mommsen in *Eusebius Werke*, II (*GCS* 24), Leipzig 1908.

The Sentences of Sextus. Henry Chadwick, *The Sentences of Sextus. A Contribution to the History of Early Christian Ethics*, Cambridge 1959.

Serapion, *Contra Manichaeos*. R. P. Casey, *Serapion of Thmuis against the Manichees* (*Harvard Theological Studies* 15), Cambridge, Mass., 1931.

Epistula ad discipulos Antonii. René Draguet, 'Une lettre de Sérapion de Thmuis aux disciples d'Antoine (A.D. 356) en version syriaque et arménienne', *Le Muséon* 64 (1951).

Severus Antiochenus, *A Homily on St. Antony*. M. Brière, *Les homiliae cathédrales de Sévère d'Antioche* (*PO* 23.1), Paris 1932.

Shenoute, *Contra Origenistas*. Tito Orlandi, *Shenute contra origenistas*, Rome 1985.

Socrates, *Historia Ecclesiastica*. R. Hussey, *The Church History of Socrates Scholasticus*, I–III, Oxford 1853; *PG* 67, 9–842.

Sozomenus, *Historia Ecclesiastica*, J. Bidez & G. C. Hansen (*GCS* 50), Berlin 1960.

Sulpicius Severus, *Dialogi*. C. Halm (*CSEL* 1), Vienna & Leipzig 1866.

Synesius Cyrenensis, *Dion Chrysostomus*. Kurt Treu, *Dion Chrysostomos oder vom Leben nach seinem Vorbild*, (*Schriften und Quellen der Alten Welt* 5), Berlin 1959

Teachings of Antony. Anbā Murqus al-Anṭūnī, *Kitāb rauḍat al-nufūs fī rasā'il al-qiddīs Anṭūniyūs*, Cairo 1899.

Teachings of Silvanus. Y. Janssens, *Les leçons de Silvanos* (*BCNH*, Textes 13), Québec 1983. (The photographs of the manuscript are published in *The Facsimile Edition of the Nag Hammadi Codices, Codex VII*, Leiden 1972).

Theodoret, *Historia Ecclesiastica*. L. Parmentier & F. Scheidweiler (*GCS* 44), Berlin [2]1954.

Vita Antonii. Coptic: Gérard Garitte, *S. Antonii vitae versio sahidica* (*CSCO* 117–118), Louvain 1949.

Greek: *Vita s. Antonii eremitae a D. Athanasio graece scripta, E Codice Boico nunc primum edita*, Augsburg 1611; *Sancti patris nostri Athanasii. Opera omnia*, I.2, Paris 1698; *PG* 26; *Vie d'Antoine* G.J.M. Bartelink (*SC* 400), Paris 1994.

Latin, Vita prima: Gérard Garitte, *Un témoin important du texte de la Vie de S. Antoine par S. Athanase. La version inédite des Archives du Chapitre de St-Pierre à Rome* (*Etudes de philologie, d'archéologie et d'histoire anciennes publiées par l'Institut Historique Belge de Rome*, 3), Rome 1939; H. Hoppenbrouwers, *La plus ancienne version latine de la vie de S. Antoine par S. Athanase,* Nijmegen 1960.

Latin, Vita Evagriana: *PG* 26.

Syriac: R. Draguet, *La vie primitive de saint Antoine conservée en syriaque* (*CSCO* 417–418), Louvain 1980.

Vita Pachomii, Arabic: E. Amélineau, *Monuments pour servir à l'histoire de l'Égypte chrétienne au IVe siècle. Histoire de Saint Pakhôme et de ses communautés. Documents coptes et arabes inédits, publiés et traduits par E. Amélineau* (*AMG* 17, I–II), Paris 1889.

Coptic: L–Th. Lefort, *S. Pachomii vita bohairice scripta* (*CSCO* 89), Louvain 1925; *S. Pachomii vitae sahidice scriptae* (*CSCO* 99–100), Louvain 1933–34; 'Glanures pachômiennes', *Le Muséon* 54 (1941); 'Vies de S. Pachôme (noveaux fragments)', *Le Muséon* 49 (1936).

Greek: F. Halkin, *Sancti Pachomii Vitae Graecae* (*Subs. Hag.*19), Brussels 1932. *Cf. Le corpus athénien de Saint Pachome* (par François Halkin avec une trad. francaise par André-Jean Festugiere), (*CO* 2), Genève 1982.

3. LITERATURE

Abbott, Nabia: *The Monasteries of the Fayyum* (*SAOC* 16), Chicago 1937.

Abramowski, Louise: 'Vertritt die syrische Fassung die ursprüngliche Gestalt der Vita Antonii?', *Mélanges A. Guillaumont* (*CO* 20), Geneva 1988.

Adam, Alfred: 'Grundbegriffe des Mönchtums in sprachlicher Sicht', *ZKG* 65 (1953–54).

Alvarez, Plácido: 'Demon Stories in the *Life of Antony* by Athanasius', *CS* 23 (1988).

Amélineau, E.: *Histoire des monastères de la Basse-Égypte. Vies de saints Paul, Antoine, Macaire, Maxime et Domèce, Jean le Nain, &^a* (*AMG* 25), Paris 1894.

De 'Historia Lausiaca' quaenam sit huius ad monachorum Aegyptiorum historiam scribendam utilitas, Paris 1887.

Assemani, Stephanus & Joseph: *Bibliothecae Apostolicae Vaticanae Codicum Manuscriptorum catalogus,* I–III, Rome 1741–1759.

Roger S. Bagnall, *Egypt in Late Antiquity,* Princeton 1993.

Bardenhewer, Otto: *Geschichte der altchristlichen Literatur,* III, Freiburg ²1923.

Bardy, Gustave: 'Antoine', *DSp* I, Paris 1937.

La question des langues dans l'Église ancienne, I, Paris 1948.

Barnes, Timothy: 'Angels of Light or Mystic Initiate. The Problem of the "Life of Antony" ', *JTS* 37 (1986).

Barns, John Wintour Baldwin: 'Egypt and the Greek Romance', *Akten des VIII. internationalen Kongresses für Papyrologie* (*MPER* New Ser. 5), Vienna 1956.

Bartelink, G. J. M.: 'Die älteste lateinische Übersetzung der Vita Antonii des Athanasius im Lichte der Lesarten einiger griechischen Handschriften', *RHT* 11 (1981).

'Echos an Platon's Phaedron in der Vita Antonii', *Mnemosyne* 37 (1984).

'Die literarische Gattung der Vita Antonii', *VC* 36 (1982).

Batlle, C. M.: 'Die *«Adhortationes sanctorum Patrum» im lateinischen Mittelalter. Überlieferung, Fortleben und Wirkung* (*Beiträge zur Geschichte des alten Mönchtums und des Benidiktinerordens* 31), Münster 1972.

Bauer, Walter: *Rechtgläubigkeit und Ketzerei im frühesten Christentum,* Tübingen 1934.

Baumeister, Theofried: 'Die Mentalität des frühen ägyptischen Mönchtums. Zur Frage der Ursprünge des christlichen Mönchtums', *ZKG* 88 (1977).

Martyr Invinctus. Der Märtyrer als Sinnbild der Erlösung in der Legende und im Kult der frühen koptischen Kirche. Zur Kontinuität des ägyptischen Denkens, Münster 1972.

de Bazelaire, Louise: 'Connaissance de soi', *DSp* II, Paris 1953.

Beck, Edmund: 'Ein Beitrag zur Terminologie des ältesten syrischen Mönchtums', *Antonius Magnus Eremita 356–1956* (*SA* 38), Rome 1958.

Bell, Harold Idris: *Cults and Creeds in Graeco-Roman Egypt,* Liverpool 1953.

Greek Papyri of the British Museum, V, London 1917.

Jews and Christians in Egypt. The Jewish Troubles in Alexandria and the Athanasian Controversy, London 1924.

Bellet, Paulí: 'Nou Testimoni de les lletres de Sant Antoni', *Studia Monastica* 31 (1989).

Beskow, Per: 'The Theodosian Laws against Manichaeism', *Manichaean Studies. Proceedings of the First International Conference on Manichaeism (ed. P. Bryder)* (*Lund Studies in African and Asian Religion* 1), Lund 1988.

Bibliothèque de manuscrits Paul Sbath. Catalogue, I–III, Cairo 1928–1934.

Bidez, Joseph: *Deux versions grecques inédites de la Vie de Paul de Thèbes,* Gand 1900.

Bienert, Wolfgang A.: *«Allegoria» und «Anagoge» bei Didymos dem blinden von Alexandria* (*PTS* 13), Berlin 1972.

Dionysius von Alexandrien. Zur Frage des Origenismus im dritten Jahrhundert (*PTS* 21), Berlin 1978.

Blake, R. P.: 'Greek Script and Georgian Scribes on Mt. Sinai', *HTR* 25 (1932).

Bleeker, C. J.: 'The Egyptian Background of Gnosticism', *Le Origini dello Gnosticismo,* Leiden 1967.

Boak, Arthur E.: '*Politai* as landholders at Karanis in the Time of Diocletian and Constantine', *JEA* 40 (1954).

'Village liturgies in Fourth Century Karanis', *Akten des VIII. internationalen Kongresses für Papyrologie* (*MPER* New Ser. 5), Vienna 1956.

Boak, Arthur E. R., & Youtie, Herbert C.: *The Archives of Aurelius Isidorus in the Egyptian Museum, Cairo, and the University of Michigan (P.Cair.Isidor.),* Ann Arbor 1960.

'Flight and Oppression in Fourth-Century Egypt', *Studi in onore di Aristide Calderini e Roberto Paribeni* (ed. Edoardo Arslan), II, Milan 1957.

Bousset, Wilhelm: *Apophthegmata. Studien zur Geschichte des ältesten Mönchtums,* Tübingen 1923.

Bouyer, Louis: *La vie de Saint Antoine. Essai sur la spiritualité du monachisme primitif,* Abbaye Saint Wandrille 1950 (2nd ed. in *Spiritualité Orientale,* 22, Abbaye de Bellefontaine 1977).

Bowman, Alan K.: *Egypt after the Pharaohs,* London 1986.

Brakke, David: 'The Greek and Syriac Versions of the *Life of Antony*', *AB* 112 (1994),

Brennan, Brian: 'Athanasius' Vita Antonii. A Sociological Interpretation', *VC* 39 (1985),

Brown, Peter: *The Body and Society,* New York 1988.

'The Rise and Function of the Holy Man in Late Antiquity', *JRS* 61 (1971).

'The Diffusion of Manichaeism in the Roman Empire', *JRS* 59 (1969), repr. in *idem.*, *Religion and Society in the Age of St. Augustine*, London 1972.

Browne, G. M.: 'Coptico–Graeca. The Sahidic Version of St. Athanasius' Vita Antonii', *GRBS* 12 (1971).

Browne, G. M., and Shelton, J. C.: *Nag Hammadi Codices; Greek, Coptic Papyri from the Cartonnage of the Covers* (*NHS* 16), Leiden 1981.

Brunner, Helmut: 'Ptahhotep bei den koptischen Mönchen', *ZÄS* 86 (1961).

Buck, D. F.: 'The structure of the Lausiac History', *Byzantion* 46 (1976).

Büchler, Bernward: *Die Armut der Armen. Über ursprünglichen Sinn der mönchischen Armut,* Munich 1980.

Burton-Christie, Douglas: *The Word in the Desert. Scripture and the Quest for Holiness in Early Christian Monasticism,* Oxford 1993.

Butler, Cuthbert: *The Lausiac History of Palladius,* I–II, *Texts and Studies* , 6,1–2, Cambridge 1898–1904.

'Palladiana', *JTS* 22 (1921).

Cadell, H., & Rémondon, R.: 'Sens et emploi de τὸ ὅρος dans les documents papyrologiques', *REG* 80 (1967).

Cameron, Alan: 'Wandering Poets: a Literary Movement in Byzantine Egypt', *Historia* 14 (1965).

Catalogue of the Greek Papyri in the John Rylands library (ed. by A. S. Hunt, J. de M. Johnson, V. Martin, C. H. Roberts and E. G. Turner), I–IV, Manchester 1911–1952.

Cavallin, Samuel: *Literarhistorische und textkritische Studien zur Vita S. Caesarii Arelatensis, Lunds Universitets Årsskrift,* Lund 1934.

Chadwick, Henry: 'The Domestication of Gnosis', *The Rediscovery of Gnosticism. Proceedings of the Conference at Yale, March 1978 (ed. by B. Layton),* I–II, Leiden 1980.

Chadwick, Owen: *John Cassian,* London 1950.

Chaine, Marius: 'Le texte original des Apophthegmes des Pères', *Mélanges de la faculté orientale (Université Saint-Joseph, Beyrouth),* V.2, Beirut 1912.

'La double recension de l'*Histoire Lausiaque* dans la version copte', *ROC* 25 (1925–26).

Chitty, Derwas: *The Desert a City,* Oxford 1966.

'Dom Cuthbert Butler, Professor Draguet and the "Lausiac History" ', *JTS* 6 (1955).

Comparetti, D., and Viletti, G.: *Papiri greco-egizii*, I–III, Milan 1906–1915.

Contzen, B.: *Die Regel des hl. Antonius* (*Beilagen zum Jahresbericht des humanistischen Gymnasiums Metten 1895/96*), Metten 1898.

Couilleau, Guerric: 'La liberté d'Antoine', *Commandements du Seigneur et libération évangelique* (*SA* 70), Rome 1977.

Courcelle, Pierre: *Connais-toi toi même de Socrate à Saint Bernard,* 1, Paris 1974.

Cox, Patricia: *Biography in Late Antiquity. A Quest for the Holy Man,* Berkeley 1983.

Crouzel, Henri: *Origène,* Paris 1985.

Crum, Walter Erwing: *Catalogue of the Coptic Manuscripts in the British Museum,* London 1905.

A Coptic Dictionary, Oxford 1939.

Daniélou, Jean: 'Les démons de l'air dans la "Vie d'Antoine"', *Antonius Magnus Eremita 356–1956* (*SA* 38), Rome 1958.

Message évangelique et Culture hellénistique (*Histoire des doctrines chrétiennes avant Nicée* II), Tournai 1961.

Théologie du Judéo-Christianisme (*Histoire des doctrines chrétiennes avant Nicée* I), Tournai 1958.

Dechow, Jon Fredrick: *Dogma and Mysticism in Early Christianity: Epiphanius of Cyprus and the Legacy of Origen,* Diss., Univ. of Pennsylvania 1975, (published by North American Patristic Society, Monograph Series 13, Macon, GA, 1988).

Delehaye, Hippolyte: *Les légendes hagiographiques,* Brussels 1905 (with a number of reprints).

Devos, Paul: 'Fragments coptes de l'Historia Monachorum', *AB* 87 (1969).

Dölger, Franz Joseph: 'Klingeln, Tanzen und Händeklatschen im Gottesdienst der christlichen Melitianer in Ägypten', *Antike und Christentum,* IV, Münster 1934.

Dörries, Hermann: 'Die Vita Antonii als Geschichtsquelle' (*NAWG,* Phil.–Hist. Klasse), Göttingen 1949 (quoted according to the revised edition in his *Wort und Stunde. Erster Band. Gesammelte Studien zur Kirchengeschichte des vierten Jahrhunderts*, Göttingen 1966).

Draguet, René: 'Butler et sa "Lausiac History" face à un Ms. de l'édition, le Wake 67', *Le Muséon* 63 (1950).

'Le chapitre de l'*Histoire Lausiaque* sur les Tabennésiotes dérive-t-il d'une source copte?', *Le Muséon* 57 (1944), 58 (1945).

'L'*Histoire Lausiaque,* une œuvre dans l'esprit d'Évagre', *RHE* 41 (1946).

'Les apophthegmes des moines d'Égypte. Problèmes litteraires', *Bulletin de l'Académie de Belgique. Classe des lettres et des sciences morales et politiques,* V, 47 (1961).

'Une lettre de Sérapion de Thmuis aux disciples d'Antoine (A.D. 356) en versions syriaque et arménienne', *Le Muséon* 64 (1951).

'Une nouvelle source copte de Pallade: le ch. VII (Amoun)', *Le Muséon* 60 (1947).

La vie primitive de saint Antoine conservée en syriaque (*CSCO* 417–418), Louvain 1980.

Les cinq recensions de l'ascéticon syriaque d'abba Isaïe (*CSCO* 122), Louvain 1968.

Ecchellensis, Abraham: *Sapientissimi patris nostri Antonii magni Abbatis Regulae, Sermones, Documenta, Admonitiones, Responsiones et Vita duplex. Omnia nunc primum ex Arabica lingua Latine reddita,* Paris 1646.

Sanctissimi patris nostri Beati Antonii magni ... epistolae viginti. Nunc primum ex Arabico Latini juris factae, Paris 1641.

Edsman, Carl-Martin: 'Origenes och själavandringen', *Meddelanden från Collegium Patristicum Lundense* 4 (1989).

Eichhorn, Albert: *Athanasii de vita ascetica testimonia collecta,* Halle 1886.

Erdinger, A.: *Epistolae septem quae sub nomine Antonii abbatis circumferuntur,* Innsbruck 1881.

Evelyn-White, Hugh G.: *The Monasteries of the Wadi Natroun,* II, New York 1932.

Festugière, André-Jean: 'La problème litteraire de l'Historia Monachorum', *Hermes* 83 (1955).

'Sur une nouvelle édition du »De vita Pythagorica« de Jamblique', *REG* 50 (1937).

Fowden, Garth, *The Egyptian Hermes. A Histotical Approach to the Late Pagan Mind,* Cambridge 1986, revised reprint Princeton 1993.

Fuhrmann, M.: 'Die Mönchsgeschichten des Hieronymus. Formexperimente in erzählender Literatur', *Christianisme et formes littéraires de l'antiquité tardive en occident,* Geneva 1976.

Funk, Wolf-Peter: 'Ein doppelt überliefertes Stück spätägyptischer Weisheit', *ZÄS* 103 (1976).

Garitte, Gérard: 'A propos des lettres de S. Antoine l'ermite', *Le Muséon* 52 (1939).

Catalogue des manuscrits géorgiens littéraires du Mont Sinai (*CSCO* 165), Louvain 1956.

'De unius ex Ammonae epistulis versione iberica', *Le Muséon* 89 (1976).

'Histoire du texte imprimé de la Vie grecque de S. Antoine', *BBR* 22 (1942–43).

'Le texte grec et les versions anciennes de la vie de saint Antoine', *Antonius Magnus Ermita 356–1956* (*SA* 38), Rome 1958.

'Les lettres de Saint Antoine en géorgien', *Le Muséon* 64 (1951).

'Panégyrique de Saint Antoine par Jean, évêque d'Hermopolis', *OCP* 9 (1943).

'Un fragment grec attribué à S. Antoine l'Ermite', *BBR* 20 (1939).

'Une lettre grecque attribuée à S. Antoine', *Le Muséon* 55 (1942).

Giamberardini, G.: 'San Giuseppe nella tradizione copta', *Studia Orientalia Christiana Aegyptiaca,* Cairo 1966.

Giardini, Fabio: *La dottrina spirituale di S. Antonio Abate e di Ammonas nelle loro lettere. Contributi allo studio della Spiritualità dei Padri del Deserto,* Florence 1957 (originally published in *Rivista di ascetica e mistica* 1957).

Goehring, James E.: *The Letter of Ammon and Pachomian Monasticism, PTS* 27, Berlin 1986.

'New Frontiers in Pachomian Studies', *The Roots of Egyptian Christianity,* Philadelphia 1986.

'Pachomius' Vision of Heresy: The Development of a Pachomian Tradition', *Le Muséon* 95 (1982).

Gould, Graham: 'A Note on the *Apophthegmata Patrum', JTS* 37 (1986).

The Desert Fathers on Monastic Community, Oxford 1993.

Graf, Georg: *Catalogue de manuscrits arabes chrétiens conservés au Caire* (*Studi e testi* 63), the Vatican 1934.

Geschichte der christlichen arabischen Literatur, I–V(*Studi e Testi* 118, 133, 146, 147, 172), the Vatican 1944–1953.

Grant, Robert M.: 'Theological Education at Alexandria', *The Roots of Egyptian Christianity,* Philadelphia 1986.

Green, Henry A.: 'The Socio–Economic Background of Christianity in Egypt', *The Roots of Egyptian Christianity,* Philadelphia 1986.

The Economic and Social Origins of Gnosticism (Society of Biblical Literature, Dissertation Series 77) 1985.

Gregg, Robert C., & Groh, Dennis E.: *Early Arianism—A View of Salvation,* Philadelphia 1981.

Grenfell, B. P., & Hunt, A. S.: *The Amherst Papyri,* I–II, London 1900–1901.

Gribomont, Jean: '*Lettres de S. Antoine. Version géorgien neet fragments coptes,* édition et traduction par G. GARITTE. (*CSCO* 148–149) Louvain 1955 [comptes rendus], *RHE* 51 (1956).

'Les apophthegmes du désert', *Rivista di Storia e letteratura religiosa* 13 (1977).

Griechische Urkunden der Papyrussammlung zu Leipzig, Leipzig 1906.

Griggs, C. Wilfred: *Early Egyptian Christianity from its Origins to 451 C.E.* (*Coptic Studies* 2), Leiden 1990.

Grillmeier, Alois: *Jesus der Christus im Glauben der Kirche,* 1, Freiburg ²1979.

Guillaumont, Antoine: *Aux origines du monachisme chrétien* (*Spiritualité Orientale* 30), Abbaye de Bellefonatiane 1979.

'Gnose et monachisme: exposé introductif', *Gnosticisme et monde hellénistique. Actes du Colloque de Louvain-la-Neuve* (ed. Y. Janssens & J.-M. Sevrin), Louvain 1982.

Les 'Kephalaia Gnostica' d'Évagre le Pontique, Paris 1962.

'Philon et les origines du monachisme', *Philon d'Alexandrie,* Paris 1967.

Guy, Jean-Claude: *Jean Cassien, vie et doctrine spirituelle,* Paris 1961.

Recherches sur la tradition grecque des Apophthegmata Patrum (*Subs. Hag.* 36), Brussels 1962.

'Remarques sur le texte des *Apophthegmata Patrum* ', *RScR* 43 (1959).

'Note sur l'évolution du genre apophthegmatique', *RAM* 32 (1956).

Gwatkin, Henry: *Studies of Arianism,* Cambridge ²1900,

Halkin, F.: 'La légende de S. Antoine traduite de l'Arabe par Alphonse Bonhomme', *AB* 60 (1942).

Hannick, C.: 'Maximos Holobolos in der kirchenslawischen homiletischen Literatur', *Wiener Byzantinische Studien,* XIV, Vienna 1981.

Hardy, E. R.: *Christian Egypt, Church and People,* New York 1952.

Harl, Marguerite: *Origène et la fonction révélatrice du verbe incarné* (*Patristica Sorbonensia* 2), Paris 1958.

Harnack, Adolf von: *Geschichte der altchristlichen Literatur bis Eusebius. Zweite erweiterte Auflage,* I.1, Leipzig 1958.

Das Leben Cyprians von Pontius. Die erste christliche Biographie (*TU* 39.3), Leipzig 1913.

Hausherr, Ireneé: 'Un écrit stoicien sous le nom de Saint Antoine', *De doctrina spirituali Christianorum Orientalium, OCA* 30, Rome 1933.

Hedrick, Charles: 'Gnostic Proclivities in the Greek Life of Pachomius and the Sitz im Leben of the Nag Hammadi Library', *Nov. Test.* 22 (1980).

Helderman, Jan: *Die Anapausis im Evangelium Veritatis* (*NHS* 18), Leiden 1984.

Henne, Henri: 'Documents et travaux sur l'Anachôrèsis', *Akten des VIII. internationalen Kongresses für Papyrologie, Wien 1955* (*MPER,* New Series 5), Vienna 1956.

Hennecke–Schneemelcher: *Neutestamentliche Apokryphen,* I, Tübingen 1959 (repr. 1968).

Heron, Alisdair: 'The Holy Spirit in Origen and Didymus: A Shift in Perspective From the Third to the Fourth Century', *Kerygma und Logos,* Göttingen 1979.

Heussi, Karl: *Der Ursprung des Mönchtums,* Tübingen 1936.

Holl, Karl: 'Der schriftstellerische Form des griechischen Heiligenlebens', *Neue Jahrbücher für das klassische Altertum* 29 (1912), reprinted in K. Holl, *Gesammelte Aufsätze zur Kirchengeschichte,* II, Tübingen 1928.

Hopfner, Theodor: *Über die koptisch-sa'idische Apophthegmata Patrum Aegyptiorum und verwandte griechische, lateinische, koptisch-bohairische und syrische Sammlungen* (*Denkschriften der kaiserlichen Akademie der Wissenschaften in Wien,* Phil.–Hist. Klasse 61.2), Vienna 1918.

Über form und Gebrauch der griechischen Lehnwörter in den koptisch-sa'idischen Apophthegmen (*Denkschriften der kaiserlichen Akademie der Wissenschaften in Wien,* Phil.–Hist. Klasse 62.2), Wien 1919.

Hunt, E. D.: 'Palladius of Helenopolis: A Party and its Supporters in the Church of the Late Fourth Century', *JTS* 24 (1973).

Ivanka, Endré von: 'ΚΕΦΑΛΑΙΑ, Eine byzantinische Literaturform und ihre antiken Wurzeln', *BZ* 47 (1954).

Janssens, Yvonne: 'Les leçons de Silvanos et le monachisme', *Colloque international sur les textes de Nag Hammdi, ed. B. Barc* (*BCNH,* Ét. 1), Quebec 1979.

Johnson, David W.: *A Panegyric on Macarius, Bishop of Tkow, attributed to Dioscorus of Alexandria* (*CSCO* 416), Louvain 1980.

'Coptic Reactions to Gnosticism and Manichaeism', *Le Muséon* 100 (1987).

Judge, E. A.: 'The Earliest Use of Monachos for 'Monk' and the Origins of Monasticism', *JAC* 20 (1977).

'Fourth–Century Monasticism in the Papyri', *Proceedings of the Sixteenth International Congress of Papyrology,* Chico, California, 1981.

Judge, E. A. & Pickering, S. R.: 'Papyrus Documentation of Church and Community in Egypt to the Mid-fourth Century', *JAC* 20 (1977).

Kahle, Paul: *Bala'izah: Coptic Texts from Deir el-Bala'izah in Upper Egypt,* I–II, London 1954.

Kaiser, M.: 'Agathon und Amenemope', *ZÄS* 92 (1966).

'Ein altägyptisches Idealbild in christlicher Gewand', *ZÄS* 99 (1973).

Kakosy, L.: 'Gnosis und ägyptische Religion', *Le Origini dello Gnosticismo,* Leiden 1967.

Kelly, J. N. D.: *Jerome. His Life, Writings and Controversies,* London 1975.

Kenyon, F. G. and Bell, H. I.: *Greek papyri in the British Museum,* I–V, London 1893–1917.

Kettler, F. H.: 'Der melitianische Streit in Ägypten', *ZNW* 35 (1936).

Klejna, Franz: 'Antonius und Ammonas. Eine Untersuchung über Herkunft und Eigenart der ältesten Mönchsbriefe', *ZKT* 62 (1938).

Klijn, A. F. J.: 'Jewish Christianity in Egypt', *The Roots of Egyptian Christianity,* Philadelphia 1986.

Koenen, Ludwig: 'Manichäische Mission und Klöster in Ägypten', *Das römisch-byzantinische Ägypten* (*Aegyptiaca Treverensia* II), Mainz 1983.

Koschorke, Klaus: 'Zur spätgeschichte der Valentinianischen Gnosis', *Gnosis and Gnosticism (ed. M. Krause)* (*NHS* 17), Leiden 1981.

Kramer, Bärbel, and Shelton, John C.: *Das Archiv des Nepheros und verwandte Texte* (*Aegyptiaca Treverensia* IV), Mainz 1987.

Kraus, Johannes: 'Der Heilige Geist in den Briefen des heiligen Antonius des Einsiedlers', *Festschrift zum 50-jährigen Bestandsjubileum des Missionshauses St. Gabriel,* Kaldenkirchen 1939.

Krause, Martin: 'Koptische Literatur', *LÄ* III, Wiesbaden 1980.

Kuhn, K. H.: *A Panegyric on Apollo, Archimandrite of the Monastery of Isaac, by Stephen, Bishop of Heracleopolis Magna* (*CSCO* 394), Louvain 1978.

Lallemand, Jacqueline: *L'administration civile de l'Égypte de l'avènement de Dioclétien à la création du diocèse (284–382)* (*Mémoires de l'Académie royale de Belgique, classe des lettres et des sciences morales et politiques* 52.2), Brussels 1964.

Lampe, G. W. H.: *A Patristic Greek Lexicon,* Oxford 1961.

Leclerq, Henri: 'Confréries', *DACL* III.2, Paris 1914.

Leclerq, Jean: 'Saint Antoine dans la tradition monastique médiévale', *Antonius Magnus Eremita 356–1956* (*SA* 38), Rome 1958.

Leipoldt, Johannes: *Shenute von Atripe und die Entstehung des national-ägyptischen Christentums* (*TU* 25), Leipzig 1903.

Leloir, Louis: *Paterica Armeniaca,* I–IV (*CSCO* 353, 361, 371, 379), Louvain 1974–1976.

Premiers renseignements sur la vie d'Antoine en éthiopien', *Antidoron. Hommages à Maurice Geerard,* Wetteren 1984.

'Le prophétisme ecclésial d'Antoine', *After Chalcedon. Studies in Theology and Church History Offered to Professor Albert van Roey for his Seventieth Birthday,* Leuven 1985.

Lewis, Naphtali: *Life in Egypt under Roman Rule*, Oxford 1983.

Lichtheim, Miriam: *Late Egyptian Wisdom in the International Context* (*Orbis Biblicus et Orientalis* 52), Fribourg 1983.

Lilla, Salvatore: *Clement of Alexandria. A Study in Christian Platonism,* Oxford 1971.

Lipenius, M. Martinus: *Bibliotheca Realis Theologica*, Frankfurt 1685.

List, Johann: *Das Antoniusleben des hl. Athanasius des Großen. Eine literar-historische Studie zu den Anfängen der byzantinischen Hagiographie* (*Byzantinisch–neugriechische Jahrbücher,* Beiheft 11), Athens, 1930.

The Lives of the Desert Father (intr. by B. Ward, tr. by N. Russell), London 1980.

Lorenz, Rudolf: *Arius judaizans. Untersuchungen zur dogmengeschichtlichen Einordnung des Arius,* Göttingen 1980.

'Die griechische Vita Antonii und ihre syrische Fassung', *ZKG* 100 (1989).

Der Zehnte Osterfestbrief des Athanasius von Alexandrien, Berlin 1986.

Louth, Andrew: 'The Concept of the Soul in Athanasius' *Contra Gentes–De Incarnatione'* (*Studia Patristica* XIII.2), Berlin 1975.

The Origins of the Christian Mystical Tradition. From Plato to Denys, Oxford 1981.

'St. Athanasius and the Greek *Life of Antony', JTS* 39 (1988).

Lüddeckens, E.: 'Gottesdienstliche Gemeinschaft in Pharaonischen, Hellenistischen und Christlichen Ägypten', *ZRG* 20 (1968).

MacMullen, Ramsay: 'Social Mobility and the Theodosian Code', *JRS* 54 (1964).

Mahé, J.–P.: *Hermès en Haute–Égypte,* I–II, (*BCNH* 3 and 7), Quebec 1978 and 1982.

Mai, Angelo: *Scriptorum veterum nova collectio,* IV.2, Rome 1831.

Martin, Annick: 'Aux origines de l'église copte: L'implantation et le développement du christianisme en Égypte (I^e^–IVe siècles)', *REAnc* 83 (1981).

'L'église et la khôra égyptienne au IVe siècle', *REAug* 25 (1979).

Meijering, E. P.: *Athanasius: Contra Gentes. Introduction, Translation and Commentary,* Leiden 1984.

Mertel, H.: *Die biographischen Formen der griechischen Heiligenlegenden (Diss. München),* Munich 1909.

Metzger, Bruce M.: *The Early Versions of the New Testament. Their Origin, Transmission, and Limitations,* Oxford 1977.

Meyer, J.: 'Über die Echtheit und Glaubwürdigkeit der dem hl. Athanasius zugeschriebenen Vita Antonii', *Der Katholik*, 1886.

Milne, H. J. M.: *Catalogue of the literary papyri in the BM,* London 1927.

Mingana, Alphonse: *Catalogue of the Mingana Collection of Manuscripts,* I–III, Cambridge 1933–1939.

Mohrmann, Christine: 'Note sur la version latine la plus ancienne de la vie de saint Antoine par saint Athanase', *Antonius Magnus Eremita 356–1956* (*SA* 38), Rome 1958.

Mokbel, Antoine: 'La règle de Saint Antoine le Grand', *Melto* 2 (1966).

Molitor, Joseph: *Glossarium Ibericum* (*CSCO* 228, 237, 243, 265), Louvain 1962–1965.

Morard, Françoise–E.: 'Monachos, Moine. Histoire du terme grec jusqu'au IVe siècle', *ZPT* 20 (1973).

'Encore quelques réflexions sur monachos', *VC* 34 (1980).

Morenz, Siegfried: *Die Geschichte von Joseph dem Zimmermann* (*TU* 56), Berlin 1951.

Moscadi, A.: 'La lettere dell'archivio di Teofane', *Aegyptus* 50 (1970).

Müller, Guido: *Lexicon Athanasianum,* Berlin 1952.

Musurillo, H. A.: 'Early Christian Economy', *Chronique d'Égypte* 31 (1956).

Nagel, Peter: 'Die parabolische Handlungen im ältesten Mönchtum. Eine formgeschichtliche Untersuchung zu den Apophthegmata Patrum', *Klio* 43–45 (1965).

Nau, François: 'La première lettre de saint Antoine', *ROC* 13 (1908).

'Le texte grec original de la Vie de S. Paul de Thèbes', *AB* 20 (1901).

'La version syriaque de la première lettre de saint Antoine', *ROC* 14 (1909).

Oldfather, A.: *Studies in the Text Tradition of St. Jerome's Vitae Patrum,* Urbana 1943.

Outtier, Bernard: 'Le modèle grec de la traduction géorgienne des Apophthegmes par Euthyme', *AB* 95 (1977).

Orlandi, Tito: 'A Catechesis against Apocryphal Texts by Shenute and the Gnostic Texts of Nag Hammadi', *HTR* 75 (1982).

'Coptic Literature', *The Roots of Egyptian Christianity,* Philadelphia 1986.

The Oxyrhynchus Papyri (ed. by Grenfell, Hunt *et al.*), I– , London 1898–.

Parson, P. J.: 'A School Book in the Sayce Collection', *ZPE* 6 (1970).

Pearson, Birger A.: 'Earliest Christianity in Egypt: Some Observations', *The Roots of Egyptian Christianity,* Philadelphia 1986.

Peeters, P.: 'Une vie copte de S. Jean de Lycopolis', *AB* 54 (1936).

Pelikan, Jaroslav: *The Emergence of the Catholic Tradition (100–600),* Chicago 1971.

Peradze, Gregor: 'Über die georgischen Handschriften in Österreich', *Wiener Zeitschrift für die Kunde des Morgenlandes* 47 (1940).

Preuschen, Erwin: *Palladius und Rufinus: ein Beitrag zur Quellenkunde des ältesten Mönchtums,* Giessen 1897.

Priessnig, A.: 'Die biographische Form der Plotinvita des Porphyrios und des Antoniuslebens des Athanasius', *BZ* 64 (1971).

Die biographischen Formen der griechischen Heiligenlegenden in ihrer geschichtlichen Entwicklung (Diss., München), Munich 1924.

Quasten, Johannes: *Patrology* III, Utrecht 1960.

Regnault, Lucien: 'Aux origines des collections d'Apophthegmes', *Les Pères du désert à travers leurs Apophthegmes,* Solesmes 1987,

'Les Apophthegmes en Palestine aux Ve—VIe siècle', *Irénikon* 54 (1981).

Reitzenstein, Richard: *Des Athanasius Werk über das Leben des Antonius. Ein philologischer Beitrag zur Geschichte des Mönchtums* (*SHAW* Phil.–Hist. Klasse 8), Heidelberg 1914.

Historia Monachorum und Historia Lausiaca. Eine Studie zur Geschichte des Mönchtums und der frühchristlichen Begriffe Gnostiker und Pneumatiker (*Forschungen zur Religion und Literatur des Alten und Neuen Testaments* 7), Göttingen 1916.

Rémondon, Roger: 'L'Égypte et la suprême résistance au christianisme', *BIFAO* 51 (1952).

The Roots of Egyptian Christianity, Studies in Antiquity and Christianity (ed. by Birger A. Pearson & James E. Goehring), Philadelphia 1986.

Roberts, Colin H.: *Manuscript, Society and Belief in Early Christian Egypt,* London 1979.

Catalogue of the Greek and Latin Papyri in the John Rylands Library, Manchester 1938.

'Two Oxford Papyri', *ZNW* 37 (1938).

Roldanus, Johannes: *Le Christ et l'homme dans la théologie d'Athanase d'Alexandrie,* Leiden 1968.

'Die Vita Antonii als Spiegel der Theologie des Athanasius und ihr Weiterwirken bis ins 5. Jhr', *Theologie und Philosophie* 58 (1983).

Rousseau, Philip: 'The Formation of Early Ascetic Communities: Some Further Reflections', *JTS* 25 (1974).

Ascetics, Authority and the Church in the Age of Jerome and Cassian, Oxford 1978.

Pachomius. The Making of a Community in Fourth Century Egypt, Berkeley 1986.

Rubenson, Samuel: 'Arabic Sources for the Theology of the Early Monastic Movement in Egypt', *Actes du 3e congrès international d'études arabes chrétiennes. Ed. par S. Khalil Samir S.J.* (*Parole de l'Orient* XVI), Kaslik 1991.

'The Arabic Version of the Letters of St. Antony', *Actes du deuxième congrès international d'études arabes chrétiennes* (*OCA* 226), Rome 1986.

'Evagrios Pontikos und die Theologie der Wüste', *Logos. Festschrift für Luise Abramowski,* Berlin 1993,

'Der vierte Antoniusbrief und die Frage nach der Echtheit und Originalsprache der Antoniusbriefe', *OC* 73 (1989).

'St. Antony, "The First Real Coptic Author"?' (*Actes du IVe congrès copte, Louvain-la-Neuve, 5-10 septembre 1988. Ed. par M. Rassart–Debergh et J. Ries, Vol II De la linguistique au gnosticisme*), Louvain-la-Neuve 1992,

Rudolph, Kurt: *Die Gnosis. Wesen und Geschichte einer spätantiken Religion,* Leipzig ²1980 (first edition 1977).

'Zur Soziologie, sozialen "Verortung" und Rolle der Gnosis in der Spätantike', *Studien zum Menschenbild im Gnosis und Manichäismus (hrsg. von P. Nagel)* (*Wissenschaftliche Beiträge der Martin–Luther Universität Halle–Wittenberg 1979/39*), Halle 1979.

Ruppert, Friedrich: *Das Pachomianische Mönchtum und die Anfänge klösterlichen Gehorsams, Münsterschwarzacher Studien 20,* Münsterschwarzach 1971.

Sachau, Eduard: *Katalog der syrischen Handschriften in Berlin,* Berlin 1899.

Samir, Khalil: *Tables de concordance des manuscrits arabes chrétiens du Caire et du Sinaï* (*CSCO* 482), Louvain 1986.

Santos Otero, A. de: 'Die altslavische Überlieferung der Vita Antonii des Athanasius', *ZKG* 90 (1979).

Sauget, Joseph-Marie: 'La collection du manuscrit 4225 de la Bibliothèque de Strasbourg', *OCP* 30 (1964).

'Le "Paterikon" du manuscrit arabe 276 de la Bibliothèque nationale de Paris', *Le Muséon* 82 (1969).

'Le "Paterikon" du MS Mingana Christian Arabic 120a', *OCP* 28 (1962).

'Un nouveau témoin de collection d'*Apophthegmata Patrum:* Le collection du Sinaï arabe 547', *Le Muséon* 86 (1973).

Une traduction arabe de la collection d'Apophthegmata Patrum de ᶜEnānīšōᶜ. Étude du ms Par. ar. 253 (*CSCO* 495), Louvain 1987.

Schoedel, William R.: 'Jewish Wisdom and the Formation of the Christian Ascetic', *Aspects of Wisdom in Judaism and Early Christianity (ed. by R. L. Wilken),* Notre Dame/London 1975.

Scholten, Clemens: 'Die Nag–Hammadi–Texte als Buchbesitz der Pachomianer', *JAC* 31 (1988).

Schoo, Georg: *Die Quellen des kirchenhistorikers Sozomemos, Neue Studien zur Geschichte der Theologie und Kirche,* 11, Berlin 1911.

Schütt, Marie: 'Vom heiligen Antonius zum heiligen Guthlac. Ein Beitrag zur Geschichte der Biographie', *Antike und Abendland,* V, Hamburg 1956.

Schulthess, F.: *Probe einer syrischen Version der Vita Antonii* (Diss. Strassburg), Leipzig 1894.

Segelberg, Eric: 'Syncretism at Work: On the Origin of Some Coptic Manichaean Psalms', *Religious Syncretism in Antiquity (ed. P. Brown),* Missoula 1975.

Les Sentences du Pères du désert. Nouveau recueil, Solesmes 1970.

Les Sentences du Pères du désert. Troisième recueil & tables, Solesmes 1976.

Seston, William: 'L'Égypte manichéenne', *Chronique d'Égypte* 14 (1939).

'Remarques sur le rôle de la pensée d'Origène dans les origines du monachisme', *RHR* 108 (1933).

Simaika, Marcus: *Catalogue of the Coptic and Arabic Manuscripts in the Coptic Museum, the Patriarchate, the Principal Churches of Cairo and Alexandria and the Monasteries of Egypt.* I–II.1, Cairo 1939–1942.

Le Site Monastique des Kellia (Basse–Egypte), Recherches des Années 1981–1983 (*Mission Suisse d'Archéologie Copte de l'Université de Genève*), Louvain 1984.

Staats, Reinhart: 'Antonius', *Gestalten der Kirchengeschichte (hrsg. von M. Greschat),* I, Stuttgart 1984.

Stroumsa, Gedaliahu: 'Ascèse et gnose. Aux origines de la spiritualité monastique', *RT* 89 (1981).

'The Manichaean Challenge to Egyptian Christianity', *The Roots of Egyptian Christianity,* Philadelphia 1986.

'Monachisme et Marranisme chez les Manichéens d'Égypte', *Numen* 29 (1982).

Tetz, Martin: 'Athanasius und die Vita Antonii. Literarische und theologische Relationen', *ZNW* 73 (1982).

Thélamon, Françoise: 'Rufin d'Aquilée, *DSp* 13, Paris 1988.

Timm, Stefan: *Das christlich-koptische Ägypten in arabischer Zeit* (*Beihefte zum Tübinger Atlas des Vorderen Orients* B 41), II, Wiesbaden 1984.

Trombley, Frank R., *Hellenic Religion & Christianization c. 370–529,* I–II (*Religions in the Graeco-ROman World* 115), Leiden 1994.

Turner, Eric G.: *Greek papyri. An Introduction,* Princeton 1968.

'Scribes and scholars of Oxyrhynchus', *Akten des VIII. internationalen Kongresses für Papyrologie, Wien 1955* (*MPER,* New Ser. 5), Vienna 1956.

Utas, Bo: 'Mānistān and Xānaqāh', *Papers in Honour of Mary Boyce* (*Acta Iranica*, Ser. II, Vol. X), Leiden 1985.

van den Broek, Roelof: 'The present State of Gnostic Studies', *VC* 37 (1983).

'The Theology of the Teachings of Silvanus', *VC* 40 (1986).

van Esbroek, Michel: 'Les Apophthegmes dans les versions orientales', *AB* 93 (1975).

van Haelst, Joseph: 'Les sources papyrologiques concernant l'Église en Égypte à l'époque de Constantin', *Proceedings of the Twelfth International Congress of Papyrology* (*American Studies in Papyrology* 7), Toronto 1970.

van Minnen, Peter: 'Pelousion, an Arsinoite Village in Distress', *ZPE* 77 (1989), pp. 199–200.

Veilleux, Armand: 'Monasticism and Gnosis in Egypt', *The Roots of Egyptian Christianity*, Philadelphia 1986.

'Monachisme et gnose', *LTP* 40 (1984), 41 (1985).

The Pachomian Koinonia, I–III (*CS* 45), Kalmazoo 1980.

Vergote, Joseph: 'L'expansion du manichéisme en Égypte', *After Chalcedon. Studies in Theology and Church History Offered to Professor Alois van Roey* (*OLA* 18), Louvain 1985.

Villey, André: *Alexandre de Lycopolis: Contre la Doctrine de Mani*, Paris 1985.

Vivian, Tim, *St. Peter of Alexandria. Bishop and Martyr*, Philadelphia 1988.

von Hertling, Ludwig: *Antonius der Einsiedler* (*Forschungen zur Geschichte des innerkirchlichen Lebens* 1), Innsbruck 1929.

'Studi storici antoniani negli ultimi trent'anni', *Antonius Magnus Eremita 356–1956* (*SA* 38), Rome 1958.

Weber, Hans-Oskar: *Die Stellung des Johannes Cassianus zur ausserpachomianischen Mönchstradition* (*Beiträge zur Geschichte des alten Mönchtums und des Benidiktinerordens* 24), Münster 1961.

Weingarten, Helmut: *Der Ursprung des Mönchtums im nachkonstantinischen Zeitalter*, Gotha 1877.

Welles, C. B.: 'The Garden of Ptolemagrius', *Transactions of the American Philological Association* 77 (1946).

Wilken, Robert L.: 'Wisdom and Philosophy in Early Christianity', *Aspects of Wisdom in Judaism and Early Christianity (edited by Robert L. Wilken)*, Notre Dame/London 1975.

Williams, Michael A: *The Immovable Race. A Gnostic Designation and the Theme of Stability in Late Antiquity* (*NHS* 29), Leiden 1985.

'The *Life of Antony* and the Domestication of Charismatic Wisdom', *Charisma and Sacred Biography, JAAR*, Thematic Studies XLVIII/3 & 4 (1982).

Williams, Rowan: *Arius. Heresy and Tradition*, London 1987.

Wilmart, A.: 'La lettre spirituelle de l'abbé Macaire', *RAM* 1 (1920).

'Une version latine inédite de la Vie de saint Antoine', *RB* 31 (1914).

Winstedt, E. O.: 'The Original Text of One of St. Antony's Letters', *JTS* 7 (1906).

Wipszycka, Ewa: 'La christianisation de l'Égypte aux IVe–VIe siècles. Aspects sociaux et ethniques', *Aegyptus* 68 (1988).

'Les confréries dans la vie religieuse de l'Égypte chrétienne', *Proceedings of the Twelfth International Congress of Papyrologists*, Toronto 1970.

'Le degré d'alphabétisation en Égypte byzantine', *REAug* 30 (1984).

Les ressources et les activités économiques des églises en Égypte du IVe au VIIIe siècle (*Papyrologica Bruxellensia* 10), Brussels 1972.

'Un lecteur qui ne sait pas écrire ou un chrétien qui ne veut pas se souiller?', *ZPE* 50 (1983).

Wisse, Fredrick: 'Gnosticism and early monasticism in Egypt', *Gnosis. Festschrift für Hans Jonas,* Göttingen 1978.

'The Nag Hammadi Library and the Heresiologists', *VC* 25 (1971).

Wright, William: *Catalogue of the Syriac Manuscripts in the British Library,* II, London 1871.

Yassā ᶜAbd al-Masīḥ, *Katālūj makhṭūṭāt Dayr al-Anbā Anṭūniūs bi-l-Baḥr al-Ahmar* (typewritten catalogue without date).

Youtie, H. C.: 'ΥΠΟΓΡΑΦΕΥΣ: The Social Impact of Illiteracy in Graeco-Roman Egypt', *ZPE* 17 (1975).

Zandee, Jan: *Death as an Enemy, Studies in the History of Religion. Supplement to Numen,* Leiden 1960.

'Die Lehren des Silvanus. Stoischer Rationalismus und Christentum im Zeitalter der frühkatholischen Kirche', *Essays on the Nag Hammadi Texts in Honour of Alexander Böhlig* (*NHS* 3), Leiden 1972.

Zanetti, Ugo: 'Deux lettres de Macaire conservées en arabe et en géorgien', *Le Muséon* 99 (1986).

Les manuscrits de Dair Abû Maqâr (*CO* 11), Geneva 1986.

Zoega, Georg: *Catalogus codicum copticorum manu scriptorum qui in Museo Borgiano Velitris adservantur,* Rome 1810.

Zotenberg, H.: *Catalogues des manuscrits syriaques et sabéens (mandaïtes) de la Bibliothèque Nationale* (*Catalogue des manuscrits orientaux de la B. N.,* 2), Paris 1874.

INDICES

Biblical Quotations and Allusions

Arabic Terms

Coptic Terms

Georgian Terms

Greek Terms

Latin Terms

Syriac Terms

General Index